How We Use Stories and Why That Matters

How We Use Stories and Why That Matters

Cultural Science in Action

John Hartley

BLOOMSBURY ACADEMIC

NEW YORK • LONDON • OXFORD • NEW DELHI • SYDNEY

BLOOMSBURY ACADEMIC
Bloomsbury Publishing Inc
1385 Broadway, New York, NY 10018, USA
50 Bedford Square, London, WC1B 3DP, UK
29 Earlsfort Terrace, Dublin 2, Ireland

BLOOMSBURY, BLOOMSBURY ACADEMIC and the Diana logo are trademarks
of Bloomsbury Publishing Plc

First published in the United States of America 2020
This paperback edition published in 2021

Library of Congress Cataloging-in-Publication Data
Names: Hartley, John, author.
Title: How we use stories and why that matters: cultural science in
action / John Hartley.
Description: New York: Bloomsbury Academic, 2019. | Includes bibliographical
references and index.
Identifiers: LCCN 2019028563 (print) | LCCN 2019028564 (ebook) |
ISBN 9781501351631 (hardback) | ISBN 9781501351648 (epub) |
ISBN 9781501351655 (pdf)
Subjects: LCSH: Culture–Philosophy. | Knowledge, Sociology of.
Classification: LCC HM621 .H3733 2020 (print) | LCC HM621 (ebook) |
DDC 306.01–dc23
LC record available at https://lccn.loc.gov/2019028563
LC ebook record available at https://lccn.loc.gov/2019028564

ISBN: HB: 978-1-5013-5163-1
PB: 978-1-5013-8329-8
ePDF: 978-1-5013-5165-5
eBook: 978-1-5013-5164-8

Typeset by Deanta Global Publishing Services, Chennai, India

To find out more about our authors and books visit www.bloomsbury.com
and sign up for our newsletters.

To Tina, Karri, Rhiannon, Sophie –

'Oh, the cleverness of you!'

Wendy Darling (Rachel Hurd-Wood), Peter Pan, 2003

CONTENTS

Prolegomenon

Cultural science in action

1

Causes and classes:

Communicative causation and mediated subjectivity

Writing a book in the twenty-first century is an increasingly delusional enterprise.

(JEFFREY SCONCE, 2019: ix)

I. Cultural science

This is a book about knowledge, in which stories play a prominent role. But it's not about the difference between true stories and fiction or lies. Instead, it's about how culture makes knowledge. A previous volume, *Cultural Science: A Natural History of Demes, Stories, Knowledge and Innovation* (Hartley and Potts, 2014), is a precursor book to this one. It brought together cultural studies and evolutionary economics to argue that

- the evolutionary function of culture is to create and sustain groups;
- the cultural function of groups is to make knowledge and act accordingly, while inter-group competitive conflict is a productive force for newness and innovation; and
- knowledge is the 'currency' of both economics (growth) and politics (contestation).

How does that work? This book, *How We Use Stories and Why That Matters: Cultural Science in Action,* takes the 'thought experiment' of cultural science further, in a series of explorations of the cultural function of storytelling in group-forming cultural systems. Together, the chapters that follow link agents (micro-scale), institutions (meso-scale) and systems (macro-scale) in a new 'model' of culture – with some new concepts, methods and ambitions for cultural studies – that acknowledges both culture's ancient provenance and its current global, digital dispersion. Where this model of culture differs from others is that it does not *confine* 'culture' to the past, to memory and to the transmission of embedded rules from one generation to the next (important though these are); it examines how culture mobilizes these resources to imagine possible futures, using stories – and the groups that make them – to stimulate disruption, innovation and change; and, with cultural science, it attempts to put the account on a systematic footing.

To accomplish its task the book draws from the social and natural sciences as well as the humanities. Specialized approaches to culture have tended to look inwards, seeing it as an autonomous or exceptional region. Cultural science looks outwards, seeking to integrate the insights gained in the arts and humanities with those from other spheres, especially the evolutionary sciences (including economics and bioscience) and complexity sciences (computational systems and networks).

What can each domain learn from the other?

- What is the role of fiction, imagination, creativity and novelty in economic and life systems?
- How does cultural conflict result in both the destruction and creation of knowledge?
- What is the agency of technology and artificial systems in human affairs?

In terms of approaches and method:

- Which scientific approaches can help us to explain planetary-scale and population-wide cultural processes and their dynamics under uncertain conditions?
- How can the methods already in use in specialist corners be synthesized towards a general model?
- How can such a model improve on individualistic, choice-theoretic and behavioural approaches?

Can we (the 'we' of scholarship) discover the extent to which culture is the *cause* of societal problems? Can understanding how it works become part of these problems' solution? If you are concerned about the economics or governance of *groups*, the negotiation and transmission of *identity*, the history and future of *communities*, the development of networked *knowledge*, or the role of social media in shaping the *creative economy*, then you have a place in the rich interdisciplinary ferment of cultural science. For a taste of cultural science work in progress, see this book's predecessor and companion volume (Hartley and Potts, 2014); and *Cultural Science Journal* (https://culturalscience.org/), whose archives go back to 2008.

Rigour + vigour: Cultural science in action

In 1974, Raymond Williams – widely held to be a founding parent of cultural *studies* – called for a new approach to the study of culture. He wanted a discipline that was 'rigorous in method' but retained a 'vigorous and general humanity' (1974: 37). He wrote: 'The approach I want to describe is that of cultural studies, which is English for "cultural science".' Williams was translating the German term *Kulturwissenschaft*, associated with philosophy (Simmel, Cassirer), history and anthropology (Dilthey), sociology (Weber) and art history (Warburg, Gombrich) (Herrmann-Pillath, 2018). Thus, for Williams, the first theorist of 'British' cultural studies (Turner, 2003), cultural science came first. We can call this 'cultural science 1.0'.

Cultural studies has enjoyed a long period of expansion and social prominence, marked by politicization and bursts of controversy, which displayed plenty of vigour but not always rigour. The relation between scientists and cultural studies deteriorated after the so-called Sokal affair in 1996, which set science (truth claims about objects) against postmodernism (ethical claims about language use) (Lucy, 2016). The details of this case are widely published and discussed (Sokal and Bricmont, 1998; Derrida, 2005: 70–3; see also Wikipedia). It began with a hoax paper, submitted by a physicist, being published (in good faith) in a journal of postmodern theory (*Social Text*), and then being revealed (by the author) as a hoax. This was taken to be 'evidence' that postmodern theory is 'not just false, it is gibberish' (Sokal and Bricmont, 1998: 23), without due recognition of the research traditions, methods, protocols and ambitions of a discipline for which the author had only contempt (his book was called *Fashionable Nonsense*). Beyond the details and denunciations of the case itself, the divisive aggressiveness of the attack left a bitter taste and a continuing gulf between science (especially in the 'Anglo-Saxon' tradition of empirical realism) and cultural theory (especially in the tradition of Continental philosophy). It became a textbook case of adversarial distrust between 'we' and 'they' groups. Neither side learnt much from the other. When Alex Mesoudi (2011) published a knowledge tree of evolutionary approaches to culture, the arts and humanities branches were missing altogether. Cultural studies was fair game, not science.

More than twenty years later history was repeated, not as farce, exactly, and certainly not as serious scholarship, in the so-called 'Sokal squared' brouhaha of 2018–19 – another hoax prank directed against identity-based research publications and postmodernism, dubbed 'Grievance Studies' by the perpetrators, to the delight of conservative commentators (Fox News) – but as provoking fears among others that the only cause served by the prank was that of racism.[1] The Sokal and 'Sokal Squared' affairs certainly demonstrated the importance of tribal allegiance and inter-group conflict in public colloquy, but it does a disservice to our understanding of knowledge to assert that truth and reason are all on one side, and the other side is merely contemptible. As David Banks put it in a thoughtful response on *Cyborgology*:

> Gender studies, fat studies, cultural studies, science and technology studies – they all have incisive criticisms of a wide array of disciplines that orbit the same idea that predicated their founding as fields of inquiry: that no one has a monopoly on truth. That science is, like all human endeavours, shot through with politics, prejudices, and cultural norms. This essential idea, that all knowledge is the result of human history, geography, and culture is much more than a splash of cold water on burning passions of ambitious scientists, although it is sometimes that and for good reason. The Cultural Turn – the name given to the moment in the 70s where the social situatedness of knowledge really began to be transformative – says that we can make better scientific breakthroughs, not less. This isn't a detour, it's the only way through that assures no one is left behind. (Banks, 2018)

In short, cultural science – like postmodernism – is part of scientific endeavour, dedicated to the improvement of knowledge, not its destruction. It's time to restart the conversation across disciplines, seeking to synthesize the best work. The particular effort of which this volume is a part commenced in 2008 under the title of 'cultural science' (version 2.0). With Carsten Herrmann-Pillath (2013), it seeks for culture a 'scientific approach that aims at establishing truthful propositions about reality' – and at finding ways for humans to *perform* themselves and their knowledge in the face of those facts (Herrmann-Pillath, 2018).

Cultural *science* is an evolutionary, complex-systems approach to culture. As such it operates on the dynamics of change ('evolutionary') and the formation and action of groups ('complex systems'), as well as on meaning, identity, relationships and power ('culture'). Within its scope is any analysis of meaning-formation and usage that is combined with social networks and institutions. It is interested in how knowledge is made, stored, distributed and contested among scalable populations, and how it is reproduced across time and space. Cultural science can be summarized as the study of how, utilizing evolved sense-making knowledge technologies (speech, writing, media, electronics and their organizational forms), human culture makes

---

[1]For the 'Sokal Squared' story and its aftermath, see: https://en.wikipedia.org/wiki/Grievance_Studies_affair; and https://www.chronicle.com/article/Proceedings-Start-Against/245431. For the fears of racism see: https://www.insidehighered.com/views/2018/10/30/sokal-squared-hoax-was-put-down-scholars-concerned-racial-issues-opinion.

groups, groups make knowledge, and innovation emerges from 'translation' within and between groups (Lotman, 1990), not simply from 'transmission' of information (Carey, 1989).

Re-reading the historical, anthropological and archaeological record, cultural science conjectures that culture is a primary causal force – ahead of both 'the economy' (forces of production) and 'politics' (organized settlement) – in human change over the *longue durée*. If so, then the conceptual framework for *communication* is in need of revision, not least because language came first, social organization and settlement (states and cities) a long time after. Communication is not a 'behaviour' of already-made individuals; it is a condition of existence for individuals. Culture is not a 'superstructure' whose causal determination lies elsewhere (in economics). Instead it is *constitutively prior* to production (economies) and settlement (polities), contrary to most developmental narratives.

At the same time, the concept of culture as used in the humanities is no longer fit for purpose. Cultural science is an attempt to reconceptualize it, based on what culture is *for*, as an evolved system. The received usage of 'culture' to refer to the works of elite artists (literature) or to the everyday practices of ordinary people (anthropology) does not address causal sequence and group formation in culture.

Following Thorstein Veblen's (1898) provocation – 'Why is economics not an evolutionary science?' – cultural science poses the same question of cultural studies, over 100 years later. The evolutionary sciences do indeed theorize about culture, but a rather impoverished version of it, compared with the 'language arts' developed in the humanities over two centuries and more of continuous thought and argument. However, the lesson of economics is that it takes a long time – say, a century – to swing a discipline around towards an evolutionary approach, and only then by rethinking evolutionary theory (as is under way in evolutionary economics).[2] The need for a clearer understanding of *cultural causation* and its *dynamic change processes* has been made urgent by the rapid expansion of user-created content, creative industries and the maker movement. These phenomena clearly carry economic, business and political implications, but at the point of production they are all culture – about identity, relationships, meaning and power, using textual-discursive codes to communicate imaginative truths, fictions (and deceptions). How do such creative systems work at population and planetary scale?

The conceptual models inherited by cultural and media studies – structuralism, political economy, production/consumption – were not well-suited to understanding global dynamics and system-level change. Following the widespread adoption of computation and the internet, in addition to

---

[2]For a beginner's guide, see: https://medium.com/@brendanmarkeytowler/what-is-evolutionary -economics-ce1dc62b74c4 (and follow the links).

globalizing commercial popular culture, cultural studies needs new tools to understand

- competitive communication in and among self-organizing groups;
- the productive agency of myriad users of social networks (Hartley, Wen and Li, 2015); and
- the principles of social network markets (Potts et al., 2008).

Of course, many studies of social media now borrow, adapt or propose numerate methods to analyse user-created systems and 'big data'. But an overall conceptual framework is still a challenge for a branch of knowledge that has relied on in-close interpretation of unique artistic works and different 'language games',[3] analysis of situated groups and their textual-discursive activities in a wider context of power (Gibson, 2007). The agency of users could no longer be researched using received cultural methods (textual-discursive; ethnographic; critical) alone, but 'big data' analytics often seemed to miss the cultural component of scaled phenomena. How to bring meaning and mathematics into imaginative dialogue?

Cultural productivity

Long decades of observing monopoly industries in the press, broadcasting and commercial media entertainment habituated critical cultural analysts to the business model of production as a sphere radically separated from consumption. From the proprietor's perspective, it seems obvious that consumers are not 'productive' because they are the 'end-user' who *uses up* products without contributing anything new to the 'value chain'. Upon this production/consumption distinction, numerous other accretions began to stick, turning a description of an industrial process into a story about culture, building in invidious assumptions about the relations between social groups:

Production	Consumption
Active	Passive
Firms	Individuals
Creativity	Behaviour
Male	Female (etc.)

---

[3]In Lyotard's (1979) sense, see: https://plato.stanford.edu/entries/lyotard/.

The familiarity of these binaries, and their structural equivalence, do not make them real; listing them confirms their origin in ideology, not nature. To counter their widespread influence (e.g. through the taken-for-granted truisms of behavioural sciences and marketing), cultural studies needed a model of 'consumption' that includes the creative – and political – productivity of everyday users, makers and social networks in interactive, participatory and sense-making media. During the broadcast era, an overarching frame that could encompass both social scale and individual meaning-making proved elusive. Cultural science seeks to build that frame, in the context of the network era, where individual actions contribute to planetary effects, many of them destructive: welcome to the Anthropocene (Wark, 2016).

Cultural science focuses on culture's function and dynamics across whole populations, seeing culture as a long-run evolving system. At micro (agent), meso (institution) and macro (system) scale (Dopfer, Foster and Potts, 2004), culture has enabled humans as a whole

- to form trustworthy groups (and to spread these out across the globe);
- to store and transmit knowledge (under conditions of uncertainty and change); and
- to generate useable novelties (innovation) in self-creating, self-organizing systems and their mutual interactions.

It investigates

- how culture makes groups (we/they boundaries) organized around identity and meaning (language, codes, customs, rules);
- how groups make knowledge (shared among 'us' but secreted from 'them');
- how knowledge is boundary-marked, proclaiming universal application while displaying parochial aggressiveness towards outsiders;
- how meaning systems, from speech and story to elaborate institutional forms, both share and restrict the distribution and growth of knowledge among populations;
- how knowledge is 'translated' (Lotman, 1990) or 'copied' (Bentley, Earls and O'Brien, 2011) across groups, not 'transmitted' (Carey, 1989; 2000); and
- how interactions (clash, competition, cooperation) between groups result in new knowledge (innovation).

It is looking for causal sequence in cultural processes, when 'micro'-generated novelties (random variation) are adopted via 'meso'-institutions (selection) in 'macro'-systems (retention). For this, it uses a 'bioscience' (complex system) model, rather than the 'transmission' model that was borrowed from physics (moving electrons along a wire), becoming entrenched in communication disciplines post-Second World War (Carey, 2000).

Rethinking user-creativity within large-scale social and technical systems entails linking language systems with industry systems, focusing on the growth/distribution of knowledge via 'translation' of meaning across boundaries (Lotman, 1990). Instead of confining cultural agency to the common distinction between culture (seen as critical) and enterprise (seen as exploitative), or as a struggle between the public sector and private interests (Oakley and O'Connor, 2015), cultural science focuses on

- groups organized as 'clubs', in the economic sense of that term (Buchanan, 1965; Sandler and Tschirhart, 1980; 1997);
- groups (including clusters of clubs), sharing knowledge via 'commons' (Hess and Ostrom, 2003; Allen and Potts, 2016; Hartley et al., 2019).

The shift from public/private to clubs/commons draws attention beyond individualism to the agency of groups and 'imagined communities' (Anderson, 1991), the Tocquevillian 'associations' that emerge and consolidate to support them and the communication media that coordinate them. Cultural science is an effort to discover how decentralized agency and self-organizing social systems (re)produce knowledge, by developing new (hybrid) methods for studying cultural systems and dynamics, combining

- 'in-close' attention to textual-discursive meaningfulness;
- 'big-data' analytics, including 'network effects' in knowledge-making systems; and
- attention to the governance of groups and their interactions in circumstances of uncertainty and conflict, both by technology (e.g. blockchain) and by socio-semiotic coordination (e.g. journalism).

Cultural science is an attempt at disciplinary modernization in the arts and humanities. In relation to policy, it seeks to shift culture, creativity, knowledge and research from 'market failure' or 'social welfare' (public) models to a model based on dynamics of groups:

- Purposeful enterprise or activist 'clubs'
- Multivalent, multi-user 'commons'

The main policy question – as yet rarely asked in policymaking circles – is: if 'culture makes groups and groups make knowledge', what are we doing to nurture excellent groups and open knowledge, while treading lightly on the planet and the environment?

The oeuvre is the artwork

This book is not a 'how to do it' scientific lab manual, nor is it a defence of 'culture as we know it'. Instead, it's an argument for a new kind of interdisciplinary cultural science that combines in-close, reflexive textual-discursive investigation, based on 'language games' in the global 'semiosphere', with 'big-data' analytics and visualization. Its 'method' is that of the humanities essay, in which I am trained, rather than computer science or bioscience, in which I am not; but it does seek to integrate those approaches with cultural approaches derived from my own disciplinary formation (literary cultural studies, critical communication studies, media studies, journalism and creative industries).

I have treated some of the topics covered in this book elsewhere; each chapter represents a foray into a different problematic; thus, numerous chapters have been published previously, in a form that has been revised here in order to develop a narrative arc across the work as a whole. I'm treating what might be called 'long-form' problems here: I worry and tug at particular items across different chapters and publications, in order to clarify what there is to worry about, and some terms, examples follow through from previous work. Self-citation is also a way of acknowledging a 'knowledge club' – I'm a serial co-author and editor, including in the 'companion' efforts of *Cultural Science Journal*, so 'my' citations invoke a now-sprawling cultural science gang. This book has emerged from that work; it represents the truism that 'the writing is the research' – what each topic amounts to emerges from considering it, in concert with others.

More important, and as Paul Frosh puts it so well in his book on digital media poetics (2019: 3), 'media are poetic forces; they bring forth worlds into presence, producing and revealing them'. Well, the same can be said for research about media; a book like this is also 'world-building', a term borrowed from production designer Alex McDowell, later a professor at the University of Southern California. McDowell has written:

> World Building is founded on three beliefs, namely that storytelling is the most powerful system for the advancement of human capability due to its ability to allow the human imagination to precede the realization of thought; that all stories emerge logically and intuitively from the worlds that create them; and that new technologies powerfully enable us to sculpt the imagination into existence.[4]

In the same way, extended thinking about the role of storytelling in 'sculpting the imagination into existence' is itself a form of world-building; the writing

---

[4]Source: http://worldbuilding.institute/about.

is the research, and the research is a participant in the world it describes. As a result, *the oeuvre is the artwork*. I'm trying to develop a coherent but flexible approach to popular culture and media, in which a cumulative body of conceptual, interpretative and polemical work is part of the explanatory apparatus, such that various parts refer to one another, while the whole is greater than its parts. The scattered items do have one overriding purpose, which is to bring culture into the mainstream of both scientific and public colloquy. Thus, it seems right to gather the discussion together under one roof in a 'poetics' of *media studies*.

After a couple of centuries of essays and arguments about culture, now giving way to multiple myriads of data, we can begin to understand what culture is *for*. The next stage – cultural science 3.0, if you like – will emerge as this approach gets down to the detail of empirical studies. That's the work of many hands, over a prolonged period. I was in at the beginning of media and cultural studies and of the 'new humanities' in the 1970s, and know well that disciplinary change – from a 'turn' to a 'transformation' – can take a generation or more to take hold. It is impossible to predict how it will turn out, which is of course the best reason for getting started; the only certainty is that the new work will be completed by new hands – yours, for example?

II. Communicative causation
and mediated subjectivity

A universe comes into being when a space is severed into two. A unity is defined. The description, invention and manipulation of unities is at the base of all scientific inquiry.

(HUMBERTO MATURANA AND FRANSISCO VARELA, 1980: 73)

Despite technological changes of unprecedented scale and acceleration, the big challenge for the communication/cultural/media/creative constellation of academic subjects is not technological; it is to understand and account for the sociocultural uses and impact of a medium as it operates in the world. This turns out in practice to be a compromise among contending forces. Analysis in both research and teaching must pick out a chain of *cause and effect* in the relations and interactions of very different phenomena, ranging from the micro-scale encounters of individual people and individual texts, through mid-level (or 'meso') institutions (firms, community organizations, activists and advocates), all the way up to the macro-level of the social and economic organization of high-tech and high-investment enterprises, government agencies and heterogeneous populations (citizens, the public, audiences, consumers), from different demographics in different countries, within an overall context of globalizing modernity (and its discontents).

Media studies commenced with this problem: How might mass communication (at societal scale, broadcast by powerful state/commercial entities) cause changes in the minds and behaviour of individuals – how will they vote, buy, riot? Can they be persuaded, deliberately or unwittingly, to make different choices, at sufficient scale to make a measurable institutional and societal difference? Early communication sciences presumed that 'mass media' exerted a behavioural effect on individuals, and that 'mass society' was both structured and changed by those media; all that remained for science was to measure the effects. However, after several generations of 'effects' studies, it is still not clear how causation works in this context (or if it does). Nevertheless, the presumption is now institutionalized: reproduced by the behavioural sciences in universities; nurtured in economics (most abstract of all the behavioural sciences), PR (public relations), advertising, marketing, HR (human resources), public policy, political persuasion and propaganda; and distributed by the very media under scrutiny. It necessarily infects news, current affairs and talk shows, not simply in partisan or biased coverage that coincides with a given interest, but also in the very stuff of news – stories about the behavioural effects of societal phenomena, and the evidence that shows these effects to be pathological.

Mention of 'stories' might have alerted the behaviourists to a quite different model of causation, but the field's investment in empirical science (measuring the effect of controlled stimuli) and instrumental knowledge (judged by its usefulness to industry, business and government as organized in the here and now) made them hostile to those branches of knowledge that traditionally dealt in stories. History, literary and religious studies, philosophy, linguistics and the arts – the humanities, in short – were amassing quite different bodies of evidence, largely made of text, discourse, story (more or less elaborate), in which the trick of analysis was to train oneself in 'astute reading', not to control the reading of others.

If you adopt the language of behavioural sciences, then stories disappear. Instead, you are faced with 'subjects' who are 'exposed' to media 'stimuli' in a controlled experimental situation where their 'responses' can be observed and measured. This is necessarily a 'reductive' science, because the variables are so many, but it is axiomatic that the individual subject under scrutiny stands for universal humanity, and that 'effects' are understood to be general and replicable. It soon becomes more important to reproduce the scientific method than to understand the story (a criticism more often levelled at economics than at psychology, but applicable to the social sciences in general). Without a properly derived and applied methodology, your observations are merely 'subjective'. Method constitutes the 'object' of study; it is therefore method (not any one finding) through which your observations may compel others, both 'upwards' (policymakers) and 'downwards' (individuals). The one participant never to suffer those effects is the analyst; the 'effect' is always on 'the other' – *them*.

If you adopt the language of the humanities, then behaviour disappears. Instead, you are studying the play of difference among texts, discourses, representations, images, ideas, fantasies and fictions. There's no 'method' here beyond copious, continuing and comparative reading (including 'reading' the visual and performing arts, popular and elite). This may have a profound 'effect' on *you*, emancipating you into intellectual freedom, stimulating both curiosity and scepticism, emotional and critical responses, changing your subjectivity, identity and knowledge, inspiring your actions, aptitudes and ambitions.

It's easy to see that 'exposure' to an experimental stimulus is quite different from exposure to stories. The formation of consciousness, astute judgement, knowledge and self-control as part of an identity in action, in society, in history, is a cumulative and contextual process, where changes may be unobserved by the self even as they are realized in life. Equally, however, individual 'exposure' to media clearly has some effect on culture (meaning systems), society (groups) and persons (as a particular amalgam of selfhood, class, ethnicity, family, gender, sexuality, age, etc., plus variable taste and experience cultures), even if methodological individualism has been unable to identify a universal causal process.

This is why *cultural science* is needed. Neither fully behavioural-objective (modernist) nor fully textual-subjective (postmodernist) approaches work. Each needs the insights of the other. Each has something to offer the analyst. Each has some instrumental utility. This book is an attempt at 'conciliation' between the two. It uses the methods associated with the textual traditions of the humanities to argue the case for a science of culture.

However, because culture is as much story as behaviour, what counts as 'science' cannot simply be imported from some other context. Luckily, rethinking science is well under way in the sciences themselves. Systems, dynamics and genetics (inherited information) have come into their own in the biosciences and computational (information) sciences. 'Science and Technology in Society' is now a recognized disciplinary array in its own right, restoring context and the interplay of technology and power to the 'story' of science. The study of media, communication and culture is not exempt from these influences, but in my opinion each field has been slow to move beyond its own founding tendencies, whether these are grounded in the US tradition of behavioural science or in the European tradition of discursive humanities, especially now that both scholarship and media have broken beyond the transatlantic dyad. As they ooze across a globalized planet, they remain oil and water: they don't mix well, and each loses its efficacy in the presence of the other.

Nevertheless, media and communication are both personal and social, technological and political, behaviour and story, with multiple sources of causation in overlapping and interacting systems, from micro to macro scale.

Is it possible to combine cultural and scientific approaches and knowledge in such a way as to add value to both culture and science? The 'story so far' is not encouraging; let it be cautionary.

Transmission as causation?

To make sense of communication in the era of mass media, mass persuasion and the social transformations following mass production, it was to simplification via reductive science that the nascent field of communication turned, especially in the United States. Claude Shannon's (1948) model of physics-based linear communication – 'sender-message-receiver' – was adopted in the 1950s, resulting in the long tradition of studying print and broadcast media via the 'producer-text-audience' model.

This model was always deficient in one crucial respect: there was no compelling theory of causation *along* the 'value chain' of meaning. Just because goods shift through a production chain, from factory to distributor to retailer to consumer, it does not follow that what a manufacturer makes *causes* what a consumer makes of it. How much less likely is it that semiosis works this way? The physics model originated from a military imperative: How to optimize the chances of getting a 'message' (e.g. 'Go!' or 'No go!') through from 'sender' (command-and-control headquarters) to 'receiver' (front-line units) with minimum 'interference' (technical or hostile)? The imperative was to understand what might degrade a 'signal' as it progresses through various bits of apparatus and along interminable tangles of wire, such that the actions of individuals and systems alike matched the intentions of 'commanders'.

Reducing 'communication' to 'information signals converted to electrons' assumes linear or mechanical (Newtonian) force, with causation running from sender to receiver. In the case of electronic communication, a single sender can transmit the same message to many receivers. It is easy to see why such a command-and-control model was needed in the era of the Second World War. However, it is not quite so clear that the enthusiasm of the nascent communication sciences to adopt it in order to study 'mass' communication was well placed. After several generations of 'effects' research, there is still no agreement on whether or how that kind of causation works. Instead, producers' intentions are one thing, textual forms another; and audience or users' actions cannot be predicted from either of them, even though the idea that mass communication can cause behavioural effects has achieved the status of myth, so much so that 'violence in the Western media' has been blamed for criminal acts by people with no access to those media, for example, in China (McIntyre and Zhang, 2003).

Now we are well into the digital age, but this too was first 'mapped' for military purposes, with Paul Baran's (1964) model of distributed as opposed to command-and-control communications: the famous reticulated-network diagram that inaugurated the age of the internet.

Reticulated causation

It was only after the turn of the twenty-first century (around 2005) that the internet could handle video and global connectivity among users as well as producers. That accelerated a shift from 'enterprise-created' to 'user-created' content. Profound changes ensued, within and among all three of the links in the old model.

- The *production* industry was no longer dominated by Hollywood studios and New York finance. Digital technologies and online networks brought in new players, who soon expanded from Silicon Valley to global dominance.
- The *textual system* shifted from one where power and profit were concentrated in the production and transmission of text (in the press, movies and broadcasting) to one where it accrued to those coordinating traffic: YouTube, games and Twitter transformed textuality itself from *a work* (made by high-investment experts) to *a relationship* (among 'influencers' and 'followers'; celebrities and fans, P2P gamers).
- At the *'receiver'* end of the chain, the already-shaky or fuzzy distinction between producers (understood as industrial) and consumers (understood as domestic) was superseded by the concept of *the user*; an 'agent' that could be an individual or an enterprise, whether commercial or activist, community-based or corporate. Now, every consumer – including domestic amateurs – is *also* producer, publisher, journalist, author (etc.).

The line between enterprise and consumption, or between audience and citizenship, is blurred to the point where new models of causation are urgently needed. The solution will not be to *define* these media, especially not in relation to their legacy technical forms or to their relative newness, but to have another crack at solving the problem of *causation*. Here, we need to start with a different model of science. This one is not directly derived from reductive science – the fields, forces and linear causation of Newtonian mechanical sciences. Instead, it uses models of evolutionary and complex systems derived from the biosciences. Here, what matters is not the direction of electrons in a wire but the *relations* and *dynamics* among components in *systems*, the *rules* by which such systems maintain themselves in some sort of equilibrium (even as they adapt to external changes), and the *interactions* among neighbouring systems that produce 'newness' or innovation.

In brief, the humanities need to become not just 'digital' but evolutionary and complexity sciences. Studying human technosemiotic systems and their dynamics of change, rather than individual behaviour and expression, has a double consequence.

First, it requires analysis at scale. An 'evolving systems' approach requires the analyst to study populations (users), change (uncertainty, dynamics) and the emergence of 'newness', as it is called by Michael Hutter (2015), where 'novelty' is one thing (new inventions or ideas) but *newness* is another (innovation of whole systems), based not on the output of producers but on cultural uptake and adaptation by users.

The second consequence is that an evolving systems approach requires the analyst to move away from 'human exceptionalism', as if humans are the only species with attributes collected under the heading of 'humanities', including culture. And last, humans can be studied *naturalistically*, as an evolved, differentiated and complex but still natural component of the matter-energy universe that also includes other life forms (the biosphere), other material systems (the atmosphere, geosphere, etc.), and natural processes that do not require explanation by reference to what is presumed to happen uniquely in an abstracted, idealized, individual human brain.

Humanity as a relation

Strangely enough, it is only at this point – when humanity is understood as a relation not an essence – that the human impact on the environment and on other species within the biosphere can be understood, leading to a growing recognition that 'natural' systems such as the geosphere are increasingly explicable only if human agency (at species level) is taken into account. Here is where the idea of the Anthropocene Epoch is gaining recognition (Wark, 2016; n.d.). The Anthropocene is a period characterized by a human-made envelope around the planet, made of biogeochemical structures and strata that are produced or transformed by human action – cities, waste, industrially induced climate change, newly synthesized substances and elements from plastic to plutonium. There's even a date for the commencement of this epoch: 1965 (Turney, Palmer and Maslin, 2018).

Further, human *animality* can now be recognized, not only by understanding *Homo sapiens* as just one of the apes but also by recognizing continuities between some of humanity's most treasured attributes and those of other creatures, including sociality, communication, culture, cooperation and toolmaking. Such a move underlies an even more radical recognition, that consciousness, intelligence, moral choice and imaginative expression are not necessarily confined to humans at all: they may be shared by other species – and they may evolve among technologies (Artificial Intelligence, machine-learning, robots, cyborgs).

'The individual' is itself a term derived from theology, where it signified the irreducible unit of divine *creation*, namely, a '*creature*' with a soul; something that couldn't be divided or shared so the individual was the 'unit' of creation. The shift from this individualistic approach to a systems approach means that this vestige of religiosity turns from first cause to an effect – input to output. Instead of human choice and rationality being the *cause* of action and behaviour, individuality itself, along with choices, actions, behaviour and the rest, turn out to be a product of planetary processes working at system scale and changing along evolutionary paths. You are a product – of systems, of evolution, of relations, and of adaptive dynamics within biological, cultural and technological environments not of your own making.

Evolutionary systems

Thinking about systems that nobody owns but everybody uses, which have become elaborate and adaptable over long periods, it is immediately apparent that there is another model of communication that was neglected throughout the broadcast era: language. Language is a human invention – language-in-general and all languages, from the most endangered Indigenous tongue to the Big 5 world languages (Mandarin, Spanish, English, Hindi, Arabic, in that order). It is an evolutionary-adaptive system and system of systems. It works at population level and it changes over time, well beyond the intentions, desires or control of any user. It is both *universal* (every society and speaker has it and each language signifies everything in its world) and *adversarial* (*our* language can be trusted; *theirs* is duplicitous). Indeed, separate languages may be a naturally evolved security system, functioning efficiently to identify 'we' groups and to unmask 'they' groups, when such things mattered in a different way from what confronts users now, in a globally connected but still divided world.

When trying to fathom how textual-cultural systems work at global scale despite local difference, I have found compelling and prescient the work of Yuri Lotman (1990), the Estonian-Russian semiotician. Of course there are many other theorists (see the references!); and I've been working intensively with evolutionary-economist Jason Potts to apply some of these insights to culture, media and communication (see our book *Cultural Science*), and with evolutionary economist, sinologist and philosopher Carsten Herrmann-Pillath on the creative economy and the 'technosphere'. Closer to home, our teams at Curtin University, and before that at the ARC Centre of Excellence for Creative Industries and Innovation at QUT, have found many new ways to explore the role of culture, groups, stories, knowledge and innovation in the digital, global, Anthropocene world, including Lucy Montgomery and Cameron Neylon's work on digital scholarly publishing, Henry Li and Michael Keane's work on the creative and digital economy in China, Marcus Foth and Jaz Choi's work on urban informatics, Jean Burgess and others' work on digital media, our colleagues' at RMIT University on digital ethnography and blockchain research (at different centres!), not to mention an international web of former PhDs, postdocs and co-authors who've gone on to publish new work on everything from *Grand Designs* to digital storytelling in Turkey, China and elsewhere. This is the dynamic intellectual mix out of which cultural science has emerged and is still in formation. In short, '*cultural science in action*' is not confined to this book or to my own publications, but is already an extensive mix of energetic practices that are taking their own directions, guided by many hands.

Media/cultural studies

One big difference between 'old' technical media studies and 'new' evolutionary-systems models is in the way they conceptualize the subject or agent of media communication. In the received modernist linear causation model, the idea of 'mass communication' was simple: *one source, many receivers*. It followed that TV and radio studies would be concerned with what (ideology) and how (psychology) 'influence' or 'effects' could be sent down the line, to change individual behaviour at scale. Such 'effects' were seen as both positive (advertising, public broadcasting) and negative (propaganda, hate speech, violence, sexual display, deviance, 'bad' language, terrorism). However, the mechanism was the same whether judged 'good' or 'bad': it was simply the private consumption by individual consumers of central/corporate 'content' or 'messages'. Audiences, reckoned at population scale, were being taught how to be a 'modern subject': individualist, competitive, consumerist, ideological, domesticated, suburban, etc. – or even the American nuclear family (Spigel, 1992; see Chapter 11).

The concerns of such a model were inevitably about power, leadership and accountability in a system where 'senders' (Network TV, then Murdoch, Bertelsmann, then Netflix, HBO – all with interconnected shareholdings) were thought disproportionately to affect 'receivers' (citizens), although still no one knew exactly how *this* text (say, Fox News, BBC World Service, *Game of Thrones*) affected *these* citizens (including the analyst, or the 45th US president) in order to produce compliant behaviour – say, voting or acting socially, not to mention rioting, purchasing, hating, loving, relating, thinking, knowing, etc. Despite a continuing scholarly tradition ('mass comm', which remains influential in health and behavioural sciences), empirical social science has never demonstrated 'beyond reasonable doubt' a direct *causation* along the chain from producer's intentions, via textual mechanisms, to audience behaviour and belief. What has happened is that the 'reasonable doubters' began to travel under a different flag from the 'behavioural scientists' (Bogost, 2019).

In the humanities rather than the social sciences, other models of subjectivity came into play, especially those associated with postmodernism, poststructuralism, Continental Philosophy, semiotics and cultural studies (Lucy, 2016). Here, the methodological individualism and behaviourism of the social sciences, yoked as they were to a Newtonian linear-force model of communicative causation, were never convincing. Instead, from structuralism onwards, there was a decentralized but increasingly compelling effort to understand culture from a systems perspective, and to introduce into human systems something that in physics had already superseded Newtonian mechanical forces, namely, relativity and 'quantum' causation, experienced in evolutionary affairs as probability rather than exactitude.

For many years, cultural studies was preoccupied with 'the subject' and 'subjectivity'; not so much that of an individual personality with behavioural agency and 'subjective' opinions, but rather subjectivity as a structurally distributed and decentred relational power system: the 'subject of modernity', or of ideology, or of many other socially constructed identities – class, race, ethnicity, gender, sexuality, age and ability. Systems that produce meanings also produce subjects (a position from which to observe); and this applies as much to the analyst as to the user, as both physics and linguistics discovered long ago. Ferdinand de Saussure pointed out in the 1910s that 'there is ... not the slightest possibility of gaining insight or of defining a linguistic fact, without first adopting a point of view' (Saussure, 2006: 9). Everyone is a user, defined through their relations with others (including relations of power asymmetry) in the system and with other systems. There's no 'fact' of semiosis that doesn't proceed from, or in turn make, eco-social relations (Thibault, 1997: 153). Rules for creative productivity are encoded in semiosis itself, but semiosis only ever occurs in eco-social space and time, via 'technologies' ranging from natural language use (organized into poetics and rhetoric) to cultural forms like broadcasting, the press and publishing, but also literature, religion, law, and other human-made 'fictions' binding on groups (Harari, 2014), or even physical objects and places (roads, walls, cities as signifiers), within specific culture-bound meaning systems (Lotman, 1990).

Although this agenda has been prefigured, proclaimed and rehearsed in semiotic and cultural theory for many decades, its *productive* potential – as a system – has not been realized so readily, and its explanatory power has not been sufficiently 'imported' by other disciplines. The challenge now is to reorientate media studies to pick up the winds of change blowing from the biosciences (evolutionary processes), systems theory (information, computer and web sciences) and complexity theory (autopoiesis, populations of rules, borders, interactions/relations), in order to understand mediated communication as a dynamic cultural system, making meaning under uncertainty, in the context of new understandings of the global extent of biological interrelationships (the biosphere), networked economic and technological systems (globalization), and planetary cultures (the semiosphere).

The user

Here, the most important *invention* of 'new media' (computation and the internet) is not their technical specification or extraordinary reach, but *the user* – one who is always a speaker and maker as well as an audience; producer as well as a consumer; citizen and publisher as well as member of the public, and only ever encountered in relation to other users, clumped and clubbed together in various more or less inescapable socioeconomic cultural groups. The challenge for media studies is to *understand the user in the context of sociality* and *group-based knowledge and action*, within a web of relations, under uncertainty.

Group-made rules apply, but innovation can come from anywhere in the system (typically, by breaking them). Here, the 'postmodern subject' is normal, just as likely to make TV as to consume it; more interested in connectivity and sociality than power; just as likely to be female, young, old, differently abled and oriented, mobile, migrant, with multiple identities and group fluidity, compared with the abstract adult-male individual of the social science imagination. New knowledge is made by difference and diversity, via inter-group interaction across boundaries between different rule-systems, not by the will of Rupert Murdoch.

In the era of the social user, when both global connectivity (universal extent) and adversarial cultural conflict (border zones of intense semiosis) are also the new normal, how does it all work? This is the question for those interested in the intersection between *communicative causation* and *mediated subjectivity*. It used to be simple: centralized media caused behavioural effects; human subjects were unitary, and media influence altered their behaviour. But despite the individualistic appeal of these formulae, they don't explain very much about communication or subjectivity. Can we come up with a better model of how it all works – based on culture, dynamics, systems and meaning, not on psychology, structure, individualism and behaviour? The following chapters represent an attempt over several years to find out. With others, I've entered the debate on how to reform media studies in the light of global economics and big data, without losing interest in the cultural aspects of media – language, text, meaningfulness, truth, identity, sociality, relationships, power and the politics of the personal – wrapped in story, drama, staged conflict and rhetorical elaboration.

The mode is exploratory and conceptual, ground-clearing and analytical, distributed and local. Beneath it all runs an abiding worry: that the

(American) communication sciences of the twentieth century have proven to be no more successful than (European) cultural studies in explaining the relations between communication and subjectivity. Both are tied to modes of explanation (amounting to ideologies) that predate the changes wrought by computational technologies and digital networks, and in turn the uses to which such technologies and networks have been put around the world. So the questions that underlie this book are not scientific in the narrow sense (hypotheses that can be tested); they are also disciplinary (how do we know?) as well as political (who are 'we' anyway?), even while attempting to build a neutral but adequate framework for communication as a field.

Outline of the book

The book is divided into two parts.

Part 1, 'System (theory): Demes and communicative causation', is concerned with the relationships among groups (or demes), stories and media systems or institutions. It works through the concepts and principles of cultural science while considering how culture, often in the form of stories, works at demic and system scale – through language, codes and genres – providing the motive or causal force for social media over very long-run time periods (Chapter 2), storytelling institutions (Chapter 3), formal and informal knowledge systems (Chapter 4), as well as showing how these systems operate through path-dependency and network effects to make certain kinds of story *prevail* (Chapter 4) or to serve certain *interests* (Chapter 5), including the countervailing cultural function of thought-coordination and critique (Chapter 6). Part 1 also sets up the terms and ambitions of cultural science, showing how thinking of culture in terms of populations, systems and dynamics (change) over the *longue durée* yields excellent food for thought. It may not yet be ready for reduction to formulae and equations, but it takes the prior scientific step, sanctioned by Karl Popper (1963), of making what he calls the 'bold conjectures' that a subsequent more meticulous testing process will need to adopt or refute.

- Chapter 2 *'Pushing back: Social media as an evolutionary phenomenon'*. This long chapter tells a long story! It sets the context for 'social media' and pushes back the timeline for that phenomenon to the furthest possible points of origin, in order to establish what Thorstein Veblen called 'causal sequence' (Hodgson, 2004: 344) in semiosis and mediation, establishing 'causal' primacy for culture.
- Chapter 3 *'Smiling or smiting? Selves, states and stories in the constitution of polities'*. Continuing the attempt to trace 'new' media and culture's continuity with the ancients, this chapter posits

two kinds of storytelling, one subject to technologization, even weaponization, as an instrument of state power, while the other remains oral and personal. The digital era brings these two types of storytelling together, with questions arising for those who wish to use digital storytelling for alternative purposes.

- Chapter 4 'Armed and wild: What hope for open knowledge?' Another twofold distinction drives this chapter, this time between two types of knowledge. Like storytelling, these emerge from the ancient and medieval worlds with different cultural functions, one to promote connectivity among demes, the other to promote productivity and organized coherence for states.

- Chapter 5 'Industry versus language? Something fishy going on'. This chapter turns to storytelling as intellectual property. Say what? Isn't storytelling an institution of language, rather than of the economy? Come to think of it, if stories can be properties, why not languages? The chapter looks for answers.

- Chapter 6 'Intellectuals: Three phases – Paris, public, club'. The cultural function of the modern intellectual, has changed from the heroic 'critical outsider' (Paris) to the administrative 'public intellectual', from whence it has dispersed among myriad social groups and clusters, where we find the function decentralized among 'knowledge clubs'. We're not in Paris anymore.

Part 2, 'Agent (Practices): Knowing subjects and mediated subjectivity', shifts focus to the agent, construed not as the behavioural individual of social science but in terms of cultural function, where 'the subject' is produced by group, class or functional processes: that is to say, in and by culture, which is thereby the evolutionary mechanism for transmitting knowledge and technology use through generations and across societies. The radical potential of this approach is that it releases cultural functions from individual attributes (the 'genius' of a 'special' elite), allowing a new analytical horizon to come into view, where class formation can be observed on the run, from the industrial era (Chapter 8) to the digital era, it's occurring in the 'world-building' activities of a new global class – girls (Chapter 12). If demes make culture, it is necessary to reconceptualize those staples of cultural subjectivity, the author (Chapter 7), the city as a site of inter-demic conflict (Chapter 8 and Chapter 9), the reader (Chapter 10), the audience (Chapter 11) and class (Chapter 12).

The book uses the modus operandi of cultural studies – essayistic in form, using text and discourse as evidence, and interpretation as method – to mount a series of arguments that link literary and cultural subjectivity with broader cultural processes organized around class, class consciousness and class struggle in an urban setting. Looking to the future, it suggests that what is meant by 'class' needs to be rethought in the context of global social media, and argues that the self-creating leadership group for forming an adequately self-conscious digital class or deme is – girls.

- Chapter 7 *'Authorship and the narrative of the self: The gods (Shakespeare), no-one* (Vogue), *everyone* (Dazed)*'*. This chapter considers authorship as the source of creativity across three different domains: literary culture (Shakespeare), popular culture (*Vogue*) and digital culture, finding that authorship itself changes radically over time and context, depending on its cultural function and institutional form.

- Chapter 8 *'Shakespearean class struggle: "The pit has often laid down the law for the boxes"'*. Shakespeare was the inspiration for early – and lethal – class struggle in industrializing America. As Alexis de Tocqueville predicted, 'the pit' – groundlings, the populace – used the theatre as the crucible for rebellion against 'the boxes' – the 'silk-stockinged' elite of New York – who responded with militia and muskets. A pattern for class struggle was set, which Shakespeare, not to mention Tocqueville, had been warning about from the start.

- Chapter 9 *'Staged conflict: Dialogic monuments and dancing difference'*. Here, the emphasis is on 'knowing subjects' knowing *where* they are, as well as what. The chapter explores the extent to which cities stage inter-demic conflicts in 3D form, using architecture, space and statuary to memorialize 'our' ancestors, and so bring fictional, fantasy and long-dead individuals into the deme, while excluding others. The chapter concludes that a better model for staging the difference between demographic groups in urban settings is the dance.

- Chapter 10 *'Reading magazines:* Death Cab for Cutie *– from shed to Dalston'*. I like magazines, but they may seem a perverse topic for a book about 'social' 'media'. Nevertheless, their history as a popular storehouse of miscellaneous knowledge for the masses does offer some salutary lessons, not least for Rupert Murdoch.

- Chapter 11 *'What is television? A guide for knowing subjects'*. Just as it passes out of its period of supremacy as the most popular medium in the world – following the earlier dominance of the press, cinema and broadcasting – television's cultural function (rather than its behavioural, economic, political or ideological effects) can be considered. This chapter argues that what TV is *for* is the creation of the modern subject.

- Chapter 12 *'World class: Girls as a problem of knowledge'*. Considering girls, social media and class struggle as one problem, this chapter argues – against the grain of the all-too-Parisian 'Theory of the Young-Girl' proposed by the Tiqqun group (2012) – that girls are the self-creating class of global digital culture. They're using the means to hand – social media – not only to make themselves into the ultimate *product* and spectacle of consumer culture (as Tiqqun wants us to believe) but also to build the organizational form required to achieve what E. P. Thompson (1963) looked for in a world-building class; namely, that 'the working class ... was present at its own making'. Behold, the digital 'world class', present at its own making.

Combining the two parts of the book, the 'take-out' from this cultural science approach is that rethinking culture in terms of systems and agents – *causes and classes* – yields productive and sometimes startling results, while preserving the specificity of the range of topics for the digital, global era. There's no need to make culture an exception to Darwinian evolution, or to think of cultural evolution as eugenic manipulation: there's no need to modify Darwin using Lamarck (learned traits can be inherited) or Galton (social Darwinism) as some recent theory attempts (Schuller, 2017).[5] *Culture* is the group-made process by which knowledge and technology are 'inherited' – semiotically, by the deme, rather than genetically, by the individual – and at the same time adapted and renewed to face uncertain futures.

---

[5]And see: https://www.thenation.com/article/the-trouble-with-white-women-an-interview-with-kyla-schuller/.

PART I

System (theory)

Demes and communicative causation

2

Pushing back:

Social media as an evolutionary phenomenon

We understand culture as the nonhereditary memory of the community, a memory expressing itself in a system of constraints and prescriptions.

(YURI LOTMAN, B. A. USPENSKY AND GEORGE MIHAYCHUK, 1978: 213)

Social media: Long story!

Taking the long-term view, 'social media' is a tautology: we were always social; all media are social; all sociality is mediated, at least among *Homo sapiens*. Of course, the current international techno-cultural arrangements are not geared to the long-term view. They distinguish online social media (like Facebook) from entertainment media (like television) and from social networks (analogue as well as digital). It may be that most readers are focused on the here and now too. However, this chapter heads in the opposite direction, out of the endless present tense of social science, to push back as far as possible in order to understand what it might mean to claim, as Zizi Papacharissi (2015a: 1) does in her opening statement for the journal *Social Media and Society*, that 'we have always been social'.

What follows in this chapter does not seek to establish a single method, but to learn from what is being achieved – and imagined – in other disciplinary fields. We must find ways to translate and enjoy each other's expertise, especially across polarized disciplinary and ideological boundaries. Thus, this is not an application of a particular branch of science; it's really about 'noetics' (Ong, 2012) – *how* we know what we know.

I. Pushing back

Let's take that 'always' literally, and see where it leads, back beyond Fernand Braudel's (2012) 'extreme long term' history (*la très longue durée*), beyond even the confines of *H. sapiens*, to a much more fundamental level, as explored in biosemiotics – that of life itself:

> Semiotics, in the process of delimiting and defining itself, has shown a noticeable trend towards a view which states that semiosis begins where life itself begins. (Kull, 1999: 115)

In other words, *'life' and 'sign' may prove to be one and the same*. It's not just that 'we' (humans) are social and thus communicative, via media from language to the internet, but also that all life is founded upon signals communicated in, by, and among biogeochemical material processes, where the 'self-creation' and self-organization of complex systems, or *autopoiesis* (Maturana and Varela, 1980: 73–123; Luhmann, 2012), produces discrete entities, bounded by difference-from-environment, from molecular level upwards.

We'll get back to the beginning of 'all life' later in the chapter, but for now let's illustrate this point with something that emerged about halfway along terrestrial life's timeline, about two billion years ago. That is when eukaryotic organisms appeared. Two billion years is a long time, but note that life lasted as long before eukaryotes as it has since. What's special about them is that their cells have a nucleus. The cells of the other two domains of living organisms, the prokaryotes – archaea and bacteria – do not (Figure 2.1). Eukaryotes are in fact the cellular 'complex systems' from which we are descended, along with most multicellular organisms, including all the big stuff that humans tend to find charismatic: algae, plants, fungi and animals. Internally, they are quite complex structures, with nuclei and other 'organelles' within each cell. These include mitochondria and (in plants or algae) chloroplasts, which are thought to derive from once-independent bacteria. They provide energy to the cell and in turn depend on it. In order to constitute and maintain themselves as entities, eukaryotic cells require communicative relationships at all levels.

- *Internally*, each cell's actions are coordinated by cell signalling.
- *Externally*, cells must communicate with the environment and its biotic load.
- In the case of *multicellular* eukaryotes like us, each cell must communicate with other cells of the same organism, and with the trillions of other microorganisms living within each organism, such as gut bacteria.

Bacteria   **Archaea**   **Eukaryota**

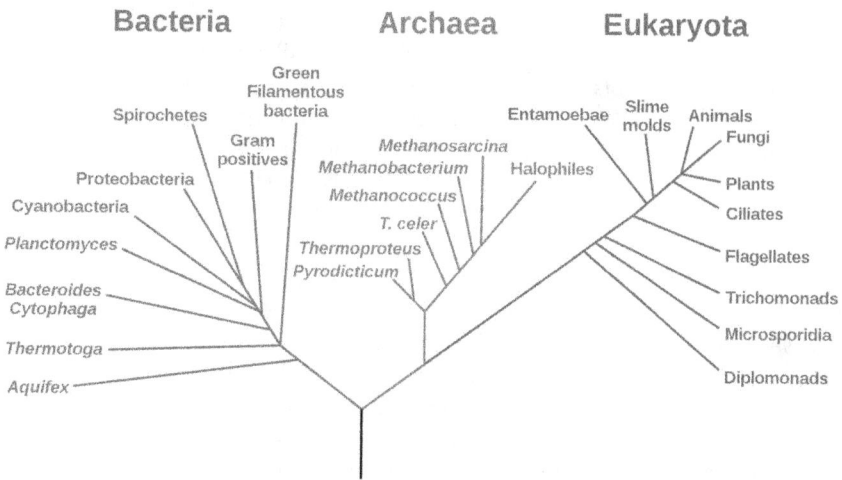

FIGURE 2.1 *The biosphere: 'To the best of our current knowledge, all organisms that are alive today or that have lived on this planet in the past are part of one large, genetically connected group: Life on Earth'* (Tree of Life Web Project). *Image credit: Wikimedia, public domain: https://en.wikipedia.org/wiki/File:Phylogenetic_tree.svg. Source of quotation: http://tolweb.org/tree/home.pages/structure.html).*

Communication connects organisms to systemic relations at much higher levels of organization too:

- relations of descent and reproduction (family/genetic information)
- relations of prey and predator (energy)
- relations of cooperation and competition (culture)
- relations of environmental adaptation or niching (knowledge)

The very constitution of eukaryotes (including *H. sapiens*), then, is based on these communicative relations, internal and external, which, at maximum, interrelate every living organism with every other, present and past, differentiating life into an evolved new 'envelope' of planetary extent: the 'biosphere' (Vernadsky, 1998). Thus, the original 'social media' must include cellular secretions – think pheromones. More generally, life cannot proceed without intra- and inter-species communication at all levels of complexity: life and sign are inseparable.

If you like, you may proceed even further back in time and in causal sequence, from life to rocks, from biogeochemistry to elementary physics, which may also be founded on communication. Elementary particles communicate with each other through 'messenger particles' (gravitons, photons, Higgs bosons, etc.) that carry force over a force field (gravitational field, electromagnetic field, Higgs field). Physics is the 'fundamental' or 'enabling' science because it describes mathematically a framework of perfect communication – of all particles with all particles – which then constructs the concepts of information and message, based on difference from randomness. Rethinking physical reality itself in terms of communication bases the natural world – physical and biological – not only on fields but also on relations.

'Social instincts'

The very glimpse of such possibilities permits an approach to communication – the thing that makes the media into media and sociality social – that is naturalistic and scientific, but does not need to rely on a model borrowed from the war-effort physics of the 1940s. That model (Shannon, 1948) reduces communication to 'transmission' of 'information' from 'sender' to 'receiver' across a field (or wire). It still underlies the dominant 'transmission' model (Carey, 1989) of social communication in the social sciences and psychology. This reduces *relations* to 'interference' and 'noise' and communication itself to individualistic behaviour. As James Carey (2000) went on to warn, such a model of science is better suited to control than to democracy, because it replaces communication with behaviour and uses science to manipulate that. In critiquing 'a science designed to rule over citizens', Carey offers an alternative: a 'science of enlightenment or citizenship, a science in society'. He writes:

> Science, under the dominant construction of what science is, deeply undercuts the democratic impulse of journalism. For a science of journalism is a science about journalism: a science of bureaucracy, of systems, of procedures, of management and of control. It is not a science of creation and construction, a science of understanding and common action. A science from without cannot connect with the creative impulse from within. (Carey, 2000: 22)

We can now do better, using relational models to develop a communication-based science of 'creation and construction', of 'understanding and common action' that connects with 'the creative impulse', developed from interdisciplinary contact (and some feats of mutual translation) with evolutionary and complexity sciences.

The evolutionist Charles Darwin (1871) called the framework of *human* communication the 'social instinct'.

> As humanity advances in civilisation, and small tribes are united into larger communities, the simplest reason would tell each individual that they ought to extend their social instincts and sympathies to all the

members of the same nation, though personally unknown to them. This point being once reached, there is only an artificial barrier to prevent their sympathies extending to the humanity of all nations and races. ... As soon as this virtue is honoured and practised by some few people, it spreads through instruction and example to the young, and eventually through public opinion.

The highest stage in moral culture at which we can arrive, is when we recognise that we ought to control our thoughts, and 'Not even in inmost thought to think again the sins that made the past so pleasant to us.'[1] (Darwin, 1871, 1(3): 100–1)[2]

Extending the 'social instinct' to non-kin and even to unmet strangers ('all the members of the same nation') is an important move, both for humans and for bioscience. It draws attention away from the *individual* and the so-called 'selfish gene' celebrated by Richard Dawkins (1976) and focuses instead on the *group*, up to population level ('all nations and races'). Instead of Dawkins's individualistic gene-centred view of evolution, Darwin is pointing to a culture-centred view, where communicative sociality – language, relationship, identity and meaningfulness – binds groups, via social media, in such a way that their knowledge and technologies can be shared, stored and transmitted through time and across space, typically in competition with those of other, external groups.

Culture makes groups, which are the 'survival vehicles' (Pagel, 2012) for all who live within their boundaries. Hartley and Potts (2014) introduced the concept of 'demes', based on terms in both bioscience (interbreeding subpopulations) and political science (the demos) (Hornblower and Spawforth, 2005), to identify inter-knowing subpopulations or 'we'-groups that are made in and by culture. Demes are cooperative and competitive – up to the point of destructive conflict – all at once. Within a deme, cooperation is not all lovey-dovey, since *H. Sapiens*, like previously evolved hominins going back two or three million years, had use of lethal weapons as well as tools. Indeed, current scientific thinking suggests that the 'big brains' of modern humans have little to do with toolmaking; they are instead the

---

[1]The internal quotation is from Alfred, Lord Tennyson (Darwin's exact contemporary): *Idylls of the King* (1859): 244–45. It is in the voice of Queen Guinevere, repenting (but still yearning for) her 'golden days' with Sir Lancelot. Valerie Purton's (2013: xii) interesting commentary on this passage – and on Darwin as a reader of Tennyson – suggests that Darwin's 'highest stage in moral culture' reveals not (only) his 'advanced human being' but (also) Tennyson's 'desperate soul striving, almost certainly in vain'.

[2]In honour of Guinevere, the only authority quoted by Darwin in this passage, the gendered pronouns (he, his) are here modernized (they, their); and generic 'man' is rendered as 'humanity' and 'people'.

result of *sociality*: they are needed for communication.[3] And with language, humans had access to deceit as well as truth.

In that situation, whatever knowledge could save a group could also destroy it. Thus, the 'social media' of any 'we'-group are crucial to the maintenance of both trust and scepticism, testing individuals' communicative intentions (Tomasello, 2014) even while telling group-binding stories, building and breaking alliances for social coordination at different scales, as well as extending knowledge and technology across increasingly large communities of non-kin and personal strangers.

This is essentially a systems approach to culture, and its germ is present in Darwin, in evolutionary bioscience. It shares components with other evolutionary sciences, from computer- and web-science to economics and linguistics. It builds on previous 'systems' approaches to culture, for example that of the sociological theorist Niklas Luhmann (2012, 2013 etc.), who analysed 'society' as *autopoietic* (following Maturana and Varela), and Yuri Lotman (1990, and elsewhere), who construed culture as a dynamic semiotic meaning-system (or system-of-systems) of planetary extent: the semiosphere, in which a major function of language is *autocommunication* – a culture communicating with itself, through texts that circulate widely, across different media, to confirm or to transgress (and thereby to delineate) the rules binding a given population (Ojamaa and Torop, 2015; Ibrus, 2015). This kind of communication is inexplicable using a linear model.

Like the 'tree of life', social media cannot be explained without reference to previous social media: they are the resultant of evolving complex systems. The mediasphere is part of the semiosphere, which is a product of the biosphere, which envelops the geosphere. Like the principle of biogenesis, or continuity of life (*omne vivum ex vivo*), by which life cannot be understood but by the existence of prior life (Vernadsky, 1998: 54–5), or like semiosis, which cannot be understood without reference to two or more pre-existing semiotic systems (Lotman, 1990), social media, as part of culture, are both self-creating and of evolutionary provenance, and cannot be understood without a principle of *autopoietic* continuity based on evolutionary processes.

These processes are indifferent to individuals – specimens or species – so you can't really do evolutionary analysis without a 'macro' model of both planetary space and geological time in which to situate your 'micro' processes and specimens, as well as the 'meso' institutions or populations in which they cluster (cf. Dopfer, Foster and Potts, 2004). The human population

---

[3]'Big brains weren't required to make simple stone tools. The evolution of bigger brains comes at least a million years after our ancestors invented the Oldowan toolkit.' 'Becoming Human: The Origin of Stone Tools'. *Smithsonianmag.com*: https://www.smithsonianmag.com/science-nature/becoming-human-the-origin-of-stone-tools-55335180/#yiaOTMwzH1C1mO6Y.99.

as a whole is 'macro', but knowledge is generated in 'meso' institutions by 'micro' individuals. For most of human history, the macro (planetary) picture was simply not known. Once they migrated 'out of Africa', humans took about 98 per cent of their historical timeline to girdle the Earth, closing the loop only about 1,000–1,500 years ago when Polynesians settled the last large uninhabited landmass, Aotearoa New Zealand. But they took with them no shared understanding of the planet as such. They developed a planetary patchwork of scattered and incommensurate cultures whose competitive interactions were marked by conflict and catastrophe. Despite *humans* being planetary, *culture* and *knowledge* long remained parochial.

Planetary extent was 'realized' *in knowledge* only in modernity, following early modern European exploration and consequent imperial exploitation from the 1500s to the 1900s. Knowledge of the planet as a single system was thus only attained as part of Western expansionism, once observations 'here' (e.g. meteorology, geology, fauna, flora, fossils, natural processes) could be correlated with similarly conceptualized observations of phenomena found 'there'. At an accelerating rate, the Earth became a coherent unit of exploration, discovery and thence knowledge. Finally, Darwin was able to conceptualize the 'social instinct' as a planetary phenomenon, with 'sympathies extending' to 'all nations and races', such that 'our thoughts' would come under the control of that knowledge, to value the macro (group) over the micro (individual) for the sake of survival through different but shared culture.

'World-historical facts'

Geology emerged as a global science in the eighteenth century, first as a by-product of religious attempts to 'prove' the biblical estimation of Earth's age (which in the event proved only that sectarians should beware what they wish for), then in the pursuit of rocks that might yield resources (coal, oil, metals, etc.). During the nineteenth century, such global 'findings' began to be consolidated into disciplinary knowledge systems (Wallerstein, 2004; Lee, 2012) by globetrotting scholars. Alexander von Humboldt's explorations in South America led to his 'invention of nature' (Wulf, 2015) and, in *Cosmos* (Humboldt, 1858, 2018), a very early conceptualization of the 'causal interconnectivity of the universe' (Walls, 2009). It was Humboldt who first understood why the plants he saw in Andean South America resembled those found in Alpine Europe: it was *altitude* and *latitude* that determined their similarity, despite then-prevalent assumptions about each species being a unique creation. Building on Humboldt, who built on Captain Cook, Darwin and Alfred Russel Wallace elaborated evolutionary science using insights they'd gathered from voyages to the Galapagos Islands, Tierra del Fuego and the Malay Archipelago – and, in Darwin's case, return visits to his home in Kent by barnacles, live and fossilized, from all over the world (Stott, 2004).

Karl Marx was an early 'collector' and synthesizer of global knowledge, reading ravenously through the burgeoning 'imperial archive' (Richards, 1993) under the dome of the British Museum Reading Room, microcosm of the noosphere (sphere of thought), to develop his notion of 'world-historical' capitalism:

> The more the original isolation of the separate nationalities is destroyed by the developed mode of production and intercourse and the division of labour between various nations naturally brought forth by these, the more history becomes world history. Thus, for instance, if in England a machine is invented, which deprives countless workers of bread in India and China, and overturns the whole form of existence of these empires, this invention becomes a world-historical fact. (Marx, 1845: Ch1.B)

Despite this discovery of world-historical 'facts' in the socioeconomic and historical domain by 1845, the implications of global scale have taken much longer to work through into widespread consciousness, especially in the arena of public thought and discourse. Darwin's vision of the diffusion of species-sociality has not yet been realized. Marx was surely one of those 'few people' who 'honoured and practised' global consciousness back in the 1840s, but strenuous efforts have been made from that day to this to *stop* 'this virtue' being copied 'through instruction and example to the young, and eventually through public opinion'. Aggressive parochialism (which is bioscientist Mark Pagel's definition of culture),[4] and ideological conflict (politics), still rule the roost. Meanwhile, the very idea of comprehensive, integrated knowledge ('scientific progress') is widely resisted, not least because it was established on the wings of nation-state imperialism, colonialism, militarism, class antagonism and gender inequality, but also because it defeats the knowledge systems that maintained 'parochial' cultures, including religions and 'we'-group self-aggrandizement (nationalism).

Global consciousness was adopted first in the natural sciences connected with the geosphere, and thence in those that served large-scale organized economic exploitation such as mining, manufacturing and trade. The next wave of knowledge-globalization took in the biosciences, which

---

[4]An article related to the launch of Pagel's (2012) book appeared in *New Humanist*, introducing his ideas thus: 'The fact that cultural allegiance is most vividly expressed not in ethical behaviour but aggressive parochialism suggests it has been instrumental in protecting human beings throughout their evolution, argues Mark Pagel.' See: Pagel, M. (2012b) 'The culture bandwagon'. *Eurozine*, February: http://www.eurozine.com/articles/2012-02-21-pagel-en.html.

were synthesized into an evolutionary framework in the 1940s (Huxley, 1942). Here, too, the integration of knowledge is followed by large-scale economic exploitation. In the most recent wave, post-Second World War, the globalization of telecommunications, broadcasting and user-centred social media took human meanings, relationships and identity around the world. Again, economic exploitation followed, such that the largest global corporations are currently the ones that 'mine' the resources of personal identity, relationships and meanings most efficiently. Individual subjectivity and global scale have at last integrated: in the culturally impoverished form of corporately owned 'big data'; but also in 'social media', where what individuals know clashes noisily against both meso (institutional) and macro (system) knowledge.

However, even though that process may be accelerating, it too is resisted. The struggle between (closed) system-control and (open) user-democracy has continued. Conceptually, it is proving as hard to separate culture from capitalism as it was to distinguish science from imperialism, because the international trade in cultural products and media platforms is market-based, putting pressure on national jurisdictions to 'open' their citizens as well as their economies to the global market. But market forces don't have everything their own way. Emergent countries such as China and India, and non-Western cultural systems such as Islam, resist open media markets for strategic as well as ideological reasons, seeing such 'soft power' systems as a means to improve their own competitiveness. The galloping corporatization of the internet, against which Jonathan Zittrain warned us way back (2008), is still resisted by myriad activists, associations and local cultures, both traditional (first peoples, civic organizations) and alternative (green activism, subcultures). Ordinary users, consumers and citizens are also resistant to such developments when they are experienced as over-intrusive because of surveillance, invasions of privacy and corporate appropriation of the 'social instinct' (and its expression) through intellectual property regimes, proprietorial platforms and marketing, or where they are corroded from within, as it were, by personal hate speech, abuse, trolling, flaming, cyberbullying, online harassment, racism, sexism and intolerance of others, all of which Emma Jane (2015) sums up in the interdisciplinary portmanteau term 'e-bile' (see also Jane, 2017, 2018).

Where social media (the tech-semiosphere) differ from the biosphere and geosphere is that here is the domain of consciousness, subjectivity and sociality itself, where all 'agents' (users) are active and productive makers of the very sphere that produces them. *They* ('consumers') cannot be 'mined' and 'exploited' in the same way that other 'resources' from the geo-biosphere are; and *we* ('citizens') cannot be trusted to form a single, global, e-bile-free 'we'-group who agree with Darwin (1871) that 'the highest stage in moral culture at which we can arrive, is when we recognise that we ought to control our thoughts'.

II. Global semiosophere

Globalization and the acceleration of difference

Despite the global extent of computers, telecommunications, media and the internet, the cultural 'sphere' remains riven, even as knowledge of its planetary extent is increasingly widespread. It is still hard even to represent the semiosphere as a single unit, since its variable components use different languages, different technologies and software, and different politics to produce what look, at first sight, like different realities, where 'difference' is construed as adversarial and antagonistic. At the level of national cultures, *your* global entertainment (America) is seen as an invasion of *our* reality (Xi Jinping's China, radical Islam). At the level of personal identity, 'difference' is not always welcome. It is just as likely to be greeted with boundary-enforcing hostility (often scaffolded by institutional frames such as journalism or political parties) as with recognition of a larger system or network within which identity can differentiate.

At best, then, the semiosphere – and the cybersphere with it – is currently going through a transitional phase, partway between 'micro' aggressive parochialism that wants to recognize difference by keeping it foreign and 'macro' global synthesis, where the characteristic communicative stance is not foe-creation but *translation*, across cultural (intermediary) and knowledge (interdisciplinary) boundaries. That process is already well under way at the level of corporate infrastructure, where proprietary platforms are often not interoperable but need to be, spawning aggregator or 'container' services.[5] But as yet much less attention has gone to facilitating 'interoperable' cultures among populations. Automated translation apps such as Google Translate, while welcome, also show how much remains to be achieved at the technical level here, and even more so at the level of social diffusion, uptake and general use. Darwin's 'artificial barrier' preventing our 'sympathies' from 'extending to the humanity of all nations and races' has proven to be formidable indeed.

All of this has a bearing on how to consider social media, which emerged in a strongly US-centric anglophone user-environment. Along with so much of modern science, as well as triumphant forms of global journalism, fiction and entertainment, the internet was developed as an English-speaking technology during its both technical (scientific–military) and commercial

---

[5]Docker.com is a Linux-based technology for packaging applications. It is supported by an unusual array of otherwise competitive companies, including Google, IBM, Microsoft, Cisco and others. Containers use shared operating systems to allow developers to create and package apps to run more efficiently, cheaply, and portably. The corporate giants are learning to standardize and automate at the level of servers.

phases, all the way up from domain names to the companies that began to dominate it. Hence, the already common habit of universalizing 'we' (anglophone America) to mean 'everyone in the world' transferred readily to social media, such that, to many users in many countries and even more so to the organized journalistic and cultural commentariat, 'the internet' *means* Google, Amazon, Facebook, eBay, and other US-born global tech giants. It's an easy enough habit to get into, because until lately the biggest firms have tended to be American. In 1995, only two of the world's top fifteen internet companies (by market capitalization) were *not* based in the United States. But by 2015, out of a total market cap that had expanded from US$17bn to US$2.4 trillion,[6] all but one of these firms had been displaced, and the top fifteen now included four Chinese companies: Alibaba, Tencent, Baidu (collectively known as BAT in China) and JD.com (Jingdong Mall). Clearly 'the universe' was changing!

Awareness has grown that 'the' internet is a world system, but it is still often expressed in old-fashioned parochial terms of nation-state competitiveness: 'Ours is bigger than yours.' In terms of firms, it is still a matter of a 'Snow White' (Google) and 'seven dwarves' (everyone else).[7] *The Economist* spells out what that means:

> America's Amazon and Facebook, ranked second and third, would be the biggest in any country save for China. Google is bigger than the peak value of the top internet firms in all other 48 countries combined. (*The Economist*)[8]

Nevertheless, business and journalism discourse registered that China was 'catching up', and has a very large pool of as-yet unconnected people to fuel further growth. Talk of a 'Mandarin-speaking internet' began to circulate in about 2010–12.[9] Meanwhile, Chinese firms were internationalizing too, led by e-commerce giant Alibaba (based in Hangzhou), and telco Huawei (based in Shenzhen), followed by games and social media company Tencent (also based in Shenzhen). The size and strength of internet companies inside China suggests there's plenty more

---

[6]A trillion is not just a very big billion: it's much bigger than that. Think of it in seconds: 1 million seconds = 12 days ago; 1 billion seconds = 31 years ago; 1 trillion seconds = 32,000 years ago: http://ihtd.org/festivalguide/resources/how-much-is-a-trillion-dollars/
[7]An echo of the 1960s–1990s, when commentators used to speak of 'IBM and the Seven Dwarves'. Afterwards, it was Microsoft.
[8]Source: 'Largest internet firms by country (2014)'. *The Economist*, 12, July 2014: http://www.economist.com/news/business/21606850-biggest-internet-companies.
[9]Source: 'Top 10 internet languages (2017)'. *Internet World Stats*: https://www.internetworldstats.com/stats7.htm.

where they came from (Hartley, Montgomery and Li, 2017). By 2018, China boasted nine of the world's twenty largest tech companies.[10]

Naturally, Western incumbents were concerned about their own primacy and market share. *The Economist* (see above) noted: 'Worryingly for Europe, of the top five countries, none is European.' That worry will only have increased post-Brexit. It is even more worrying for some first world, anglophone countries like Australia and Canada. They didn't appear in this list at all. Indonesia, Kenya, Costa Rica, Kosovo and Ethiopia all outranked them. The writing is on the wall.

'Disproportionately influential'

Apologists for the (American) English language have sought to explain these changes away, insisting that what really counts is not populations but 'influence' (Fisher, 2015). Researchers had put some numbers on this assertion (Ronen et al., 2014). They investigated the links between languages, across three chosen 'GLNs' or Global Language Networks. These are (1) translated books (from UNESCO's *Index Translationum* project), (2) Wikipedia, and (3) Twitter. The familiar visualizations from 'big data' ensue, showing 'three global language networks' (Ronen et al., 2014).[11] That visualization does the necessary ideological work for you: never mind the details, just know that the fat lines all lead to English, and that the fattest connections are between English and the imperial European languages, French, Spanish and German in particular. Note also that Chinese, Arabic and Hindi hardly figure at all. Job done! English is top language! Right?

But there is something circular and self-fulfilling about this approach. The authors, one of whom is Steven Pinker (senior author is César Hidalgo of the MIT Media Lab), start with an 'intuition': 'Our method formalizes the intuition that certain languages are disproportionately influential because they provide direct and indirect paths of translation among most of the world's other languages.' 'Formalizing' an 'intuition' sounds suspiciously like dealing in foregone conclusions. Here are those conclusions:

The GLNs [Global Language Networks], mapped from millions of online and printed linguistic expressions, reveal that the world's languages

[10]China's largest internet companies (2014), *China Internet Watch:* http://www.chinainternetwatch.com/13008/top-20-internet-companies-value-2014/. Largest companies worldwide (2018): https://www.marketwatch.com/story/china-has-9-of-the-worlds-20-biggest-tech-companies-2018-05-31.
[11]Sources: visualization: https://www.pnas.org/content/111/52/E5616/F1 (original article: https://www.pnas.org/content/111/52/E5616); critique: https://www.pnas.org/content/112/15/E1814; reply: https://www.pnas.org/content/112/15/E1815.

exhibit a hierarchical structure dominated by a central hub, English, and a halo of intermediate hubs, which include other global languages such as German, French, and Spanish. Although languages such as Chinese, Arabic, and Hindi are immensely popular, we document an important sense in which these languages are more peripheral to the world's network of linguistic influence. (Ronen et al., 2014)

The authors do admit the possibility of 'bias', not on their own part but in the chosen datasets. However, they dismiss it, because these data come from 'forums' of 'recognized importance':

One might argue that the peripheral position of Chinese, Hindi, and Arabic in the GLNs stems from biases in the datasets used, such as the underrepresentation of these languages and of some regional languages to which they connect. However, although these languages may be central in other media, their peripheral role in three global forums of recognized importance—Twitter, Wikipedia, and printed book translations—weakens their claim for global influence. Moreover, Chinese, Hindi, or Arabic would not qualify as global hubs even if their connections to regional languages were better documented in our datasets, because a global language also links distant languages and not just local or regional ones. (Ronen et al., 2014)

On the basis of 'intuition' and 'recognized importance' – in other words, preconceived ideas and a circular argument – the conclusion is that Chinese, Arabic and Hindi are 'local or regional' languages, despite being 'immensely popular', ranking first, fourth and fifth among the world's most spoken.[12]

What's going on here is both recognition of the global interconnectedness of languages, media, firms and technologies and, through them, meanings, and simultaneously a refusal to see the planetary system in overall terms, but only from the perspective of competing places, each of which is compared invidiously with the others. This is an old error – mistaking historical power asymmetries for natural processes, thereby converting power (imperial languages of the past two centuries) into nature ('global' languages), but missing the marginal, emergent and as-yet-unnoticed (where one might find innovation and future-forming).

The trouble with this approach, despite its sophisticated grasp of 'big-data' methods and systems science, is that it does not take the word 'global' seriously. It sees only a set of competing locals. Such thinking leads inevitably to speculation about the extinction of 'local' languages and the continuing dominance of today's 'winner', English.

---

[12]English is third; Spanish second: Ethnologue: https://www.ethnologue.com/statistics/size.

It would be easy to stop the analysis there, pointing out that picking winners is evolutionarily impossible and politically ineffective. But there is more going on than that. I'm taking this example of one-language supremacism as evidence of a transitional period, when global meanings, media and communications are of intense interest, but the conceptual and ideological frameworks to explain what's going on are stuck in a prior (nationalist) mindset. The phenomena are 'universal' (planetary) but the explanatory perspective is still parochial, aggressive and adversarial. So what we need here is not 'winners and losers' (because today's self-proclaimed 'winners' are in for a big surprise), but a new model.

To the extent that knowledge of culture at planetary scale and evolutionary time may produce understanding that supersedes the parochial aggressiveness of individual and local protectionism, it can nevertheless be observed that the expanding knowledge systems of modernity, which must periodically be self-corrected by bouts of reflexivity, activism, decolonization and revision, can extend planetary-scale knowledge from the geosphere (resources) and biosphere (life) into the semiosphere and mediasphere (cultural and mediated meaning), to the sphere of knowledge itself – the noosphere – as 'globalization' accelerates further, across the economy, technology and media-culture.

III. Waves and continuity

Meet the ancestor

Vladimir Vernadsky, who coined the terms 'biosphere' and 'noosphere' (sphere of thought), and who elaborated these concepts in the early twentieth century as part of what he called biogeochemistry, knew of no geological epoch that was 'azoic' (devoid of life). Despite advances in earth sciences since then, it is still not known *when* life arose on Earth (never mind *how*). All that is known is that it was surprisingly early, within the Hadean Eon (Figure 2.2), once thought to be entirely devoid of life, but not strictly a 'geological' period, since no Hadean *strata* survive, only organic (carbon) traces metamorphosed into other minerals such as zircon crystals (see Bell et al. (2015), Figure S3).

Recent evidence of undisturbed carbon in zircon from the Jack Hills of Western Australia, reported by Elizabeth Bell et al. (2015), suggests a date earlier than previously imagined: 4.1 billion years ago, a mere half-billion years after the Earth's initial formation, and within the timeframe of cosmic bombardment from asteroids (rocky) and comets (icy), which may have caused, catalysed, or concentrated the formation of complex molecules

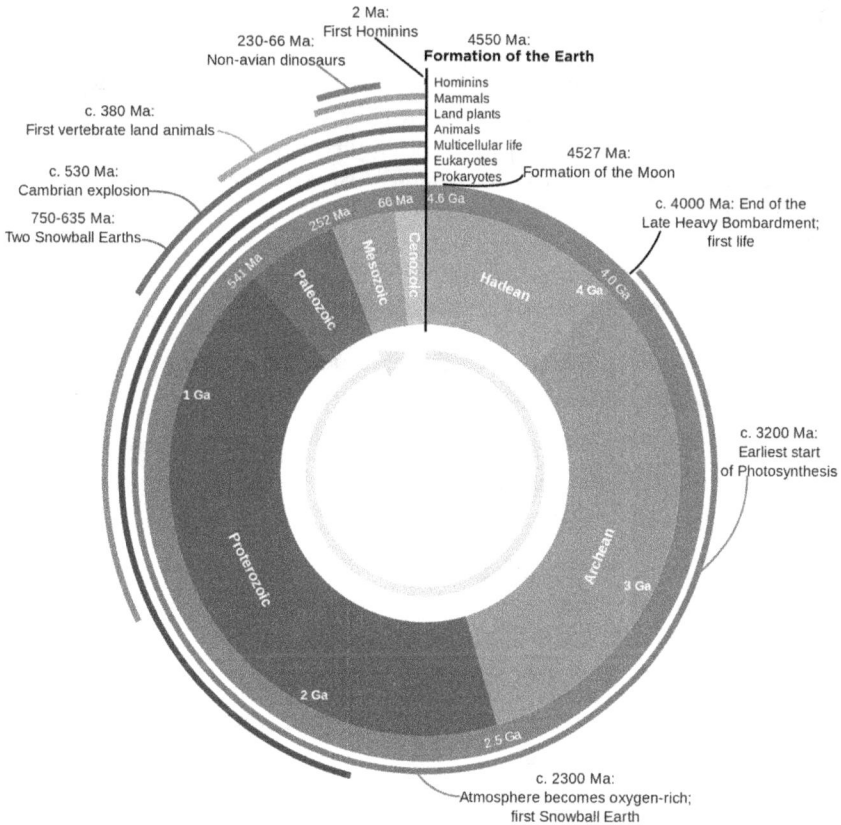

FIGURE 2.2 *The Geological Clock*

Source: *Wikimedia (public domain): https://en.wikipedia.org/wiki/Geologic_time_scale#/media/File:Geologic_Clock_with_events_and_periods.svg.*

(organic polymers), and thence life. Bell and her colleagues conclude that 'a terrestrial biosphere had emerged by 4.1 Ga [billion years ago]', and note that 'confirming such a connection would represent a potentially transformational scientific advance'. However, they warn that 'establishing a Hadean carbon cycle and its possible bearing on the origin of life will require enormous and sustained efforts'. Thus, for the time being, there is still no 'standard model' for the origin of life, so it remains 'empirical' to claim that all observed life comes *ex vivo* – from life, even though its most likely origin is abiogenetic (geochemical). Dating the emergence of the biosphere to 4+ Giga years ago pushes the commencement of *autopoietic* communication even further back in time, such that 'we' have a stake in processes once thought 'Hadean'.

Durée, cycle, wave

These ancient evolutionary processes are still active in human life, which in turn is a much longer story than is usually told, albeit one with multiple timeframes and rhythms operating simultaneously. The idea of very long-term history is associated with the *Annales* historian Fernand Braudel (2012; and see Lee, 2012). He argued that human sociality does not run to the beat of a stopwatch. He proposed a 'plurality of social times', where each moment thrums to rhythms of different 'duration' (*durée*). The *frequency* of these carries different types of historical process:

- *Events* – political history (highest frequency duration)
- *Conjunctures* – economic cycles
- *Structures* (the *longue durée*) – social life
- *Humanity* ('*la très longue durée*') – anthropological or species-system truths (lowest frequency duration)

Events concern not humankind but individual humans, whose history is '*l'histoire événementielle*' – 'the history of events: surface disturbances'. *Conjunctures* are medium-term 'slow but perceptible rhythms', such as Kondratieff waves and Schumpeter's business cycles. The *longue durée* is 'history whose passage is almost imperceptible', that of social life 'in relationship to the environment, a history in which all change is slow, a history of constant repetition, ever-recurring cycles'. By contrast, *la très longue durée* introduces an 'extreme long-term' timespan, 'such as to be found in the work of Claude Lévi-Strauss' (Braudel, 1972, Vol. 2: 20–1; qtd in Lee, 2012: 2–3). This pushes history back yet further, into territory previously given over to anthropology or, mistakenly, to 'timeless, eternal truths'. Changes observed across this timespan concern humanity as an organism, but nevertheless the period remains *history*: that is, even the most extreme *durée* exhibits beginnings, development and transformations.

Currently, 'social media' are treated as a mere 'event' – an irritation – concerning individuals and their behaviour, and are thus consigned to political history (or to universal present-tense scientism). But Braudel's 'plurality of social times' reminds us that they are also directed by these longer-term rhythms, slowing from 'surface disturbances' to the extreme long-term, where changes occur at population scale and anthropological speed.

Is it possible to study *social media* at these low frequencies? Where or whether such superficial 'events' have a longer-term impact is uncertain; do they come and go, or do they drive longer-term cycles? A proponent for the latter position was Joseph Schumpeter (1942) – of 'creative destruction' fame. His large-scale work *Business Cycles* (1939) sought to mount a mathematically compelling case for the argument that the ceaseless changes in capitalism are driven by entrepreneurial innovation; that is, surface events may drive conjunctural or long-term change. Schumpeter specified business cycles at three frequencies: the Kondratieff wave (about fifty years); the Juglar cycle (nine to ten years) and the Kitchin cycle (three-and-a-third years) (Mee, 2009). Since Schumpeter's day, Kondratieff waves have been periodized thus (Figure 2.3):

You will notice that Schumpeter's 'economic waves' (five since the Industrial Revolution) are triggered by *technological* innovations:

1   steam power (see Mokyr, 2009);

2   railways;

3   a cluster including electrical, chemical and automotive engineering;

4   petrochemicals and automobiles (the split between waves 3 and 4 is not clear-cut); and

5   information technology (computation, broadcasting, the internet, social media, blockchain).

Following this logic, economics has long considered technology – but not culture – as a causal force in economic evolution and growth. Cultural science aims to add culture's group-making, knowledge-making capacity for disruption and innovation to the picture, seeing technology as embedded knowledge.

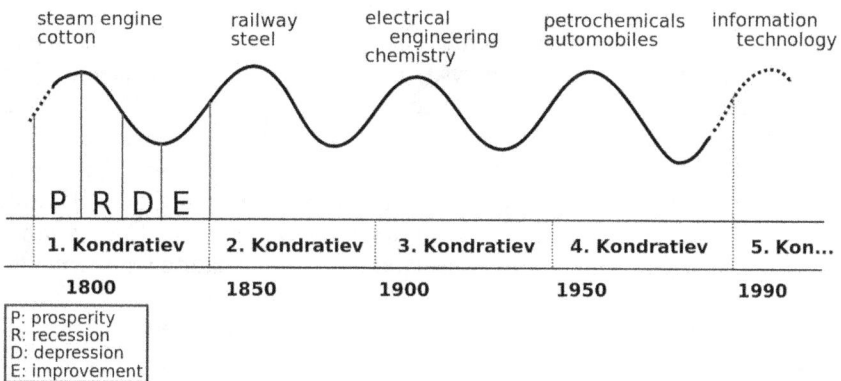

FIGURE 2.3 *Kondratieff Waves, updated. Only the first three waves were identified by Schumpeter himself, writing in 1939. Image by Rursus, Wikimedia: https://co mmons.wikimedia.org/wiki/File:Kondratieff_Wave.svg.*

Waves and frequencies of communication

You will note also that only one of these technologies, the last, is communication-based. The others are focused on energy and mobility. But 'waves' in communication technologies have a very long history, across the widest historical span – that of the *'très longue durée'* (see Fig. 2.4. below) – so 'information technology' is not the first. General changes in communication technologies trigger epochal changes, not only for humanity's active edge (literate elites) but for whole populations (users), albeit at different rates of uptake and uneven 'translation' across different societies. These changes occur when one general technology of communication is augmented by another (speech to writing to print, etc.), to which it may yield productive primacy. Epochs follow very long (but accelerating) waves, which have never been broken or rescinded, thus presenting a growth pattern stretching over millennia and across the planet. The uses and impact of such innovations are not exhausted at the moment of invention; it may take years, decades or much longer for new ways of communicating things to be absorbed, transforming social (group) relations and thus the lives of individuals, whether they are adept practitioners of a given mode of communication or not. For instance, printing with moveable type, invented in about 1450, took a couple of centuries to incubate across and beyond Europe before it played a transformative political role in the English Civil War (1640s), when sectarian pamphlets and religious texts recruited partisans to the cause; another century before the French Revolution of the 1790s, when political pamphlets and journalism came to the fore; and a further century before the same impetus stirred revolutionary changes in imperial Russia and colonized China. In each case, it was social uptake and use that proved transformational, not the technological invention alone.

Meanwhile, it is worth remembering that communications themselves – the textual form – operate at systematically different frequencies, all of which signify in a present moment. Thus, some of the meaning of journalism, academic writing and ancient monuments, respectively, comes from the 'frequency' of their mode of public address – high frequency (electronic), mid-range (print) and low frequency (stone/ruin) (Hartley, 2008: 36–60). This means in turn that 'fast' media online are *linked to*, and not distinct from, 'slow' media inscribed on stone. Human communication is an evolving, technologically distributed system where high-frequency forms (say, Twitter) and low-frequency forms (say, architecture), can only be understood relative to each other. At the same time, human communication is a continuing unity, from prehistoric ruins to internet sensations in music, sports and celebrity lifestyle, because the cultural *function* served by the latest 'mass communication' technology may remain the same – both Stonehenge and Ariana Grande signal in-group identity, belonging and pre-eminence within and beyond the boundaries of their group. Once again, the celebrity baton is shifting from West to East: *Time*'s list of the internet's 'most influential people' for 2018 was topped by K-pop band BTS.[13]

Continuities

Recent discoveries in other fields have revealed some of these continuities and pushed back the supposed origins and milestones of human history, as well as those of life more generally. The *très longue durée* keeps getting longer. In the process, we learn that what was once described as 'primitive' life and culture were no such thing; 'we' are now what we were then (it's technology, communication and economics that have changed). Some persistent truisms about the past are turning out to be scientific myths; while modern thought turns out to have ancient lineage, upon which it builds combinatorially (Arthur, 2009).

One such modern scientific myth, of prime importance to how we think about historical change, is the concept of the 'Neolithic Revolution'. This idea has been accepted as a 'world-historical fact', in Marx's terms, for a century now. Indeed, it is routinely hailed as the *'most important'* fact of human history, although, in the timeframe of this chapter, you might want to argue that the *really* critical moment was a bit further back, when our ancestor eukaryotic cells did that surplus energy deal with mitochondria.[14] Nevertheless, the 'Neolithic Revolution' has become 'common knowledge'. To illustrate, here is an online example of the genre, where an essay by Senta German repeats a big claim for 'the cultural advances brought about by the Neolithic revolution'. She says that this was 'the most important development in human history', and explains:

> The way we live today, settled in homes, close to other people in towns and cities, protected by laws, eating food grown on farms, and with leisure time to learn, explore and invent is all a result of the Neolithic revolution. ... Before the Neolithic revolution, it's likely you would have lived with your extended family as a nomad, never staying anywhere for

---

[13]Source: http://time.com/5324130/most-influential-internet/; and see: https://variety.com/2019/digital/asia/bts-youtube-record-boy-with-luv-halsey-1203188877/.

[14]Every nucleic cell – and organism – that ever lived (and that's a big number) owes its life to this tiny organelle. Originally independent bacteria, then accidental 'visitors' that overstayed in cells, mitochondria are 'essential to the *life* (they provide most of the chemical energy as ATP) and *death* (they can release a chemical that triggers programmed cell death) of a cell'; and they also exercise the power of life and death over every potential new human: 'Mitochondria are also thought to influence, by exercising a veto, which eggs in a woman should be released during ovulation and which should be destroyed by programmed cell death (apoptosis)'; http://bscb.org/learning-resources/softcell-e-learning/mitochondrion-much-more-than-an-energy-converter/.

more than a few months, always living in temporary shelters, always searching for food and never owning anything you couldn't easily pack in a pocket or a sack. The change to the Neolithic way of life was huge and led to many of the pleasures (lots of food, friends and a comfortable home) that we still enjoy today.[15]

Great story! (unless you're an Australian or other Indigenous person living a traditional life), speaking powerfully for the continuity of history. But where did the idea come from; why is it thought so important; and did it actually occur?

IV: Cultural causation: 'Neolithic revolution' or Göbekli Tepe?

Childe's children

The theory of the Neolithic Revolution was first propounded by Vere Gordon Childe, an Australian archaeologist and socialist (1925, 1936).[16] Childe is widely forgotten in his native Australia, except by playwright John Doyle (aka comedian 'Rampaging Roy Slaven'), whose play *Vere [Faith]* was inspired by Doyle's own discovery of Childe's existence.[17] But Childe ranks as one of the world's most important archaeologists of the twentieth century: if not Indiana Jones then certainly his teacher.[18] He was reputed to loathe actual digging (no 'digger', he), although he excavated Skara Brae in the Orkney Islands. His strength was synthesis of knowledge. He performed for archaeology the 'modern synthesis' that Julian Huxley (1942) achieved for the biosciences, at about the same time. Childe was able to gather piecemeal discoveries and sites across Eurasia into a coherent story: the story of the Neolithic Revolution.

---

[15]Source: German, S. 'The Neolithic revolution,' in *Smarthistory*, June 8, 2018, https://smarthistory.org/the-neolithic-revolution/; previously published by the Khan Academy (https://www.khanacademy.org/humanities/prehistoric-art/neolithic-art/a/the-neolithic-revolution). Neither organization is being criticized here – I'm trying to show how influential ideas are diffused and naturalized. For German's scholarly credentials, see: https://smarthistory.org/author/dr-senta-german/.
[16]A useful summary of Childe's publications, by Judith Treistman, to which this section is indebted, can be had from the *International Encyclopedia of the Social Sciences* (1968), archived at *Encyclopedia.com*: http://www.encyclopedia.com/doc/1G2-3045000185.html.
[17]Story at: www.sydneytheatre.com.au/magazine/posts/2012/september/feature-vere-gordon-childe.aspx.
[18]See: http://indianajones.wikia.com/wiki/Vere_Gordon_Childe.

Childe was a progressive cultural evolutionist, especially in relation to the mutually determining forces of technology and food production. He drew attention to the *longue durée* continuity of technological evolution, through the discovery of

> insignificant bits of flint and stone, bronze and baked clay [in which] are revealed the preconditions of our gigantic engines and of the whole mechanical apparatus that constitutes the material basis of modern life. (1925: xv)

For Childe, using Marxist theory, this 'material basis of modern life' was determined by the economy or mode of production, not by culture or mode of communication. Thus, the Neolithic Revolution named the shift from hunter-gathering to farming, when 'mankind' (humanity) became

> master of his own food supply through the possession of domestic animals and cultivated plants, and shaking off the shackles of environment by his skill in fashioning tools for tree-felling and carpentry, by organization for co-operative labour, and by the beginnings of commerce. (Childe, 1925: 1)

Childe drew the lines of continuity back in time to show that the Stone Age was part of the story of how we came to be modern ('our gigantic engines'). The mode of production (domesticating animals and cultivating plants), technology (tools), along with the social organization of cooperation and trade, were all well established before copper and bronze were first smelted (*c.* 5,000 years ago).

Childe's 'modern synthesis' of archaeology turned a patchwork of mutually disconnected digs and findings into a coherent story of developmental causation (aka modernist progress). His was an anti-racist and anti-elitist explanation of human origins at a time when racial supremacism was mainstream intellectual thought. Childe was careful and erudite, integrating previous knowledge. He developed an inferential method for associating archaeological finds with the material conditions of prehistoric 'cultures' (his term) that convinced many professionals; and he was a good science communicator at a time when popular learning was being stimulated and extended to 'the masses' via cheap paperbacks. The 'Neolithic Revolution' became 'common knowledge', faithfully taught in academies from that day to this.

In line with his commitment to modernist progress, Childe didn't much like the Stone Age, at least prior to the Neolithic Revolution, seeing Mesolithic hunter-gatherer societies, dependent on the environment and with low levels of technological and social organization, as closer to animality than to 'civilization'. The Neolithic Revolution introduced *growth*. The 'gigantic engine' of history sputtered into accelerating motion.

'Most important'; or 'worst mistake'?

Childe's dream of 'shaking off the shackles of environment' proved to be a modernist delusion. His desire to find a complete break between the Stone Age and civilization was also mistaken: we are just as dependent on the environment as ever – including the geology, climate and biota – that we are busy manipulating, without ever having addressed the problem of how to reabsorb waste into the biosphere, or how to harness energy, resources and space without despoiling the planet. In fact, Childe's characterization of the invention of agriculture as a 'revolution' owed more to Marxist theory of his own times than to Mesolithic or modern realities. He wanted the term to carry its full revolutionary weight. Transition from one economic epoch to another had to be rapid, transformative and general, precipitating new class antagonisms (in this case between surplus-producing farmers and surplus-consuming specialists such as elite warriors and priests). But was it?

Agriculture's diffusion from the 'Fertile Crescent' across Eurasia and Africa was uneven. Even where it was introduced, it also mattered whether cultivation was mainly of wheat (Eurasia), rice (East Asia), maize and potato (America), millet (Africa) etc., or, as in Papua New Guinea, the much less nutritious taro, because cereals produced a greater surplus of energy (starch), although not necessarily of protein.[19] Agriculture was invented more than once, across different continents and islands, using different crops. Some cultures developed herding but not crop cultivation (Saami), while in some places, like Aboriginal Australia, Inuit Canada, or Kalahari Africa, agriculture was invented not at all. But Aboriginal people who live traditionally do not reject as primitive or supersede the idea of living 'with your extended family as a nomad, never staying anywhere for more than a few months, always living in temporary shelters, always searching for food and never owning anything you couldn't easily pack in a pocket or a sack', as German puts it. This is not a primitive dystopia but a description of aspects of the oldest continuing cultures in the world, which value 'country', 'dreamtime' and ceremony above a suburban semi-detached.

Meanwhile the progressivism inherent in the idea that today's 'pleasures (lots of food, friends and a comfortable home)' are confined to post-farming cultures has been thoroughly critiqued. Jared Diamond, borrowing

[19]Jared Diamond: 'Highland agriculture was based on crops like these taro roots, which are very different from cereal crops. Taro is much more work. You've got to plant it one by one, unlike wheat where you throw your hand and spread the seed, and these New Guinea crops can't be stored for years the way wheat can – they rot quickly, they have to be eaten in a short time. They're also low in protein compared to wheat, so these farmers of the New Guinea highlands suffered from protein deficiency.' http://www.pbs.org/gunsgermssteel/show/transcript1.html.

ideas from anthropologists like Marshall Sahlins and Eric Wolf, is the best-known critic:

> Now archaeology is demolishing another sacred belief: that human history over the past million years has been a long tale of progress. In particular, recent discoveries suggest that the adoption of agriculture, supposedly our most decisive step toward a better life, was in many ways a catastrophe from which we have never recovered. With agriculture came the gross social and sexual inequality, the disease and despotism, that curse our existence. (Diamond, 1987)[20]

Note that Diamond isn't disagreeing with Childe's thesis about the *importance* of the Neolithic Revolution. It's just that he values its outcomes negatively instead of positively. He also accepts the Marxist narrative of increased class antagonism. Thus, his intervention (including subsequent criticisms of his work) does not alter the idea of a 'revolution' but strengthens it. Alternative explanations are not sought. Even counter-evidence doesn't upset the model, which has surely by now been reified into myth. For example, economist Samuel Bowles (2011) found that the first farming was *not* more productive than foraging, but he still calls the period in which farming was adopted the 'Holocene technological revolution', and repeats the idea that this was 'arguably the greatest ever revolution in human livelihoods'. His own results suggest *piecemeal* not *revolutionary* adoption, and ascribe 'causes' that come from culture (childrearing) and politics (military procurement), not economics (productivity). He concludes:

> Social and demographic aspects of farming, rather than its productivity, may have been essential to its emergence and spread. Prominent among these aspects may have been the contribution of farming to population growth and to military prowess, both promoting the spread of farming as a livelihood. (Bowles, 2011)

The evidence flatly contradicts the theory, but the theory – zombie-like – lives on. As Egyptologist John Romer put it:

> The 'Neolithic Revolution' ... that most useful phrase, was concocted by the Australian archaeologist Vere Gordon Childe in the 1920s ... specifically to combat the then current climate of ethnic stereotyping in European archaeology. ... Not surprisingly, perhaps, given the

---

[20]Diamond is the best-known critic, but not the first. See Jason Antrosio (2013) for a useful review of the salient literature.

contemporary climate, Childe's newly invented Neolithic Revolution, a two-word adventure story in itself, soon became part of Western history. (Romer, 2012: 32–3)

Childe's story – that 'material prosperity ... brought social and artistic progress in its wake' (as Romer summarizes it) – exerted its own powerful influence on scientific thought. The science may be 'tricked out with fashionable neo-evolutionary economics', as Romer points out, but 'the very language of the inquiry' determines what will be found: the *story* precedes and determines the evidence, which is largely a work of the imagination, ascribing causal sequence to 'the relics of the past'.

Gordon Childe was interested in 'civilization', which included urbanization. Not content with the Neolithic Revolution in economics, he also coined the term 'Urban Revolution' to explain politics, marking changes in settlement patterns from dispersed farms to trading towns; thereby adding politics to economics as determining forces, ahead of culture; an axiomatic presumption that, shorn of Marxist language, remains in force across the social sciences.

Among urban innovations, Childe was impressed by the European system found in prehistoric Greece:

An international commercial system linked up a turbulent multitude of tiny political units. All these, whether city-states or tribes, while jealously guarding their autonomy, and at the same time seeking to subjugate one another, had none the less surrendered their economic independence by adopting for essential equipment materials that had to be imported. (1958: 172)

The 'Urban Revolution' introduced the development of international markets, which managed to combine political competitiveness with economic cooperation through trade. Here, then, is the full developmental picture, projecting twentieth-century Marxist orthodoxy into the premodern past: the economy led to growth, class division and concentrated 'political units'; accompanied by the development of mutually antagonistic classes (internally) and competitive states (externally), which nevertheless continued to trade, in ideas as well as goods.

The arrow of causation

The question to be asked by any student of communication, culture, media, or social media – not to mention economists, geographers and anthropologists – is whether it is safe to rely on this story. The answer is no, as archaeologists have recognized (Watkins, 2010); but not because it's a story. The problem is not with the 'grand narrative' of progress as such, problematic though that has proven to be (Lyotard, 1979; Lucy, 2016), but with the *arrow of causation* in history. If you're a student of social media, you're going to need a theory of causation. Childe's is the one in general use. But it places culture at the receiving end of a causal chain that separates it from most of human history (the tens of thousands of years before the Neolithic Revolution; and those cultures that didn't have one), and it places causal priority on labour (mode of production) over both knowledge and sociality, including mediation (language, culture, story). 'Productivity' has become an economic term rather than a cultural one, despite the astonishing and continuing productivity of language, customs, practices, relationships, identities, meanings, ideas, stories, myths and fictions produced by our species – without economists or political scientists seeking to explain that, or to use it to explain how human systems evolve. The question that is seemingly beyond question is simple: What if the arrow of causation points the other way? What if the Neolithic Revolution was primarily about *social media*, and *mode of production* was a side effect, or means to an end?

In both of his revolutions – economic (mode of production) and political (ordered settlement) – Childe explains causal sequence in human history (and Diamond follows him) by using Marx's 'base and superstructure' model. In a justly famous passage Marx wrote:

> In the social production of their existence, humans enter into definite, necessary relations, which are independent of their will, namely, relations of production corresponding to a determinate stage of development of their material forces of production. The totality of these relations of production constitutes the economic structure of society, the real foundation on which there arises a legal and political superstructure and to which there correspond definite forms of social consciousness. The mode of production of material life conditions the social, political and intellectual life-process in general. It is not the consciousness of humanity that determines their being, but on the contrary it is their social being that determines their consciousness. (1857: 4–5)

Marx was not interested in 'structure' or 'consciousness' as such; he was more interested in the causes and dynamics of historical *change*. He wanted a scientific explanation for social change, and he thought the 'base and superstructure' model supplied it:

> At a certain stage of their development, the material productive forces of society come into conflict with the existing relations of production [property relations]. ... From forms of development of the productive forces these relations turn into their fetters. At that point an era of social revolution begins. With the change in the economic foundation the whole immense superstructure is more slowly or more rapidly transformed.

In considering such transformations it is always necessary to distinguish between the material transformation of the economic conditions of production, which can be determined with the precision of natural science, and the legal, political, religious, artistic or philosophic, in short, ideological, forms in which humans become conscious of this conflict and fight it out. (1857: 4–5)

That's a terrific piece of synthesizing analysis, its ambition, reach and rhetoric still commanding admiration after all these years. Like his previous comments on 'world-historical' facts, it is also an amazingly early attempt to put history on the footing of 'a natural science', complete with laws arising from observations, and to consider it at planetary scale. But is it true? Does the conflict between forces and relations of production drive historical change, transforming in turn the 'whole immense superstructure' of culture, communication and consciousness?

'Göbekli Tepe changes everything'[21]

Social groups certainly were transformed in the Neolithic period, but the crucial question for present purposes is about the chain of causation. Did farming produce surpluses, classes, antagonism, growth, settlement, states, and thus set humanity on the uneven road to modernity? And even if it did (albeit not as a 'revolution', but 'piecemeal'), what 'caused' the invention of farming, and then of cities?

A way of posing the problem most starkly is to turn causation around, and ask: Did *culture* 'cause' the need for large-scale resource gathering and ordered settlement in order for large Mesolithic demes to perform large-scale acts of meaningfulness, which required concentrations of people who were occupied in building ceremonial 'mass media', as well as feasting (and offering)? And was it this ceremonial activity, perhaps marking the demic boundaries of large, highly organized groups and 'broadcasting' their strengths, which necessitated more intensive modes of food gathering, herding, and residential settlement? Such possibilities were out of the question for Childe.

We can only ask them now – a century later – because we now know that the so-called Neolithic Revolution came *after*, not before, *cultural innovations* on a literally monumental scale. The first great stone buildings in the world were put up not by farmers, as was the case for Stonehenge (Parker Pearson, 2012) and the pyramids (Romer, 2012), but thousands of

---

[21]Ian Hodder, director of archaeology, Stanford University: http://www.academia.edu/468134 9/Göbekli_Tepe_Changes_Everything; and see Hodder (2018).

years earlier than that – further back in time before Stonehenge and Saqqara than these sites are remote from today – in Turkey, Syria and the Fertile Triangle, by *Mesolithic hunter-gatherers*, before farming was invented, although it was invented, soon after, thereabouts.

The arrow of causation may have to be reversed: the causal force for change is culture, as has been recognized by those closest to the scene (Watkins, 2010). It is based not on 'surplus labour' but on *concentration and intensification of communication, by self-identifying groups* called demes – inter-knowing subpopulations, made coherent by shared and competitive culture. This precipitated intensive food requirements and the need to house large bodies of people in a particular place.

Recent discoveries, especially at Göbekli Tepe ('Potbelly Hill') in Turkey, excavated by the late Klaus Schmidt,[22] suggest that the Childean chain of causation is the wrong way round. The limestone monuments at Göbekli Tepe are about 12,000 years old. Stonehenge and the Great Pyramid are not yet 5,000 years old. The Turkish site's monumental scale – both in terms of the size of individual stones and circles and in terms of their number– is astonishing, as is the precision and beauty of construction. There's no sign of it being used for military, economic or residential purposes, as was also the case for Stonehenge, millennia later. It seems to be have been designed as an expression of 'symbolic culture' (Schmidt's term) and communal activities that were organized around *gathering* people, resources, knowledge and performance, into one place, for one purpose: *communication*. It may have been internal, confirming the 'we'-group, with feasting and shared ritual – not to mention the collaborative work and organization of making the monument, or external, 'costly signalling', especially to foes or competing neighbours who may have been building something of their own.

Altogether, the site is a boundary-making exercise, possibly one designed to include the dead (burial levels are not yet excavated). Indeed, following Parker Pearson (2012), it may have been a prehistoric technology for *linking* the living with the dead, making demic 'honorary relatives' (Pagel, 2012) out of ancestors, by drawing a new, capacious boundary around the deme to include within the community both time (beyond death) and place, 'sanctifying' (as we might now say) the country where they inhabited (and see Griffiths, 2018, for Australian Aboriginal parallels). Once boundaries were drawn around the 'we' community, it proved practical to do the same to the land required to support it. The crowd was so big that they had to invent farming and settlement to cope with the pressures created by congregating,

---

[22]See, for instance: http://beforeitsnews.com/blogging-citizen-journalism/2013/08/gobekli-tepe-f antastic-new-photos-of-12000-year-old-temple-complex-the-oldest-known-2448608.html. For a tribute to Schmidt, see: http://antiquity.ac.uk/tributes/schmidt.html. And for the continuation of his work at Göbekli Tepe, see: https://www.dainst.blog/the-tepe-telegrams/.

building stone monuments, feasting and ritual activities. Mesolithic nomads, without metals or even pottery, began the process of 'abstracting' symbolic culture into *new media* – in this case, limestone – so that everyone could find their thrill on Potbelly Hill. Klaus Schmidt concluded:

> The evolution of modern humanity involved a fundamental change from small-scale, mobile hunter-gatherer bands to large, permanently co-resident communities. The factor that allowed the formation of large, permanent communities was the facility to use symbolic culture, a kind of pre-literate capacity for producing and 'reading' symbolic material culture, that enabled communities to formulate their shared identities, and their cosmos. (Schmidt, 2010: 253–4)

What Schmidt calls 'shared identity' was *performed* here: in the monuments themselves, in the work needed to make them, and in the attendant ceremonies. Göbekli Tepe was an improbably early site of *mediation*, and in terms of causal sequence, it suggests that culture produced the polity and economy, not the other way around.

Neolithic mass communication

Throughout the twentieth century there seemed to be no need to *argue* the primacy of economics or the concomitant corollary, that culture was dragged along 'in its wake', until the discoveries at Göbekli Tepe. The upright stones may resemble ancestors, who may be gathered in a ceremonial (story) circle, perhaps linking the living and the dead.[23] Now, it seems, we may need to reverse the flow of causation, because the monument-builders there were hunter-gathers, who neither farmed nor settled. It turns out that symbolic ritual, including gathering, dancing, feasting and ceremony, was staged in massive, elaborate stone-built circles that seemed to have no economic or residential function. Schmidt's colleagues at Göbekli Tepe are quite explicit on this point:

> Repetitive feasting at Göbekli Tepe may have played an essential role not only in creating and strengthening social bonds among the individuals and groups meeting there, but must also have stressed the economic potential of these hunter-gatherers to repeatedly feed such large crowds. In response to this pressure, new food resources and processing techniques may have been explored, subsequently paving the way for a complete

---

[23]'Pillars at the temple of Göbekli Tepe – 11,600 years old and up to 18 feet tall – may represent priestly dancers at a gathering.' *National Geographic*: http://ngm.nationalgeographic.com/2011/06/gobekli-tepe/musi-photography; and see: C. Mann (June 2011) 'The Birth of Religion'. *National Geographic*: http://ngm.nationalgeographic.com/print/2011/06/gobekli-tepe/mann-text.

change in subsistence strategy. In this scenario, the early appearance of monumental religious architecture motivating work feasts to draw as many hands as possible for the execution of complex, collective tasks is changing our understanding of one of the key moments in human history: the emergence of agriculture and animal husbandry – and the onset of food production and the Neolithic way of life. (Notroff and Dietrich, 2017)

The megaliths, like others, are constructions of the *polity* – an expression of meaningfulness for the demes (groups) that built them. More important, they offer intriguing evidence that the received standard formula has it wrong. It is not that 'the economic base determines the cultural and political superstructure', but that *culture constitutes the polity*, and the expression of the resultant facts (in organization and logistics, as well as stone and story), may have precipitated epoch-changing economic and political arrangements. These feats of construction both organized and represented what can be described as the earliest known political narrative: the very earliest 'mass communication' (one 'sign' broadcasting powerful messages to many). They predated and likely precipitated both farming and settlement.

Once farming had been invented and put on an efficient footing, the resources were so much the greater for continuing with cultural and political activities. Nick Card – director of the Ness of Brodgar dig in Scotland (6 miles southeast of Skara Brae on Orkney's Mainland), another recently unearthed wonder that is older than Stonehenge – told PBS in August 2015 that the artefacts unearthed over the years of the dig had led him to change his view of its function, from 'something to do with life and death' to the suggestion that 'people traveled long distances to the imposing complex people to perform rituals, but also to feast, trade goods, gossip and celebrate'.[24] Perhaps there's no need to choose between these options. After all, even the most revered ancient Greek *temples* like the Parthenon were also *treasuries* – Bronze Age Reserve Banks – storing 'cash reserves for the construction of buildings and the erection of statues, as well as for a series of wars'.[25]

From the perspective of cultural science, the first great stone monuments erected by our species, from Göbekli Tepe to Stonehenge, are nothing less than *mass media*. Why is communication so important? The answer appears to be that culture and communication perceive the world for us and shape our demes as high-trust 'we'-groups with a collective identity, such that the

---

[24]Lorna Baldwin (2015) 'Keeping up with the Joneses, Neolithic Scotland edition'. *PBS Newshour:* http://www.pbs.org/newshour/updates/uncovering-neolithic-mysteries-one-dig-season-time/#.

[25]*Greek Reporter*, July 9, 2015: http://greece.greekreporter.com/2015/07/09/parthenon-might-h ave-served-as-athens-treasury/.

'we' community encompasses ancestors and the dead, but not neighbours and potential enemies. Identity is realized through shared language, knowledge and technologies, including practical know-how and processes to make technologies and societies work, and the collective actions required to make and maintain them. 'We' groups are distinguished from adversarial or low-trust 'they'-groups by recognized differences in language, knowledge and communicative systems. Social media are group-forming institutions of inclusion and exclusion, and demic groups are powerful both internally (they 'crowdsource' new ideas) and externally (they protect knowledge and culture from incursions – 'ours' can beat 'yours'). But equally, they are vulnerable to lethal force and duplicity, both internal and external. They don't even exist 'in nature' (they're made not found), so they need elaborate rituals, stories, ceremonies and 'sacred sites' to sustain their centrality in the group, whether that is a tribe, a city or more diffused 'imagined community'.

'Talking animals'

Culture-made groups are the survival vehicles for knowledge and technology. They are, as it were, the prime directive for humans. In modern society, they are what Alexis Tocqueville, at the outset of global democratization, identified as one of its great features – 'associations':

> Americans of all ages, of all conditions, of all minds, constantly unite. Not only do they have commercial and industrial associations [firms] in which they all take part, but also they have a thousand other kinds: religious, moral [intellectual], serious ones, useless ones, very general and very particular ones, immense and very small ones; Americans associate to celebrate holidays, establish seminaries, build inns, erect churches, distribute books, send missionaries to the Antipodes; in this way they create hospitals, prisons, schools. If, finally, it is a matter of bringing a truth to light or of developing a sentiment with the support of a good example, they associate. (Tocqueville, 2010, Vol. 3: 896)

Here, even as we think forward from the Neolithic to the modern era, it is helpful to push back yet further, to what Yuval Harari (2014) calls the 'Cognitive Revolution', which he dates at about 70,000 years ago (but it may be much earlier), when humans found a clever way to use their vocal apparatus, energy-guzzling brains and group-making habits to discern and manipulate the communicative intentions of others (Tomasello, 2014), and to create and communicate realities that did not exist in nature, which Harari calls 'fictions'. These are big-deal presences in human life, not trivial illusions: gods, law, money, nations, the economy and firms, to name a few.

It may be wiser to call Harari's 'Cognitive Revolution' *cultural* (following Lotman (1990, 2009); Dor (2015); Evans and Levinson (2009) and others) rather than *cognitive*; and, learning from Childe, perhaps not a 'revolution' at all, but an *evolutionary* change. Harari follows modernist history ('revolution') and behavioural psychology ('cognitive'), but the logic of his argument points to a communicative, collective and cultural explanation: he nominates a *use* for cognitive powers – speech – which is not primarily produced by individual cognition (brainwork), but by social relationship and cultural function (Dediu et al., 2013). Thus, despite his disciplinary biases, Harari is on to something! He observes that humans are distinguished among animals by their ability (or need) to create group-binding *fictions*, which he does not dismiss as 'superstructural' luxuries. Indeed, the 'fictions' Harari has in mind make the world go round (albeit in a direction not much to his liking). Here we can see in action a tentative consilience of evolutionary sciences with the humanities, combining evolution, history and fiction in a way that takes the full weight of each and, in the process, re-ordering human history in the name of *stories*. This is the emergence of *Homo sapiens* as the '*talking animal*', as Shakespearean critic Terence Hawkes put it (1973; and see Chapter 8). What distinguishes the talking animal from others is the ability to organize social life and processes, from micro to macro scale, by means of these fictions and their embodiment in stories.

V. Social media, demes and children

Evolution of media technologies

Harari's placement of 'fictions' at the centre of *Sapiens*' species being, his willingness as a historian to push 'history' back very much further than its traditional limit, to an evolutionary not a documentary point of origin, and his recognition that 'fictions' (human ideas and institutions) have material, historical, biogeochemical effects, point the way for us to bring culture, communication, media – and knowledge itself – back to the centre of scientific inquiry. This is the terrain being explored in cultural science, where an attempt has been made to account for the growth of knowledge within the context of technological and economic evolution (Hartley and Potts, 2014: 215). Harari's 'Cognitive Revolution' is but the first of several accelerating changes in knowledge technology that can be seen to co-evolve with human culture (Figure 2.4).

Knowledge grows exponentially with the discovery and general adoption of new knowledge technologies. From the extreme long-term perspective, and despite various 'mass extinctions' of particular languages, writing systems and media forms, the overall story of knowledge – like that of the human population – is one of continual growth in scale and complexity. In each stage, fears are expressed that continued growth cannot be accommodated,

Technology of Knowledge	Economic epoch	Timeline
1. Primate animality	Pre-economic subsistence	before 200K years ago
2. Speech/stone	Hunter-gatherer economy	before 70K years ago
3. *Göbekli Tepe*	*Ceremonial economy*	*~12,000 years ago*
4. Writing/maths	Agricultural economy	~3100 BCE
5. Print (moveable type)	Industrial economy	1450 CE
6. Electronic/broadcast	Information economy	1895 CE
7. Internet/network	Creative economy	1970 CE

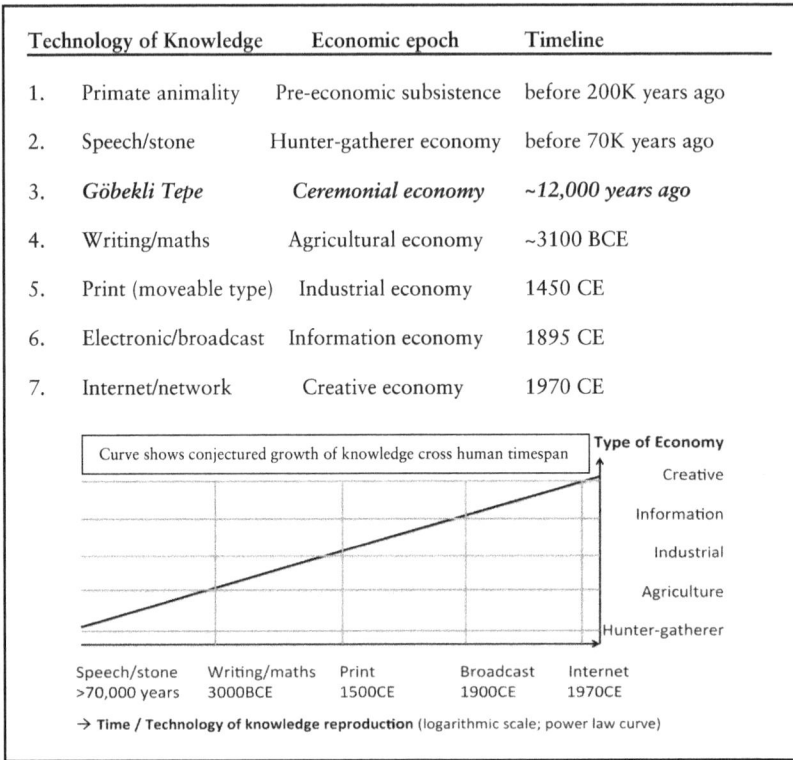

FIGURE 2.4 *Communicative epochs and the growth of knowledge. Technologies of knowledge communication, correlated with economic epochs. Adapted from Hartley and Potts (2014: 215).*

because it threatens either the existing social order or, more recently, the natural capacities of the planet. So far, at least, growth has nevertheless continued, in terms of both 'outward' flows (more of the population know more about more), and 'upward' stocks (there is more knowledge now than there was before and it is more accessible). These step-changes correlate with successive economic epochs (Figure 2.4). Thus, human history can be reckoned by reference to various stages of the evolution of knowledge-making communications technology, a tradition of inquiry going back to Harold Innis, Marshall McLuhan and Walter Ong (the 'Toronto School').

The epochal growth of knowledge by means of successive media technologies cannot be explained as 'revolution'. Media uptake and use cannot be explained by reference to technology alone, or to economics alone. To make a societal difference requires unprecedented literacy – in writing and making as well as reading – and it creates its own groups, going well beyond received boundaries of culture, nation or class. In fact, group-making is what social media '*do*'. The resultant groups sometimes resemble demes (*culture*-made, inter-knowledge commons), sometimes 'clubs' (purposeful, knowledge-*making* groups), and sometimes classes (action-oriented, *group*-making groups). These groups can be evanescent (they come and go, like crazes) or ancient (following 'tribal' affiliations); they are 'real' (organized around a city, an activity or purpose) or 'virtual' (affiliation in media, whether fanship or the 'republic of letters'). They can share economic interests, resources and rewards, or ignore these completely, linking people across the world, across divisions of gender, class, age, race, nation or occupation in a community of affect and action, often as audiences and readers of the performing and creative arts. Sometimes groups 'leak' into one another, as when fans – often children or teens – are caught up in political action, either through sudden catastrophe (bombing Ariana Grande's Manchester gig) or from slow-burn dissatisfaction with existing political discourse (gun violence; climate change; environmental pollution; extinctions). Here we see young people, with only the resources of communication at their command, and 'fictional' ideas in their heads, forming new demes, new clubs and commons and a new class (see Chapter 12), marking their difference from the past with new language, new rules of conduct (whether dance moves or interpersonal ethics), new associations, new celebrities. Making groups is culture-led, but its consequences are political and economic, social and human.

It is important therefore to consider how *longue durée* the history of *social media* really is, pushing decisive changes back, beyond the Neolithic Revolution to *language evolution*, and at the same time bringing the process forward to the era of the internet, recognizing that some of what we know is embedded in rule-systems so ancient and over-coded that we don't know that we are using them. These systems include grammar, storytelling, deme-formation, mediated communication, and technologies. Another implication is that the current era is witnessing the growth of knowledge at unprecedented scale and speed, and that changes in economic epoch are accelerating too. Knowledge is growing at logarithmic scale (power law curve), and it has been since humans first migrated 'out of Africa'.

Caveat

Assumptions are built into the culture-made knowledge-technology-economy sequence (Figure 2.4); each of them poses a problem that needs further attention in cultural science. For example:

- Many '*knowledge technologies*' are not listed: not just experimental or short-lived ones (e.g. magic lanterns, magnetic tape), but also those carrying different orders of knowledge. There are those that are associated with *embodiment*: ceremony, drama, music, apparel, gender; those appropriate to *the city* and to *travel* (sailors' stories from the sea, rather than peasants' stories from the soil) (Buonanno, 2005, 2012); *'maker'* or artisanal practical know-how and the use of technologies and the visual and plastic arts. These deficiencies follow a bias of the originating McLuhan-Ong model of communication technology studies, which focuses on the most abstract of knowledge technologies – writing, print and broadcasting. But as John Romer puts it, in a 'pre-literary environment', 'the manipulation of stone, wood and pigment was a prime mover in the processes of human thought' (2012: 372–3). Even as that manipulation worked tirelessly to imagine and represent the order of the pharaonic state, it 'allowed the practical free-flow of intelligence' (trial and error; innovation), rather than conforming to 'a sternly centralizing organization' (2012: 376). These and other knowledge-technologies need to be integrated.

- A further gap in the model at Figure 2.4 is the *time lag* between invention and impact, as I've mentioned in the case of print. More generally, industrialization was made possible by the invention of the steam engine, but it was made *real* by the application and absorption of that invention's potential uses, first in Britain over the ensuing fifty years, and then globally in national and imperial competition (Mokyr, 2009). Similarly, broadcasting, computers and the internet were invented decades before their socioeconomic decisiveness became apparent. The invention of a technology doesn't coincide with its importance, which can only be observed when it is taken up as a *social* technology.

- Over the long span of the growth of knowledge, the *number of demes* accessible by any individual person has increased, perhaps exponentially. It's not just 'knowledge' (abstract) that grows but the *number of groups* which make it; and the *number of demes per person* that give individuals access to different kinds of knowledge and to multiple literacies. Demes may once have been organized principally around language, ethno-territorial descent and divisions of labour, starting with gender ('when Adam delved and Eve span')[26]

---

[26]Priest John Ball's sermon at the Peasant's Revolt (England), 1381: 'When Adam delved and Eve span, Who was then the gentleman? From the beginning all men by nature were created alike, and our bondage or servitude came in by the unjust oppression of naughty men. For if God would have had any bondmen from the beginning, he would have appointed who should be bond, and who free. And therefore I exhort you to consider that now the time is come, appointed to us by God, in which ye may (if ye will) cast off the yoke of bondage, and recover liberty' (McIntire, 2009: 104). Things didn't turn out well for John Ball or the peasants in 1381, but you can see here the ideological and rhetorical foundation for the American Declaration of Independence. See http://www.bbc.co.uk/radio4/history/voices/voices_reading_revolt.shtml.

and age-group (the old governed the young), and thus there were few 'we'-groups to which the Neolithic savant *could* belong. Today's knowledge agent can belong to demic groups and knowledge-making associations by choice, affinity, education and experience, not just by social position, and can access both groups and archives beyond the reach of people from earlier economic eras, many of whom, incidentally, are still alive, so rapid is the pace of change. It follows that new ways of thinking about how knowledge is distributed and accessed are more important than ever. It's no longer sufficient to assume that whatever the local elite knows goes for the generality of the population (as has been the default setting in print/industrial culture), because knowledge is specialized, dispersed (across language and other boundaries), and is very easy both to avoid and to hide (e.g. behind secrecy, privacy, and other new deme-making barriers). Thus, a 'policy' setting for contemporary knowledge systems would focus on how many different 'demes' or 'knowledge clubs' are simultaneously open to everyone. Cultural science must move from an interest in 'the growth of knowledge' to concern for *'open knowledge'*.

- The *aggressive parochialism* of culture, which produces the familiar 'universal-adversarialism' (where 'our' knowledge is universally accessible, applicable and adequate; while 'their' knowledge is mistaken, malicious, or murderous), is inadequate to the scale and pace of change. It's important *not* to associate knowledge with 'we' groups that seek to defeat others, but to think at species level.

- The *accelerating pace* of change needs to be taken seriously. Economic epochs used to last longer than human lifetimes. They don't now. Scholarship needs to be mindful of both 'ends' of this problem. Looking back, it is important not to cut off the past as if its steps don't lead directly to the here and now. But equally, and this is new, it is important to note that 'consciousness' now includes individual, personal consciousness of planetary systems of difference and change. We need to attend to dynamics, difference and the increased force of noetic uncertainty in this context: everything you know is going to be proven wrong – while you're alive and probably more than once. It's keeping up that matters; learning how to navigate knowledge groups and archives.

Children invent demes

From this model of culture, groups, knowledge and long-term growth patterns, we may follow some clues about how to think about social media as the process continues to unfold. In that context, it is illuminating to focus attention on children. *Discourses about* children tend to focus on control; *representations of* children tend to focus on innocence, especially when it is thought to be under threat. What children do for themselves, as a population with a cultural function, is rarely considered. Here's where cultural science differs from social and behavioural science. Cultural science accords a central conceptual place to children, observing that they – as a group, or cultural function – perform the activities required to make future-facing groups and thus knowledge, thereby maintaining dynamism in cultural systems. They are *culturally* productive.

Empirical social science, in contrast, barely notices children when thinking about social structures and agency; they only enter the picture as problems – vulnerable victims or disruptive youth. Social sciences have accepted the idea that children are defined by a lack: they are *required* to be unproductive, asexual, irresponsible and incomplete. Only if their uselessness is reduced – by child labour, sexualization or 'adult' responsibilities and experiences – do the social sciences intervene. Social sciences are part of the control system applied to childhood; 'letting children be children' comes to mean 'preventing children from experiencing labour, sexuality or family management'; or at least, preventing outsiders from seeing any of this.

Nevertheless, children are *semiotically* active from an early age, and this is encouraged (until technology outpaces parental control): they become speakers, readers, audiences and makers not only within a family and neighbourhood but also, via media, in schooling, sport, entertainment, friends, rivals, in direct interaction with a much wider world, including fantasy and fictional worlds in which they may research their senses of self. They are early adopters not only of technological devices and crazes but of groups, which they may go through in bewilderingly quick succession, from princess to Potter to punk and, before parents know it, straight to politics.

Thus, an evolutionary perspective on *social media* asks how young people form groups (off- and online), both passively (where they belong) and actively (what they do). When children start to make groups among non-kin they are modelling or experimenting with deme-formation, and also developing real links for future social networks, marked by new languages and argots. Children's play, mischief, language-games, purposeless creativity and daydreaming are creative of the next set of demes or culture-made groups, bound together by sociality and mutual knowledge, encoded and signalled through systems ranging from personal attire to celebrity culture. Demic groups are also divided from others (foreign and parental versions) by asymmetries of trust, comprehension and cooperation, codes for which are learned in childish play, including playing with online social media.

Here, 'play' is mistaken in social science as inconsequential and unproductive behaviour, using *economic measures* to determine culture, and thus posing a 'biological puzzle' for those who seek a 'rational choice' account of childhood activity (Konner, 2010: 500). Play needs to be reconceptualized, using *cultural functions* to explain a dynamic process of group-formation, code-creation and thence transmission of knowledge, know-how and technologies through time, where, again, economic productivity is a consequence, not a cause.

Nevertheless, 'children' and 'young people' are generally *represented* in both media and scholarly 'fictions' about society in a rather different guise, that of 'innocence' – unknowing irresponsibility and analytic inconsequentiality. Instead of being seen as future-forming agents they are looked at with anxiety and rarely permitted, even in semiosis, a creative, productive role, even while childish innocence is the preferred image of euphoria for capitalist marketing. When children *are* productive, economically and creatively, from underclass child labour in field, farm and factory to 'under-age' models and actors, they attract discourses of disquiet, protection and correction. Economic productivity in children is represented as going beyond the limit of the social, thereby *setting* that demic limit.

'Letting children be children!' means confining them to uselessness: politically unenfranchised, economically unproductive, behaviourally inconsequential, sexually impotent and creatively sterile, most themselves when most idle and irresponsible. They are very much a latter-day Veblenesque 'leisure class', their conspicuous wastefulness an index of their society's affluence (or, where they are exploited as a labour force, its poverty).

Actual humans have to turn these values upside down, traversing from child to adult by exchanging unknowing unproductivity for social, political and economic responsibility. They perform that trick in public, always being looked at and looking (Hickey-Moody, 2015: 145), both among peers (where it matters 'internally' to their deme) and by 'external' institutions interested in enforcing certain choices upon them, from what might be called 'honorary parents' (children's rights activists) to corporate marketing to law enforcement. As they experiment with the possibilities of social media, they are building selves and society: longing for love, fearing death, combining identity ('me') and belonging ('we'). Their collective creative and communicative dynamism demonstrates that the uncertainty, anxiety and difference associated with coming of age *drive* economic productivity in the creative epoch.

Science has inherited a view of children as underperforming or incomplete economic assets, to which the only response is control, combined with a knowledge-regime that discounts whatever they produce. Such a tradition not only mistakes the role children are playing in social reproduction but it also misconstrues social media and associated institutions, such as celebrity, entertainment and games, dismissing them as unproductive leisure, distraction, even delusion. But if we think of young people as a class of collective-action deme-forming agents of future social networks for the growth of knowledge, creative of groups, meanings, sociality, relationships and identity, then we may need to re-set the predominant governance mechanisms, moving the needle further along from 'control' to 'openness'. It may even be that social media are themselves a 'natural experiment' in this very enterprise, blindly looking for ways to make newness count, which is why children stand in for more general anxieties about what will happen to 'us' and 'our' deme in times of dynamic uncertainty and accelerating change. We need to rethink how our inherited knowledge systems understand (and discount) both 'primitive' culture and 'childish' behaviour (see Chapter 12). Both of these might have something to teach us.

3

Smiling or smiting?

Selves, states and stories in the constitution of polities

The story of the United States has been the continual expansion of rights to more and more groups claiming them, as well as continual resistance to that expansion. When conservatives object to this historical reality ... it is to America that they are objecting.

(ROBERT KAGAN, 2019)

This chapter investigates the role of storytelling in political narrative, taking a very long-term perspective, where 'political narrative' does not mean 'coverage of the politics of the day' but rather 'stories about the foundation of "our" polity and its heroes'. The archetypal polity is a tribe, city, nation (etc.), but in principle the term may apply to any group that identifies itself as coherent and as differentiated from neighbouring, competing groups, in fact or fiction. Thus, it may apply to informal or virtual groups organized around identity and affinity politics, including fans and taste cultures as well as communities based on ethnicity, sexuality, age and the like. I argue that this cultural role of narrative is not secondary or descriptive of social and political arrangements that have their origins and causes elsewhere (in the economy, or politics) but, on the contrary, that story is primary, generative and creative in that it *constitutes* the polity.

Stories include the Constitution, for countries that have one, for example, the United States (together with the Declaration of Independence). They take 'these truths' to be self-evident (Lepore, 2018), projecting the 'we'-group out into nature ('natural law') and beyond, into the supernatural ('under God'). These are *fictions* in the strong sense offered by Yuval Harari (2014). They literally tell insiders and outsiders alike who 'we' are, and hence what kind of political arrangements are appropriate, such that these can gain general acceptance and thus consent. It's the story that makes the polity; fictions make groups.

The question posed in this chapter is whether contemporary *digital storytelling* – in principle the most democratic mode of narration yet – can call new kinds of polity into being without the use of state apparatuses based on violence. If digital storytelling is going to 'count' in public (which now simply means 'online'), it needs to develop its own community, within which its particular kinds of knowledge may be communicated.

I. Smiling and smiting

Storytelling seems to be a very personal accomplishment, requiring a narrator and an audience, as one talks to the other. Interpersonal or conversational storytelling is no doubt a pleasure for individual participants, but its function is primarily social. *Groups* that share stories are pulled and glued together by them. Storytelling is part of 'natural pedagogy' or 'communicative teaching', identified as a specifically human evolutionary adaptation:

> Despite the huge variability in child-rearing practices, all human cultures rely on communication to transmit to novices a variety of different types of cultural knowledge, including information about artefact kinds, conventional behaviours, arbitrary referential symbols, cognitively opaque skills and know-how embedded in means-end actions. (Csibra and Gergely, 2011)

In other words, cultural knowledge is reproduced through time and across demographics by communicative means, often by copying, but also including narrative. Cultures as whole units are shaped in and by their stories. In traditional societies and also in oral components of modern ones (such as mother–child interactions), stories are a chief means for cultural and knowledge reproduction. In literate cultures (i.e. since 3100 BCE) stories begin to 'migrate' to extra-somatic technologies: clay, stone, papyrus etc. (Figure 3.1). Here, another transformation occurs. A distinction emerges between stories told by 'selves' (persons) and those told by or on behalf of 'states' (institutions). In addition, the category of 'selves' bifurcates into stories by 'natural persons' and stories by *personae ficta* or 'juridical persons' (institutional agencies). This happened over 4,000 years ago.

FIGURE 3.1 *The 'Flood Tablet' (*Epic of Gilgamesh*), Library of Ashurbanipal (seventh century BCE), photographed at Perth, Western Australia (February 2016). The shadow of the author's iPhone camera, latest in a long line of extra-somatic communication technologies, can be seen on the right. Photo by author. The tablet is held by the British Museum: http://www.britishmuseum.org/research/collection_o nline/collection_object_details.aspx.*

More recently, 'states' too have bifurcated, into 'public' (national, governmental) and 'private' (commercial, corporate) versions, with the emergence of commercial markets in narrative entertainment. This was an early modern development, from the time of Shakespeare (around 1600 CE), who was an early capitalist, a shareholder in a joint-stock company.

Within the institutional distinctions between self/state and private/public, stories themselves – in form and content – can be categorized into what I'm calling, for reasons explained below, *'smiling'* (community-building, caring, personal self-realization) and *'smiting'* stories (adversarial stories of conflict between groups). Persons are in the 'smiling' category, while 'smiting' stories belong to the state (when claimed to be true) and corporations (when presented as fictional). Thus, the entire *mediated* apparatus of storytelling (fiction, films, TV, drama) belongs to the 'smiting' side, while self-expression and thus digital storytelling belongs to the 'smiling' side of a long-term history of what might be called 'story capture' (Figure 3.2). Structurally, this casts digital storytelling as part of culture (subjective expression), while institutional storytelling, whether factual or fictional, counts as knowledge (objective truth). Structurally, the distinction may also be gendered: 'smiling' stories being domestic, vernacular, kitchen-table (or locker-room talk) rather than public sphere.

In economic terms, we may say that the otherwise unimproved cultural resource of storytelling was subjected over millennia to a division of labour and specialism. It grew into a productive industry, first as a 'state owned enterprise' (actually a monopsony: lots of bards/priests, but only one 'market' – the king/god). Later it expanded as 'private enterprise' (literature, history, science, games, etc.), in myriad local/national markets, which in turn expanded and integrated to reach global scale. Further specialization meant that different story forms and content (e.g. entertainment, science, journalism, religion) seem to belong to different 'industries', with little mutual dialogue, although all of them use the story form to reproduce their knowledge and their communities, and also to call out to others, whether

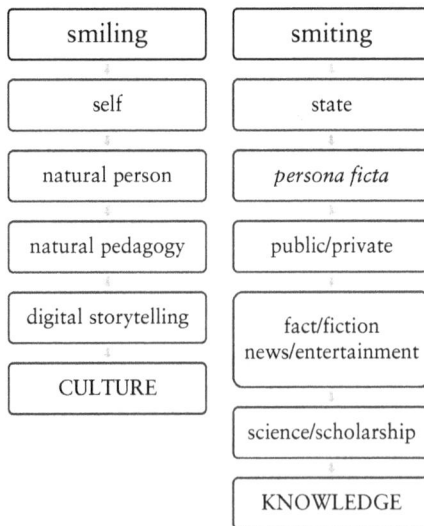

FIGURE 3.2 *Bifurcations of stories: Selves (smiling) = culture; states (smiting) = knowledge.*

for recruitment or conflict. The general or 'reading' public has access to many different story-types in which to recognize its own identity and to archive accumulated wisdom.

Smiling selves

Culture remains the source and destination of storytelling. But stories *by* unrehearsed ordinary people expressing themselves are not the same as stories *about* them or those told *to* them. These latter types are, in contemporary societies, fully institutionalized at corporate, state, and global scale. The personal aspect ('smiling') is appropriated to signal non-threatening communicative intentions, carrying messages that would likely be rejected if the tale were understood to be on behalf of industry or government. Hence, 'smiling' is now part of the corporate productive apparatus as well as being a tool of 'natural pedagogy'. The 'smiling professions' – where a chief skill is an appealing demeanour in the face of customers or audiences – include media jobs such as anchor, presenter, newsreader, actor, comedian, host, compère, MC, DJ, model, PR and all forms of marketing. 'Smiling' occupations are not confined to media. Often feminized, they extend to physical personal/bodily services: fitness trainers, 'cosmetic' services (from hair, make-up and skincare to waxing and surgery), retailers, hospitality, care-work, sex-work, teaching (which has evolved from a 'caning' to a 'caring' order). The smiling professions, especially in the media, are adept at telling 'smiling' stories, personalizing everything from prices to princesses in 'like us' scenarios, in order to convert citizens into consumers. So there isn't necessarily anything 'personal' about personal stories, despite the ubiquity of agreeable and attractive women and girls in them, who seem so naturally to represent 'us'. The important distinction is the one between those stories told *by* and those told *to* the ordinary citizen/audience.

Corporately produced 'smiling' scenes are central to the marketing, celebrity and media industries, public and private. But these use the very kind of 'personal' stories that the digital storytelling movement or community has tried to get away from, seeking to help people to tell their own stories, with self-expression, authenticity and freedom from institutional pressure. Such ambitions have however put a different kind of pressure on digital storytelling, and on the resultant stories themselves: it has become imperative to avoid initiating conflict, hate, partisanship and violence (although it's okay to tell of the negative personal effects of these, as for instance, in the memorialization of war). Digital storytelling systematically avoids 'smiting'! Nobody talks about the Fight Club.

Despite the desire to facilitate self-representation, individual digital stories are coloured if not determined by the type and purpose of the organization commissioning or facilitating the telling (Thumim, 2012; Chouliaraki, 2012; Couldry et al., 2014; Thumim, 2018). This is not a criticism; it is simply meant to demonstrate how hard it is to consider digital or any other storytelling without reference to its institutional form and semiotic environment. Given that digital storytelling is competing with a long-established, elaborate and highly capitalized system, everyone involved is always literate in 'state' as well as 'personal' narratives, requiring alertness to and scepticism about corporate communicative intentions, a scepticism that people will carry with them into the digital storytelling world itself.

Hence, a 'natural' person telling a 'smiling' story that 'realizes' or represents a 'self' is nevertheless unlikely to be a purely 'innocent' experience, because seeing and hearing the story is always preceded and surrounded by the 'critical reading' skills of a media literate audience. Now that consumers are increasingly also producers, a level of reflexivity about the 'self' and scepticism about *personae ficta* is built into 'smiling' itself, even at personal level: *'the self' is a performance*, to such an extent that 'scepticism' might now be a separate form of narration (to add to smiling and smiting), especially in social media commentary platforms like Facebook.

Smiting states

Many nation-founding stories, which are about the *constitution* of the polity, are stories of violence. Perhaps 'the people' (of 'our' polity) rebelled against an oppressor, home-grown tyrant or foreign invader, or all three, as may be claimed for the most charismatic modern revolutions (United States, France and Russia); or perhaps the 'national character' was forged in war, under threat of extinction (this is said to apply to Australia). Similarly, stories of national supremacy ('we' are better than 'they') are based on force (moral truth asserted by military victory), for example, the United States after the Second World War. It seems that such 'smiting' stories are exclusive to states and their corporate 'bards'. I have never seen a self-made digital story that celebrates this version of narrative. It does seem that self-made storytelling is more pacific or irenic in mode. Even stories about war are more likely to be about mateship or family than about defeating enemies. This is not to say that people in general don't harbour prejudicial, adversarial or bloodthirsty thoughts about their neighbours, internal or international. Of course they do. But such sentiments are somehow absent from digital storytelling, which seems dedicated to an alternative narrative, perhaps based on family not 'tribe'.

Nevertheless, everyone in popular culture is all too familiar with *smiting state* stories, since they are the staple of both history and drama, and have been since Gilgamesh (2700 BCE – nearly 5,000 years ago). Recent fiction tends to displace the enemy to the past, the future, to other planets or fantasy worlds, and the state to some fantasy version of 'us' (the 'free world') as a polity.

In a global marketplace this displacement is only to be expected: any nation or even an ideological system (political or religious) that is cast into a 'they' or enemy role is going to be a lost market. Thus, China routinely bans foreign films that denigrate China:

> Published reports have pinpointed at least a half dozen recent films where Hollywood has given in on demands from Chinese censors to alter content for political or other reasons, ranging from the James Bond feature "Skyfall" – where unflattering references to the sex trade in the Chinese territory of Macau supposedly landed on the cutting room floor – to "World War Z," starring Brad Pitt, in which the Chinese origin of a plague of apocalyptic zombies was said to have been excised. And that doesn't take into account ostensible instances of self-censoring, like last year's remake of the 1984 film "Red Dawn," where producers changed the nationality of bloodthirsty soldiers invading the United States from Chinese to North Korean, apparently to cater to their perception of Chinese political sensitivities.[1]

'Smiting' stories need to be careful where they create foes. But that doesn't deter them from the story form, only from naming specific enemies. Just look at the blockbuster movies on a screen near you. They are, as ever, dominated by individual struggle against alien adversaries thought to be stronger (or more duplicitous) than 'our heroes'. Protagonists are rarely shown as political or national leaders, but as 'ordinary' people, representing 'everyone', not the state. National character is also displaced onto children, of the type whose mettle proves true under pressure. Girls represent an 'innocent' version of 'us', despite the fact that, after *The Hunger Games* and *Game of Thrones*, they can even be depicted as killers (albeit 'moral' murderers) although never as sexual (see Chapter 12). In short, 'smiting' is not typically perpetrated *by* kings or leaders anymore; and it's not applied *to* national adversaries or competitors as it was in the World War and Cold War eras. It is no longer patriotic, religious or nationalistic in mode. Now, it is 'just personal', done by 'our' toned-bodied heroes, so these stories tell us,

---

[1] Source: http://asiancorrespondent.com/2013/04/hollywood-yielding-to-chinas-growing-film-clout/.

in democratic, egalitarian, or representative mode. This is also the ground for videogames, where participants are not only 'consuming' a story but also creating it as they go along. In the process, the biggest-selling first-person shooter franchise can boast that its users have 'thrown' *300 billion* in-game grenades between 2010 and 2015, in *Call of Duty*.[2] And here is a list of 'All Time Box Office' top ten movies:[3]

Rank	Title	Year
1.	*Avatar*	2009
2.	*Titanic*	1997
3.	*Star Wars: The Force Awakens*	2015
4.	*Avengers: Infinity War*	2018
5.	*Jurassic World*	2015
6.	*Marvel's The Avengers*	2012
7.	*Furious 7*	2015
8.	*Avengers: Age of Ultron*	2015
9.	*Black Panther*	2018
10.	*Harry Potter and the Deathly Hallows Part 2*	2011

The list is dominated by narratives where 'we' (compromised selves) smite 'them' (superhuman monsters).

The top-selling single-volume fiction books of all time are a slow-burn list in comparison with movies. Book stories are more focused on self-realization (smiling) than on 'smiting' enemies, but in most cases self-realization (English doesn't even have a word for it – in German it is called *Mündigkeit*: responsibility, maturity) can be achieved only at peril of mortal danger from a monstrous other. Even children must fight to the death to prevail against the odds. Here are those that have sold over 100 million copies:[4]

[2]Source: https://blog.activision.com/community/games-blog/call-of-duty/blog/2015/03/26/call-of-duty-infographic-over-300-billion-grenades-thrown/.
[3]Source: http://www.boxofficemojo.com/alltime/world/, December 2018.
[4]Source: https://www.ranker.com/list/best-selling-books-of-all-time/jeff419 and see: https://en.wikipedia.org/wiki/List_of_best-selling_books.

Rank	Title, author	Year
1.	*A Tale of Two Cities*, Charles Dickens	1859
2.	*The Lord of the Rings*, J. R. R. Tolkien	1954–5
3.	*Le Petit Prince* (*The Little Prince*), Antoine de Saint-Exupéry	1943
4.	*Harry Potter and the Philosopher's Stone*, J. K. Rowling	1997
5.	*The Hobbit*, J. R. R. Tolkien	1937
6.	*Alice's Adventures in Wonderland*, Lewis Carroll	1865
7.	*Dream of the Red Chamber*, Cao Xueqin	1754–91
8.	*And Then There Were None*, Agatha Christie	1939

In whatever medium, *smiting* remains the stock-in-trade, the business plan, of the most successful story-machines ever invented.

II. Constituting the polity

Polities: Demes

How can scholarship account for this, and thereby accurately explain the place of digital storytelling in this ancient but still evolving dynamic? In cultural science, *culture* is the primary means for making *groups*, and culture-made groups or demes are the primary makers of *knowledge*. In order to understand why and how this new approach to culture may be useful in relation to storytelling, it is best to start with what culture *makes*:

- *Polities*, which we call demes. The term refers to 'interbreeding subpopulations' in bioscience, and to 'the demos' or politically coherent decision-making groups (tribes, cities, nations) in political science. A deme is an 'inter-knowing' population or 'we'-group, linked by shared language and its institutions – including storytelling genres, conventions and archives – to produce individual identities that nevertheless gain meaning only in a group context, which includes potentially hostile competing groups, with well-defined boundaries between 'we' and 'they'.

- *Knowledge*, which is understood to comprise meaningfulness, not just information, data and transmission. In cultural science, culture makes groups and groups make knowledge. Cultural science conceives of knowledge as 'externalized' – not confined to the individual mind or brain, but produced by *linked brains*, through communication, cooperation and competition, and also technologized (Ong, 2012) over a very long period such that speech, writing (including maths and art), print, electronics and the internet (which supplement each other; the successor medium does not supplant its predecessor) provide external resources of knowledge in the ultimate 'open access' archive: culture.

Thus, culture (group identity, semiosis and knowledge) *precedes* politics: *Homo sapiens* is a groupish animal (Bowles and Gintis, 2011) and that is what makes it a 'political animal' (Aristotle). Group survival (culture) is more important than individual survival (Pagel, 2012), because that's how knowledge and technology can be reproduced across generations and across distance, just as genes survive but individuals die. In fact, it is culture (within and between demes) that *produces* individuals and knowledge, not the other way round.

Recent advances in linguistic theory (Tomasello, 2014) have begun to rethink the origin of language, focusing not on 'universal grammar' (as Chomsky did) or on the 'smallest signifying unit' (as Saussure did), but on the *'communicative intentions'* of which these arbitrary sounds and abstract rules become the external signs. As Paul Ibbotson and Michael Tomasello (2014) have put it: 'Language is not the unique thing in itself – it is an expression of what is unique: the ability to put our heads together and collaborate.' Humans use it to organize and conduct collective action while simultaneously probing the communicative intentions of others – gaining the ability not only to discern what a given signal or string is meant to convey but also to test those signals for deceit, duplicity and falsehood (masked or treacherous intentions).

Language is not at all straightforward: it doesn't simply name things. It can only tell the truth about the world because *all signs can also tell lies* (Eco, 1976: 7). But, especially in the hands of skilled 'users', it is efficient for monitoring the honesty of others' intentions (Bowles and Gintis, 2011), and thus for developing trust among groups comprising non-kin, for strategic intentions and collective action, to an extent not achieved by any other sublunary animal.

But because hominins (prior to and including *H. sapiens*) developed the ability to use lethal force (projectiles, stones, sticks) that could kill dominant 'alpha-males' (of the kind familiar among gorillas) by stealth, humans could only achieve group coordination through cooperation and what Herbert Gintis (2012: 7) calls 'individuals who could command prestige by virtue of their persuasive capacities'. Thus, culture has co-evolved with 'military' (lethal) technologies, not just in the contemporary era of the 'military-industrial complex' but as soon as *H. sapiens* emerged as 'the talking animal'

(Hawkes, 1973) several hundred thousand years ago. Language proved to be an efficient means to enable speakers to check whether their interlocutor was friend or foe (trustworthy or deceitful), and to spread throughout a community the necessary consent for leadership under uncertainty (thus, leadership = persuasion, not simply lethal power, since that particular 'power' can be returned by stealth). The 'technology' or 'institution' for these elaborate functions appears to have been the arts of rhetoric, storytelling and ceremony.

Language was – and remains – the ready-made marker to determine the boundaries of 'our' deme. Foreign accents are immediately detectable and routinely untrusted. But the boundaries of a deme are not just spatial; they are also social. One individual might belong to numerous demes, and it is reasonable to conjecture that the number of demes per person has accelerated with each successive techno-economic epoch, making multiple group-membership an index of the growth of knowledge.

Boundaries between our demes and other demes (we and they) are also temporal. Until very recently (say, since Darwin), human groups were not sure *when* they stopped, and this problem remains forceful to this day. 'We' continue to include ethnic or national heroes from the past, and ancestors (some of them 'honorary' rather than genetic) remain present from time immemorial. The relations between place, ancestors, knowledge and present possibilities are often remarked upon in relation to traditional societies, such as Indigenous 'dreamtime' cosmologies, but they are also built into modern polities, whose 'sacred sites' include public spaces and buildings (see Chapter 9), where national 'ancestors' keep watch from their monuments, which are often accorded special seasonal ceremonies. Despite Darwin, we're still uncertain (as a species) about the boundary between life and death, and some demes – for example, organized religions – reckon they can communicate with the dead (saints, spirits, ghosts), making the 'afterlife' or supernatural world a living part of the deme.

Certain cultural functionaries – priests, soothsayers, seers, shamans, augurs, clairvoyants and storytellers – act as intermediaries between the living and the dead. They assist past and future persons to talk to us through the medium of voices, smoke, shells, entrails, written signs: and Arnold Schwarzenegger! Despite Darwin, and notwithstanding the materiality of modern technological culture, we still invest inert things with ghostly 'liveness' and 'presence'; we worry that machines (robots) have independent or 'sovereign' agency (today they take our jobs, tomorrow they take over our polity), and we anthropomorphize technologies to produce wild fantasies of cyborgs and androids that will render 'our' deme as utopian or dystopian. Electronic technologies remain as alive with ghostly presence as was any Classical woodland (Sconce, 2000).

This unresolved ambivalence about when and where 'we' stop, what is 'live' or alive, what will become of our deme, and what 'they' might be plotting, sustains storytelling in industrial quantities. The big blockbuster franchises, fantasy and science fiction are all displacements of 'when' as well as 'who' we are – past, present, future, alive, dead, or cyborg – and so is plenty of non-fictional storytelling including journalism, political debate and academic publications. They're all on the lookout for signs we can trust, duplicity we should fear, or 'others' who – like winter – are coming, either from the past, for revenge or redemption, or from the future, for destruction or hope. The 'deme' and its dangers – the cultural polity – is a widely shared and endlessly reiterated fiction, and a fantasy fiction at that.

The origins of smiting

'We'-groups or demes are constituted in opposition to 'they'-groups, and 'our' knowledge' is tested against 'theirs', sometimes to destruction. Thus, conflict and warfare can be seen as a chief means for generating new knowledge (by competition), repurposing the knowledge of other demes (by conquest) and scaling knowledge up to higher levels of general abstraction or to larger units (by consolidation). This is destructive as well as constructive, because individual persons, demes and cultures, all the way up to the scale of empires and civilizations, can be and are destroyed in the process. Knowledge is lost. *New* knowledge is most intensively generated along the contested borders between communities, where the immediate goal is the destruction of adversaries. Despite the casualties, however, such conflict and even conquest can be seen as forms of *cooperation* at species or system level, where the scattered knowledge systems of small groups are aggregated and integrated into larger units that can better survive external attack. Each successive civilization contains lessons learnt by predecessors, even though these have been obliterated. Peter Turchin (2016) argues that the co-evolution of culture and warfare explains history, which is crucially the story of how states got larger in order to counter weapons that were getting more dangerous (e.g. horses, chariots). According to Turchin and his colleagues, warfare is a chief 'selection pressure' on cultures over a 10,000-year period, leading to ever larger or 'ultrasocial' units (empires):

> The conceptual core of the model invokes the following causal chain: spread of military technologies → intensification of warfare → evolution of ultrasocial traits → rise of large-scale societies. … Costly ultrasocial institutions can evolve and be maintained as a result of competition between societies: societies with traits that enable greater control and coordination of larger numbers will out-compete those that lack such traits. (Turchin et al., 2013: 16385)

Hence, and as Siniša Malešević and Kevin Ryan (2013) have convincingly pointed out (and see further discussion in Chapter 4), the oft-imagined violence of premodern societies, based on the 'natural' aggression of human beings, is a myth: 'Recent research on the behaviour of individuals in violent situations shows that our species is neither good at nor comfortable with the use of violence.' It is *civilization* – the smiting state – that explains warfare, not any 'natural' Hobbesian brutishness:

> Collective violence entails sophisticated coordination, organization, control and at least some degree of planning. ... The goal-oriented use of physical force requires cool headedness, instrumental rationality and self-control. Hence ... complex forms of organized violence, such as warfare, revolutions and terrorism, are only possible with the development of civilization. ... It is civilization, not the lack of it, that is at the heart of the organized and protracted mass slaughter of millions of human beings.

How do we know our representative heroes will protect us and provide for us, such that our deme and knowledge can continue into the future? The answer was settled by the time the recognizable entity of Egypt emerged in the reign of King Djoser (3rd Dynasty, *c.* 2675 BCE), who is credited with establishing 'the first state' in the world (Romer, 2012: 291). For Egyptologist John Romer, Djoser *personifies* 'Egypt' for the first time:

> Here, then, is pharaoh, the provider and protector of his realm, shown as the conduit linking the landscapes of his kingdom to this world and the next, a single image marking the physical and metaphysical extent of a new-made universe. (Romer, 2012: 249)

To signify the latter, Djoser is depicted as the '*smiting* king', following the very first dynastic pharaoh, Narmer, who is depicted on the famous Narmer Palette (*c.* 3100 BCE) in smiting mode (Figure 3.3). More than 2000 years after farming first appeared along the Nile, and over 400 years after Narmer, the image of 'smiting pharaoh' preceded the referent (the state of Egypt) by about fifteen generations or six lifetimes. The oldest personalization of civilized violence is the figure of the king.

Smiting kneeling enemies became the sure sign of power, and remained so for more than two millennia, up until the time of the last pharaoh, Cleopatra VII, who died in 30 BCE, when Egypt was absorbed, Turchin-style, into a larger empire. The semiotic shorthand of the smiting king, signifying the vigour of the state, was 'expanded' during the period of Egypt's imperial aggrandizement by multiplying manyfold the number of identical victims the pharaoh grasps by the hair; for instance Thutmosis III (r. 1479–1425 BCE) is shown smiting enemies in six multiples of seven (Figure 3.3), on the seventh pylon at Karnak, depicting the Battle of Megiddo (biblical Armageddon).[5] Storytelling – stories of protection and

---

[5]See: https://en.wikipedia.org/wiki/Thutmose_III#/media/File:Thutmose_III_at_Karnak.jpg. See also: USC Archaeology Research Center: http://www-scf.usc.edu/~grantdix/WhatIsAKing ToDo/HistoricalUses.html.

(a)   (b)

FIGURE 3.3 *Smiting pharaoh. (a) The Narmer Palette (3100 BCE); the first sign of the state. (b) Thutmosis III on the 7th pylon at Karnak, multiplying state power.* Source: *Wikimedia Commons.*

provision, security and victory, personal dangers faced and overcome – is the glue that holds subjects together in *states* that face external threats, real or imagined.

The growth of knowledge

Culture can be described as the evolution of meaningfulness, and even among all the waste and destruction, knowledge has grown cumulatively or exponentially, along with human populations and economic–technological epochs. Each continuing culture absorbs and supplements the knowledge of the last, so that modern material culture retains long-held knowledge (animistic beliefs, organizational forms, story genres) while simultaneously expanding the sum of knowledge via technologies from writing to computers and 'big data', and extending ubiquitous access to knowledge via technologized communication forms, most recently the internet, social media and open access.

But throughout, cultural evolution seems to be correlated not with a nostalgic notion of 'telling tales' around a comforting campfire but with something much more compelling: knowledge of 'our' lethal hunting party or armed band, allegiance to 'our' warlord, and motivation for inter-demic conflict designed to destroy 'them'. Stories are 'machines' for asserting the smiting-supremacy of 'our' band and 'our' knowledge against 'theirs'. This seems to be a constant in storytelling, from the oldest stories known to us (*The Epic of Gilgamesh*) to the latest news bulletins (Donald Trump, Daesh), which, oddly, constantly refer to the same bits of territory as were once travelled by Gilgamesh (Figure 3.4).

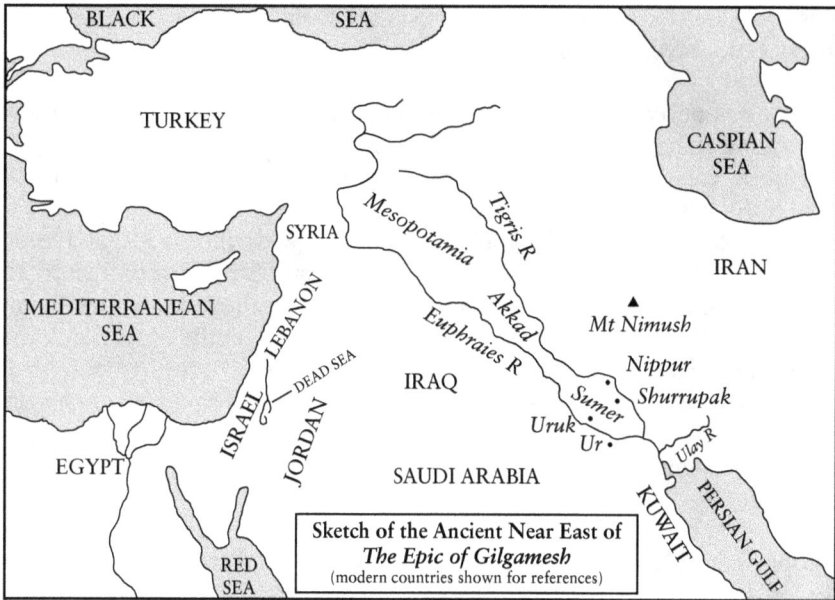

FIGURE 3.4 *The lands of Gilgamesh (king of Uruk, in modern Iraq).*
Source: *The Assyrian International News Agency: http://www.aina.org/books/eog/ eog.htm. Used with permission.*

We know how powerful stories are, because they can impel otherwise 'selfish' individuals (and their un-reproduced genes) to go willingly to their deaths in great numbers, on the promise of nothing more than that, if victorious, their names will be remembered in future stories. This does not suggest that individuals are overtaken by irrational enthusiasm, but that *cultures* (be they small demes or large cities or giant imperial states) are understood to be more important than the survival of individuals or even of their genes. The survival of culture, language, knowledge, and their enabling technologies takes precedence over everything else, and stories are the vehicle for binding a community together in that knowledge. Shared language, and 'institutions of language' are the apparatus for demic bonding, which turns out to be a matter of life and death.

Further, stories themselves (not just language but the demic uses to which it is put, and the knowledge of which stories become the archive) are 'general technologies', not the vehicles of political intentions alone. As Harari (2014) has argued, 'Sapiens' is unique among animals in developing 'fictions' as a technology for organizing knowledge and directing collective action, across some of the most important categories of life: *gods, nations, the law, money, human rights, firms* (and, we might add, *science*) – which exist only in 'our collective imagination', not out there, as it were, in the forest. But, notwithstanding its immateriality,

> fiction is nevertheless of immense importance, because it enabled us to imagine things collectively. We can weave common myths such as the biblical creation story, the Dreamtime myths of Aboriginal Australians, and the nationalist myths of modern states. And it is these myths that enable Sapiens alone to cooperate flexibly with thousands and even millions of complete strangers. ... The end result is that in contrast to all other animals, we Sapiens are living in a dual reality. On the one hand, the objective reality of rivers, trees and lions; and on the other hand, the imagined reality of gods, nations and companies. As history unfolded, the imagined reality became ever more powerful, so that today the very survival of rivers, trees and lions depends on the grace of imagined entities such as Almighty God, the European Union and Google. (Harari, 2014: chapter 2)

Fictions not only bond groups; they 'imagine' the most compelling realities we live by. They are the mechanism for organized, collective thought, and thence action.

III. Rich and the GG: New stories for new times?

A bit Rich

In this context, what of the personal 'smiling' story? It's pretty obvious that not all stories are equal, and nor are they meant to be. There's a big difference between, say, village, pub or kitchen stories concerning a tearaway boy called Rich Jenkins who lived with his sister Cis in industrial Port Talbot, South Wales, on the one hand, and, on the other, the most famous person in the world, movie star Richard Burton, who fell in love with his co-star Elizabeth Taylor, to the endless fascination of the world's press, while both were filming the most expensive movie ever made: *Cleopatra* (1963).[6]

Of course Rich Jenkins from Wales (objective reality) and movie star Richard Burton (imagined reality) are, or were, one and the same person (dual reality), and the link between them is itself an amazing story (Bragg, 1988). But local family and community stories ('Rich') and global celebrity

---

[6]Source: http://web.archive.org/web/20130629230642/; http://www.forbes.com/2006/12/18/movies-budget-expensive-tech-media-cx_lr_1214moviebudget_slide.html.

entertainment ('Burton') remain distinct, because they serve different purposes. On the one hand, blockbuster stories are centred on conflict: they are 'smiting' stories. They extend beyond media fiction (the film *Cleopatra*) to realist history (that of the last pharaoh, Cleopatra VII), to journalism and celebrity media (the 'myth', if you like, of Burton and Taylor), whose famously conflicted marriage(s) were in turn fictionalized in *Who's Afraid of Virginia Woolf* (1966), where the couple play 'themselves', to the peril of their actual marriage. On the other hand, personal stories by and about private individuals are rarely set up this way; they are centred on collaboration: they are *'smiling'* stories, often of redemption (I once was lost but now I'm found), self-realization (identity politics), or authenticity (eyewitness experience), evoking sociality and fellow feeling ('affect') in the construction of a 'we' community and personal acceptance into it. An example might be Richard Burton's own story about his childhood, *A Christmas Story* (Burton with Burton, 1991) – a short memoir for children. The likelihood of such private tales accruing demic status is low (although the *form* may be general, indeed, formulaic). Had this story been published under Richard Burton's real name (Rich Jenkins) it would no doubt have disappeared without trace.

New stories, new polities?

As in Hollywood, so in digital storytelling: whatever people's personal stories might be, they are produced and published in an institutional setting, often with an ulterior 'communicative intention', however benign. Whatever the form and content of a given story might be, it is necessarily linked to the facilitating organization's function and purpose, which is often social and political ('education' is a means, not an end). The digital storytelling movement (Lambert, 2006) is already very diverse, serving multiple purposes (but never *no* purpose). It includes Californian counter-culture (Dana Atchley), British public broadcasting (Meadows, Heledd and Evans, 2006; Meadows and Kidd, 2009), community arts and media (Woodrow et al., 2015), screen arts at the Australian Centre for the Moving Image (Simondson, 2009), the Turkish women's movement (Şimşek, 2012, 2015), 'at risk' youth (Podkalicka and Staley, 2009), education (Drotner, 2008), therapeutic healthcare (Hardy and Sumner, 2014), organizations (Dush, 2013), and self-representation for various demographics, from children (Skinner and Hagood, 2008) to seniors (T. Jenkins, 2015), whether for political emancipation (Vivienne, 2015), personal self-realization (Spurgeon and Burgess, 2015) or for 'digital literacy' and self-expression (Ohler, 2013).

Further, given the now global extent of 'digital culture', especially videogames, it hardly needs mentioning that 'digital storytelling' cannot be confined to the pre-internet, community-based, Atchley-Lambert-Meadows model of facilitated workshop practice (Thumim, 2012). The term can of course refer to any kind of narrative using 'new media' (Lundby, 2008), and to the computer-design disciplines devoted to creating them, in games, anime, movies, or social media for 'interactive entertainment' (C. Miller, 2014). A scholarly field has developed, and is rapidly specializing into subfields (Hartley and McWilliam, 2009). While games (and their attendant scholarship) have emerged out of a 'smiting' ('first-person shooter') tradition, digital storytelling seems to belong to the peace camp. It is seen in terms of social engagement, participation, activism and change; it is not simply 'story for story's sake'. Somewhere in the process someone wants to reach out to an existing or imagined 'we' group – to form a new deme, to make a polity.

It could be argued that any story with an intended interlocutor is seeking to call a group into being, whether a well-known existing deme ('us') or a new one with a new narrative. Thus, Richard Burton's *A Christmas Story* was evidently intended to signify his allegiance to his native Wales, using the model of Dylan Thomas's 1952 *A Child's Christmas in Wales*. Perhaps digital storytelling is trying to call new communities into being. But the scholarship associated with it has not paid much attention as yet to this 'political' (polity-forming) aspect of the form. It requires further investigation to understand how new forms of political association (new demic groups) may be created in contemporary digital culture, where potential storytellers number billions (many stories with few interlocutors) even as global media seek to capture everyone for *Hunger Games*, *Star Wars*, etc., (few stories with many interlocutors).

The question is, can DIY digital storytelling 'constitute' *new* 'polities'? And if so, what kind of political narrative is this? For what kind of polity and what kind of citizen? Societies are now held together by the consent of citizens, who can speak for themselves in unprecedented numbers, over globally accessible networks with billions of users. They need to reproduce in their own peer-to-peer interactions what was previously an institutional monopoly of states and corporations, namely the development of trust, coordination and cooperation across social systems that are now so large that they even exceed empires in scale.

Since the world-as-a-whole was first brought into the domain of knowledge in the nineteenth century, 'we' have started to get used to the idea that 'our' deme extends to the entire species, across the whole planet, on which it is having a material effect. There is no 'they'. As of the present moment, even the strongest empires have not sought to integrate the planet into a single winning state. The closest they came was during the period of 'Mutually Assured Destruction' in the Cold War, but both sides pulled back. Actually existing states do not have 'global domination' as their aim. Nevertheless, global trade and communications are integrating 'us' at species scale. So what happens now? What can be the function of deme-forming storytelling in a global, digital, egalitarian environment where

'they' are also 'we'? This is the challenge for centralized states and the
distributed digital storytelling movement alike.

Selfie state

Although history seems to have left us with little choice about stories at
demic or representative scale – they are stories of conflict and conquest –
there are signs that things are changing. The 'self' has begun to infect 'the
state'; smiting is giving way to smiling – or Mars to Venus, as Robert
Kagan once put it (2003). It's an inevitable consequence of democratization
(where 'democratization' is understood as expansion and decentralization
of control and governance, not as the tyranny of a majority, however
concocted), where consent to leadership is achieved as much as ever by
rhetorical and narrative persuasion, but now the representative of the state
is not always or necessarily a 'smiting king' – it can encompass 'me, myself'
and the responsibilities (*Mündigkeit*) that go with that.

In Australia, for example, the head of state is the British monarch. The
Queen has no powers other than ceremony (she's all smiles, no smiting),
and is represented by a resident deputy, the Governor General. When Dame
Quentin Bryce held that office, she delivered the annual broadcast 'Boyer
Lectures' on ABC Radio National (Bryce, 2013).[7] Her theme throughout
was that of storytelling, and digital storytelling at that. Using broadcast
media and the internet to talk directly to 'her' citizens, she said:

> Access to a computer and Internet connection can provide the marginalised
> and silenced with an outlet to speak truth to power, to participate in civic
> life. Increasingly, our capacity for circulation and activism is enhanced.
> The mechanisms of storytelling aren't perfect, but they are hopeful,
> and I think they are our best hope of building a more inclusive and a
> more responsible citizenship. ... Storytelling is in all of us. It is a natural
> human response to the experience of living and witnessing. It's how we
> talk to one another, and how we feel like we belong to something bigger
> and wiser than ourselves. It is instinctive and powerful, and foolishly
> underrated. (Bryce, 2013)[8]

Arguing that 'good leadership and good citizenship are intrinsically
connected', she linked storytelling to advocacy for human rights: 'How we
voice our ideas and concerns to the group, and how we engage one another

---

[7]The Boyer Lectures are the Australian equivalent of the better-known BBC Reith Lectures in
the UK. They're a kind of 'constitutional podcast', invented long before there were pods to cast.
[8]Source: Lecture 2: http://www.abc.net.au/radionational/programs/boyerlectures/watching-the-
women/4998504#transcript.

around ideals and around action' (2013: Lecture 2). Finally, she spoke about young people:

> When I ask young people about how they want to participate, whether in virtual or physical spaces, they say they're looking to be involved in a dialogue. They're not interested in being talked at. They want a genuine opportunity to respond. This is the idea of citizenship as communication; talking as a way of doing. Where ideas and action emerge from young people's everyday experiences and conversations. (Bryce, 2013)[9]

'Wake up everybody'

This is the challenge for digital storytelling, posed by the head of state of an existing national polity, but looking much more widely towards a group that may be as large as humanity (i.e. expressing 'human rights'): 'Our storytelling is our unique kind of advocacy as a citizen.'

Can the story, form and content of digital storytelling, reviving some of the personal communicative intentions of 'natural pedagogy', rise to the challenge of calling into being a globally distributed 'selfie state', organized around citizenship, leadership and communication, without 'they' adversaries? Joe Lambert, certainly wishes so: it is a core motivation for the digital storytelling movement he co-founded.[10] Listing a gloomy string of contemporary political, environmental and humanitarian disasters, Lambert predicts that 'it will look more like this for the rest of my life, and the lives of my children, and my children's children'. Nevertheless, he writes: 'And yet, oddly, I think we may be ready for all of this, we humans can meet this tipping point by tipping in the direction of hope, of justice, of compassion' (Lambert on Facebook, 5 March 2016).[11]

He links his comment to a 1975 R&B track by Harold Melvin & The Blue Notes, using song and story to call together a new version of the polity: the song is called 'Wake Up Everybody'.[12] This 'smiling' answer to 'smiting' is offered as the antidote to force (understood as literally hopeless), where *semiotic* cooperation among 'we humans' encourages action at

---

[9]Source: Lecture 4: http://www.abc.net.au/radionational/programs/boyerlectures/advance-aus tralia-fair/4998512#transcript.
[10]See: http://www.storycenter.org/.
[11]Source: https://www.facebook.com/joe.lambert.94801?fref=ts. The song can be heard here: https://www.youtube.com/watch?v=2HhV3Slqtvw.
[12]For the band, see: https://en.wikipedia.org/wiki/Harold_Melvin_%26_the_Blue_Notes; and for the song: https://en.wikipedia.org/wiki/Wake_Up_Everybody_%28song%29. 'Wake Up Everybody' featured in the 2004 US Presidential election when a cover version was released to encourage young people to vote.

unprecedented scale – by 'everybody' – to extend the 'we'-group to the whole species.

It is an abiding hope. As Friedrich Schiller had put it in his 'Ode to Joy' (1785), immortalized in Beethoven's Ninth Symphony (1824):

Seid umschlungen, Millionen,
Diesen Kuß der ganzen Welt!

> *Oh you millions, I embrace you*
> *– here's a kiss for all the world!*[13]

Will it work? In the equally immortal (albeit equally fictional) words of Zhou Enlai,[14] 'It is too early to say.'

---

[13]See: https://en.wikipedia.org/wiki/Ode_to_Joy.
[14]Chinese Premier Zhou was taken to be referring to the impact of the 1789 French Revolution, although that may not be the case. See: http://news.bbc.co.uk/2/shared/spl/hi/asia_pac/02/china _party_congress/china_ruling_party/key_people_events/html/zhou_enlai.stm.

4

Armed and wild:

What hope for open knowledge?

Civilization has not yet fully recovered from the shock of its birth – the transition from the tribal or 'enclosed society,' with its submission to magical forces, to the 'open society' which sets free the critical powers of humanity. ... The shock of this transition is one of the factors that have made possible the rise of those reactionary movements which have tried, and still try, to overthrow civilization and to return to tribalism.

(KARL POPPER, 1945: Preface to 2nd edition)

Within the theme of culture and technology, and in the context of planetary-scale and population-wide digital connectivity, this chapter discusses 'open knowledge', from the perspective of semiotic history and the history of ideas. I distinguish between two kinds of knowledge, which I trace back to pre-modern antagonisms: 'productive' or 'armed' knowledge and 'connective' or 'tribal' knowledge.

I argue that 'open knowledge' depends on a new synthesis of these types, which understands their difference and tension as a source of innovation. My aim is partly to show how important culture is in determining what knowledge means and who gets to share it, and partly to compare formal knowledge institutions (universities, publishing, libraries, etc.) with informal knowledge systems (popular culture and social media). Can knowledge ever be 'open' if it is at once cultural and institutionalized? If so, then how should we model openness?

I. Productive versus connective

Productive (armed) and connective (tribal) knowledge

In this chapter I introduce a way to characterize and compare two types of knowledge. My purpose is to demonstrate that in the 'deep history' of Western thought systems, in this case going back to the Roman Empire and the ensuing 'Dark Ages', these two types of knowledge have coalesced around very different groups, purposes, users and values, thence into opposing institutions and discourses. One, I call 'productive' and the other, 'connective', which I characterize as 'armed' and 'wild' respectively:

- 'Productive' knowledge (*Gk. gnosis – 'special knowledge of mysteries'*) is deep, specialist, expert, disciplinary and literate. It is state-supported, organized into sciences, taught at universities and used for economic growth. If you want to *understand* and *exploit* something, you need this kind of productive knowledge, together with its authorizing certification or 'metadata'. In its ancient forms, it is nothing less than *armed knowledge*, necessary for early states and empires to fend off incursions from marauding barbarians (Turchin et al., 2013).[1] In its modern industrial-productive mode, it is enforced intellectual property, trade secrets and private data, backed by legal frameworks that 'arm' firms and 'disarm' civilians.

- 'Connective' knowledge (*OE cnāwan – 'to acknowledge, to recognize'*)[2] is broad, circulating in everyday language and popular culture, open to everyone and shared orally. Connective knowledge is the glue of the cultural 'semiosphere' (Lotman, 1990), linking 'we'-groups internally, and setting them apart from 'they'-groups. In its ancient forms, this is the origin of *tribal knowledge*, needed to cohere and keep big groups of non-kin together (and distinct from adversaries) in uncertain times. In its modern form, it is thoroughly mediatized, digital, commercial, global, and circulated in the most popular social media. If you want to *enjoy* the *experience* of something, you need to know how to share it (both socially

---

[1]For example, the invention and evolution of the chariot was part of an ancient arms race between early empires and mobile marauders: See the TV-documentary *Secrets Of The Chinese Chariot*, Prod. Han Zhang; Dir. Giulia Clark; Lion Films, 2017: http://www.pbs.org/wgbh/n ova/ancient/chinese-chariots-revealed.html (PBS USA); https://www.sbs.com.au/ondemand/vid eo/1089120835771/Secrets-Of-The-Chinese-Chariot (SBS Australia).
[2]For etymologies of 'knowledge', going back to *gnosis* and *cnāwan*, see the *OED*, or https://www.etymonline.com/.

and technologically). This kind of 'common knowledge' is carried in language and is careless of copyright. The more popular it is, with the greatest network-effect, the better. It is that stock of oral–aural wisdom that includes myth, story, music, proverbs, jokes, sayings, folklore, etc., and their current equivalents coming out of celebrity and entertainment culture, including rumour, gossip and, increasingly, hate speech.

Productive knowledge is propagated as property; connective, as language. Both kinds operate on proprietorial platforms, public and private, and on the basis of excluding outsiders. Yet both have major commitment to openness of some kind. How might they be conceptualized as at once ordered and open? How might their contrasting features be characterized as part of an overall system in which 'open knowledge' is the outcome?

At stake is the opportunity to clarify why knowledge needs to be understood socio-culturally (not just technologically), and how, in a world that is far from 'open' in terms of borders, languages, rivalry and trust, knowledge can nevertheless travel far and wide, to be available for use in conditions unimagined by those who produced it. These questions are prompted by the Open Access movement in publishing and cognate developments around 'open source', 'open science', 'open campuses', etc. Since the technical means for openness are available with digital and internet technologies, and since there is a strong and successful international activist movement to promote openness (Montgomery et al., 2018), why is 'open knowledge' still elusive at global scale and among populations as a whole? And what can be done about that?

Universities and armed knowledge

The chief open platform for productive knowledge is the university, with a strong interest in 'branding' itself as an agent for effective knowledge-based action in the world, and an equally strong interest in avoiding contamination by purposeless, playful, piratical, person-to-person popular knowledge, which has no proprietorial or scarcity value. 'Connective' knowledge is kept at arm's length (downstream, for marketing).

Universities have descended from and still value (i.e. trade in) productive/armed knowledge (Edgerton, 2006). They continue a centuries-old tradition, where the sciences were conducted in Latin, separating the all-male public world of learning from feminized and infantilized domestic life (Ong, 1971: 113–41), making expertise an arcane 'mystery', beyond the ken of 'vulgar' people (L. *vulgus = common people*), vernacular expression (L. *verna = home-born slave*) and private life (L. *privatus = withdrawn from public life*, for which the Greek term was *idiot*). Expert, professional and scientific status required a prejudicial attitude towards popular knowledge. It is still routinely dismissed as inconsequential, childish and wrongheaded, suitable for consumers but not producers.

The 'value proposition' of universities is tied closely to their ability to translate individuals into 'knowing subjects', and method into a productive tool. The market in which universities compete is not based on knowledge 'outputs' as such, but on proxies that measure something else: 'excellence', exclusivity and 'quality' (Moore et al., 2017). In practice, prestige and branding follow the contours of imperial power, not invention, innovation, or discovery. The socioeconomic clout of a country, gender, class, or other favoured group is translated into 'neutral' league tables.[3] Such a system rewards scarcity, not openness. It is designed to convert 'the republic of letters' (where ideas can originate from anywhere in a system) into status hierarchies (Darnton, 1984), where only certain institutions, countries, disciplines and persons 'count'.[4]

The individualist-competitive process of research funding invokes the general population (the 'taxpayer') to justify, naturalize and subsidize a knowledge system that systematically excludes them. Instead, a complex network of *specialist* (as opposed to *general*) knowledge has emerged, whose 'basic structure' is 'surprisingly robust' (Rafols, Porter and Leydesdorff, 2010). The resulting 'map of science' organizes knowledge that is *influential*, useful for exploitation at scale. Despite the fact that taxpayers pay for many of the enabling inventions underlying corporate profits (Mazzucato, 2015), often with initial defence (war department) funding, the public are reengaged in the productive-knowledge system as consumers, not as coeval 'knowing subjects'.[5]

Popular culture and wild knowledge

On the other side, connective/tribal knowledge has been used by 'we'-groups (at any scale) among general populations for identity, entertainment, sociality and mutual recognition, but not so much for credentialed authority. Popular knowledge may be expert, but it is randomly distributed,

---

[3]This is a straightforward Bourdieuvian conversion of economic into cultural capital: the reputation of the very best institutions comes not from their research but from their alumni. Who has studied at Vassar or Harvard sends a more powerful market signal than who knows what among their professors.

[4]I cite Darnton (1984) here to acknowledge that one of the first contemporary descriptions of the modern 'Republic of Letters' was produced by *police surveillance*: the reports of Joseph d'Hémery, police inspector of the book trade for Paris (1748–53): See Darnton's chapter 'A Police Inspector Sorts His Files: The Anatomy of the Republic of Letters' (1984: 145–89).

[5]The US military is a major sponsor of technological research, much of it carried out in universities. See: https://www.businessinsider.com.au/the-us-military-is-responsible-for-almost-all-the-technology-in-your-iphone-2014-10?r=US&IR=T.

hence 'undisciplined'; it can be 'street-smart' practical or household know-how and artisanal 'rule of thumb', but it is not a 'precise science'. It may include inherited wisdom, 'common knowledge' and 'common sense', but also fabrication, faking, falsehood, delusion, superstition, supernaturalism, ideology, marketing and self-promotion. It does not disavow story, anecdote and fiction, as scientific method purports to do.

In connective knowledge at large, stories may be 'true' or 'true to life', but always need interpretation, such that the position of the observer is as important as that of the object (a characteristic it shares with relativity and quantum physics rather than Newtonian physics). Connective knowledge is coded into various 'institutions of language' that are oral, mobile, virtual and changeable without need of centralized direction, from small-scale rules and discourses (ready-made phrases, truisms, idioms, proverbial formulae, registers), to large-scale thought systems (genres, myth, fairy-tales, 'old wives' tales', folklore, 'quote-lore').

Social media expand untutored knowledge-seeking practices at scale (e.g. folksonomies), resulting in findings that circulate unchecked, in both senses. Institutional (aggregated) forms that emerge from online environments – for example, BuzzFeed, Vice, Wikipedia, Pinterest, Reddit – are disallowed as sources within most formal systems, although Wikipedia is making inroads (*Nature News*, 2017), despite criticism (Gauthier and Sawchuk, 2017). They are seen as unreliable and contaminated not only by their proximity to celebrity entertainment and fake news but also by their very popularity, which defies disciplinary systematization and allows personality, dreams, fantasy, fiction, illusion, anxiety, fear, desire, posturing, aggression, harassment, abuse – and creative art – to flourish alongside (indeed, as part of) truth-seeking endeavour.[6]

In the print era, it was physically possible to separate formal and informal knowledge systems into different parts of the library (or, different libraries). Since the emergence of broadcasting, this has not been so easy. Formal knowledge, from journalism to education, has had to coexist with entertainment, fact with fiction, the wonders of science with gameshows.

Social media have taken that heterogeneity to new levels. The costs of publication are effectively zero; everyone online is an author, a journalist, a publisher. The marble-clad institutions that for so long acted as filters and gatekeepers can simply be bypassed, not only by 'everyone' but also by the 45th president of the United States, whose use of Twitter cuts out 'Washington' as a complex check/balance system for political communication.[7] The rules of the game are changing. The irruption of social media 'wildness' and

---

[6]Hear, for instance, screenwriter Charlie Kaufman's BAFTA lecture (September 2011): https://soundcloud.com/bafta/charlie-kaufman-screenwriting-lecture.

[7]'Washington' is a mix of government agencies, public servants and elected representatives, lobbyists, the press and commentators, as well as academic analysts and political scientists.

'the new tribalism' (Reich, 2014) into the domain of politics has begun to destabilize established reputations among legacy forms, from 'the press' to 'Washington' – and beyond, as the similarly complex knowledge system of 'Hollywood' is disrupted by #MeToo and #TimesUp.[8]

Tribal truths

As the two kinds of knowledge clash and destabilize each other, it is important to acknowledge how much of productive, specialist knowledge is merely a certificated and branded version of the very same stories, prejudices and delusions that infect popular knowledge, and, conversely, how much connective, informal, popular knowledge strives to attain insight, certainty or explanatory power, albeit un-propped by disciplinary scaffold and institutional repute. Neither 'side' has a monopoly on truth-values or compelling stories, or even on reflexive, critical mechanisms for self-correction over time. What might each learn from the other? The question is rarely asked because the structure of their mutual relationship is adversarial (centrifugal, not centripetal).

The difference between the two kinds of knowledge goes back to ancient times, and yet it persists. Productive knowledge is still *fortressed*, answerable to the central organizational, administrative, defensive and economic apparatus of states (and increasingly to those of 'stateless companies'),[9] dedicated not only to the advancement of 'our' group but also to the defeat of rivals, and very far from 'open to all'. From that perspective, connective knowledge is construed as *wild* (unfenced, shunned, unpredictable, threatening). It works through fantasy and fiction and the knowing look of mutual recognition, where the line of trust between groups is marked by what each takes to be true, that is, where 'troth' (faithfulness to a cause or leader) trumps 'truth' (abstract). According to those watching from the fearful fortress, wildness means 'anything goes'. Beliefs are driven by superstition and undisciplined notions are expressed in barbarous tongues, requiring not dialogue but control, administered by state agencies that are affronted by ungoverned sociality. 'Wild' populations, including (successively) the labouring classes, women, colonized subjects, children

---

Like 'Hollywood' it is a culture-complex, not an institution. Insiders see it as well-connected influencers; opponents see it as a 'swamp' full of 'corruption'.

[8] 'Hollywood' as a knowledge system was prised open by sexual politics, with 'what every insider knew' becoming public knowledge via #MeToo (October 2017), to transformative effect (#TimesUp, January 2018), which produced political effects well beyond 'Hollywood'. See https://www.theatlantic.com/entertainment/archive/2018/01/beyond-metoo-can-times-up-effect-real-change/549482/; and see https://www.timesupnow.com/.

[9] For an observant discussion of 'stateless companies', see this column by John Gapper: https://www.ft.com/content/e9b4a640-b2e5-11e5-b147-e5e5bba42e51 (*Financial Times*).

(and also, in a different register, postmodernists and cultural theorists), have not historically been accepted as knowing subjects at all, unless they were *schooled*. Thus, to understand *productive knowledge*, we must talk about *warfare*. And if we want to understand *connective knowledge*, we must think again about *tribes*.

II. Modelling knowledge on violence

Violence: Social not individual

Productive knowledge emerged with administrative literacy in the rise of early states and empires. To understand what it was *for*, it is instructive to compare its 'career' with that of organized violence. The historical sociologist Siniša Malešević's study of *The Rise of Organised Brutality* (2017) opens this line of thought for us. His study offers a typology that, I argue, may be applied to organized knowledge.

Malešević begins by taking issue with recent claims, headlined by Steven Pinker, that 'today we may be living in the most peaceable era in our species' existence' (2011: xxi); that is, that violence within and between societies – both murder and warfare – has declined over the *longue durée*, from prehistory to today. In *The Better Angels of Our Nature* (2011), Pinker uses historical statistics to argue that individuals are much less likely to be killed by another human than ever before. Pinker derives his approach from social theorist Norbert Elias, whose *Civilizing Process* (1939/1969) is still used to authorize the idea that *H. sapiens* has achieved a measure of self-control and social restraint (via a complex network of social connections) over the extreme long term and across many cultures, such that the purportedly 'natural' propensity of individual humans towards 'caveman' violence was gradually transformed into so-called 'civilization', without which, *Lord of the Flies* style, humans will inevitably regress to primitivism (but see Goudsblom, 1994, on Elias; and Dekker, 2016, on 'civilization').

Pinker has picked up on the individual (behavioural) rather than social (power) aspect of this supposed process, to argue that person-to-person violence, as measured by homicide, its most extreme indicator, has declined over the past couple of generations and, more slowly, over the past several centuries. Looked at through the lens of murder, even the United States, the last bastion of an armed citizenry (in the name of freedom), is a haven of safety compared with medieval Switzerland (Malešević, 2017: 135). But that kind of calculus ignores other *forms* of violence – for example, suicide, sexual violence, coercive power, conscription, exposure to infection, starvation – and, more fundamentally, it ignores the *social* aspect of violence. If violence is not restricted to personal physical/verbal aggression (individual behaviour), but is instead understood, first and foremost, as a social phenomenon (organized power), then the picture changes radically.[10]

Studying violence as socially produced does not take individual action out of the picture, but it does change the theory of *causation* (Pierson, 2004); it focuses attention on *groups* and their organized coherence, and it foregrounds the importance of *change*, since societies wax and wane, unlike supposed 'human nature'. In a social approach, the causes of violence are sought in social *organization*, in *cultural* meanings and ideologies, and in the perceived *relations* within and among groups, often very small units. Instead of violence being seen as a universal, trans-historical and transcultural constant, underpinned by a moral philosophy that casts 'Man' (used advisedly) as a fallen (not a 'better') angel and apt to lash out in 'primitive' rage, it can be analysed through organizational arrangements, ideologies and group relations.

Accordingly, Malešević (2017) proposes a threefold key to understanding violence:

- Large-scale social *organization*, including effective *bureaucracy*, a centrally directed apparatus for coordinating and mobilizing collective action (see also Ostrom, 2000);
- An *ideology* that unites an otherwise heterogeneous group into an abstract 'we' identity, often opposed to one or more conflicting 'they' groups (see also Althusser, 1971);
- A further characteristic that Malešević calls '*microsolidarity*', typically the intense mutual loyalty among platoon- or company-sized groups, enabling warfare to be conducted (under hierarchical direction) by individuals who have little natural propensity to kill.

Social organization: An arms race

Supportive of Malešević's approach is the work of cultural-evolutionary historian Peter Turchin, who argues that it was increasing organizational complexity and scale that allowed successive ancient empires to withstand attack and incursion by external enemies wielding new kinds of technology of ever-increasing lethal capability (horses, chariots, weapons of bronze and iron, crossbows) (Turchin et al., 2013). Small, autonomous bands were no match for Rameses II or Genghis Khan, but 'ultrasociality' worked, where

> centralized, hierarchical chiefdoms ... scaled up into early states and empires, and eventually into modern nation-states. At every step, greater

---

[10]Indeed, it seems that Elias may have been arguing along these lines from the start: 'The crux of the theory lies in the observed relationship between changes in individual discipline ("behaviour") and changes in social organization ("power")' (Goudsblom, 1994: 1).

size was an advantage in the military competition against other societies. (Turchin, 2016: 38–9)

In short, the driver of 'civilization' since Neolithic times has been *organization*, honed by sporadic but increasingly damaging cross-border warfare among ever larger, complex, militarized states and 'marauding' (unorganized) 'barbarians'. Personal self-control over a supposed 'caveman' propensity to wield a club doesn't explain anything about historical change: it is not a dynamic, organizational attribute. Malešević concludes:

Modern polities have at their disposal enormous coercive organisational capacity, intertwined with deep ideological penetration, that tap into grassroots microsolidarities, all of which allow for the unprecedented use of violence. (2017: 310)

The militarization of everyday has proceeded so far that coercion can still work by indirect means:

When one is in possession of highly advanced military technology, worldwide organisational reach and a great deal of popular justification at home ... such modern coercive organisational machines might kill less but displace, injure, deprive, torment, agonise and ultimately control more people. (2017: 310)

Organized knowledge: An ideological state apparatus?

It is possible to apply Malešević's criteria for 'organized brutality' across from violence to knowledge, because knowledge (technology, weapons) and violence (organized states) share a long history. Like violence, knowledge must be understood as an evolutionary process of increasing complexity in organization, bureaucratization, ideological coherence and learned 'microsolidarity', coordinated over the past 6,000 years or so by states, themselves of ever-increasing complexity as a *longue durée* arms race has upped the technological ante for those who wanted to survive and prevail.

   Both violence (e.g. slavery) and knowledge technologies (writing) really took off at the point in the development of social complexity when states (kings) emerged (Lévi-Strauss, 1955/1961), as the Neolithic disembogued into the Bronze Age. Historically, armed knowledge and its knowledge technologies (writing, libraries, archives, academies) are a social effect of state-formation, not individual propensities. Organized knowledge requires

- large-scale social *organization* (typically, state-funded universities and private research institutes), including effective *bureaucracy* (internal to the university and at system level) – a centrally directed apparatus for coordinating and mobilizing collective action. Knowledge is more loosely coordinated than violence (although enforcement regimes and coercion are available to the authorities).

  Also needed is

- an *ideology* that unites otherwise heterogeneous groups into an abstract 'we' identity, typically opposed to one or more conflicting 'they' groups. 'Ideology' can take more than left/right or progressive/ reactionary political form; it can be (a mix of) gendered (Beck, 2017), religious (historically, the sine qua non of universities), or allegiance to science itself (rationalist), patriotism (nationalist), etc.

  Also needed is

- the further characteristic of *microsolidarity*, typically the intense mutual loyalty in departments and disciplines, enabling research to be conducted (under hierarchical direction) by individuals who as individuals may have little natural propensity to create 'state apparatuses' that 'reproduce the relations of production' (Althusser, 1971), but who operate in overlapping small-world networks (Ormerod, 2012) that reward solidarity and punish defection.

Converting the useful concept of microsolidarity into the language of economics, Potts et al. (2017) and Hartley et al. (2019) have proposed the notion of *knowledge clubs*, following James Buchanan's and Elinor Ostrom's treatment of 'club goods' and 'common goods' (differing from private and public goods), which allows for purposeful groups (clubs) and identity-sharing groups (commons) to cooperate in sharing and creating new knowledge (Allen and Potts, 2016).

Universities and violence: Organization, ideology, microsolidarity

Centralizing forces set the rules of the game, which link across disparate ideological state apparatuses (ISAs).[11] Louis Althusser used a broad brush when naming the ISAs. He lists them as follows:

- *religious*
- *educational*

---

[11]See also: http://ghostprof.org/wp-content/uploads/2013/09/Althusser-on-ISA-and-RSA.pdf.

- *family*
- *legal*
- *political*
- *trade-union*
- *communications and cultural*

Each is understood as a social system or cultural complex, not just one organization, and not under centralized control. The array is not a conspiracy, but an *uncertain order*.

That is why, as he put it, 'the unity that constitutes this plurality of ISAs as a body is not immediately visible'. There's a dynamic tension between various forces and systems that are by no means unified in purpose or method. 'Knowledge clubs', for instance, may operate under a general ideological and bureaucratic order, but nurture quite other purposes (critical, scientific, communitarian, or commercial). That is why knowledge cannot be socially organized by administrative (state) means alone. It needs appeal, not regimentation.

Here is where Malešević's model is so compelling, because it shows that organization alone is not enough. Both ideology and microsolidarity are also needed. However, where once religion provided a population-scale unifying story, in modernity, 'the educational apparatus is in fact the dominant Ideological State Apparatus in capitalist social formations' (Althusser, 1971). Thus, *education* (not just in universities) rather than gods or monarchs, provides the ideological function, loose enough to accommodate different allegiances and ambitions among those involved, but coherent enough to win assent from otherwise antagonistic social groups. Universities serve a double purpose in the social organization of knowledge: they *produce* knowledge for state development and defence; they *teach* populations the ideology of education. This explains why research and teaching remain yoked together, when they could have specialized out into separate 'industries'.[12] Their system-level functionality means that universities are not really (or not only) making individual 'knowing subjects'; they are making a productive-knowledge culture.

Inside the university, teachers, researchers and the increasing army of part-time, short-contract adjuncts are encouraged to develop microsolidarity, despite the reduction of academics to the 'precariat'.[13] What generates

---

[12]See also: https://theconversation.com/civilisation-as-we-dont-know-it-teaching-only-univer sities-28505; and: https://theconversation.com/teaching-only-roles-could-mark-the-end-of-your-academic-career-74826.

[13]Precarious professors are now 'worth' less than janitors and pet-sitters. Janitors: http://gawker.com/the-academics-who-are-treated-as-less-than-janitors-1775518734; pet-sitters: https://www.theguardian.com/commentisfree/2015/jun/22/adjunct-professor-earn-less-than-pet-sitter.

social cohesion and authorizes collective action in these contexts is learned loyalty to one's immediate colleagues and students, not necessarily to the stated purposes of the university hierarchy or desires of the funding agency. Thus, just as individuals are 'reluctant killers' (Malešević: 302), requiring organizational scale, bureaucracy, ideology, and well-honed microsolidarity to ensure military effectiveness (capacity and willingness to kill on command), so too individual academics are routinely reluctant to pursue knowledge in the interests of 'power' (to which they may wish to 'speak truth'). Nevertheless, in the collective, they remain effective agents of centralized purposes (or, at least, functions). Knowledge is routinely produced by small, intensely self-loyal groups (labs, colleagues, clubs), organized into larger units over which their members do not exercise control. Dissemination (teaching) is part of the control structure, not in the gift of knowledge-makers directly.

Thus, making knowledge must be explained by reference to the *organization of groups*, the *imperatives of ideology* and the *trust-loyalty* processes *of microsolidarity*.

III. Tribal knowledge: Troth over truth

Self-organized groups: Glued by culture, language

What of the wilder side of knowledge? Actually, being 'ungoverned' by strong-state apparatuses does not mean living in the wilderness. In fact, here is a good place to look for *self-organized* groups, for 'autopoiesis' or self-creation (Luhmann, 2013, 2012), for decentralized complexity rather than command-and-control order. Connective knowledge is a chief means for creating cohesive and resilient (but externally adversarial) groups in the first place, using the oral–aural resources of language and other semiotic systems and technologies. This process is not reserved to elites, but extends across – and so *constitutes* – subpopulations of 'inter-knowing' individuals, institutions and cultures, called *demes*.

Connective knowledge is therefore 'demic'. Demes can be identified with clans, tribes, nations, language groups, etc. (Evans, 2009), but also with class, gender, ethnic, political and other social 'tribes' of complex societies. These are held together by 'fictions', which include gods, nations, law, money, corporations and universities. Demes, then, are *constitutional* of society rather than 'institutional' or 'individual' within it. They share 'our' knowledge as common language, not as property, and provide ready-made mechanisms for avoiding or distrusting 'their' knowledge. They are held together by informal but formulaic talk (phatic communication), including in-jokes, etc., designed not so much to impart information as to keep open the communication channel (Li, 2015).

For most of what James Scott calls 'species history', humans were '"unadministered" peoples assembled in what historians might call tribes, chiefdoms, and bands' (2017: 15) – that is, what cultural science would call demes. For 'ninety-five percent of the human experience on earth, we lived in small, mobile, dispersed, relatively egalitarian, hunting-and-gathering bands' (Scott, 2017: 5). It is during this long period that culture was established and evolved – along with technologies – as the prime mechanism for the production and transmission of knowledge: internally among band members, externally between groups and temporally across generations.

However, in the relatively short period since states and then writing first emerged, prejudice *against* 'tribal' (or 'barbarian') knowledge systems became almost compulsory among those who would pursue productive knowledge. Written literacy emerged with monarchies, but it eventually lost its association with tax-collection, slavery and monarchical-imperial coercion, becoming an autonomous platform for storing and communicating abstracted knowledge across time and space. In the process, 'here and now' know-how was downgraded.

Folklore, myth, song, story, formulaic genres, ritual, together with their stores of culture-coded knowledge, were gradually excluded from the formal 'regime' of knowledge, even though these oral traditions were the tools – and repositories – for one of humanity's 'most creative periods', as Claude Lévi-Strauss pointed out:

> This stage [the Neolithic era] could only have been reached if, for thousands of years, small communities had been observing, experimenting and handing on their findings. This great development was carried out with an accuracy and a continuity which are proved by its success, although writing was still unknown at the time. (Lévi-Strauss, 1955/1961: 391–93)[14]

Thus, connective knowledge developed for the cohesion, survival and reproduction of limited-scale, self-organizing groups, and was dispersed in trade and conflict with others. It is endowed with various coding tricks to keep it memorable for insiders but hidden from competitors, and it can be reduced to formulae that allow it to be applied in unpredictable or uncertain circumstances, according to the needs of the moment. It has been shaped by continuous evolutionary forces and accidents over many millennia. It is produced anonymously, in flux of active use, and it 'belongs' to no state or property regime but to the whole population who share its language and, at macro scale, to the species whose history it records.

---

[14]And see: http://neamathisi.com/literacies/chapter-1-literacies-on-a-human-scale/levi-strauss-on-the-functions-of-writing.

Medieval ISAs

It is by exactly these means that medieval monks across Europe were able to cast the Vikings as 'marauding barbarians', bent on rape, murder and pillage, the very epitome of wild, tribal, natural aggression in action. Standing against them was something that looked like the weakest possible defensive weapon: *the Book*. But of course, that book – the Bible – linked a network of emerging states across Europe from Rome to Constantinople, from Lindisfarne to Sicily. The chief 'ideological state apparatus' of these states was religion, of which monastic clergy were the 'research and teaching' arm. The 'Church Militant' supported warlords (kings) against heathens, pagans, etc. Eventually, using complexity, organization, bureaucracy, literacy and church–state institutional monopoly on knowledge (i.e. ideology), maintained at micro-level in monasteries where microsolidarity could be nurtured, Europe absorbed the Norsemen: buying them off, redrawing borders in their favour, submitting to conquest (far-flung Viking kingdoms included the Danelaw, Normandy, Sicily and the Rus states) and at last Christianizing them. But it was the monks who wrote the histories, not the Vikings, whose children were taught to vilify their own ancestors' exploits:

> Monks and clerics well-nigh monopolized early medieval literacy, so preserved chronicles and other literary works preserve their perspective, which understandably was utterly hostile to their attackers. The Vikings thus earned an unfavourable reputation as 'a most vile people' and 'a filthy race'. In contrast, I argue that their violence, seen in broad historical context, was no worse than that of others in a savage time, when heroes like Charlemagne (d. 814) killed and plundered on a much greater scale than the northern raiders. (Winroth, 2014: 12)

Anders Winroth (2014) doesn't let the monks have the last word. He allows us to glimpse a contrary reality: that the Vikings were doing post-Roman Europe a favour, their particular version of Schumpeterian 'creative destruction' literally liquidating otherwise sunk capital (i.e. melting down ecclesiastical silver) and opening up the continent to trade (not least in monkish and civilian slaves). In short, against the rigid and defensive 'fortress' knowledge of Dark Age states, 'wild' or 'tribal' knowledge favoured trade, internationalism and expansive liquidity. But the myth held sway, even as the economics told a different story. Although many Roman cities were abandoned and modern European states and towns emerged directly from barbarian settlement and trading patterns, a centuries-long and still continuing tension – turbocharged every now and then (Charlemagne, the Italian Renaissance, Ruskin) – persists between Classical (control, proportion, precision) and Gothic (savageness, changefulness, artisanship), expressed in art, literature and architecture – as well as on Netflix.[15]

Modernizing medieval myths

The monkish myth ('fake news!') continues to appeal, 1,200 years later. Along with other 'barbarians' who swept through Europe after the fall of the Roman Empire, Vikings and Goths were cast in mythical roles that still resonate today. You can't use words like Goth, Vandal, Hun – or Dothraki – without a frisson of monkish fear or Latin enmity. The die – 'barbarian' versus 'civilization' – was cast. It has entered modernity as received truth. Here's a particularly telling example of it from 1848:

> We must not forget that these same Bedouins were a nation of robbers, – whose principal means of living consisted of making excursions either upon each other, or upon the settled villagers, taking what they found, slaughtering all those who resisted, and selling the remaining prisoners as slaves. All these nations of free barbarians look very proud, noble and glorious at a distance, but only come near them and you will find that they, as well as the more civilised nations, are ruled by the lust of gain, and only employ ruder and more cruel means.[16]

It may surprise the modern reader, familiar with left/right and Cold War politics, to find that this opinion was written by the co-author of *The Communist Manifesto*, in the same year. This is how Friedrich Engels, addressing the radical readers of the British Chartist paper *The Northern Star*, reported on the French conquest of Algeria in January 1848. Like Marx, Engels was convinced of the progressive role of the bourgeoisie, and felt that he was observing it in action, such that the cruelties of conquest were the price to be paid for modernization, making the Marxist modernizers early proponents of what might be called 'conquest as cooperation', and thus of

---

[15]An unusually direct statement of this tension can be found by Mark Bernstein, an editor of *The Victorian Web*: 'Classical architecture is a universal architecture of precision, planning, and control. Each element has its proper place and size, and each is subordinated to the greater plan. In antiquity, classicism was the architectural language of empire; in the nineteenth century it was the language of manifest destiny and of a Republic taming the wilderness; in the twentieth century, it became the language of fascism. Ruskin expounded an (admittedly ahistorical) vision of the Gothic in opposition to the Classical, emphasizing savageness and changefulness as the touchstones of the Gothic. Changefulness refers to continuous change, as the vaulted rib has no single radius of curvature but changes continuously as it flies. Savageness refers to clean breaks, to asymmetry, to unique work expressed by different hands where structural constraints allow such variation.' http://www.victorianweb.org/art/architecture/classical/bernstein.html.
[16]Qtd in the blog of René Merle: http://merlerene.canalblog.com/archives/2014/08/27/3196 4882.html.

'newness' as an outcome of clash and conflict, a kind of 'dialectic' that in economics is called 'creative destruction'. Engels continued:

> And after all, the modern bourgeois, with civilisation, industry, order, and at least relative enlightenment following him, is preferable to the feudal lord or to the marauding robber, with the barbarian state of society to which they belong.

This became the formula – the *algorithm* (Finn, 2017) – for *any* 'uncivilized' threat to 'progress', uniting imperialists and Marxists, bourgeoisie and revolutionaries, in the pursuit of systemic modernization. The formula remains readily to hand for application to any group, whether real (Bedouin) or virtual (the new 'tribes' of populist politics): 'our' side is civilized (so mass killing/subjugation is okay), 'theirs' is barbarian (so individual attacks are sensationalized). The stories used to sustain one side in those conflicts, and to belittle or insult the other, are coded in our narrative forms, from movies and science fiction to 'fake news' and the conflict between science and populism.[17] But the narrative is toxic. After 170 years, the evidence is in: crushing 'nations of free barbarians' in the name of modernity (Marxist or capitalist) has not delivered 'industry, order, and ... enlightenment', only more violence, on a scale no 'tribal' group could imagine (Daesh excepted, perhaps). In such circumstances, knowledge is not 'free', it is not open. It is constituted in adversarial conflict and divided by boundaries that we preserve in stories, codes and rules that last for generations and millennia, using them to authorize atrocities.

The digital era has ushered in further polarized conflict. One camp's 'reason' is another's 'mental disorder'.[18] After Trump, a commitment to truth has had to vie with medieval 'troth': remaining true to a cause, where 'recognition' and 'acknowledgement' (*cnāwan*) are the currency, 'trumping' Enlightenment reason (*gnosis*). The walls of 'civilization' are going up against 'tribal' outsiders again. Migrants, refugees – and 'cosmopolitan' scientists – are cast as wild and dangerous. States act to stop ideas crossing their borders. Internal difference is recast as treachery. Hate speech and trolls dog the heels of 'free' expression (Jane, 2017, 2018). Knowledge is used to

---

[17]It should be noted that although many Hollywood movies (of the *Star Wars, E.T.* tradition) line up imperial power against 'tribal' outsiders, they routinely take the side of the rebels, making a strange amalgam out of modernism (corporate–institutional power and technology = evil, but with terrific special effects) and romanticism (wish-fulfilment at individual level = good, but childish). Perhaps this is why such movies are less politically consequential than their literary forebears.

[18]'Liberalism is a mental disorder – our borders, language, culture make America great!' – the message on a placard brandished by Milo Yiannopoulos at the University of California, Berkeley, USA, September 24, 2017: https://www.buzzfeed.com/josephbernstein/heres-how-breitbart-and-milo-smuggled-white-nationalism?utm_term=.byBRn7jyG#.xt8JMqbNZ.

defend borders, not cross them. Meanwhile, in pursuit of connective, demic knowledge, fantasy fiction puts the 'marauding barbarians' in attractive costumes, from *Vikings* to *Game of Thrones*.

In such a setting, there is a danger that the two kinds – 'armed' and 'connective' knowledge – will find themselves on opposing sides of the wall.

IV. Open borders

Here in fact is the space – *between two systems*, not choosing one or the other – where open knowledge can prove to be of crucial importance, providing a new intercultural space where each can learn from the other. Open knowledge is a means to integrate productive and connective capabilities. Instead of adversarial cultures, productive systems need to embrace their wild cousins, recognizing that 'tribe' is just another word for a culture-made group. Groups are essential to human survival. They make, preserve and transmit knowledge to succeeding times, not only about the world and how to act in it but also about personal meaning, identity, social relationships and trust. They don't have to be treated as uncivilized. Knowledge that binds a group together and sets it apart from outsiders is following ancient rules, using oral and ceremonial codes, carried in language, story, song, spectacle and ritual. 'Tribal' knowledge is coded to trust insiders but to distrust outsiders.

Scientific society is not exempt from this history. Universities too depend on internal 'tribal' markers of group identity, to facilitate trust and connectivity. Social media are re-establishing oral–aural modes of thought in public discourse, including restoring the primacy of groups and borders (for good and ill). Nor are moderns as emancipated from 'magical thinking' as they like to think. Indeed, as Ed Finn (2017) has argued, magical thinking underpins the computational turn:

> It's as if we think of code as a magic spell, an incantation to reveal what we need to know and even what we want. Humans have always believed that certain invocations – the marriage vow, the shaman's curse – do not merely describe the world but make it. Computation casts a cultural shadow that is shaped by this long tradition of magical thinking. (Finn, 2017)

There's nothing new in this. Electricity was once thought to be literally 'alive', and electronic media, from the telegraph to television and computers, were thought to be haunted (Sconce, 2000). In other words, from the perspective of users, electronics and computation are part of continuing oral culture and a world inhabited by uncanny powers, not experienced, as print was, as a specialized technology in the cause freedom, equality and reason. Knowledge is bounded by distance and death, 'presence' is transcendent, and technologies are incorporated into patterns of identity-formation, expression and relationship that owe little to 'deep' knowledge systems. Indeed, social media platforms, protocols and apps are facilitating what some observers have identified as a post-Gutenberg 'restoration' of a longer-term media history that had been 'interrupted' by print (Pettitt, 2013), and perhaps, for many outside the fortress of productive knowledge, never displaced throughout the print-era Enlightenment.

Not surprisingly, social media extremism has added further to the already bad name reserved for 'tribalism' as some sort of primitive throwback. But while opposition to right-wing populism and radical terrorism alike may be justified, it may not be fair to blame tribes. I hope I've said enough to indicate that knowledge of both kinds – productive and connective – is marked not by universality but by very tight ties to identity, both social and individual, and to the construction and continuation of culture-made groups.

We need to think much more thoroughly about groups, and also about why prestige attaches to one kind of knowledge while the other is fair game for denigration and abuse. As in culture, so in knowledge: prestige and power seem to be in inverse proportion to openness and popularity. Reputation adheres to the winners, because 'we' (educated opinion) judge prestige knowledge and culture by their best efforts (Shakespeare, Einstein), but attack popular culture and media for their worst (Rupert Murdoch, Milo Yiannopoulos). One we call 'civilized' (despite its violence), the other we call 'barbarian' (despite its innovative energies) – a distinction reaching back to Classical times, which forgets that the barbarians in question may have enjoyed more freedom and comfort than the average imperial urban citizen (Scott, 2017), because the very terms belong to those who feared incursion, not to those who roamed under 'open' skies.

Biosociality: 'Diversity out of similarity, uniformity out of diversity'

In contrast with ancient adversarialism, it should hardly need arguing that each 'side' needs the other. The lesson in all of this is not to pick winners but to understand contrasting strengths and weaknesses in order to promote an integrated 'best-of-both-worlds', within which global knowledge might thrive 'in the open'. In other words, somewhere in the fraught relations between them lies a way forward for 'open knowledge'. 'Open knowledge' doesn't mean that everything is accessible to everyone. Rather, it could mean knowledge is open to both the learned and the popular, productive and connective, disciplined and wild.

That version of openness signifies a cultural tendency to *value the loss of control* as knowledge crosses demic boundaries. 'Open' is not an access key but a cultural orientation that values *translation* over *transmission* – learning from difference and increasing border-zone traffic. What's needed is not the myth of the universal individual, whether monkish or marauding, or that 'globule of desire' at the heart of 'rational' *Homo economicus*.[19] Instead, the model of openness needs to be derived from semiotics (Lotman, 1990; Eco, 1989), namely, *open dialogue* between different, incommensurable, mutually untranslatable texts, authors and users, within a complex system (aka semiosphere) that imposes its own order, path-dependency, borders and dynamics. The differences and tensions between armed and wild knowledge are themselves productive of innovation.

The 'open society' depends on the two being *integrated*, not polarized. However, 'integration' does not mean consolidation into an overall uniformity. Language doesn't work like corporate mergers and acquisitions. As Nicholas Evans and Stephen Levinson (2009) have shown, there are no 'linguistic universals' but only a human-made 'communication system which is fundamentally variable at all levels'. They speculate:

> Recognising the true extent of structural diversity in human language opens up exciting new research directions ... with new opportunities for dialogue with biological paradigms concerned with change and diversity, and confronting us with the extraordinary plasticity of the highest human skills. (Evans and Levinson, 2009)

Evans and Levinson's survey of language variability reveals that there are no universals. *Cultures are different from each other*, despite the biological uniformity of the species. At the same time, *intra-cultural uniformity* can be observed, despite the variability of neural 'machinery':

> But that is the human cognitive specialty that makes language and culture possible – to produce diversity out of biological similarity, and uniformity out of biological diversity. (Evans and Levinson, 2009)

Opening up knowledge is hard because of the *nature of knowledge*. Knowledge is not like information or data. President Reagan claimed in 1989 that 'information is the oxygen of the modern age. It seeps through the walls topped by barbed wire, it wafts across the electrified borders' (Chadwick, 2006: 1). That Californian confidence is based on a 'transmission' model of knowledge. As an abstract commodity, requiring no 'knowing subject',

---

[19] Cf. Thorstein Veblen's justly celebrated critique of *Homo economicus* (1898): 'He' is assumed to be 'a lightning calculator of pleasures and pains, who oscillates like a homogeneous globule of desire of happiness under the impulse of stimuli that shift about the area, but leave him intact.'

information can flow across borders as an exploitable or tradable resource (McKinsey Global Institute, 2016). But what applies to data does not work for knowledge and culture. These do not 'seep' or 'waft'. They need to be translated (Lotman, 1990), allowing for the *reproduction of diversity*. As Evans and Levinson put it:

> Structural differences should be accepted for what they are, and integrated into a new, broadly evolutionary approach to language and cognition that places diversity at centre stage.[20]

Diversity at centre stage – 'open' knowledge needs to be understood in these terms, with new attention to the productive (and also destructive) relations between diversity and uniformity. Knowledge needs to retain wildness even as it is ordered for global use.

---

[20]Source: http://www.mpi.nl/news/news-archive/the-myth-of-language-universals. See the full paper at: https://www.princeton.edu/~adele/LIN_106:_UCB_files/Evans-Levinson09_preprint.pdf.

5

Intellectual property:

Industry versus language? (Something fishy going on)

The movement of nations is caused not by power, nor by intellectual activity, nor even by a combination of the two as historians have supposed, but by the activity of all *the people who participate in the events.*

(LEO TOLSTOY, *War and Peace*, 1869: 1327)

This chapter contrasts *cultural value* (Frow, 1995; Crossick and Kaszynska, 2014, 2016) with *economic values* (Potts, 2011) in relation to creativity and intellectual property. It argues, on the model of language (Lotman, 1990), that the very tension between these incommensurate systems is the source of innovation and new knowledge in the creative economy. Arguing that intellectual property law (copyright in particular) is no longer fit for purpose in a creative economy, the chapter proposes that a much better strategy would be to concentrate not on *individuals, works and property* but on *groups, uses and networks*, or on 'knowledge clubs', in order to incentivize, diversify, extend, grow, regulate and communicate new knowledge among globally scaled and conflicted populations.

I. Something fishy about language

Two systems

The Estonian-Russian semiotician Yuri Lotman (1990) had a novel view of how language operates, quite different from the linear, instrumental way that it is usually conceptualized in the West. In his model, language is impossible without *two* systems, mutually untranslatable, interacting in such a way that communication is nevertheless possible. He illustrates a very sophisticated process with a simple example: the earliest meaningful interaction for any human, which Lotman charmingly calls the 'language of smiles' – the first encounter between newborn infants and their primary carers, typically their mother. Neither understands the other directly, neither has words that the other already knows, and yet they communicate with each other, each creating 'approximate equivalences' of the other's meaning. For each party, 'communication' comprises not 'message received' but a combination of *incoming* information (signals) and *internal* processing, neither of which is directly accessible to the other party as the encounter unfolds. Meaning emerges from 'simultaneous translation' in the context of each participant's intentions and purposes (Tomasello, 2014), which may be to delight – or they may be deluded, duplicitous or dangerous. So much so that it is not long before each side knows how to 'lie' to the other: a baby will cry, using a tone that *says* 'I'm hungry!', when what it really *wants* is a cuddle; a carer will coo and soothe and pet a baby in order to facilitate the execution of an anxiety-inducing procedure. And each soon learns to see through the other's tricks! Meanwhile, knowledge and relationships grow; and mastery is gained not only over the codes by which signals are sent and translated but also over the 'special knowledge of circumstances' that turns knowledge into value in the here and now, otherwise known as 'planning' (Hayek, 1945: 521).

Lying is the precondition for truth

According to the great Italian semiotician Umberto Eco,[1] this is the moment when language comes into its own as a semiotic system: 'If something cannot be used to tell a lie, conversely it cannot be used to tell the truth: it cannot in fact be used "to tell" at all' (Eco, 1976: 7). Lying is the condition of existence for truth, because that which is true or 'real' (nature) must become 'sign' (culture), else there is no language, only behaviour.

---

[1]See my entry on 'Eco' in Lucy (2016: 56–62).

As Lewis Hyde observes, the very first human act of deception (and hence signification) precedes verbal language, because the interlocutors are *fish*, requiring successful lying across incommensurable systems (predator and prey):

> A worm with no hook in it ... has ... no significance, but the worm that says 'I'm harmless' when in fact it hides a hook tells a lie and by that lie worms begin to signify. ... Only when there's a possible Lying Worm can we begin to speak of a True Worm, and only then does Worm become a sign. (Hyde, 2008: 60)

Thus 'language' in semiotics is very much broader than speech: Eco defines semiotics as 'the discipline studying everything which can be used in order to lie'. It is not just an abstract set of rules for naming self-evident objects; it's a cultural relation, belonging to no one and everyone – a means to store, share and deploy knowledge. Babies – like fish – must learn to differentiate between a tasty morsel (cooked food) and lethal danger (fire), friend and foe, 'our' clan and theirs. That is the job of language, and language is translation.

Dialogue (not utterance) makes new meanings

The business of 'telling' turns out to be more fundamental than you might expect. As Lotman puts it, 'Human intelligence ... cannot switch itself on by itself.' It needs interaction with another, external system: 'Intelligence is always an interlocutor' (1990: 2). *Meaning* – both true and false, scientific and fictional – is a dynamic interactive process, not just a system of signs.

So how does language work, *in use*? How, for example, does *new* information emerge and get across from one agent to another? Lotman finds the minimal conditions for language in the encounter between two 'asymmetrical' systems at any scale – signifier and signified, mother and baby, text and reader, French culture and Russian culture – based not on naming the world but on translation across incommensurable boundaries that both connect and divide, inform and deceive.

Such communication is always approximate, imprecise and to some extent accidental (open to chance), and this in turn is the *source of dynamism and creativity* and thus new information. New ideas emerge in the clash of difference between systems, not from the intention of a creator (which an interlocutor may wish to thwart, abate or encourage) or the accuracy of a message. Trickster *says* 'Let me help you!' but *means* 'I want to eat your children.'[2] Thought is embodied and enacted, knowledge is cunning, new ideas are the spoils of theft.

---

[2]From Hyde (2008), see excerpt here: http://yin.arts.uci.edu/~studio/readings/hyde.html.

Communication on these terms is social not individual in mode. *Groups* are formed *internally* by self-communication, sharing codes, genres, content, knowledge and technologies. Group-members *know who they are* in terms of their semiotic difference from *external* groups. Personal identity and knowledge alike grow out of group-belonging, sustained by semiotic networks which 'our' group can trust but untrusted strangers will find it hard to use undetected (on the model of spoken languages).

Social relations are to a practicable extent governed and regulated by the way that the limitless possibilities of semiosis are codified and institutionalized into a viable order, which is robust and flexible enough to allow for unforeseen uses, but reflexive and canny enough to allow for the possibility of deception. *New* ideas emerge in *inter*action (not simply individual action) within that overall order, but in breach of established rules or codes.[3]

Copying as cultural (group-based) learning

How then do agents get their ideas across, and how do interlocutors receive new ideas? What is it that goes on between them? How, in short, do humans learn new things, and how do cultures process and store useful knowledge?

The first answer is *copying* – and un-purposeful, *random* copying at that (Bentley, Earls and O'Brien, 2011), which is another way of saying that copying belongs to the *system* in action, not to individual agents' intentions:

> Imitation is arguably the simplest form of culture transmission ... which occurs when each individual acquires his or her behavior simply by copying from another individual within the population. Copying is a predominant human behaviour. (Bentley et al., 2007: 151)

Individually (or in gangs and cliques), copying *this* rather than *that* is an expression of independence, the more original and exciting the more it thwarts the rules of authority, aligning learning with appetite and getting away with something unintended.

Successful learning includes the pleasures of larceny, and 'theft' is more efficient than 'toil' (Cangelosi, Greco and Harnad, 2002). But the outcome of such exploits is to transmit the group's overall self-communicating know-how to new users and generations.

Translation is a systematic process

Copying – cultural teaching, transmission and learning, using any signifying system (including but exceeding language) – is not a mechanical process. For

---

[3]See also Vološinov (1929); and see my entry on 'dialogue' in Lucy (2016).

an idea to get across a semiotic boundary and to be 'internalized' as *my* idea (as opposed to being foreign and therefore *their* idea, potentially untrustworthy or threatening), it needs to go through a series of transformations.

How does it work? Lotman has a model for the translation process, again a very different one from simple behavioural mimicry. It is based instead on a dynamic process of dialogic turn-taking, each stage involving creative transformation. For Lotman (1990: 144–7), translation-as-copying involves five stages. In this abstract model the stages are presented sequentially, but they may jostle and clash in social life, overlapping and contradicting one another. I summarize the stages thus:

1. *Strangeness*. The 'text' retains its 'strangeness'. It is read or watched in the foreign language, which is considered superior to the receiving language (seeing a film in the original language confers higher prestige than watching a dubbed version).

2. *Transformation*. A new foreign film may spark an entirely new genre, its format and feel copied extensively by local producers. This is not mechanical imitation but a process of mutual transformation: the imported text and home culture begin to restructure each other. The foreign text is valued because it offers the local culture an opportunity to break with the past, spurring local experimentation. It reveals some previously unnoticed aspect of 'our' culture. Translations, imitations and adaptations multiply.

3. *Abstraction*. The value of the imported text is seen in its own 'higher content' (rules, codes) rather than in its foreignness (performance). Thus, its true potential is realized only when it has transcended its local origin to attain universal appeal (e.g. Shakespeare). The valued component of the work itself is renewed in the copying.

4. *Productivity*. Once the text and its potential have been thoroughly assimilated, it is no longer experienced as distinctive. Instead, the local culture produces new and original texts based on dynamic transformations, where previously 'peripheral' ideas become 'core' (innovation from the margins).

5. *Transmission*: The dialogic turn-taking process reverses its polarity: now, the 'receiving' culture becomes a 'transmitter'. A 'flood of texts' is directed beyond its own borders, transforming the world.

The five stages can be illustrated readily by thinking about a game-changing foreign filmmaker – for example from China. What is first imported for its strangeness shakes up the home system until the time comes when something new can be exported. Witness the career of Zhang Yimou in the West:

(1) Strangeness: *Red Sorghum* (1987).

(2) Transformation: *House of Flying Daggers* (2004).

(3) Abstraction (universalization): 2008 Olympics, Opening and Closing Ceremonies.

(4) Productivity: *Coming Home* (2014).

(5) Transmission: *Great Wall* (2017).[4]

Bear in mind that this is an abstract model: its stages will be encountered in social flux in mixed and remixed form, and across multiple applications. What goes for valued work in cinema applies equally to other cultural forms and inventions, including new scientific theories, political movements, musical genres, etc., all the way down to the micro-scale of ideas that are new to an individual as s/he enters social life.

II. Something fishy about flows

It has seemed necessary to rehearse this model of language and learning because it emphasizes the extent to which creativity, innovation and knowledge are collective, group-based acts of sociality, relying on populations and systems that no one owns or can control, just as language itself cannot be copyrighted.

The economics of flow

Because it relies on the complicatedness, contextual contingency and unreliable facticity of culture-in-history (rather than on algorithms), this model has not proven very influential in economics, which is an arithmetic transliteration of behavioural science.

Despite that impediment, some economists – including Nobel Prize winners from F. A. von Hayek to Elinor Ostrom – have sensed the connection between culture and knowledge. In an important paper with Charlotte Hess, Ostrom considered 'information' as a 'human artifact, with agreements and rules, and strongly tied to the rules of language itself'. Information has a 'cultural component' as well as economic and other 'functions'.

How to establish the economic value of information? Hess and Ostrom call it 'a "flow resource" that must be passed from one individual to another

---

[4]See: http://www.ew.com/article/2016/07/28/great-wall-first-look; http://www.ew.com/article/2016/08/04/great-wall-director-addresses-whitewashing-controversy-matt-damon. The 'meaning' of Zhang Yimou in China may be quite different from what it is among those in the Hollywood system.

to have any public value' (2003: 131). They distinguish 'flow' resources from 'stock' ones, using the example of 'common pool resources' like fish – who are no longer wily interlocutors but 'stocks'.

Hess and Ostrom argue that the economic exploitation of these resources requires one set of rules to enable *access* to the stock (often held in common or public ownership) and a different set of rules to regulate the *flow* of 'units' (often privately owned) that can be appropriated by any one user (121). Value – at least in economic terms – comes from *use* – from 'flow'.

As in fish, so in language. Language is a stock, owned by no one and not copyrightable. Also, like fish stocks, languages come and go, their numbers wax and wane; there is an evolutionary and environmental aspect to their existence that escapes economic valuation. On the other hand, 'text', a string of words or composition or design that uses semiotic materials, is a flow subject to private ownership and exploitation. Flows can be *regulated* and so priced.

Fair enough? Certainly this is the basis on which industrial publication operated, in both the press and broadcasting/cinema. Language is the stock, writing is the flow and copyright is the gate that regulates the *value* of the flow. In order to protect their rents, copyright-holders must restrict copying, which they call by another seafaring term: 'piracy'.

Digital copying changes everything (except institutional behaviour)

But in digital media, the difference between 'original' and 'copy' is zero (unlike analogue media, where copies typically degrade original images). Copying is perfect, automated and can be accomplished easily and cheaply at infinite scale.

Further, the difference between 'speaking' and 'publishing' is also set at zero, because chatting online is an act of publication (under the Berne Convention): *all users are publishers*. The industrial distinction between producer and consumer is undermined. *Everyone is an author* (Chapter 7).

Since the achievement of near-global ubiquity of access to online, mobile and social media via the internet, the *use* of 'flows' from the 'common pool resources' of culture, language and media have become hotly contested territory because there's no mechanism to staunch the flow. The more *social* value people get out of copying stuff online, the less is the *commercial* value of the flow.

The response of the incumbent corporations has been predictable: to defend artificial scarcity (and thus their rents) by whatever technical, legal and market mechanisms they can command (including predatory lawyers, who will enforce corporately held copyright well beyond the extent desired by the original artists and authors).

At the same time, they are massively extending copyright from its industrial-era status as a B2B (business-to-business) arrangement, of whose existence the general population was largely ignorant, to its current status as a consumer-micropayment harvesting tool for international firms, whose future seems secure now that micro-contracts can be recorded at scale through blockchain. No more free riders in creative industries (Potts and Rennie, 2017)!

III. Something fishy about creativity

Creativity as property

The trouble with the concept of 'creativity' in 'creative industries' is that the very idea is founded on an idealist notion of creativity derived from nineteenth-century German Romanticism (riffing on Kant), where 'creative genius' is revealed in the spark of *originality*, that is, the very opposite of copying.

Originality is anti-utilitarian, arising from 'individual talent'. Artefacts created by means of original talent are far from 'common' property or knowledge. They can be traded, but not duplicated. That's the value proposition that drives the art market – and the plots of some pretty good movies too, from Jean-Jacques Beineix's *Diva* (1981) to more recent international offerings such as Abbas Kiarostami's *Certified Copy* (*Copie conforme*, 2010) and Giuseppe Tornatore's *The Best Offer* (*La migliore offerta*, 2013).[5]

Cultural value and economic value were thought to have been integrated with the emergence of the idea of the creative industries in the 1990s (Leadbeater, 1999). It was a simple proposition: creative work has *private* as well as *public* value. Where 'art' had survived on public subsidy, 'creative industries' could, it was confidently predicted, extend the commercial reach of the economy (and 'public culture' could be privatized).

For that to be achieved, someone has to own something, from which value can be extracted. Who is entitled to the rents arising from licensing access to creative work? Why, the author, of course (Chapter 7); and we've already got legislation for that, not to mention bands of corporate lawyers

---

[5] *The Best Offer* (*La migliore offerta*), 2013, directed by Giuseppe Tornatore (Italy), stars Geoffrey Rush (Australia), Donald Sutherland (Canada) and Sylvia Hoeks (Netherlands); *Certified Copy* (*Copie conforme*), 2010, directed by Abbas Kiarostami (Iran) stars Juliette Binoche (France) and William Shimell (England).

scouring the countryside hunting down 'copyright bandits'.[6] If even the agents formerly known as the audience can be re-cast as 'bandits' (making pirates out of media corporations' own customers), then perhaps it's not so surprising to discover what can be understood as 'creative' and 'authored' in law, and therefore recognized as intellectual property and put behind a paywall. A string of words (or notes) is copyrightable; a single word can be trademarked if it names a business. Colours can be copyright. Blank forms too. And tattoos. Life itself can be owned as intellectual property: yeasts, bacteria, all the way up to human stem cells.[7]

For policy purposes, the 'definition' of the creative industries starts not from culture, language, etc., but from the economic individual:

> Those industries that are based on individual creativity, skill and talent with the potential to create wealth and jobs through developing intellectual property.[8]

And of course 'individual' doesn't mean a 'natural person' but a 'legal person' or *persona ficta* – that is, a corporation posing as an author (Chapter 3) – in order to secure the 'industries' bit of the term 'creative industries'.

D'oh!™[9]

Unfortunately, the standard definition reckoned without two things. First, it 'forgets' that *culture* is the source of creativity, not individual talent. Individual talent is real, of course, but you can't deploy it outside of cultural

---

[6] 'Copyright bandits' is a News Corp term: https://torrentfreak.com/illegal-downloading-is-sc umbag-theft-by-copyright-bandits-says-media-giant-ceo-120821/.

[7] For colours, see Jack Calill (December 8, 2014) 'Meet Pantone, The Company that Owns Almost Every Colour You Can Imagine'. *Junkee*: http://junkee.com/meet-pantone-the-compa ny-that-owns-almostevery-colour-you-can-imagine/46819. For blank forms, see: K. Bowery 'The Outer Limits Of Copyright Law – Where Law Meets Philosophy and Culture' (2001) 12:1 *Law and Critique* 1–24; and see *Kalamazoo (Australia) Pty Ltd v Compact Business Systems Pty Ltd* (1985) 5 IPR 213. For tattoos, see: L. Etter (1 January 2014) 'Tattoo Artists are Asserting their Copyright Claims': *American Bar Association Journal* www.abajournal. com/magazine/article/tattoo_artists_are_asserting_their_copyright_claims. For life itself, Australia recognizes human cell lines as patentable, but awaits legal clarification on whether stem cells are excluded on the grounds that 'human beings and the biological processes for their generation' cannot be patented: http://www.alrc.gov.au/publications/15-stem-cell-technologies/ application-patent-law-stem-cell-technologies.

[8] This formula is now axiomatic, claimed as 'the UK's definition': http://creativecities.britishc ouncil.org/creative-industries/what_are_creative_industries_and_creative_economy.

[9] Meaning 'annoyed grunt', 'D'oh' has a longer history, but it is now firmly associated with the character Homer Simpson of *The Simpsons*. As a spoken word, it is a trademark of 20th Century Film Corporation, 10201 West Pico Boulevard Los Angeles, CA 90035 (http://tsdr.us pto.gov/#caseNumber=76280750&caseType=SERIAL_NO&searchType=statusSearch).

relations and systems, because *culture creates groups and groups create knowledge*. The artist, like the entrepreneur, may be an energetic, daring individual, operating – like opera – at or beyond the outer limits of human passion, technical capability and economic risk. But what happens when *everyone is an artist* and *anyone an entrepreneur*? What happens, in short, if you reassign creativity to *populations*, not to 'talented' (as if we aren't all!) individuals?

Second, the 'creative industries' definition, originating in the UK, 'forgets' *digital* culture, possibly because the UK did not develop the 'tech giants' which we associate (for the time being, until China asserts itself internationally) with the American wave of digital culture: Google, Facebook, Amazon, Apple, Microsoft, Intel (even though WiFi is an Australian invention and Skype comes from Estonia).

'Authorship' works okay in certain analogue situations, but it has been totally transformed in and by digital culture. The thing about digital culture is that it leaves traces (data) of planetary and population-wide extent. Now, it is possible to map and to visualize the *systems* in which meanings emerge, jostle, are used and die. We can see that *semiotic productivity* has shifted from *author* to *reader* (user). And now that all users are authors, journalists and publishers as well as readers and audiences, we see that creative productivity is a function of something we haven't legislated for: the *system* or *network*, which has remained proprietorial rather than public from the start.[10]

Creativity an effect of system interaction

Here, as Barthes (1977a) and Foucault (1984) foresaw, the *meaning* of a given work is no longer determined by an author or even by readers as individual agents; it is an *effect of the system*. The system itself imposes the rules of the game. Even personal identity is a performance. Authors' names are a branding function for publishers based on a discursive 'truth-effect' of identity, as Judith Butler put it (1990).[11]

Some cultural scientists have responded to the 'forgotten' aspects of creativity to redefine the creative industries as '*social network markets*' (Potts et al., 2008). Here, the usual economic presumptions don't apply. Supply precedes demand (you can't 'like' a string of text that Shakespeare or whoever hasn't written yet). Consumer choices are not based on price but on prestige – the status and choices of other users in the system. Celebrity is a coordination mechanism. Economic value lies in 'thin air' (Leadbeater,

---

[10]Including regulatory organizations, for example, ICANN: https://www.icann.org/ (Internet Corporation for Assigned Names and Numbers).
[11]Butler brings gender, and therefore bodies, into discourse (1990: 136): see also Chapter 7 of this book.

1999). Instead of catching and selling fish, you can generate wealth by selling the *recipes* (knowledge) for cooking fish, a move that spawned the TV chef. In short, digital culture and the 'knowledge economy' clarifies the extent to which *publishing* has begun to take on the characteristics not of an *industry* but of *language*.

IV. Plenty more fish in the sea?

Over on the other side of the equation, there is language. Language is useful, therefore not copyrightable (it's like fashion in that regard): 'No reasonable person could claim to own something like English, Spanish, or Mandarin'

(ROBERTSON, 2014).

Live long and prosper™ [12]

This well-established principle is in the news again as users resist the overreach of copyright lawyers. Now, these cunning predators want control not only of language 'flow' but of its 'stock' as well: not a specific use of language systems but the systems themselves. The chosen legal battleground is over *constructed languages*, especially those dear to the American fannish heart, from beloved film and TV franchises such as Klingon (from *Star Trek*), Na'vi (from *Avatar*), Dothraki (from *Game of Thrones*) and others.[13] Naturally, Tocquevillian *associations* or 'we-groups' have sprung up to defend and promote the rights of 'constructed languages' ('conlang'). One such is Language Creation Society (LCS). On behalf of *users* of the Klingon language they are in dispute with Paramount, *owners* of the *Star Trek* franchise.

According to a legal brief on behalf of LCS:

> What is a language other than a procedure, process, or system for communication? What is a language's vocabulary but a collection of words? The vocabulary and grammar rules of a language provide instructions for a speaker to articulate thoughts and ideas. … Vocabulary and grammar are no more protectable than the bookkeeping system. … Plaintiffs are free to register copyright any particular expression that they create using the [Klingon] language … but they cannot claim ownership of the building blocks of the language.[14]

---

[12]Trademark CBS Studios: https://trademarks.justia.com/851/11/live-long-and-85111052.html.
[13]See, for instance, Dothraki: http://wiki.dothraki.org/Main_Page; Na'vi: http://learnnavi.org/.
[14]Cited here: http://www.technollama.co.uk/can-you-copyright-the-klingon-language. See also: http://www.seattletimes.com/nation-world/klingon-legal-brief-says-a-language-cant-be-owned/.

There are other, older constructed languages, from Esperanto to J. R. R. Tolkien's experiments with Elvish,[15] which have never been subject to copyright claims, either because the whole idea is to promote the use of the language (Esperanto) or because corporate enforcement lawyers are not involved. In either case, the language is the winner, because its use and elaboration in unforeseen circumstances by any and all users allows it to survive and evolve.

Reconstructing Indigenous languages

There are older languages still, ones that require all the protection they can get, including an element of *reconstruction*, as have Modern Hebrew and Cornish, and certain 'endangered' Australian Aboriginal languages.

The custodians of one of these, Palawa kani, have reached out for legal protection for their language. Palawa kani is neither an 'original' language nor a 'constructed' one. It is an amalgam of up to dozen Tasmanian languages not spoken since the end of the nineteenth century, of which only fragments survive. The Tasmanian Aboriginal Centre (TAC) is seeking to revive and protect the language and to promote its use among Aboriginal people.

The TAC is *not* keen on non-Aboriginal users appropriating the language. They complained (unsuccessfully) to Wikipedia, protesting against it for publishing an entry on Palawa kani.[16] Their claim is that 'policies determining Aboriginal language use are based on the principle of Aboriginal control'. Thus, they appeal not to US or Australian copyright law but to the UN Declaration on the Rights of Indigenous Peoples, which includes 'the right to revitalise, use, develop and transmit to future generations their ... languages'.[17] The TAC protocol reads:

> Any non-Aboriginal person, group or organisation wishing to use Aboriginal language for any purpose must make formal application in writing to: The Administrator, Tasmanian Aboriginal Centre, PO Box 569, Hobart, 7001. The application must state the purpose for which the language is to be used, and by whom.[18]

---

[15]See: http://esperanto.org/; http://www.elvish.org/.
[16]See: https://en.wikipedia.org/wiki/Palawa_kani. And see: http://tacinc.com.au/programs/palawa-kani/.
[17]See: https://www.humanrights.gov.au/publications/un-declaration-rights-indigenous-peoples-1, especially Articles 13, 14 and 16.
[18]See: http://tacinc.com.au/wp-content/uploads/2016/05/POLICY-PROTOCOL-for-use-of-palawa-kani-Aboriginal-Language.pdf.

Commenting for *The Verge*, Adi Robertson (2014) writes:

> For Indigenous groups, copyright is a way to preserve the traditions of cultures that have often been scattered and brutally suppressed, preventing outsiders from trivializing or copying them. Establishing control over language, religious ceremonies, and art is a way to draw boundaries around a community that's trying to reconstitute itself.

In short, copyright is being drawn into a much more fundamental struggle for any 'we-group': the need to draw clear boundaries around communities that have stared down extinction, in order for their knowledge, identity and survival – their language and culture – to be secured against all comers, including well-meaning global organizations like Wikipedia.[19]

V. Gone phishing

What have we here? a man or a fish? dead or alive? A fish: he smells like a fish; a very ancient and fish-like smell. ... A strange fish! (Caliban)[20]

Well, you can see where this is heading. There's an argument for copyright as the appropriate form of intellectual property for authors, and for its extension to cover audio-visual media, especially in the case of elaborate works like stories, plays, movies, games, etc. But copyright has been captured by international corporate players, who use it to enforce market dominance by squeezing other players – including playful users – out of the game (not just out of the market).

Meanwhile, copying means something very different in both digital terms, where it is not a degradation of some valuable original but merely one instance of an infinite series, and in cultural-semiotic terms, where it is the very basis of social learning and identity. There is clearly a case for reconceptualizing the 'definition' of the creative economy, to expand it beyond individual property based on 'talent' (authorship).

What if the myriad acts of semiotic copying and translation among a whole population of users, doing their own thing with their own 'special knowledge of circumstances', were coordinated not as a market but as a language? What increases in creative productivity may follow?

---

[19]Declaration of interest: I am a Chief Investigator on an ARC-funded project that aims to produce the world's first version of Wikipedia in an Australian Aboriginal language, the Noongar language of SW Western Australia. See: https://meta.wikimedia.org/wiki/Noongarpedia.

[20]William Shakespeare, *The Tempest* Act II Scene ii: http://shakespeare.mit.edu/tempest/tempest.2.2.html.

Allowing *just anyone* to use the group-made resources of each other's creativity, as a language does, would provoke change on the scale of the Industrial Revolution, which also took off on the wings of utility via anonymous artisanal tinkering (Mokyr, 2009).

Emancipated or emaciated?

However, the model of language does not suggest that 'anything goes'. Indeed, the model of language suggests that the tension between incommensurate systems – in this case between meanings and markets – is a *source of innovation and new knowledge* in the creative economy.

That being so, any new arrangement that *emancipates* the billions-strong population of *users* into creative freedom must at the same time put such constraints in their way that they are obliged to take their turn as *producers* of something new. Is this what copyright is good for? To *irritate* citizens into rebellious larceny, otherwise known as art? (Hutter, 2015).

Any new arrangement might want to ensure that the incumbent cadre of professional 'creatives' are not *emaciated* in the process. It has to be said, however, that history is not compassionate on this point. Who remembers what happened to copyists when print came along, or to the legions of illustrators when photography took hold?

Knowledge clubs

A much better suggestion would be to concentrate not on individuals, works and property but on groups, uses and networks, or on what some cultural scientists (Potts et al., 2017) are calling 'knowledge clubs', based on James Buchanan's (1965) model of 'club goods' (Hess and Ostrom, 2003). The main thing to remember is that if *everyone* is an author, everyone a publisher, then it is not the ownership of an idea that gives it value but its use, not the individual but the system. It is the coordination of 'flow' and utility that needs regulation, not the 'protection' (rental terms) of corporate catchphrases like D'oh!™

If knowledge is produced in groups among those with shared language and other codes, in competition with other such groups, from which they nevertheless 'trade' in copied ideas, then 'intellectual property' doesn't come near to what's needed to incentivize, diversify, extend, grow, regulate and communicate new knowledge. It has instead become a tool of corporate hegemony (over authors as much as users). That's where 'clubs' come in. Good public policy would focus on finding out more about how 'knowledge clubs' work, both as an abstract model and in local circumstances, in order to figure out how best to nurture their formation, interaction and openness in the digital, global, creative knowledge economy.

Unruly thinkers on both sides of the culture/economy divide have pointed the way. It's time to inter-translate the two knowledge systems (using Lotman's five stages). The language model suggests that among the first acts of coordination for a creative economy should be the *exemption of educational uses* of copyright material, since it is only by copying that the system as a whole – what Lotman calls the 'semiosphere', a planetary envelope of meaning (on the model of the biosphere) – can reproduce itself. And it is only by breaking the rules that it can adapt and renew; a process that disrupts and tears the existing fabric of sociality, just as vulcanism tears tectonic plates apart and renews the geosphere. Corporate overreach cannot prevent that process for long. The semiotic equivalent of earthquakes and eruptions will occur. What should intellectual property law do about that? The history of art may provide an *entrepreneurial* (Schumpeterian-Shakespearean) answer. As Pablo Picasso famously put it, asserting the claims of modernism to do whatever it likes: 'Good artists copy; great artists steal.'[21]

---

[21]Cited at: http://www.bbc.com/culture/story/20141112-great-artists-steal, a BBC review of the *Sturtevant: Double Trouble* exhibition at MoMA, New York (2014): https://www.moma.org/calendar/exhibitions/1454?locale=en.

6

Intellectuals:

Three phases – Paris, public, club

*All people are intellectuals ... but not all have in society the
function of intellectuals.*

(ANTONIO GRAMSCI, 1971: 9).

In the context of the growth of knowledge, it is instructive to trace changes
in the cultural function of the knowledge professional. There are many types
of 'knowledge workers' emerging from information and data industries, but
this chapter follows the career of 'the intellectual': past, present and future.
First, it describes an archetypal 'Parisian' myth (the heroic outsider); next,
the dissolute present or 'public intellectual' (the administrative functionary);
finally, a future vision based on the new concept of decentralized 'knowledge
clubs' (the questing group).

The chapter considers the consequences of hanging on to names from
the past, for instance by adding the word 'public' to 'intellectual', which
suggests that intellectuals remain what they once were: charismatic
persons. The 'public intellectual' label may blind contemporary analysis to
the direction in which to look for 'public thought' in the future. In fact,
the chapter argues, the cultural function of the intellectual needs to be
rethought according the approach of cultural science, where knowledge-
agency – including transgressive disruption, 'creative destruction' and the
critical contemplation of alternatives – belongs to culture-made groups, not
individuals.

Intellectuals I: Paris

Within the very limits of the teaching space as given, the need is to work at patiently tracing out a pure form, that of floating (the very form of the signifier); a floating which would not destroy anything but would be content simply to disorientate the Law. The necessities of promotion, professional obligations (which nothing then prevents from being scrupulously fulfilled), imperatives of knowledge, prestige of method, ideological criticism – everything is there, but floating.

(ROLAND BARTHES, 1977A)

Something in the coffee?

Roland Barthes had a point when he wrote an essay on 'Writers, Intellectuals, Teachers' (1977a: 190–215), in which he contrasted speech and writing, and assigned teachers and writers to opposing 'sides' of the contrast. The teacher, he argued, 'is on the side of speech', while the writer is 'every operator of language on the side of writing'. Between the two Barthes placed the intellectual, defined in his 'neutral' mode(Barthes, 2005), as 'the person who prints and publishes his speech' (1977a: 190). The function of the intellectual, then, is to convert speech into writing. Rather a bathetic definition, you may say, but this is part of a paradigm-baffling project to deconstruct the binary oppositions that make discourse meaningful. Accordingly, Barthes is not content to accept such binaries. He connects 'the intellectual' not with ideas but with *speech*, and speech with *teaching*. Barthes had a lot to say about speech, including a structuralist concern for the extent to which 'language speaks us', as they used to say, as well as poststructuralist pleasure in disrupting the *doxa* or 'Law' of language – a task he gave not in the first place to intellectuals, but principally to writing (of the 'writerly' kind that could produce *jouissance*). So here is a three-part distinction of terms that plays almost no part in current (twentyfirst-century) discussions of the topic: the typology of Writer, Teacher, and Intellectual.

These days, in discussions of the role of the intellectual, the 'teacher' is almost forgotten, perhaps in line with the reduction of status of teachers in many universities to an abject figure of the proletarianized precariat. But Barthes reckoned that 'between the language of the teacher and that of the intellectual there is hardly any incompatibility (they often co-exist in a single individual)'. Over against the speaker/teacher/intellectual, the one who 'stands apart, separate' was the *writer*: 'Writing begins at a point where speech becomes *impossible*' (Barthes, 1977a: 190). He was quick to gloss '*impossible*' as 'a word that can be understood in the sense it has when applied to a child' (see Chapter 12).

But before we get to writing as language's law-breaker and 'impossible child', it is instructive to consider more closely the context in which

Barthes can claim that teacher and intellectual are coeval, with 'hardly any incompatibility'. Despite the vigour of other national intelligentsias in the 1960s, the 'preferred reading' of 'the intellectual' was that of Parisian cosmopolitan café-society, of which Barthes himself was an archetype. In the 1970s, anglophone cultural studies became highly Francophile: structuralism, semiotics, deconstruction, psychoanalysis and Marxism were all read with a French accent. Paris had the 1960s – 'years of hope, days of rage', as Todd Gitlin eloquently put it (1987) – written all over it. Here was a heady combination of Jean-Luc Godard's *À Bout de Souffle* (*Breathless*), 'Continental' philosophy, *Les Évènements* of 1968, where you might bump into Althusser (or his shrink Lacan) in the café,[1] or catch the bus over to the revolutionary Paris University VIII to see Judith Miller, Lacan's daughter (until she was fired for handing out course credits to someone she met on a bus, as an anti-capitalist gesture), or else to see head-of-department Michel Foucault, when he wasn't busy joining in a student occupation and throwing projectiles at the police. Or, you might attend one of Foucault's weekly lectures at the Collège de France (Foucault, 1977), which Barthes himself joined in 1977, nominated by Foucault (Barthes, 2005) and where, just outside, he was run down in 1980 by a laundry van (*cleaned up* by the binary-loving *bourgeoisie*) while walking back from Sunday lunch with soon-to-be President François Mitterrand. In the Parisian air, there's the whiff of insurrection as well as *Gitanes*. In the coffee *crema*, there's philosophy – literally, in the case of Godard's 1967 film *2 ou 3 choses que je sais d'elle* (*Two or Three Things I Know About Her*) (Ford, 2013). Amidst these titans of intellectual ferment, something new was stirring.

In such a climate, the link that Barthes makes between teachers and intellectuals is much easier to 'read', as it were. Intellectuals were hot. Foucault's Collège de France lectures were packed out, as much a part of pop culture as intellectual, not least because of the Collège's rule that such events should be free and open to the public. This kind of teaching, you might say, was not outsourced, low-value, high-audit drudgery, but part of the *avant-garde entertainment complex*, a mass medium in its own right. You spoke, you published, you were hyphenated: teacher-intellectual, entertainer-celebrity, militant-hero, film-star-philosopher; it was all the same, as modelled by an amazing roll call of intellectuals whose names still resonate (Lucy, 2016). So when 'the youth of the day' crowded into the lecture hall from the demo or the café, to critique the present, to capture the future, to make love and life, in pursuit of what Barthes calls 'an *art of living*, the greatest of all the arts' (1977a: 215), Barthes was talking directly to them.

---

[1] As here, perhaps? – https://chaiselonguetheorists.wordpress.com/2013/12/04/exam-one-post-marxism-2/.

Despite the sectarianism that makes and then mars progressive politics, and which had riven the intellectual Left after 1968 in France as elsewhere, Barthes could still claim in 1977 that 'one of the things that can be expected from a regular meeting together of speakers is quite simply *goodwill*' (1977a: 213). What optimism! What ambition! Goodwill among the many different parties, causes – and intellectuals – of 'the' Left was never secure. In this period, Left politics was gradually transforming from class-based vanguardism and militancy, agitated by parties well to the left of parliamentary socialism, towards issues-led 'new social movements', aiming (for instance) at liberating subjectivities, opposing patriarchy, colonialism, racism, etc., demonstrating for (anti-nuclear) peace, environmental and social causes, or seeking new forms of personal enlightenment through sex, drugs, rock 'n' roll and Eastern mysticism. Each of these movements and issues threw up its own intellectuals, few of whom were based in universities or even political parties: some were gurus, others pop stars or film stars, still others writers. Leadership in new ideas was passing from politically constituted parties to *the market*: radicalization was more likely to follow from hearing John Lennon than John Maclean.[2]

At this time, in Germany (Red Army Faction), Italy (Red Brigades), Britain (IRA and others),[3] and Spain (ETA), political militancy spilled over into terrorism. Some intellectuals sympathized, holding fast to the Bolshevik notion of party-and-class as the agent of change, without renouncing violence. Most controversial among these, perhaps, was the Italian philosopher Antonio Negri, who served a substantial term of imprisonment on charges of terrorism (later downgraded). Negri is still regarded with deep suspicion by some commentators.[4] He retained a commitment to party-led class politics. But, as Timothy Murphy, editor of Negri's revolutionary writings (2005) has shown, his conceptualization of what 'the party' comprised changed with the times:

- from a Leninist, command-and-control vanguard elite, centred on the proletariat (male factory workers);

---

[2]John Maclean was a schoolteacher and Marxist hero of 'Red Clydeside'. His fame lasted into the 1970s via popular music: Dick Gaughan's rendering of Hamish Henderson's 'Ballad of John Maclean' (1972), celebrating MacLean's release from prison in 1918 after anti-war agitation and refusing conscription: www.dickgaughan.co.uk/songs/texts/johnmacl.html.

[3]For instance, the Free Wales Army (active and convicted in 1969). See: www.walesonline.co.u k/news/wales-news/images-spark-interest-forgotten-free-2087129.

[4]See, for instance, the exchange between Negri and Alexander Stille in *New York Review of Books*: http://www.nybooks.com/articles/archives/2003/feb/27/apocalypse-soon-an-exchange/, following a review by Stille in which he had written: 'In his homeland, Negri is the most notorious of what the Italians call *i cattivi maestri*, the bad professors who poisoned the minds of a generation, sending tens of thousands of young people to the barricades to destroy themselves for a Communist revolution that could never happen': www.nybooks.com/articles/archives/2002/nov/07/apocalypse-soon/.

- to a middle position where it was seen as what he called a 'party of mass vanguards', being the 'totalization of mass initiatives and workers' leadership', that is, the workers not the party called the shots in deciding what struggles to pursue; and finally,
- to the party as 'an external and subordinate tactical appendage of the class', that is, an action squad with no control over proletarian 'self-valorization' (Murphy, 2005: x).

In other words, to keep hold of an idea of the party at all, Negri has to concede, first, that the *composition* of the class of which it is the party must expand to include 'students, women, the unemployed, prisoners, and other subordinated groups', that is, it has to co-opt the new social movements that it had played no role in engendering. Second, it slowly dawns on Negri that these folk can think and speak *autonomously* for themselves. As Murphy puts it, what links his writings over the period is 'Negri's gradual recognition of the self-sufficiency of the proletarian masses themselves: their ability to conceptualize, produce, and organize their own forms of struggle without the need for external command of any kind' (2005: x). What need of a party at all?

In 1983, Negri fled to France from Italy, gaining sanctuary – and a new audience – at Paris University VIII and at Derrida's new Collège International de Philosophie. Was he still, but now in the guise of an international intellectual celebrity and teacher, the *'cattivo maestro'* – bad teacher/ evil genius and corrupter of youth, as his prosecutors alleged (Murphy, 2005: xvi)? He certainly sounded like it, producing his own version of the aphorism associated with Robespierre as well as Lenin: 'You can't make an omelette without breaking eggs.' In Negri's case the suffering of the egg is valued for its breakage, whether or not an omelette results from the requisite 'destruction or sabotage': 'Every act of destruction and sabotage redounds upon me as a sign of class fellowship ... nor does the suffering of the adversary affect me' (Negri, 2005: 259).

Is this the point 'where speech becomes *impossible*', in Barthes's sense? Is Negri, with his fantasy of 'fellowship' in 'destruction and sabotage' (rather than Barthes's 'goodwill' among speakers), one of those teachers who encourages the class to be as unruly as possible, or is he himself merely the naughty child of speech and teaching? Where does the 'speech-teaching-intellectual' combination go from here? For Barthes's distinction between speech and writing, the answer is clear: the intellectual must go across to the 'separate' domain of writing, where destruction and sabotage are only semiotic signs of solidarity. That is exactly what happened to Negri. As Verso's blurb for *Books for Burning* puts it, his texts of the 1970s 'were later misread and misrepresented by the Italian state in its attempt to frame Negri as responsible for the assassination of former Italian president Aldo Moro, as the leader of the Red Brigades, and as the mastermind of an armed insurrection against the state'.[5] His defence against these charges of terrorism was, of course, to argue that his *writings* belonged to an autonomous domain of ideas and were not an incitement to literal violence.

The activist intellectual retreated from both class and classroom action, to take refuge in textuality and metaphor (not violence but 'violence'). But the cat was out of the bag. As Gramsci (1971) had known, *everyone* is an intellectual because everyone can think. Now, with 'the personal as political' and activism dispersed across the social domain, up to and including the global markets in entertainment (especially music), there was no place left for professional revolutionaries (or philosophers) any more than for 'traditional' or 'universal' intellectuals (Foucault, 1977).

Now, 'the' intellectual was dispersed among myriad causes with no central leadership, 'organic' in a way that even Gramsci (1971: 9) may not have wanted to concede, because the principle of *organization*, a party function, was deleted. The command and control of ideas passed from professional elites to the *market* (which of course had always dealt in them, out of the sight of intellectuals perhaps), and henceforth were *self-organizing*, which also meant that they were subject to trends, crazes, marketing, branding, investment, the vagaries of consumer taste and manipulation by vested interests. But still, ideas could spring from anywhere, and gain adherents from anyone. 'The intellectual' could not operate without *mediation*, and the 'mass media' were by now an ascendant force in society, with their own rules and routines. The system of mass media (public and commercial entertainment and information across print, broadcast, cinema, music media) was the only one capable of coordinating such complex interactions, and so the claim that intellectuals could hold themselves apart as outsiders or exiles (except in Barthes' sense, as writers) was more than ever untenable. The intellectual function was *marketized, mediatized* and *democratized*.

It follows that intellectual and pop culture could no longer be separated, in practice or theory. Again, this was not new, for even in the days of Vietnam and revulsion against imperial 'Amerika' (as its own Yippies called it), the canniest European intellectuals and artists – Godard, say, or Nabokov, or Eco – were fascinated by American popular culture, the movies, the music, the cars, even as they used the sign of America to signal the end of everything their own cultures had held dear. Godard's *2 ou 3 choses* had set the theme in train, back in 1967 (Ford, 2013). Among plenty of other examples, a memorable emblem of this mode of (non-binary) thinking is Jacques Tati's canny film *Trafic* (1971), where America is the source of both soaring hope and crushing reality.[6] It sends up car culture while frankly acknowledging the Americanness (and TV-mediation) of the next quantum leap in human

---

[5]See: www.versobooks.com/books/24-books-for-burning.
[6]Note that the title of *Trafic* is an Americanism, for the French for 'traffic' is 'circulation'.

FIGURE 6.1 *Monsieur Hulot watches the moon landings: Screen grab of* Trafic, *by Jacques Tati (www.orbit.zkm.de/?q=node/378).*

mobility that is already upon it, in the shape of the 1969 moon landings. Bumbling Monsieur Hulot (for it is he, in his camper van) meets 'giant leap' Neil Armstrong or, at least, coexists with him. One monopolizes every TV set in the car-clogged city, while the other is stuck in traffic, destined neither to reach his destination nor to lose his faith in gadgetry.

So let us leave that apparition, the Parisian intellectual, lost in suburban space, in the company of the harbinger of another kind of modernity, M. Hulot. What to do, but to join the global audience, sit back in wonder, and watch? (Figure 6.1).

Intellectuals II: Public

I define the Neutral as that which outplays the paradigm, or rather I call Neutral everything that baffles the paradigm. For I am not trying to define a word; I am trying to name a thing. The paradigm, what is that? It's the opposition of two virtual terms from which, in speaking, I actualize one to produce meaning.

(ROLAND BARTHES, 2005: 12–13)

'A fellow of doubtful nature'?

The charisma of Paris in the 1960s and 1970s remains strong – as does that of America too, when it comes to that (Gitlin, 1987). But as I've argued, this was just the moment when 'the' intellectual had dissolved into *popular culture, the market, and the media,* and when political leadership was devolving away from parties and towards autonomous groups and networks. Among those most sceptical about the function of the intellectual as outsider, or *bande à part* (as Godard might have put it), were these very intellectuals, Barthes (and Foucault) prominent among them. In his inaugural lecture at the Collège de France, Roland Barthes did not mount the stage in his Che Guevara T-shirt, but modestly dubbed himself 'a fellow of doubtful nature'. He felt his every 'attribute' was 'challenged by its opposite'. Of course this doubtfulness was strategic as well as autobiographical. Chief among the opposites Barthes wanted to challenge was the one he discerned between the *freedom* of speech (and of teaching at the Collège) and the *power* of structure, which he attributed ultimately to language itself:

> We discover then that power is present in the most delicate mechanisms of social exchange: not only in the State, in classes, in groups, but even in fashion, public opinion, entertainment, sports, news, family and private relations, and even in the liberating impulses which attempt to counteract it. I call the discourse of power any discourse which engenders blame, hence guilt, in its recipient. Some expect of us as intellectuals that we take action on every occasion against Power, but our true battle is elsewhere, it is it is against powers in the plural, and this is no easy combat. (Barthes, 1977b)

Already we have entered the present: a world characterized by anxiety about the 'public intellectual'. For Barthes, *media, networks* and *celebrity* are already hard at work, often in the name of those 'liberating impulses'. But the duty of 'us as intellectuals' is not, as the phrase now has it, to 'speak truth to power'. Barthes knows there's no doing that, for speech is co-present with power, and he chooses to do battle with language itself: 'To speak, and, with even greater reason, to utter a discourse is not, as is too often repeated, to communicate; it is to subjugate' (Barthes, 1977b). Nevertheless, Barthes presses on with his investigations, albeit in the pre-scientific form of essays – that 'ambiguous genre in which analysis vies with writing' – knowing that intellectuals are not exempt from the powers they contest. He sees the 'true battle' for intellectuals here, in combatting powers that they themselves cannot avoid. This is the moment of the 'impossible' child: the moment when 'analysis' gives way to 'writing' (Figure 6.2).

How is that combat faring today? Coming up to date, it is instructive to note the language changing as we speak. The talk is not of 'the' intellectual, but of the 'public' intellectual. Barthes's original tripartite distinction between *speaker/teacher*, *intellectual* and *writer* has transformed into one between *academic*, *mediator*, and *celebrity*. Celebrity becomes a goal – and a profession (e.g. Richard Dawkins).[7]

---

[7]See: www.theguardian.com/science/2015/jun/09/is-richard-dawkins-destroying-his-reputation.

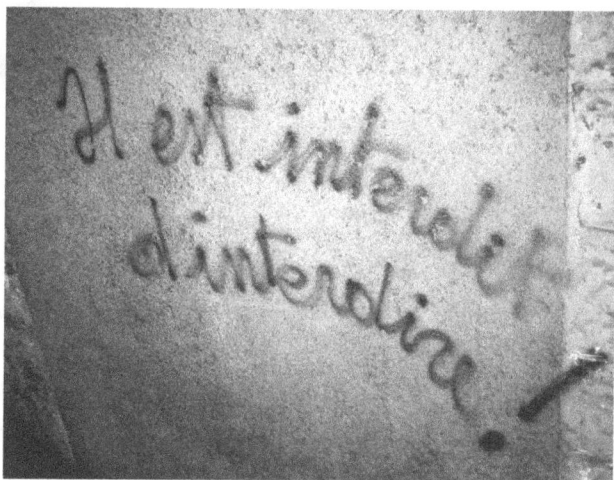

FIGURE 6.2 *Politics trumps philosophy:* May 1968 slogan, Paris. 'It is forbidden to forbid!'

Source: *'Situationist' by Espencat – Own work. Licensed under Public Domain via Wikimedia Commons: http://commons.wikimedia.org/wiki/File:Situationist.jpg#/med ia/File:Situationist.jpg.*

Barthes designated *writing* as a separate domain. For him it was perhaps the only place (in discourse) where, recognizing that power cannot be evaded, he could nevertheless evade it: 'The only remaining alternative is, if I may say so, to cheat with speech, to cheat speech' (Barthes, 1977b) – to cheat it with *writing*, which Barthes is bold enough to call both a 'grand imposture' and '*literature*':

> This salutary trickery, this evasion, this grand imposture which allows us to understand speech outside the bounds of power, in the splendour of a permanent revolution of language, I for one call literature. (Barthes, 1977b)

Barthes turns the writer into a latter-day trickster (Hyde, 2008). This cheating imposter is the one who can survive within writing, which itself, as literature, keeps language unfixed: here's how you can 'disorientate the Law' (Barthes, 1977a). This is the 'literary' intellectual, as opposed to the 'public' one who opposes power by using 'a discourse which engenders blame, hence guilt' to achieve celebrity.

Perhaps the problem lies in the word *public*. It changes the intellectual into something else: a fame-seeking, media-savvy academic. As a modifier of other terms, 'public' can signify public functions where private ones might also be expected: for example, access to a place (public house, public bar, public toilets); or it can signify a public office (public hangman). A pair of Google Ngrams (Figure 6.3) shows the frequency of various versions of the

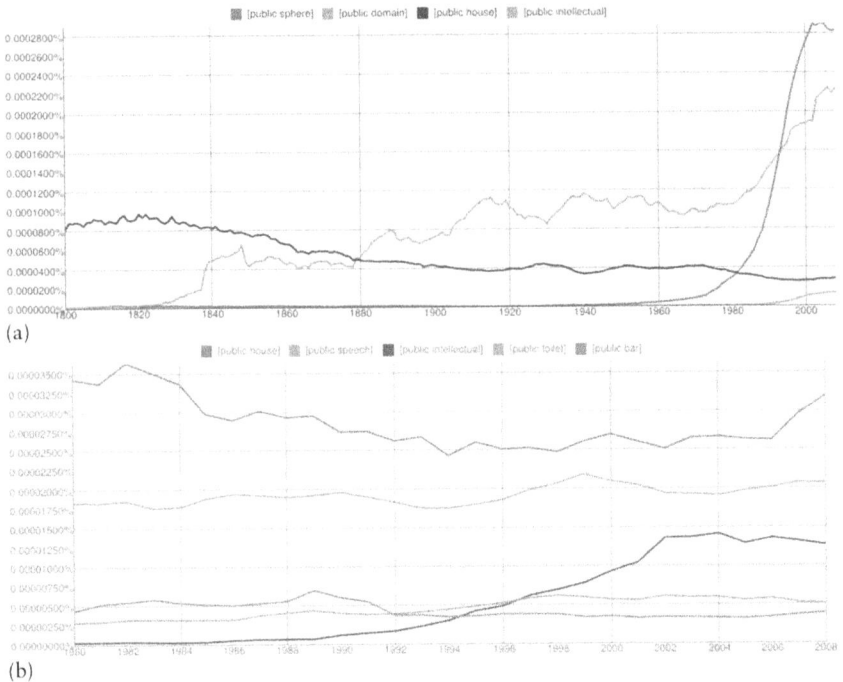

(a)

(b)

FIGURE 6.3 *Public frequencies. (a) Chart shows frequency of the terms 'public house', 'public speech', 'public intellectual', 'public toilet', 'public bar' (books in English, 1980-2008), Google Ngram. (b) Chart shows frequency of the terms 'public sphere', 'public domain', 'public house', 'public intellectual' (books in English, 1800-2008), Google Ngram.*

modifier 'public'. The first runs from the 1980s to 2007, in books in English. Most frequent in this sample is 'public house', followed by 'public speech', with 'public intellectual' rising from nothing (about 1990) to third place, overtaking 'public toilet' and 'public bar' along the way. This shows that the 'public intellectual' is a recent coinage, trending upwards but still playing second fiddle to the pub, at least in books. The second Ngram, at greater scale and over a much longer timeframe, runs from 1800 to 2000, shows how 'public domain' overtakes 'public house' in the nineteenth century, while the much more recent 'public sphere' (which has replaced the older and more neutral 'public affairs' – not shown here), far outstrips 'public intellectual'.

How might one explain the recent growth of the terms 'public intellectual' and 'public sphere'? Their appearance in the wake of Reagan-Thatcherism is doubtless significant, at a time when deregulation, privatization and neoliberalism were ascendant in the Western political sphere, both in policy and in rhetorical politics, provoking an opposing reaction among the defenders of public culture and institutions, from public housing, education and welfare to public service broadcasting and public culture. Since then, the term 'public' has become adversarial, a marker of left/right allegiances. Because this is politics, 'our' side of the opposition is treated as universal and self-evident, while 'theirs' is duplicitous and dangerous: in short, the knowledge involved is *tribal* – or 'demic', belonging to culture-made groups (Figure 6.4).

At once, the 'public' intellectual is caught up in opposition of exactly the kind that Barthes refused. If you're 'public' then you're an opponent

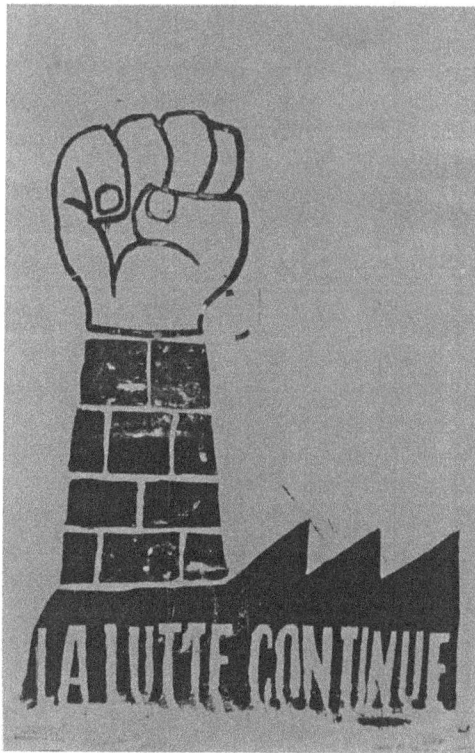

FIGURE 6.4 La lutte continue (The Struggle Continues), *May1968. Atelier Ecole des Beaux-arts: (anonymous poster).*
Source: *http://gallica.bnf.fr/ark:/12148/btv1b9018349b. The citation attached to this poster in the collection of the Musée Carnavalet – Histoire de Paris makes clear the direct line of filiation from revolutionary, political design to subsequent market leadership in the art of publicity: These posters showed a 'graphic inventiveness … which, paradoxically, then permanently influenced the world of advertising [la publicité]'. www.carnavalet.paris.fr/fr/collections/la-lutte-continue.*

of 'private' – the private sector, private enterprise, privatization. Binary opposition speaks through the *'public'* intellectual, whatever they may say. So much so that *a* 'public good' (a neutral term from economics for 'non-rivalrous' and 'non-excludable' goods) becomes *the* public good (a moral economy associated with the public sector). A structurally oppositional stance is presented as universally binding, as if the public sector is preferable to the private in all circumstances.

The ideological adversaries of 'big government' (i.e. opponents of the public sector), including pro-corporate interests in newspapers and media groups as well as ideologues in political parties of the right, encourage and foment public scepticism about the claims of partisan intellectuals, with the results that all can see: public-sector scientific, intellectual and cultural groups and individuals are politicized whether they like it or not, and there's a chasm between what is known (science) and what is enacted (policy). If this is a 'knowledge-driven economy' it's a pretty partial kind of knowledge, and its bearers are defeated by the very value that they espouse.

If the 'public intellectual' is partial, then where is its opposite: the 'private intellectual'? Private enterprise and its apologists simply do not use this discursive register or lexicon. Their terms are 'public opinion', 'public relations' and *marketing*, that is, an important sector of the market economy devoted to the communication of ideas. Here a 'private' intellectual might range from ideological warriors to advertising gurus. 'Brand ambassadors' include the many celebrities who make their name in one sphere (the performing arts) and then rent their fame for product promotion or partisan endorsements, some of them for public institutions or causes. While such figures are familiar enough, they are not often thought of as 'intellectuals', private or otherwise, despite what we know about their importance in the circulation of new ideas. Whether such figures are thought of as *cattivi maestri*, evil geniuses and corruptors of youth (e.g. Silvio Berlusconi and other politically active media moguls), or as figures of hope and identification with good causes (e.g. Dame Angelina Jolie, DCMG),[8] they don't call themselves intellectuals – and neither do academics, who are more likely to denounce them than to welcome them as fellows. This may be a strategic mistake if you're trying to understand the function of intellectuals in society.

But in fact there's not much discussion about what a 'private intellectual' might be, even among those who are interested in 'public' ones. Sometimes the term is applied to the scholar whose knowledge is produced for a specialist peer group only, circulated in publications that the public never see, and who plays no part in public affairs or public life. That figure, once again, is the negative polar opposite of the public intellectual. Such a view motivates one of the most important developments in scholarly communication of

---

[8]See: http://en.wikipedia.org/wiki/Order_of_St_Michael_and_St_George.

recent times, the drive towards Open Access, where knowledge is made public using the capabilities of digital archives and internet connectivity. The argument goes that most research is produced by scholars employed in public institutions using public funds, but published in privately owned journals that these institutions then buy back at great cost to the taxpayer. Surely such knowledge ought to be a 'public good' too? Here, we do begin to see a shift from the intellectual as moral warrior to a system-based interest in the public state of knowledge. Unfortunately, the idea that *all* scholars are – or should become – public intellectuals is not practical in the current adversarial climate. To be able to imagine such an extension of the intellectual function we need to rethink the whole set-up.

Intellectuals III: Clubs and commons

Though it is true that I long wished to inscribe my work within the field of science – literary, lexicological, and sociological – I must admit that I have produced only essays, an ambiguous genre in which analysis vies with writing.

(ROLAND BARTHES, 1977B)

Baffle the paradigm!

Roland Barthes was on to something when he sought to 'baffle the paradigm', where meaning is made by opposing 'two virtual terms from which, in speaking, I actualize one to produce meaning' (2005: 12). This is the problem with 'public' – it cannot be uttered without 'meaning' *opposition*. It doesn't specify what an intellectual is or does, but recruits intellectuals to a cause of faith (troth) rather than that of making knowledge (truth). However, while refusing to be conscripted into the action brigade of those who are 'against Power', Barthes was still making a distinction between two kinds of intellectual, the fighting one and the literary one. Despite his own doughty struggles against bourgeois thought, going back to the 1950s, he clearly preferred, and indeed was, the latter, even though he 'desires the Neutral' (2005: 12).

   But that doesn't help us to find what 'outplays' (the word he uses is *'déjoue'*: outsmarts, thwarts, foils, outwits) the oppositional paradigm. Perhaps the problem lies in the word *intellectual*. Whether public or private, literary or militant, Paris or publicity, the problem is that it refers to a person, an individual, and therefore to a character, subject, identity, persona, etc., which doesn't necessarily help us to analyse the production and distribution of critical and literate thinking in the digital age, for which we may need to get away from 'intellectuals' altogether, so long as they persist as ghosts in the machine, posing as humans. Only then can we move towards what

Barthes wanted for his analytical work: to 'inscribe' it 'within the field of science' (1977b).

Clues, directing us to the path we should have been taking to get there, can be retrieved from the preceding sections of this (pre-scientific) essay. First, we need to abandon humanist individualism. Second, we need to abandon the public/private (or any other) opposition. And third, we need to get out of Paris. Instead of using 'intellectuals' at all, my own preferred term is 'public thought'.[9] The reason is that thought is produced, exchanged and diffused in *systems*, where the concept of speaker, writer, teacher, intellectual, even 'person' as the cause, originator or author of ideas is barely relevant. As soon as we turn to the global internet and digital media, we find that public thought has escaped confinement to the human individual. Furthermore, the internet is not structured in oppositions, nor does it respect previous hierarchies of prestige or authority. Public thought can come from anywhere, originated by anyone. Some ideas come from celebrities at the head of Anderson's (2008) long tail, but myriad more are made at the tail, any of which (and according to the mathematics of probability, not the politics of opposition and exclusion) can trade places with the head and become celebrated.

So far, so good. We've left the public/private opposition behind, for the internet is made of private (proprietary) platforms in which expression of thought is public (albeit constrained by and generative of new political differences based on digital divides, IP rights, privacy/surveillance and the like). We've left Paris behind (although, because it is 'liked' by so many, its traces are all over the internet, which is always just a few clicks away from nostalgia). We've left the 'metaphysics of presence' behind too, for agency here is systemic and distributed, such that 'thought' is no longer a function of persons but a human–machine hybrid, readily detached from one 'owner' or context and transferred to myriad others, where its productivity may be greater but unpredicted by the originator. And we've put in place instead a model of a large array of complex systems, in which scale and dynamism, regularities and turbulence, clash and conflict, as well as collaboration and cooperation, demand a mode of analysis unlike that of literate critique by individual intellectuals, and more akin to the science of meteorology (i.e. probability), where forecasts rather than linear predictions are possible, using immense numbers of data-points and constantly modified computational models.

But we're not there yet, for the internet is not a uniform space. In other words, it's not an open 'public sphere', where public thought can be universally created and accessed, or where new ideas *enlighten* the system from one end to the other without let or hindrance. This means, while we're

---

[9] I borrow the term 'public thought' from Clay Shirky (2010b).

on the subject, that calls for Open Access of knowledge, welcome as they are, only go so far, because this model is still operating the private/public binary. Its proponents want scholarly knowledge to come out from behind publishers' IP, DRM, paywalls and other mechanisms for creating artificial scarcity, that is, to be converted from *private goods* to *public goods*, available to all. But market forces still apply, and 'private' intellectual work does not enter a smooth 'public' universe but one that is already lumpy.[10] Incumbent players seek to maintain their position by capturing public thought as it shifts from analogue to digital mode. Clumps include former news-media mastheads (*Guardian* for thought, *Daily Mail* for celebrities), born-digital sites devoted to creating an 'invisible college' among the digerati (*The Edge*), and hybrid forms like TED Talks and airport bestsellers. As has been widely noted, professional expertise gives way to crowd-sourced, socially networked production and distribution of ideas. The logic of the system shifts from the authority of the author to the spreadability of the idea and its uptake among users (Jenkins, Ford and Green, 2013).

Attention becomes its own measure: you're a thought leader if sufficient participants 'follow', 'like' or 'comment' on your ideas; if not, not. Thought that is sufficiently liked might end up in a YouTube or FB 'university'; ideas that are well distributed (Wikipedia) may trump disciplinary knowledge. Folksonomies outwit taxonomies; self-organizing groups regulate knowledge practices online. Everyone can play (and so 'outplay' the paradigm), from celebrity Tweeters to anonymous originators of new 'memes' that flash across the world from anywhere in the system. Innovation may be most intensive not in metropolitan centres like Paris but at the margins, in neglected or isolated regions along contested borders, among unfavoured populations, or in the clash of difference among groups.

Such phenomena are widely noticed and have begun to be understood in descriptive detail, but much of the critical attention that is devoted to them is still organized around the public/private binary, including the special issue of *MIA*. A way out of that impasse, however, may be to hand. Cultural scientists are investigating new models of publishing Open Access scholarly knowledge and the sociocultural economics of the growth of knowledge. As well as Jason Potts and Ellie Rennie at RMIT, they include Lucy Montgomery, Cameron Neylon and me at Curtin, among others (Potts et al., 2017; Hartley et al., 2019).

Instead of continuing with the distinction between public and private goods, we have begun to organize our approach around 'club' goods (Buchanan, 1965) and 'common goods' (Ostrom, 1990; Ostrom and Hess, 2007). This is not the place for a detailed exposition of a nascent research program, but we think it points to a much more robust model of how

---

[10]For the 'lumpy universe', see: http://imagine.gsfc.nasa.gov/science/questions/lumpy.html.

innovations and 'newness' – new ideas – are produced, and how they are distributed and taken up in the overall process of knowledge growth, which itself underlies economic growth and cultural improvement alike. We are developing the concepts of 'knowledge clubs' and 'knowledge commons', deriving them from our attempt to identify a *cultural science* based on naturalistic, evolutionary and complexity principles, to arrive at a new understanding of communication and culture. This is probably not quite the science that Barthes dreamed of, but that's really the point: in the 1970s the evolutionary and complexity sciences were not where they are now, and the effort to link critical humanities with them was hampered by opposition to evolutionary theory ('social Darwinism').

While the sciences have made amazing progress since the 1970s, in the humanities we're still reading essays from Paris. If we are to understand how ideas are made, by what kinds of agency, and how they are distributed across whole populations to effect changes at system level, then we're going to have to have another go at science. This is not just a matter of gaining the numeracy to be able to deal with the big data generated by the internet, social networks and digital media. More important is the problem of how to establish and trace causal sequence in such a complex and variable object of study as knowledge, and of how to constitute a field where new work adds to what has been achieved in a systematic way, rather than vying for adherents based on ideological affiliation.

How, in short, can we achieve 'Neutral' status for intellectual inquiry about public thought itself? Cultural science attempts a first-approximation answer to that question by linking culture with the economics of discovery and innovation, seeking to understand the role that culture plays in the growth of knowledge. The conclusion we come to is that culture makes groups, groups make knowledge, and the way in which knowledge is constituted bears all the traces of that process across the span of human history. However, successive adoptions of new communications technologies – speech, writing, print, electronic and internet – have enabled quantum leaps in the *growth* of knowledge, generating successive economic epochs: hunter-gatherer, agricultural, industrial, information and creative.

All along, *groups* are the key to both culture and knowledge. Cooperative and competitive groups of non-kin are our species' unique survival mechanism (Pagel, 2012). They are constituted and bound together in language, culture, shared codes, know-how, technology and sociality – *fictions*, including religion, nation, the law, money, firms. They are differentiated from and hostile to competing groups, a stance that is signalled by incommensurable languages and knowledge systems, such that 'our' knowledge is trusted but 'theirs' isn't. It follows that knowledge, meaningfulness and new ideas (innovation) are the products of *groups*, which also determine individuality and thus 'personae' (of the kind that David Marshall studies) within their bounds (culture). The fact that individuals these days have access to unprecedented numbers of groups – not only family, language-community and ethno-territorial descent but also groups affiliated by taste, affinity and difference – means that identity itself is due for a rethink. This work is well under way of course: for example, (among many) Tama Leaver's project on 'the ends of identity',[11] Eleanor Sandry's on robots and communication (2015) and, more widely, the work of Zizi Papacharissi (2010, 2015b); Nancy Baym (2010), Alice Marwick, Kate Crawford and others (e.g. in Hartley, Burgess and Bruns, 2013; Papacharissi, 2011).

If the individual is not the *source* of action and choice but the *product* of systems and connections, this suggests that newness, innovation and the growth of knowledge need to be looked for in the actions and interactions of groups, along with the motivations. The motivations, talents and achievements of individuals are not decisive. Naturally, talented, specialist, expert individuals are vital to the production of 'newness', but it's the system that decides on value: you get the Nobel Prize because the group recognizes the merit of your work, not for your merit as such (as many non-winners will attest!).

Here is where the new concept of 'knowledge clubs' comes in; where knowledge is 'non-rivalrous' but 'excludable'. People form clubs for a purpose. Some clubs are organized for the purpose of growing knowledge and ideas. They retain the characteristics of culture: common language, adversarial competitiveness with external clubs, producing not just neutral or inert information but culture-made asymmetries of trust (with various tests and punishments to ensure group coherence), and reluctance to share 'our' knowledge with 'them'. They are also apt to resort to a discursive version of the traditional solution to the problem of how to scale up and consolidate knowledge across multiple demes or groups – namely, conquest and the forcible assimilation of other groups' demic knowledge. The same model can be observed in corporate takeovers, and even in the takeover of academic disciplines from the arts/humanities to the sciences – as has happened successively to economics, psychology, geography, but not, yet, to culture.

But now global connectivity and the potential for species-wide social networks offers new possibilities for group formation based on affinity as well as adversarial opposition. Here, we think a powerful explanatory concept is the other term from the economics of goods that has not yet been taken up, that of the knowledge *commons* (Ostrom and Hess), and more recently the idea of an 'innovation commons' (Potts, 2012, 2019; Allen and Potts, 2016). We think that the drive towards Open Access and 'public intellectuals' alike needs to be augmented by urgent attention to how *knowledge clubs and commons* form and interact. With that will come a

---

[11]See: www.tamaleaver.net/research/the-ends-of-identity/.

new perspective on the intellectual. Our guess is that such a figure will turn out to be a group, or rather a cluster of interacting groups, part human and part technological-media network. We don't think it will be an oppositional figure. It might be entrepreneurial. It might play a regulatory role in system self-correction processes. 'Public thought' is in experimental development in many different group-enterprises, from research groups and advocacy/ activist groups to firms (large and small) and systems (small-world networks and planetary social networks).

The task at hand is not to pine for the individualism of the intellectual, Parisian or public, nor to fall for opposition as the purpose of the knowledge agent, but to identify where and how new ideas are propagated, and what mechanisms are in place to encourage the development of a 'club' and 'commons' approach to knowledge, one that encourages the formation of new knowledge clubs while sharing knowledge gains. We need also to identify the 'critical' functions of self-organization, self-regulation and self-correction in groups, looking to system-automation (autopoiesis) for the organizational principle that Negri assigned to the command-and-control party. Public intellectuals have not proven effective agents for these functions. Meanwhile the scientific, publicity and political 'spheres' have drifted further apart, mutually repelled by low-trust adversarial out-group hostility. Instead of reproducing such oppositions unwittingly, the intellectual function of large-scale social networks needs to get clubby.

PART II

Agent (practices)

Knowing subjects and mediated subjectivity

7

Authorship and the narrative of the self:

The gods (Shakespeare) → no one (*Vogue*) → everyone (*Dazed*)

Three-act drama

This chapter conforms to the plot scheme recommended by Frances Taylor Patterson, instructor of silent-movie photoplay composition at Columbia University in the 1920s, who (using the gendered language of the day) summarized it as follows:

- Act 1 – get a man up a tree;
- Act 2 – throw stones at him;
- Act 3 – get him down (Patterson, 1920: 8).

In this chapter, the 'man' in question is 'the author'.

- Section I of the chapter sees our hero transform historically from divine status (in oral media) to economic institution (in print media);
- Section II 'throws stones' by questioning the need for such a figure at all (in modern visual media);
- Section III restores a certain level of narrative equilibrium by describing the return of the author – now expanded to whole populations (in contemporary digital media).

This plot structure enables a conceptual and textual investigation of authorship under three headings:

- *God* as the Author (Shakespeare);
- *No one* as the Author (*Vogue*);
- *Everyone* as the Author (Jefferson Hack).

That each of these apparently mutually exclusive propositions may be true, even at the same time, and also contestable, is the problematic addressed by the chapter as a whole. The long history to which this brief plot gestures may, I argue, indicate profound shifts in what it is that authorship creates:

- *Nature*, the world, and truth (premodern);
- *Intellectual property* and thus economic wealth (modern);
- *The self* (contemporary).

I. God as the author

I think that, as our society changes ... the author function will disappear.

(MICHEL FOUCAULT (1984: 119))

A matter of life and death

There's an eons-old mystery at the heart of authorship – that of life and death. In pre-modern societies, the mystery of origination belonged to gods; and from the gods authorship gained its own existence and authority. The author, godlike, is a giver of life. But in modern society, gods have died (Nietzsche, 2006). The death of the author has also been proclaimed (Barthes, 1977a). However, as Mark Twain nearly said, reports of these deaths may have been exaggerated (Burke, 1998; Gallop, 2011). The author remains alive and well, outliving the gods and retaining a certain generative mystique. If we are to understand contemporary authorship we shall need to be mindful of this myth of origins, because it continues to animate the otherwise strongly institutional and economic context in which the term operates.

Despite the mysteries hinted at here – life, death, gods, eons, rebirth – there is a reasonably straightforward way to demonstrate the relation between gods and authors, simply by looking at the way that the word entered the English language. From the original Latin word '*augere*' ('to make to grow, originate, promote, increase' – think 'augment'), the word 'author' signifies 'the person who originates or gives existence to anything' (*Oxford English Dictionary (OED)*: 'author,' sense 1). It appeared in English around 1380 in the writings of John Wyclif (theologian and Bible translator) and Geoffrey Chaucer (English poet):

Chaucer (c.1374): *But oh thou Jove, oh author of nature!*
Wyclif (c.1380): *If holy writ be false, truly God author thereof is false.*[1]

The author is thus a figure of great antiquity, linking mortal people to the divine attribute of immortality and the ability of nature to create anew. It was the personification of singular origin: the beginning or first cause of everything that was made, and of nature itself with its own life-giving or generative properties of germination, growth and increase. This mystique still resonates in the ideas that authorship immortalizes a writer and that authors have the power to immortalize the characters they create, whether our hero(ine) is factual or fictional. Thus, authorship as *causal agency* assures the immortality of one who can *bring to life* a world imagined in words; and it *confers* immortality, or life *without* death. In Judeo-Christian tradition, God is not only understood to be the author of all things but, as the quotation from Wyclif makes clear, is also taken as the literal author of specific written texts, called simply *The Books* (from the Greek βιβλία; thence the Bible), known to Christians as 'holy writ'. From this sacred or originating model, a more mundane sense of authorship emerged, as 'one who sets forth written statements; the composer or writer of a treatise or book' (*OED*, 'author' sense 3).

That such a being, albeit mortal, remains invested with some of the mystery of the divine original, cannot be doubted. It was standard procedure in medieval rhetoric to deny personal originality. Another name for *that*, in those days, was *heresy*, for which the consequences could be fatal for the author. From the love letters of Abelard (d. 1142) and Heloise (d. 1162) to Chaucer's (d. 1400) *Canterbury Tales*, it was important to link ideas to *authorized* figures in the system, by ascribing them to ancient or venerated authors, sanctioned by church or state as the *authority* for both words and action, a later version of which was the *Authorised Version* (aka the King James Bible of 1611). 'Authority', in turn, is the 'power to enforce obedience,' (*OED*), but its etymology is the same as that of 'author' – an authority that belongs to God but can be *represented* by others such as the Pope, since 'authority' also includes 'derived or delegated power; conferred right or title; authorisation'.[2] Thus, the history of the word shows that an author never was a simple individual, but *one who channels system-level or*

---

[1]Chaucer: *Troilus and Criseyde*, iii. 1016; Wyclif, *English Works*, 267. Spelling updated: the quotations are given in the *OED* as: 'ʒif holy writt be fals, certis god autor þer-of is fals' (Wyclif) and 'But o þou Ioue, o autour of nature!' (Chaucer).
[2]*OED*, 'authority', sense 2. The earliest *OED* quotation for this sense is from *c.* 1375: 'Reprovede him sharpli bi autorite of God.'

institutional authority into text. The 'one who sets forth written statements', as the *OED* puts it, is endowed with an authority conferred by the textual system of writing itself, reaching back through previous masters to its natural and ultimately divine origins.

Adventurers in 'setting forth'

Of all mortal authors, William Shakespeare is perhaps the most famous 'one who sets forth', in the English tongue at least. He attained this status despite the fact that he produced rather few written statements. Most of his output comprised plays, whose published versions were notoriously uncertain in terms of provenance and textual accuracy. One set of written statements that used the authority of his name in his own lifetime was published in 1609 under the title of *Shake-speares Sonnets.*[3] The first edition bears an

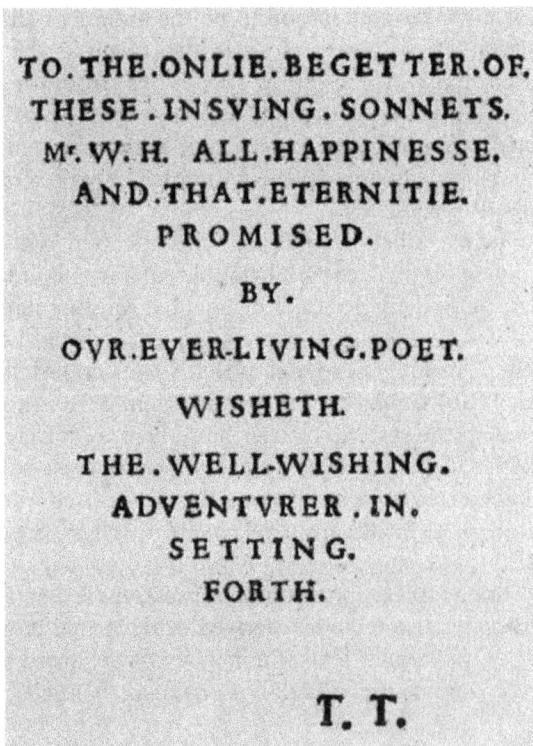

TO. THE. ONLIE. BEGETTER. OF.
THESE. INSVING. SONNETS.
Mr. W. H. ALL. HAPPINESSE.
AND. THAT. ETERNITIE.
PROMISED.

BY.

OVR. EVER-LIVING. POET.

WISHETH.

THE. WELL-WISHING.
ADVENTVRER. IN.
SETTING.
FORTH.

T. T.

FIGURE 7.1 *Who is the author…?*

---

[3]See www.gutenberg.org/cache/epub/1041/pg1041.html for the sonnets.

enigmatic inscription (Figure 7.1), thought to have been written by the book's publisher, Thomas Thorpe ('T T.'), not by Shakespeare himself, although it is impossible to be sure. This strange dedication seems to preserve the promise of authorial godhead: the 'only begetter' (echoing the 'only begotten' son of the biblical God) – the immortality or 'eternity promised' by our equally immortal or 'ever-living' poet. But at the same time, the inscription is beset with doubts about its own and the sonnets' authorship, the identity of the author (is 'Mr. W. H.' a typo for W. S., William Shakespeare?), and even the meaning of the words – an uncertainty that has sustained 400 years of unresolved speculation.[4] It seems that authorial authority and immortality alike are compromised and undermined by the very means of their own expression: we have it on good authority that authors are immortal; but we don't really know who the author is, even when he's the most celebrated author of all time.

Why would anyone be so careless as to have the means of immortality at their fingertips and yet fail to capitalize on it? William Shakespeare is instructive in this regard. He lived in a period of turbulent transformation between the medieval and modern eras, and while he might earn undying repute as an 'ever-living poet,' he actually earned his daily crust as a commercial entertainer, not as an author. This early modern period saw the organizational emergence of many now-familiar features of the ascendant market economy, even as it retained strongly medieval characteristics and beliefs. Shakespeare displays medieval and modern characteristics at once.

He writes, but only rarely as a published author in the tradition of Classical learning. His published books, *The Sonnets*, *Venus and Adonis* and *The Rape of Lucrece*, were poetic meditations on the vicissitudes of courtly love. Some say that Mr. W. H. was William Herbert, Third Earl of Pembroke, a poet himself, who went on to sponsor the publication of the First Folio of Shakespeare's works in 1623; or alternatively the handsome Henry Wriothesley, Third Earl of Southampton, to whom both *Venus and Adonis* and *The Rape of Lucrece* were dedicated, the latter fulsomely. In all of this, Shakespeare's mode of authorship is aristocratic, amateur, and part of the web of courtly patronage that sustained great families. As an *author*, he remained carelessly medieval, content for the most part with what Richard Lanham would call, for a later age, 'the economy of attention' (Lanham, 2006) – an economy in which literary fame and reputation are valued, but not directly convertible to cash. Thus, the value of Shakespeare's *books* was cultural rather than pecuniary, connecting his name to established status-based learning and aristocratic culture, which was itself on the make

---

[4]See: www.shakespeares-sonnets.com/dedication and: www.folger.edu/template.cfm?cid=926 for discussion of the dedication and the work. And see Wikipedia for a helpful summary: http: //en.wikipedia.org/wiki/Shakespeare's_sonnets.

in this period, transforming from medieval arms (the sword) to modern administration (the pen), motivating some aristocratic patrons to add poets – like Shakespeare – to their adornments. Shakespeare showed little personal interest in his books as publications, except perhaps in lean years when the bubonic plague closed the theatres and income could be augmented by publication, as indeed occurred with the *Sonnets* in the plague year of 1609.[5]

If that type of authorship was all there was to Shakespeare, he may well have gained poetic immortality, but most of us would never have heard of him.

The play's the thing

Of course, this was not all there was to Shakespeare. His plays are the cause of his enduring reputation, but at the time they were, for practical purposes, *unauthored*. They were written for performance, not publication, and were staged under the brand name of licensed companies of players like Pembroke's Men or the Lord Chamberlain's Men. Only half were published in his lifetime, often in pirated editions based on actors' or prompter's copies (known as 'foul papers'). Shakespeare, the famous actor and part-owner of the companies that staged his plays, does not appear to have had a direct hand in the publication of any of them; and the first collected edition, edited by fellow-actors, was not published until seven years after his death.

Shakespeare the dramatist was not an *author* but a *media producer*. In that respect he was altogether modern (see Chapter 8). He was a shareholder in one of the first English capitalist joint-stock companies, and he combined with others – writers, actors, entrepreneurs and shareholders – to make money by providing commercial entertainment to anonymous consumers for profit. He was, in short, among those who gained first-mover advantage in the commodification of culture. We tend to call such folk not authors but capitalists.

Among the emergent features of the era was a new conceptualization of both property and authorship, leading eventually to the modern notion of 'intellectual property' (Hamilton, 2003; and see Chapter 6). What had been a 'common pool resource' (Ostrom, 1990) in medieval culture, including common land, common learning (in Latin), and a common stock of popular culture, began to be 'enclosed' (May, 2010), giving rise to the notion of an individual owner of *expression* as well as *estates*.

As James Hamilton (2003) has pointed out, the Elizabethan theatres in London pioneered new modes of commercial organization, and were

---

[5]The London theatres were closed throughout 1609, when the *Sonnets* were published; see www.globe-theatre.org.uk/globe-theatre-closed.htm.

uniquely sensitive to the demands of the market, because 'box office receipts were collected and tallied each night, thus immediately linking revenues to audience sizes in ways unavailable to then-current print modes' (2003: 304). This enabled the commercial value of individual plays to be realized (in both senses of that word) immediately. That capability remains in place to this day for popular drama, when TV ratings and first-weekend cinema box-office takings still organize production decisions in a way that publishers have never been able to match, at least until the launch of Nielsen's BookScan in 2001.

Then as now audience size was influenced by multiple considerations other than authorship – drawcards included the reputation of the theatre, the company, the actors and the play, as well as that of the playwright. However, immediate feedback on individual productions did hasten the 'professionalization of writing,' which 'only emerged when authors saw themselves as having something valuable to sell and conducted themselves accordingly, and when the legal, economic and cultural frameworks were present which enabled such a validation' (Hamilton, 2003: 304–5). In other words, Shakespeare was ahead of the game as a playwright, but behind it as an author: he made his money, and plenty of it – enough to buy himself the status of a gentleman – in the popular, commercial theatres as an entrepreneur-actor-writer, not through book sales, as an author.

Shakespeare followed the money when he pursued success in the popular media of the day. Perhaps this is also why he neglected his status as a literary author. There was little money in literary publishing, at least for authors. The real 'adventurers in setting forth' were *publishers*, like Thomas Thorpe, who may or may not have secured his author's consent to publish *Shakespeares Sonnets*. No one knows whether Shakespeare himself was paid. As yet the book trade was not developed as a popular commercial industry, in the way that the London theatres were, not least because the reading public was small (albeit expanding). Paper was expensive, so books were priced according to the number of pages, without economies of scale, or pricing according to demand. Compared with the theatres, where a play might attract a thousand or more paying customers a day at a penny a person, books were rare, slow and expensive.[6]

Some books were profitable, including popular plays that were published *as* books. But here again the author was not necessarily the organizing figure for an oeuvre, or even for the meaning of a given play. Zachary Lesser has argued that some publishers sought that status for themselves. They wanted to be known for a certain type of play (no matter who it was written by), and so their catalogues 'form a corpus as much as any author's

---

[6]The Globe held 1,500 to 3,000 paying customers. See: www.william-shakespeare.info/william-shakespeare-globe-theatre-structure.htm. The 1623 First Folio, unbound, cost a pound (£1).

work does' (2004: 77). In Shakespeare's day, the idea that strings of words were heritable by writers alone, and thus tradable in their name, was not well established, which is presumably why he took no action to protect his strings of iambic pentameters. However, publishers were quicker off the mark.

Enclosures and clearances of culture

Following Henry VIII's dissolution of the monasteries and the accelerating enclosure of common land in the seventeenth century, private property among the landed gentry rapidly extended, including that of one W. Shakespeare of the county of Warwickshire. It entailed the right to put up 'keep out!' notices over land previously held and worked in common. The effect was not only to privatize the produce of the land (chiefly wool) but also to 'buttress the master-servant relationship' by forcing commoners to become employees (Hawkes, 1986: 8–13). Enclosure was an important catalyst of the modern industrial workforce, separating work from land and creating a pool of available labour.

In the same way, and at the same time, intellectual property began to take shape, conferring the right to privatize creations of the mind, and to exclude others from the use of that property. Here began the very modern clearances of non-owners from both real and intangible properties, including assets previously regarded as common pool resources, resulting in an increasing dissociation between producers (construed as active owners, generative agents of growth, firms) and consumers (seen as individual, passive recipients of products that they may purchase but not make their own).

This process was spearheaded not by writers but by publishers, who acted on behalf of authors. At the heart of the system was a (legal) fiction – that of the author as agent of creation – because the real producer was the publishing firm. In fact, the producer/consumer pairing does not map very convincingly on to the author/reader one. *Authors* played only a limited role in the establishment of intellectual property rights compared with the corporate agencies to whom they assigned those rights; and *readers* do not use up (i.e. consume) what they read. But this was a necessary fiction, required to organize the chain of causation, from creation to consumption, *as a property right*. Henceforth, authors were construed as agents of creation, consumers and readers were effects. This division of labour between producers and consumers reproduced in abstract, secular and economic form the status differential between gods and humans (ancient), and master and servant (medieval). Thereby a glimmer of pre-industrial mystique – and mystification – is preserved in a modern, institutional system.

Authorship emerged into modernity not as an attribute of persons but as a device for the efficient operation of a market. In other words, the author is a device for *limiting* rather than *expanding* meaning, reducing what any text or discourse means to the intentions of its designated originator, including their pecuniary intentions; the very opposite of the godlike polysemic liberality of the premodern author and postmodern reader (Barthes, 1977a).

This kind of 'author-function,' as Foucault calls it (1984: 108), was itself the *product* of a system of commodification that, even as it limited signification, vastly increased the *productivity* of the domain of writing – just as land clearances increased the economic productivity of land – bringing more publications from more authors across more subjects to more readers than ever before in recorded (written) history. The primary agents weren't authors but publishers, now operating through the *persona* of the author. As the commercial book trade developed during the seventeenth and eighteenth centuries, publishers 'found in the assertion of *authors'* rights to reap the fruits of their labours a convenient cloak for their own interests' (Hammond, 1997: 34–5). Hence, the mark of modernity is the *corporatization* of authorship as an *economic institution*. The publishing industry required the *concept* of authors as the originators of something that could be held as private property in order to be exploited.

Once established, by the time of Dr Johnson, authorship became an increasingly entrenched social institution, comprising a professional elite working for public prestige or the commercial market, sometimes both. What counted as authorship became both more specialized and more abstract. The relationship between authors and readers was itself highly mediated, because the specialist work of the author was routinely accompanied by other skills that enhanced it but were never *counted* as authorship, including the minutiae of font design and the other crafts of bookmaking, graphic design, illustrations and layout, all the way out to marketing and distribution, without which few books would prosper as they may deserve. The author is but one part of this industrialized system, and an abstract one at that, because the sign of the author (the name on the cover) works not to identify a corporeal person but as a branding device for a specific market niche.

II. No one is an author

The author is the principle of thrift in the proliferation of meaning.

(MICHEL FOUCAULT, 1984: 118)

Turning from early modern to what some think is 'late' modern society, but staying with popular entertainment, we must also turn from the written word to pictorial publications like magazines, audio-visual forms like film, TV and digital media, and non-literary genres such as news, science, the movies and games. Here, even though it is recognized that such forms and genres rely on the talents of writers, the concept of authorship dwindles to the point of meaninglessness. In the most prolific, popular and pervasive media of the press and broadcasting, *no one is an author*. It seems that the 'death of the author' can be observed as an empirical fact. So it might be worth pausing here to explore just how the modern media manage without it. This is necessary before moving on to discuss the 'return of the author' in another guise, as 'new' media emerge with a different dynamic (see Section III).

Although the most prominent of the contemporary media are audio-visual ones like TV and cinema, for the purposes of this chapter I will stick to the magazine press (and see Chapter 10), simply to show that here too the concept evaporates, just where you might expect to see it claimed, at the very place where capital investment is highest. Authorship falters where a print publication can work at the top level of professional creativity and name-branded talent without needing the concept to organize the way that readers respond to the text.

'How do I mine it?'

I'm looking at *Vogue* (USA) for September 2011.[7] At 758 pages this is undoubtedly a book, and of course it is published: the print form of *Vogue* is still dominant. The online version is used to persuade browsers to buy the ad-laden print edition (although times are said to be changing). The cover proclaims that here is 'something for everyone', thereby hailing (as Althusserians put it), *everyone* as the reader – an act not of possessive *enclosure* but of journalistic *disclosure*. The authority for – and, in terms of copyright, the legal author of – all that follows is *Vogue*, which has its own carefully nurtured identity, an accumulated 'point of view', a position in the expectations of readers and a copyright sign over the entire contents (see p. 757).

Despite the cover's interpellation of the *reader* through that familiar masthead, no one would expect to find an *author* here, as Barthes seemed to predict (1977a). Indeed, the occlusion or endless displacement of any point of origin for the meanings broached by this cover, never mind those let loose within, serves to exemplify the general point of how fugitive the *causal agent of creative generation*, the agent previously known as the author, has become in contemporary media.

It's not that there are no candidates for authorial status here, if by that is meant the creative genius behind the words and images on the page;

---

[7]'Unfortunately this image is unavailable for licensing' (Condé Nast Image Licensing). Cover can be viewed at https://www.vogue.com/article/looking-back-vogue-covers-2011 (image 10 of 13).

rather, there are too many. Here too are stories, the traditional province of the author, even though the primary medium of communication is visual and graphic. But while these stories and images are produced by creative individuals, many of whose names are well known in the fashion world and carefully credited in the magazine, none of them qualifies as an author.

It isn't wise to divide the people responsible for meaning-creation into those on the business side (publishers) and those on the editorial side (suits and creatives). More than a century after Condé Montrose Nast bought *Vogue* in 1909, each side understands and works to the needs of the other. Thus, on the business side, there is Si Newhouse, octogenarian billionaire and co-owner of Advance Publications, Condé Nast's parent company.[8] In the September 2011 issue he is listed as chairman, along with CEO Charles Townsend and recently hired president Robert Sauerberg (p. 314). These corporate grandees had brought in Susan Plagemann as publisher of *Vogue* magazine, who had worked on the business side of *Marie Clare*, *Cosmopolitan*, *Esquire* and *Mademoiselle*.

Despite being the real bosses, these people would not be well known to *Vogue's* readers, and do not produce the magazine itself. They are not its authors, even though they have godlike powers of life and death: they cause the title to exist in the first place and they have the power to close it. Between those extremes, they create its narrative in the marketplace, deciding on its position, strategy and performance as a corporate asset. They are also the corporate custodians of its goodwill – its story in the heads of the public – accumulated over many years by *Vogue's* brand name and reputation.

Where does *Vogue* fit into the Condé Nast equation – what is its meaning as a business proposition? CEO Townsend had recently spoken to *WWD* on a change in corporate strategy, from the title's reliance on print advertising, at 70 per cent of revenue, towards a fifty-fifty split between ads and direct income from consumers:

In a nutshell, the publishing company now wants to wring 'as much out of our consumer margin generation potential' as possible, Townsend told WWD. … 'I'm charging [Sauerberg] with leading the company in the creation of a new business model, which is technology-enabled, consumer-centric and concerned with the monetization of that consumer relationship.' … He emphasized the importance of digital initiatives in this model. … 'There's gold in those hills somewhere,' Townsend said. 'How do I mine it?'[9]

---

[8]See: www.forbes.com/profile/samuel-newhouse.
[9]Nick Axelrod, 'Robert Sauerberg Named Condé Nast President.' *WWD*, 23 July 2010: www.wwd.com/media-news/fashion-memopad/robert-sauerberg-named-conde-nast-president-3193144.

That question remains open, but, for the time being, the gold standard of fashion publishing remains the September issue on the newsstands.

The September issue

The September issue is important to all the glossy monthlies, because it launches the fashion year. It faces the future and sets trends. In terms of advertising, which is what fills most of those many hundreds of pages, it can set records. For corporate *Vogue*, a lot rides on it: it is a statement of – and an investment in – *their* confidence in the magazine's editorial direction. *Vogue*'s way of doing the September issue was immortalized in R. J. Cutler's 2009 film of the same name.[10] The film followed the magazine's production process for the September 2007 issue – at 832 pages, the biggest fashion magazine ever published to that date.

The job of producing each issue falls to the editor-in-chief, Anna Wintour, who is much better known than her corporate bosses. An Englishwoman from a journalistic family, she has held that post since 1988.[11] Wintour became a celebrity in her own right, partly through portrayal in Cutler's documentary and *The Devil Wears Prada*, a rom-com based on a tell-all novel by Lauren Weisberger (the only author in this story, and not universally admired for that).[12] With Meryl Streep as the Wintour-like Miranda Priestly, ruthless editor of fictional *Runway* magazine, and Anne Hathaway as the ingénue with a lot to learn, *The Devil Wears Prada* was a surprise box-office hit. A speech about a cerulean blue sweater, delivered with withering contempt by Streep to Hathaway, has become justly famous:

> *[Miranda and some assistants are deciding between two similar belts for an outfit. Andy sniggers because she thinks they look exactly the same]:*
>
> - **Miranda Priestly** [Meryl Streep]: Something funny?
> - **Andy Sachs** [Anne Hathaway]: No. No, no. Nothing's … You know, it's just that both those belts look exactly the same to me. You know, I'm still learning about all this stuff and, uh …
> - **Miranda Priestly**: 'This … stuff'? Oh. Okay. I see. You think this has nothing to do with you. You go to your closet and you select … I don't know… that lumpy blue sweater, for instance,

---

[10]See *The September Issue* (2009): www.arp.tv/production.html?production=septissue.
[11]Wikipedia has a full entry on Anna Wintour, relying on Oppenheimer (2005).
[12]David Frankel's *The Devil Wears Prada* (2006: www.imdb.com/title/tt0458352/) is based on Lauren Weisberger's 2003 novel of the same name, based in turn on Weisberger's experience as an intern working for Anna Wintour. For a pro-Wintour review of the book, see fellow-author Lauren McLaughlin's blog: www.laurenmclaughlin.net/2006/01/26/the-devil-is-an-ungrateful-brat-who-should-be-so-lucky/. *Vogue*'s annual Met Gala features prominently in the all-female heist romp *Ocean's 8* (2018), also starring Hathaway, where Wintour plays herself.

because you're trying to tell the world that you take yourself too seriously to care about what you put on your back. But what you don't know is that that sweater is not just blue, it's not turquoise. It's not lapis. It's actually cerulean. And you're also blithely unaware of the fact that in 2002 Oscar de la Renta did a collection of cerulean gowns. And then I think it was Yves Saint Laurent, wasn't it, who showed cerulean military jackets? I think we need a jacket here. And then cerulean quickly showed up in the collections of eight different designers. And then it, uh, filtered down through the department stores and then trickled on down into some tragic Casual Corner where you, no doubt, fished it out of some clearance bin. However, that blue represents millions of dollars and countless jobs and it's sort of comical how you think that you've made a choice that exempts you from the fashion industry when, in fact, you're wearing the sweater that was selected for you by the people in this room from a pile of … stuff.[13]

This speech has been widely cited as an accurate depiction of how the fashion system works, still channelling divine authority down to the individual as in medieval times, such that even fashion laity can't escape its sway. It's not simply that what goes into the *magazine* is decided by 'the people in this room'; it's also, much more significantly, that a consumer's entire look, and with it her very personality, may be determined not by her own choices but by theirs. That kind of authorship goes well beyond the creation of strings of words. The word 'author' doesn't really catch it unless you remember the premodern origins of the term.

The real Anna Wintour is known to exercise tight control over photographs published in *Vogue* (Oppenheimer, 2005: 244), especially the cover photo, a genre that she had reinvented with her debut issue:

In her first year at Vogue, Wintour gave the magazine a facelift. In contrast to the bland headshots of mostly blond models favored by [outgoing editor Grace] Mirabella, Wintour's covers were fresh: The frame was almost always pushed back to encompass more of the model's body, and the shoot itself was often done al fresco, in natural light. (Fortini, 2005)

In short, Wintour has a signature style and the magazine's covers are recognizably hers, including the September 2011 one to hand, which conforms exactly to the specifications quoted above. Even the headlines bear comparison over more than twenty years: Wintour's 1988 debut featured a

---

[13]See: www.imdb.com/title/tt0458352/quotes.

cover story called 'Color Catches On',[14] while September 2011 has one called
'How to Wear Color'. Wintour will have decided in advance just what the
cover would say, down to the last details of colour, composition and graphic
design; of mood, model and make-up; of garment, stylist and photographer.
But she was no more its author than were her Condé Nast bosses or her
fictional alter ego. A sizable company of talented creative personnel was
needed to create the reality.

From the reader's point of view, the most important element is the 'cover
girl' (p. 218), who embodies and personifies the look of the month. Kate
Moss (for it is she) would be a safe bet, you might think, despite the fact
that, at 37, she was well above the average age for a contemporary fashion
model. Since her debut in *The Face* in 1990, Moss has graced innumerable
covers worldwide, including thirty-one *Vogues* in her native UK.[15] Although
now diversified into other areas of the business, she remains one of the
best-known faces in fashion – an icon. She is a thriving business brand in
her own right. Her company, Skate, posted a £2.4m pre-tax profit for the
previous year.[16]

It was not for her iconic value alone that she was chosen for the all-
important September cover. This time, Moss was *newsworthy*, because she
had just married, and *Vogue* had the story. The cover copy duly proclaims:
'Exclusive: KATE MOSS: an inside look at the most romantic wedding of
the year.' Quite a claim, considering, as Wintour's customary 'letter from the
editor' puts it, that 'she wasn't the only famous Kate to marry this year' (p.
234), the other having been Kate Middleton marrying into the British royal
family. But the tone is set; the word is not 'royal' but 'romantic'.

Kate Moss married a musician called Jamie Hince. Her daughter Lila
Grace was a bridesmaid at the wedding and prominent model in the fashion
shoot. Lila's father, Jefferson Hack, himself editor or publisher of fashion
bibles *Dazed & Confused* and *AnOther Magazine*,[17] was pictured as a guest
in *Vogue*'s online photo-gallery – but not in the print edition – in company
with *Vogue* writer Hamish Bowles. No mention is made of his relationship

---

[14]See: http://upload.wikimedia.org/wikipedia/en/thumb/e/e6/November_1988_Vogue_cover.jp
g/250px-November_1988_Vogue_cover.jpg.

[15]Moss had most recently featured on the cover of *Vogue* UK in August 2011, also photographed
by Mario Testino. See all thirty-one covers at: www.vogue.co.uk/magazine/archive/search/
Model/Kate%20Moss.

[16]Moss's company, Skate, had filed sales of £3.2 million for 2010 (£2.4m pre-tax profits) in
February 2011: www.vogue.co.uk/news/2011/02/14/kate-moss-profits-and-sales-for-2010.

[17]When Lila Moss turned 16, *Dazed* featured her as its cover model. It credits Lila to the Kate
Moss Agency (http://www.katemossagency.com/lila-moss). 'Lensman' Tim Walker is clearly
channelling Kate Moss's breakthrough photographer Corinne Day (p. 146). Lila is 'styled
by her godmother Katy England'. Jefferson Hack, *Dazed*'s co-publisher and Lila's dad, isn't
mentioned (Who's That Girl?' *Dazed* (Winter 2018), 138–51 (http://www.dazeddigital.com/f
ashion/article/42296/1/lila-moss-first-cover-shoot-tim-walker-katy-england).

to Moss or their daughter. He is merely captioned as 'journalist'.[18] Man of mystery? Or anonymous hack? We'll meet him again, in another role, in the last section of this chapter.

A corporately authored story of redemption

Model mother marries musician: so what? Without a single author, a clear storyline nevertheless emerges. In her editorial letter, Wintour muses on the romance of 'experience': 'simply engaging in real life can lead us somewhere delightful and magical' (p. 218). Specifically, it can lead to the extensive coverage of the ceremony and associated fashions in the magazine's main fashion section: 'Kiss Me, Kate', pp. 676–91. Here, we see something *not* shown on *Vogue*'s cover, namely, the wedding dress (pp. 682–83). The only nuptial sign on the cover itself is a glimpse of Moss's outsize engagement ring. She wears not bridal white but a maroon hand-frayed organza-and-ostrich feather dress by Alexander McQueen (pp. 172, 756). Inside, however, she models *several* wedding outfits, specially created for this set to channel previous iconic wedding pictures. As one celebrity blog reported, even before the 'highly anticipated' issue was published: 'Anna told about 10 designers to pick out their ideal dresses for Kate. ... Since Anna made the request, that meant they had to do it.'[19]

All this seems predictably generic, but that only masks the true meaning of the story. In fact, 'real life' proved a little too gritty to be shown on the cover, because Kate Moss's actual wedding dress was made by British designer John Galliano. This too was highly newsworthy, but not in a romantic way. At the time of the wedding and *Vogue*'s publication, Galliano was awaiting trial in France on charges of 'casting public insults based on origin, religious affiliation or ethnicity'; in other words, anti-Semitic and anti-Asian hate speech, which is illegal in that country.[20] This celebrated story, scooped by the Murdoch tabloid *Sun* in the UK in March 2011, had already cost Galliano his job as chief designer for Dior. It was dealt with by the French courts in September, while the September issue itself was still on the world's newsstands, meaning that the issue was being prepared between the charge and the verdict. Galliano was convicted.

How does *Vogue* deal with such a tricky story? As far as Galliano's racial abuse is concerned, it keeps absolutely *schtum*: not a word on the case.

---

[18]See: www.vogue.com/magazine/article/kate-moss-kiss-me-kate/#/magazine-gallery/kate-moss-wedding/23 (this gallery has since been deleted).
[19]See: www.hollywoodlife.com/2011/07/25/kate-moss-vogue-september-issue-wedding-dress-spread-sex-and-the-city-carrie-bradshaw/.
[20]See: www.independent.co.uk/news/world/europe/john-galliano-found-guilty-of-racial-abuse-but-escapes-jail-and-fines-2351642.html.

But is it embarrassment that keeps the Galliano dress off the cover, and its details unlisted in the customary list of suppliers (p. 757)? We'll never know. The scandal isn't ignored, however: a very particular and *corporately authored* meaning is constructed across the different elements of *Vogue* – the cover, editor's letter, feature story and fashion shoot. Kate's wedding dress emerges as the *agent of redemption* for Galliano. It is modelled by Moss with Galliano himself holding up the veil (pp. 682–83). In the accompanying feature by Hamish Bowles, we learn:

> In the flurry of pre-wedding madness and nerves, the one thing that is keeping Kate sane is the dress. With her characteristic loyalty, she has asked her beleaguered friend John Galliano to work on this. 'When I put the dress on, I'm really happy,' says Kate. 'I forget about everything.' (p. 686).

That single word – 'beleaguered' – is the only concession to the real-life story throughout this issue of *Vogue*. The romance of the dress, it seems, magically makes *everyone* 'forget about everything'. Kate's 'loyalty' engenders nothing less than a rebirth for Galliano: '"She dared me to be John Galliano again," the designer tells me. "I couldn't pick up a pencil. It's been my creative rehab."' Apparently the dress works its magic at both wedding and reception. In Bowles' words:

> [*At the wedding*]: When Kate appears in her Galliano finery, with her flotilla of bridesmaids and flower girls in their Bonpoint dresses, there are wolf whistles and applause in the church. (p. 691)

> [*At the reception*]: When Kate's father, Peter, thanks John Galliano for 'the beautiful dress', every guest stands in a spontaneous ovation, and John's eyes well up. (p. 755).

The ultimate beneficiary of the experience, then, is not the new 'Mrs. Jamie Hince' (p. 691), but John Galliano. In telling Galliano's story as a romance of redemption, *Vogue* is out on its own. More typical was the generally hostile reaction when he was sentenced to a token fine and costs rather than doing six months in chokey. The *Sun* fulminated about the court's lenience: 'The soft treatment of Brit Galliano – worth £20million and a close pal of top models including Kate Moss — triggered uproar last night.'[21] News of Galliano's conviction reached New York on the very day of Fashion's Night Out, culmination of the season for which the September issue is the 'bible'.[22]

---

[21]Nick Parker & Dan Sales (2011) 'Dior havin' a laugh: £20m Galliano fined £2.64 for racist rants.' *The Sun*, Sept 9: www.thesun.co.uk/sol/homepage/news/3804233/Dior-havin-a-laugh.html.

[22]Biblical status can inspire resentment as well as devotion: See 'Vogue: Fashion Bible, or Pravda?' by stylist Alison Jane Reid: www.ethical-hedonist.com/vogue-fashion-bible-or-pravda_380.html.

Despite its editorial line, *Vogue* remained institutionally tight-lipped. A reporter for *New York* magazine canvassed reactions from, among others, *Vogue*'s photo director Ivan Shaw:

> Q: What was the mood in the Vogue office today with the Galliano verdict?
> A: I couldn't tell you.
> Q: Is the magazine planning on addressing the story?
> A: No comment.[23]

The rest, as Shakespeare knew, is silence.

'The photographs will be forever'

Returning to the season's 'energy and optimism' (p. 280), and to *Vogue*'s cover, various people may qualify as its potential authors, should any Foucauldian 'principle of thrift' (1984: 118) be required. Chief among them is the Peruvian photographer Mario Testino, responsible for the cover photo, 'Kiss Me, Kate' feature, and Kate's wedding portfolio. Like Wintour and Moss, Testino was a celebrity in his own right, so well known that Moss, we are told, 'shifted her [wedding] date from Saturday to Friday to accommodate his schedule, reasoning, with a model's canny logic, that the ceremony will last minutes but the photographs will be forever' (p. 681).

Testino is no author, even though the art/photography publisher Taschen had released a book of his photos called *Kate Moss by Mario Testino*. That book's online blurb quotes Testino's own story of how he first met Kate wearing Galliano:

> I met Kate very early on. Shortly after her first Galliano show I went backstage to congratulate her, only to find her crying: she was disappointed that she had only been given one outfit to model in the show. My answer to her was this: 'In life there are perfumes and colognes. You need to use lots of cologne as the scent fades away; with a perfume you just use a drop and it lasts all night. You are a perfume, you will go on and on.' Little did I know just how true that would become! And that I had made a friend for life. [24]

---

[23]'Models, Actors, and Designers React to the Verdict in John Galliano's Trial.' *New York* magazine: 9 September 2011. Online: http://nymag.com/daily/fashion/2011/09/galliano_re actions.html.

[24]*Kate Moss by Mario Testino* (Berlin: Taschen): www.taschen.com/pages/en/catalogue/photo graphy/all/06344/facts.kate_moss_by_mario_testino.htm. Following unrelated #MeToo allegations, Wintour later severed *Vogue*'s ties with Testino (and Bruce Weber); January 14 2018.

In *Vogue*, Hamish Bowles recycles the same story:

> Mario has known her since she was a fragile sixteen-year-old, crying her
> eyes out backstage at John Galliano's first Paris show. In that dim, distant
> past, when a model's success was judged by the number of changes she
> had in a show, Kate had been given only one outfit and was feeling
> unloved. Mario comforted her. 'You know, in life, there's perfume and
> there's cologne', he told her. 'Cologne, you have to spray every fifteen
> minutes. Perfume, you put a drop and it lasts a week. You're perfume.'
> (p. 681).

Here we encounter another kind of authorship – Bowles's rather free
rendition of words from a book that *Testino* had published. Bowles recasts
Testino's personal (or at least, self-serving) anecdote into the form of an
interview with himself. His story in *Vogue* continues with 'Mario' saying:
'"I had seen her out, and she had nothing of the waif," he remembers.' (p.
681). In Taschen's online blurb, this line goes to Kate Moss herself, who
reports: 'He was the first to say "Oh, she's quite sexy. I've seen her out!
I know she's not just that grungy girl."' In scholarly authorship this sort
of thing might look suspiciously like *plagiarism*, but in *Vogue* it is simply
promotion. Bowles gives Testino's book a plug, and Testino gets to be the
guy who invented Kate Moss's image, although that is a reinvention of
history. Without mentioning the late Corinne Day by name, Bowles, Testino
and Moss are all made to give Testino 'authorial' rights over Moss's career,
thereby distancing her from the photographer who made her famous in
1990, for the waif or grunge look (Hartley and Rennie, 2004; Hartley,
2007), but who had died in 2010.[25]

Nonetheless, Testino is not the author of the September cover. Like any
professional, Testino works to the brief: on this occasion, as dictated by
Anna Wintour, it was to be 'romantic.' On another occasion, he might be
called upon to urge his models to 'look Breeteesh!'[26]

Helping him to fulfil the brief is a small army of specialists, some of
whose contributions are acknowledged by *Vogue*. Most important is the
stylist who chooses the outfit (under Wintour's watchful eye), in this case
Vogue's contributing fashion editor Camilla Nickerson. The Rimmel make-
up is by Charlotte Tilbury (Art Partner); hair is by Sam McKnight (Pantene),
and manicure by Sophy Robson (Streeters). The technical grades include
production by 10-4 Inc. and set design by Gideon Ponte (Magnet Agency).

---

[25]See Day's obituary, which gives a very different account of Moss's early career, and a good
account of Day's importance, here: https://www.theguardian.com/artanddesign/2010/aug/31/
corinne-day-obituary.
[26]Mario Testino, giving direction to models on a cover-shoot for British *Vogue* (January 2002:
100); see Hartley and Rennie (2004: 477).

Those responsible for graphics and printing are not credited; the only such information given is that the magazine itself is 'printed in the U.S.A.' (p. 757).

Thus, like any other commercial media product of our time, the cover of *Vogue*, like a medieval potentate, is attended by expert and expensive talents in depth, all renowned in their own field, some celebrities, and many of them represented by agencies which would also have 'skin in the game'. Everyone's a maker; everyone's on the make, with no sign of thrift in sight. They all assist in telling the story, but not one of them is an author.

III. Everyone is an author

What difference does it make who is speaking?

(MICHEL FOUCAULT, 1984: 101, 120)

Where there is death, there is often also a birth, especially in fiction. The 'death of the author' was announced by Roland Barthes (1977a) in his influential essay of that name. This demise turned out to be highly contagious: 'the author' was done for among a whole complex of disciplines and a whole generation of critics. Among them, Jane Gallop (2011: 30) has observed: 'The last clause of Barthes's manifesto is taken as the definitive statement – not only Barthes's but poststructuralism's – on the question of the author.' Citing Seán Burke (1998: 19), she sees it as 'the single most influential meditation on the question of authorship in modern times.' It was 'so perfect that it has been taken as the last word.' (Gallop, 2011: 29–30). However, this death was not so final. Even when it was first announced, Barthes did not proclaim it as a stand-alone event. What he actually wrote in that 'definitive' last clause was about a *birth*: 'We know that to *give writing its future* ... the *birth of the reader* must be at the cost of the death of the author' (Barthes, 1977a: 148; my emphases).

Gallop takes Barthes's 'manifesto' as a call to *critical* action – '*critics* should no longer be concerned with the author; he should be dead to *us*' (2011: 30; my emphases); a call that was taken up in the discursive experiments of avant-garde postmodernism. But I want to consider a different way of thinking about Barthes's provocation; as an emancipationist expansion of the categories of 'writing' and 'the reader' (albeit at the expense of that of the author) to include, in principle, *everyone*.

In announcing an authorial death, Barthes was facing the future; the future of *writing*. He was interested in a birth – the birth of the *reader*. Since his intervention, both writing and the reader have superseded the author in a spectacular way: partly aided by game-changing technological developments unimagined in his day, associated with digital media, online connectivity and the internet; and partly abetted by the economic and political ascendancy of individualism in the wake of Reagan-Thatcherism and the end of the Cold War. These epochal changes wrought their own effects on authorship, because now, for the first time, *everyone* linked to digital media, including those billions who were previously confined to the status of readers or consumers, are endowed with the agency of *publishers* for every single utterance they make online, from phatic chatter to elaborate artifice.

In this context, authorship – as the sign for one who is *responsible* for published writing – expands to the point of meaninglessness. The accumulated assumptions associated with the modern socioeconomic institution of authorship are set at naught when, in principle, *everyone* is an author. Where in this formula is the scarcity value on which price must be based? Where does it leave the investment of publishers? What happens to copyright? How is it possible to retain professional status for authors? These are economic questions, and the turbulence of the publishing industry tells us that answers are still at the experimental stage.

The *Götterdämmerung* scenario?

'We live, for the first time in history, in a world where being part of a globally interconnected group is the normal case for most citizens.' So says Clay Shirky (2010a: 24). Billions of people are authors, producing more works than anyone could possibly imagine, archive or classify, much less consume or use. What's new may not be that people are doing this for the first time; rather that for the first time they are leaving digital traces of doing it, which can be tracked, mined and monetized. Many of their utterances are published within the confines of social networks, whether small-world groups like family-and-friends or giant-scale operations like Facebook, YouTube or Twitter, which themselves are not authored by any single individual, but nonetheless share creative agency with their users.

Semiotic productivity shifts: from author to reader, user to system, and is shared among all agents within the system. Readers (users) are productive of meanings, interpretations and uses for text, which is disconnected from the person or even the function of the author. Instead, discourses or textual systems – complex dynamic language-networks – could be said to 'speak us' even as we speak them. Here, as Barthes and Foucault saw, the meaning of a given work – its interpretation in the mind of the reader – is no longer determined by an author; it is an effect of the system, in which both author and reader are agents, and where the system itself imposes the rules of the game. In short, *publishing* has begun to take on the characteristics not of an *industry* but of *language* (see Chapter 5).

Thus, we are witnessing another of those steep increases in the productivity of communication technologies. This one is of even greater scale than the modernizing property enclosures of Shakespeare's era, when print started to outpace speech, and intellectual property supplanted orality. Then, the combination of print technology, publishing industry and authorial function served to increase the productivity of textual systems in line with an *industrial* model. Now, the combination of online/mobile technology, complex information/data systems and the user function of communication technologies has increased the productivity of expression in line with a *network* model.

In fact, following the Copernican and Darwinian revolutions, which dethroned humanity from the centre of the physical and the biological universe respectively, the emerging revolution in culture, presaged by the structuralists, has decentred the individual from the 'universe of the mind' (Lotman, 1990). Meaningfulness is not an outcome of individual intentions, authorial or otherwise. Methodological individualism, the analytical system based on being able to identify the 'author' of actions and behaviour, fails in its grasp just at the very moment when the agency of individuals as micro-producers is extended from a few privileged professionals to encompass *whole populations*. Not surprisingly, the extension of authorship this far out troubles many observers. Surely, more means worse? Here's Clay Shirky again (2010b):

> This shock of inclusion, where professional media gives way to participation by two billion amateurs … means that average quality of public thought has collapsed; when anyone can say anything any time, how could it not? If all that happens from this influx of amateurs is the destruction of existing models for producing high-quality material, we would be at the beginning of another Dark Ages. (Shirky, 2010b)

The 'shock of inclusion' that Shirky describes here is of course felt by current beneficiaries of the modern industrial system, not by the 'influx of amateurs' themselves. They are not bent on the 'destruction of existing models' but are simply exercising new-found opportunities for participation. If a process of Schumpeterian creative destruction is under way, it isn't *intended* by the entrepreneurial (or authorial) 'influx'; nor is anyone seeking to hasten the decline and fall of public thought, or to bring on another Dark Age (see Chapter 4). Those who adopted this *Götterdämmerung* (twilight of the gods) scenario were authors and publishers, not users, for the obvious reason that they operated the 'existing models'. Here's a typical expression of the prevailing anxiety, from author Ewan Morrison, speaking at the Edinburgh Book Festival of 2011:

> Will books, as we know them, come to an end? Yes, absolutely, within 25 years the digital revolution will bring about the end of paper books. But more importantly, ebooks and e-publishing will mean the end of 'the

writer' as a profession. ... The digital revolution will not emancipate writers or open up a new era of creativity, it will mean that writers offer up their work for next to nothing or for free. Writing, as a profession, will cease to exist.[27]

To which lament, one unsympathetic reader added this comment: 'Well, might as well give up then. ... Alternatively ... use your bloody imagination. I understand that writers are supposed to be quite good at this.'

Can we imagine something other than the end of the world as we know it? What if those billions of new authors are not barbarians at the gate but *citizens*? Unlike authorship, citizenship is a concept where more participation is generally valued positively. But like authorship, citizenship is experiencing radical changes in the wake of technological and social dynamics. Here too an *emergent* change is occurring that massively expands the practice of citizenship even while displacing some of its most *elaborate* modernist manifestations.

Zizi Papacharissi (2010: 19) called attention to the 'emerging model of the digitally enabled citizen', a model that is 'liquid and reflexive' in relation to 'contemporary civic realities', but also 'removed from the civic habits of the past'. Papacharissi argues for a reconceptualization of the public sphere, where the Habermasian tradition would place authors, and its relocation into the erstwhile private sphere, where one would previously have looked only for amateurs and consumers. She writes:

> Privately contained activities with a public scope, like online news reading, lurking in on political conversations, or following opinion leaders' blogs or tweets, take place within the locus of the private sphere. Publicly oriented activities, like posting a blog, sharing a political opinion, voting or signing a petition to support a cause, or uploading exclusive news content on YouTube, are also increasingly enabled within the locus of a digitally equipped private sphere. (2010: 20–21)

It should be noted that these two types of activity, 'privately contained' and 'publicly oriented', are – respectively – *reading* and *writing*: they are two sides of the *authorship* coin, albeit stripped of its association with intellectual-property-grabbing publishers. That is, public and private are not two warring systems, but two sides of the same communicative coin, and everyone can practise both of them. Papacharissi argues that *digital literacy* is practised with 'greater autonomy, flexibility, and potential for expression'

---

[27]Ewan Morrison, 'Are Books Dead, and Can Authors Survive?' *The Guardian online*, 22 August 2011: www.guardian.co.uk/books/2011/aug/22/are-books-dead-ewan-morrison. And see: http://ewanmorrison.com/.

in private than in public, which 'challenges the fundamental supposition that humans, in order to be social, and by consequence political, must possess public face' (2010: 21).

Within the private sphere, as traditionally conceived, people are more often seen as consumers than as citizens; but now, in order to practise digitally enabled citizenship, people *must* also be consumers. Papacharissi examines 'the centrality of consumption in emerging civic behaviors, enabling individuals to claim citizenship through the possession of commodities and thus blurring democratic and capitalist narratives' (2010: 19). In this world, 'public face' and private identity are one and the same.

Thus it is arguable that authorship too is evolving beyond the need for 'public face' and publishers. It is another of those seeming paradoxes, where citizenship, the public sphere, authorship and politics are all conducted in what used to be thought of as the sphere of private, amateur, personal consumption. What's new is that this private space of identity is the locus for digitally enabled micro-productivity, where one-person creativity is scalable through digital connectivity.

Putting your face on: Self-authored bodies

Among the commodities produced in this context is personal identity. When you 'put your face on', with the help of products advertised in consumer outlets like *Vogue*, you are creating an identity, and simultaneously setting yourself up as an actor in a digitally enabled social network that is both your own and the public sphere. As a fashion magazine, *Vogue* is part of a larger world of lifestyle and fashion journalism that occupies a mediating space between public and private life. This isn't front-line political journalism, although politics may ruffle the glossy surface unexpectedly (as we've seen) nor is it fiction, an interior imaginary world (where you might expect to find a modernist author).

From the point of view of the *reader*, style journalism brings together (i.e. mediates) these external and internal worlds. To that extent, then, *Vogue* is a participant in the practice of privatized citizenship. External sociality, celebrity and style, with attendant status-competition, attention-seeking and immersion in the flow of time and trends, connects with internal identity, the formation not just of a personal style but also of a self with its own public face that, in turn, enables the self to connect with the world. *Vogue* mediates the world and the self, offering social learning cues (Thomas and Brown, 2011) for an emergent *narrative of the self* for every reader, if they so choose. Not only is everyone an author, they are *the author of the self*.

Increasingly, that kind of authorship is being professionalized. Here is where the *elaborate* (professional) practice of authorship links with the *emergent* (user-created) variety – experts of all kinds are on hand to teach myriad emergent selves how to inscribe their own story, whether directly on the body or by mediation through online networks. Judith Butler argues,

> If the inner truth of gender is a fabrication and if a true gender is a fantasy instituted and inscribed on the surface of bodies, then it seems that genders can be neither true nor false, but are only produced as the truth effects of a discourse of primary and stable identity. (Butler, 1990: 136)

The surface of bodies themselves – the very *subject* of *Vogue* – is textualized on each individual body as a 'truth effect' of self-authored gender discourse. How and what to write on that surface is becoming professionalized on both sides of the emergent/elaborate pairing: for professional writers it is a business opportunity; for citizen authors it is a competitive arms race in which everyone's signalling performance is judged, requiring professional input into self-improvement and thus a new service industry.

The Cartesian 'turn to the self' in philosophy and religion (Simpson, 2001: 309) meets the 'production of the self' in consumerism. From the resulting textualization, 'self-authorship' emerges. It combines lessons from top-down style-bibles and self-help media, where selfhood is literally modelled by celebrities, with bottom-up or DIY digital literacy, where people exploit textual resources (platforms, connections, apps) to make themselves up as they go along. Ordinary selves are re-made in the image of expertise, which stands, like Jeeves, at the elbow of every domestic endeavour, from the disciplining and care of the body to its adornment in fashion, extending ever outwards to cooking, singing, purchasing a house, parenting, dating and gardening (Taylor, 2008). Makeover media are thus virtual versions of aristocratic servants: like Jeeves – or Shakespeare – they know more than those they serve, but it's the patron-client who has to play the game of competitive individualism.

Along the way, Cartesian dualism has been overcome: body and consciousness are one. Now, selfhood is an *autopoietic* outcome of performative actions and interactions, inscribed in, on and by the body including in its language-performances, through a creative process that exploits diet, lifestyle, exercise, garments, hair and make-up, and the rest, as well as the discursive, textual and audio-visual affordances of online media, to produce daily performances of a narrative of the self, via texts, blogs, emails, Facebook, Twitter, etc. Scattered across digital devices and online networks, users establish a trans-media, public–private 'cloud self' that interacts with the bodily self in unpredictable ways, requiring constant updating and adjustment, and that is subject to critical scrutiny by both internal and external surveillance. Digitally enabled citizens work to integrate consciousness and corporeality into story, in a competitive process of micro-productive creativity.

The professionalization of self-authorship is not a new phenomenon in itself. For instance, the avant-garde filmmaker Jean-Luc Godard, a contemporary of Barthes and Foucault, caused his on-screen characters to make themselves up as they went along in his movies of the 1960s (e.g. Jean-Pierre Léaud in *Masculin-Féminin*). What's new is the extent to which this departure from psychological realism has been driven throughout society, by both market and moral forces: if your 'real' self is no good, make a new one – using these products and services. Help is available, not only to present positive role models (often celebrities) but also to teach the limits beyond which a well-governed self cannot go, often personified by reality TV contestants.

Here, sociologist Bev Skeggs has argued that discourses and shows about loud-mouthed women, including 'White Trash TV', media portrayals of chavs or Essex Girls (Jones, 2011), and even hen-parties out on the town, are a contemporary manifestation of class struggle in the UK: 'We now have the loud, white, excessive, drunk, fat, vulgar, disgusting, hen-partying woman who exists to embody all the moral obsessions historically associated with the working class now contained in one body; a body beyond governance' (Skeggs, 2005: 965). Racial politics produces a different unruly subject in the United States (e.g. on *Jerry Springer*), although it serves the same discursive purpose. Skeggs argues that such portrayals do more than mock certain taste formations; they also give onlookers a 'position of judgment' to set the limits of propriety, by placing these women beyond it:

> It is not just a matter of using some aspects of the culture of the working class to enhance one's value, but also maintaining the position of judgement to attribute value, which assigns the other as immoral, repellent, abject, worthless, disgusting, even disposable. (Skeggs, 2005: 977)

The lesson here is that there will be a price to pay for unruly self-authorship that transgresses taste boundaries. That price may be public, provoking old-fashioned divide-and-rule politics, providing a handy image of the 'undeserving' poor, who 'deserve' welfare cuts (Skeggs, 2005: 968). Those targeted may in turn flaunt gross behaviour as a sign of co-subjective resistance. On the other hand, those 'beyond governance' provide a negative incentive to everyone else, encouraging onlookers to *professionalize* their self-created self-responsibility further, by 'governing' their own narrative of the self. This is the 'generalization of the risky self', where 'life now depends on knowing how to behave in the distance between everything that may happen and what is more probable of happening; it depends on the restriction of possibilities' (Vaz and Bruno, 2003: 287). Here, as elsewhere in the creative industries, individual choices are determined by the choices of others (Potts et al., 2008).

How *do* you script yourself to tell others that you *follow* fashion but *face the future*? Luckily, Kate Moss's daughter's father is on hand to help. A feature in the London *Standard* tells all. Jefferson Hack is 'the man who knows everyone, and who everyone wants to know. *The Guardian* wasn't joking recently when it asked: "Is this the coolest man in the UK?"' Hack belongs to 'the digital generation, where the boundaries between disciplines and functions have broken down, where producers, customers, commercial sponsors and critics have formed "new relationships."' Co-founder of *Dazed & Confused* and editor-in-chief of *AnOther Magazine*, Hack knows what this generation needs: 'In this "post-post-modern" world, he says … the "ongoing story" is out there competing in cyberspace. Yet in the age of information-overload, "consumers have never had more need for a filter like *AnOther*"' (*Standard*).

This guide doesn't write your story for you, as *Vogue* might. It 'filters' (edits) the digital overload and you create the 'ongoing story' for yourself. That story is not about taste discrimination – between the chavs and the chav-nots, as it were – but something more structural: '"The story we're always talking about is the bigger divide between the haves and have-nots," he says. … *AnOther*'s mission is "not to tell the reader to make themselves feel better by buying stuff they can't afford but to give value through the reading experience"' (*Standard*). Why should you filter your reading experience through Hack? Because he practises what he preaches: he *made himself up as he went along*; he's 'living on thin air' (Leadbeater, 1999), 'it cannot be denied that his edge-cutting attitude allows him to punch way, way above his weight' (*Standard*). Jefferson Hack is a new kind of model: that of the self-author. His person, life and career all represent his own story. But as with any kind of fashion modelling, the take-out message for onlookers is not about him. His self-authorship stimulates the competitive market in self-authorship. The message is that *you* – dear reader – can make *yourself* 'grow, originate, promote, increase'. The once godlike power, to be 'the person who originates or gives existence to anything', has democratized, to become everyone's own responsibility, and tradable.

8

Shakespearean class struggle:

'The pit has frequently made laws for the boxes'

One advantage of being on the periphery is that you know where the centre is. ... A simpler, if no less disturbing way of putting it is to say that Shakespeare has become, both metaphorically and literally, an American institution.

(TERENCE HAWKES)[1]

I. Invidious comparison

Terry Tocqueville

Alexis de Tocqueville's *De la démocratie en Amérique* (*Democracy in America*), published in two volumes in 1835 and 1840, was really about France. Tocqueville thought it might be possible to think through the problems that bedevilled the French polity (between the two Napoleons) by learning from both Britain and America, despite their manifold shortcomings; the one for liberty, the other for democracy. Tocqueville's

[1]This epigraph conjoins two reviews written by Hawkes for the *London Review of Books*: The first, 'Putting on Some English', *LRB* 24:3, 7 February 2002, 25–6: https://www.lrb.co.uk/v24/n03/terence-hawkes/putting-on-some-english; the second, 'Bardbiz', *LRB* 12:4, 22 February 1990, 11–13: https://www.lrb.co.uk/v12/n04/terence-hawkes/bardbiz.

anglophile tendencies were unusual in French public life, which habitually shared with the Americans a desire to 'fight free of Englishness' (Brogan, 2006: 399). His motivations were political: he wanted to balance order and liberty, avoiding both dictatorship and revolution (a trick that is still puzzling transatlantic polities); but they were also personal. He thought that it was his own aristocratic Norman ancestors who had introduced into England the conditions for *liberty* to develop (by *conquering* it, in 1066 – it's a long story) (Welch, 2001: 128–9, 162 n. 11). His personal interest in English liberty may have been extended further by his marriage to an English Protestant commoner, Marie Mottley, six years his elder. Such a match went against the grain of his own nation, religion and caste, but by all accounts the marriage was a successful and lifelong union of opposites.

The Shakespearean critic and literary theorist Terence Hawkes, my lifelong mentor, who died in 2014, analysed the condition of democracy through drama; he analysed Britain by comparing it to America; and he analysed Shakespearean drama through the lens of class, as did Tocqueville in Volume 2 of *Democracy in America*. Terry Hawkes was Tocquevillian in temper – astute, wry, literary, transatlantic and worried. He was adept at using 'America' to effect what Thorstein Veblen (1899: 27–8) would have called 'invidious comparison' (1899: 15–16) with 'England'.[2] What worried Hawkes in this comparative method was that neither side of the Atlantic provided a satisfactory solution to the problems that he wanted to figure out. But Americanness and Englishness might begin to explain one another. Britain was the colonial power from which the Americans had wrested their liberty. As Hawkes put it: 'To fight free of Englishness by turning to things French has, after all, been a major transatlantic ploy since the eighteenth century' (2002: 125). In that instance, he was discussing Duke Ellington, jazz, and the future of literary criticism, but of course, Alexis de Tocqueville's *De la démocratie en Amérique* was one of the 'things French' towards which the Americans turned, as soon as the two volumes were published.

In a fascinating section on 'the influence of democracy on intellectual movement in the United States', Tocqueville devoted a chapter to 'Some Observations on the Theatre of Democratic Peoples' (2010: 845–52), where he recommends:

When the revolution that changed the social and political state of an aristocratic people begins to make itself felt in literature, it is generally in

---

[2]These shifting signifiers – 'America', 'England' – are uncomfortable equivalents for the United States and United Kingdom. What each may have meant in Shakespeare's or Tocqueville's time, never mind Hawkes's, is indeterminate. Both carry imperial baggage, which Hawkes, an Englishman living in Wales, eventually confronted in his 'Blyn Glas' and 'Aberdaugleddyf' (Hawkes 2002).

the theater that it is first produced, and it is there that it always remains visible. ... If you want to judge in advance the literature of a people that is turning toward democracy, study its theatre. (846)

On re-reading Tocqueville with Terry in mind (or turn-about) – a pleasure I can recommend – it is remarkable how often Tocqueville's insights shine with a Hawkesian glint; a glint in the eye that surprises, amuses, instructs and illuminates all at once, revealing previously unsuspected tensions about the state of reality at play. Both of them employ (or enjoy) what one of Tocqueville's critics describes as a 'paradox-seeking tone',[3] infuriating to some but an efficient rhetorical vehicle for the 'invidious comparison' method.

Postmodern thunder

You may say that my suggestion of a Hawkesian glint in Tocqueville's text smacks of the ludicrous time-inversion of Persse McGarrigle, a character in David Lodge's 'academic romance' *Small World* (1984). McGarrigle studied 'the influence of T.S. Eliot on Shakespeare', to the general amusement of the common room until the Eliot scholar Jason Harding pointed out that the fictional McGarrigle's paradoxical arrow of time was in fact pointing the right way: 'Had Persse been a more attentive student of Eliot, he'd have known that the author of the dictum "the past should be altered by the present as much as the present is directed by the past" anticipated his postmodern thunder by half a century' (Harding, 2012: 160). On the principle that many a true word is spoken in jest, let Lodge's canny insight authorize us to investigate Hawkes's influence on Tocqueville, since the burden of Hawkes's own later work, on what he called 'presentism' (Hawkes, 1999, 2002, 2003), was that canonical texts say what *we* mean, albeit with a sting in the tail of that particular truth:

Let's get it straight. It's not what the plays say that counts, but the uses to which they are put. We wonder about what they 'mean'. But the truth is much starker. We mean. Worse, we mean it by the plays.[4]

---

[3]Christopher *Caldwell*, '*Even God Quotes Tocqueville*'. New York Times, July 8, 2007: http://www.nytimes.com/2007/07/08/books/review/Caldwell.html.
[4]A post by Terence Hawkes on the *Shaksper* website, 10 August 2007 (http://shaksper.net/archive/2007/256-august/25677-washpost-ourselves-in-shakespeare-sp-2088857046). This comment was part of a short discussion string in which the Shakespeare Riots and Nigel Cliff's (2007) book were mentioned in someone else's post, to which Hawkes's comment is a response. See also Hawkes (2002).

'We mean it by the plays' is 'worse' because it is *our* 'uses to which *they* are put'. They are an alibi. The same is true of Tocqueville. The uses to which he has been put include his status – up there with Shakespeare – in the United States. Blithely, commentators endlessly repeat:

> *Democracy in America* is at once the best book ever written on democracy and the best book ever written on America. (Mansfield and Winthrop, 2000)

Democracy and America become 'convertible terms', as Walt Whitman had asserted in *Democratic Vistas* (1871),[5] no matter that Tocqueville had doubts about democracy as a system of government, or that America no longer practises the backwoods egalitarian version that he observed. In the name of Tocqueville, minority elites and corporate raiders cloak undemocratic practices in democratic theory, simply by invoking Americanness. It seems high time to subject the uses of Tocqueville to some Hawkesian, air-clearing, 'postmodern thunder'.

Totus mundus agit-prop

Both Hawkes and Tocqueville had something to say about Shakespeare. Tocqueville claimed him for the enterprise at hand, calling him 'the democratic author par excellence' (2010: 868 n.). Even as America was 'struggling to fight free of Englishness', Shakespeare ruled its public rostrum and log cabin alike:

> The literary genius of Great Britain still shines its light into the depths of the forests of the New World. There is scarcely a pioneer's cabin where you do not find a few odd volumes of Shakespeare. (803)

This may be characterized as a literary (read-only) or *pedagogical* Shakespeare, rather than a *people's* Shakespeare. A more riotous version was also to hand across America: a dialogic, dramatic one, playing in the theatres. Tocqueville had a theory of the theatre that was straightforwardly political. In an early performance of Hawkesian cultural studies, Tocqueville subjects the theatre of the 1830s to class analysis:

> It is only in the theater that the upper classes have mingled with the middle and lower classes, and that they have agreed if not to accept the advice of the latter, at least to allow them to give it. It is in the theater that

---

[5]See: http://xroads.virginia.edu/~hyper/whitman/vistas/vistas.html, third paragraph.

the learned and the lettered have always had the most difficulty making their taste prevail over that of the people, and keeping themselves from being carried away by the taste of the people. There the pit has often laid down the law for the boxes. (846–7)

Drama co-evolves with democracy, no matter that theatres themselves were class divided between 'the pit' and 'the boxes':[6]

If it is difficult for an aristocracy not to allow the theater to be invaded by the people, you will easily understand that the people must rule there as a master once democratic principles have penetrated laws and mores, when ranks merge and minds like fortunes become more similar. (847)

Not only was this true for Shakespeare's own theatres (groundlings commingling with lords), as Alfred Harbage (1947) noted at length, but it is also true for contemporary mediated societies. The radical potential of the 'popular dramatic tradition' – first noted in relation to movie musicals by S. L. Bethell (1944), one of Hawkes's own teachers – was also inherent in the popular drama of the television era, where, 'once democratic principles have penetrated laws and mores', 'the boxes' had been thoroughly 'carried away by the tastes of the people'. This is of course where Terence Hawkes came in (1973: 215–41).

II. The Shakespeare Riots

The riotous potential of the popular dramatic tradition in Tocqueville's America was soon on spectacular – and lethal – display, in New York City, May 1849. Tocqueville had been prescient:

The tastes and instincts natural to democratic peoples … will show themselves first in the theater, and you can predict that they will be introduced there with violence. In written works, the literary laws of the aristocracy will become modified little by little in a general and so to speak legal manner. In the theater, they will be overthrown by riots. (847)

The 'Shakespeare Riots' duly ensued (Cliff, 2007; Dobson, 2007). The fatal disturbance included a strong dose of anti-British sentiment, but one particular manifestation of Englishness – Shakespeare – was exempt. Indeed, as 'the democratic author, par excellence', Shakespeare was appropriated,

---

[6]Tocqueville (2010) translates the sentence this way; the (more familiar) Mansfield and Winthrop translation (2000) has it as: 'The pit has frequently made laws for the boxes.'

according to the logic of Whitman's 'convertible terms,' as the *American* author 'par excellence'. No matter what the machinations of *la perfide Albion*, Shakespeare was henceforth 'translated' as a universal soldier of the American way.

The crisis extended over several days. It was ostensibly provoked by a dispute between two Shakespearean actors, the American Edwin Forrest and the Englishman William Charles Macready, who were appearing in different theatres in New York City. Both were playing the role of Macbeth (Figure 8.1). Forrest had genuine working-class credentials and a loyal following in the New York 'popular dramatic tradition'. He saw himself in the rugged individualist mould of the American pioneer. In the process he played a further dramatic role, popularizing the template for the rugged-individualist film star of the later Hollywood studio system, paving the way

(a)   (b)

FIGURE 8.1 *Duelling Shakespeareans. (a)* Mr. Edwin Forrest as Macbeth. *(b)* Mr. William Macready as Macbeth. *(a) Forrest: R. Thew, engraving, 1856. (b) Macready: T. Sherratt after H. Tracey, engraving, nineteenth century. Folger Shakespeare Library. Illustrations used by permission of the Folger Shakespeare Library, Creative Commons Attribution-ShareAlike 4.0 International License (CC BY-SA 4.0).*

for the likes of John Wayne, Charlton Heston, Ronald Reagan and a certain kind of Americanism that recovered from Vietnam (Wayne, *The Green Berets*), eventually to take over the National Rifle Association (Heston) and the presidency (Reagan).

Apparently Forrest had clashed previously with Macready who had insulted him in London four years earlier, and whom he now cast in the villainous role of English toff – an effete, simpering aristocratic fop. Macready was playing at the Astor Place Opera House, which was associated with New York's well-to-do elite. Local matinée idol Forrest was having none of that. He was out for revenge (Cliff, 2007). But the scale and violence of the showdown far exceeded the bounds of professional jealously. Forrest had whipped up patriotic fervour among the Bowery Boys or B'hoys, an early spectacular subculture of urban, alienated youth in a New York City that was undergoing the painful transformation from an artisanal to an industrial economy, and thus to a full-blown class distinction between workers and capitalists (Adams, 2005: 39–45; Zecker, 2008: 25–6). The Bowery Boys were motivated by inequality, nationalism, class hatred and urban subcultural swagger. They spilled out of 'The Republic of the Bowery' in spectacular style, precursors of Martin Scorsese's *Gangs of New York*,

> dressed in outlandish manner, with slicked-down forelocks, gaudily colored suits, expensive walking sticks, high working boots, and tall beaver hats set at a jaunty, defiant angle. Avid drinkers, carousers, and battlers with rival gangs, the Bowery toughs comically asserted their place in the urban landscape, with stage plays devoted to their exploits and their aggressive aping of their betters (Zecker, 2008: 25–6).

The stage was set for three convergent provocations to civil war: the dramatic conflict unleashed by Macbeth with the murder of King Duncan in the Scottish Play; class war in a city newly marked by industrial inequality; and a continuing war of decolonization between what an incendiary poster at the time, seeking to inflame the disturbances, called American 'Workingmen!' and 'English Aristocrats And Foreign Rule' (Adams, 2005: 42–3).

The climax was Shakespearean – bodies strewn everywhere (Figure 8.2). Except that these were the corpses of the audience, not the characters. Before order was restored, the forces involved on both sides had glimpsed nothing less than revolution. Faced with an unarmed crowd estimated at between 15,000 and 20,000 people from 'the pit', New York's mayor called out the National Guard. For the first time in US history (but not the last), the Republic's own soldiers 'shot point blank at American citizens' (Adams, 2005: 42):

> A crowd of Forrest's partisans gathered early in the evening before the theatre, and waiting till the performance had begun, attempted to force

FIGURE 8.2 *The Shakespeare Riots. Riot at the Astor Place Opera House, New York 1849. Wood engraving. Folger Shakespeare Library. Used by permission of the Folger Shakespeare Library, Creative Commons Attribution-ShareAlike 4.0 International License (CC BY-SA 4.0).*

a way inside and put a stop to it. The police were powerless and sent for the military; the Seventh Regiment (New York militia) came up, and was assailed by the mob with showers of brickbats and stones. Before the fray was ended, 34 rioters were killed, a great number wounded, and 141 of the regiment injured by the missiles.[7]

'Partisans' versus 'pedigree': 'High working boots' meet the 'silk stockings'

Confronted with their own fellow democrats, protesting a colonial power they both opposed, what motivated the National Guard to shoot down so many citizens? Their theatrical excess? Not entirely, threatening though visible otherness has seemed to security forces in American cities from that

---

[7]Source: *Encyclopaedia Americana*, 1920. Archived at Wikisource: (https://en.wikisource.org/wiki/The_Encyclopedia_Americana_(1920)/Astor_Place_Riot).

day to this. But here, at the 'hated elite' Astor Opera Theatre, it seems that *class supremacy* played a role. 'The boxes' were shooting into 'the pit':

> [National Guard] units had historically played a central role in the social and political lives of the localities, regions, and social communities in which they were based. The 7th Regiment of the New York National Guard, for example, carried on its muster rolls the names of so many scions of New York City's socially prominent families that it was commonly known as the 'Silk Stocking' or 'Blue-Blood' Regiment. The unit's strict peacetime entry requirements endowed it with the character of an exclusive club for New York City's patrician elite, the regiment's membership being limited only to recruits able to produce evidence of proper pedigree or social connections. (Lukasik, 2008: 84)

Throughout the nineteenth century, these patrician scions of 'proper pedigree' continued to keep order among unruly industrial workers. The Seventh Regiment was called out to support state or municipal authorities for one emblematic disturbance after another:

- Execution of James Reynolds, 1825
- Election Riots, 1834
- Abolition Riot, 1834
- Stevedore Riot, 1836
- Flour Riots, 1837
- Anti-rent War, 1839
- Croton Water Riot, 1840
- Astor Place Riot, 1849 (the Shakespeare Riots)
- Police Riot, 1857
- Dead Rabbits Riot, 1857
- Draft Riots, 1863
- Orange Riots, 1871
- Labor Riots, 1877
- Motormen's Strike, Brooklyn, 1895
- Strike, Croton Dam, 1900.[8]

The Shakespeare Riots were provoked by feuding Shakespeareans; they ended as a modern tragedy of Shakespearean proportions. And *Macbeth*

---

[8] 7th New York Militia, *Wikipedia*. https://en.wikipedia.org/wiki/7th_New_York_Militia.

was just the play to use for thinking through such matters. As Terence Hawkes has pointed out:

> Most modern critics agree that the play exhibits … concern with the diagnosis of evil in the modern world. … Macbeth's reduced world, its language, its politics, are instantly familiar to us. Yet that familiarity perhaps becomes the play's most complicating factor, making it difficult to 'see' Macbeth as the self-damned wretch its structure demands. He looks too much like someone we know. (Hawkes, 1977: 11)

For in the end, as Hawkes has been arguing all along, it is the uses to which the plays are put that counts. What *Macbeth* may say is no guarantor of what it may mean, but what it means certainly includes the politics of class, nation and industrialization that played out in Manhattan in 1849. There's even a play, *Two Shakespearean Actors* (R. Nelson, 2019), which dwells on this incident as the basis for an examination of the theatre in a postcolonial era.

III. Antidemocratic evils lurk

'You might want to work on that little roar of yours, hmm?'

The face of evil as 'someone we know' is one legacy of the Forrest-Macready feud. Springing from the craggy heights of tragedy, Shakespearean villainy ran quickly into the fertile alluvial plains of popular culture. For the American popular dramatic tradition has never quite resiled from the model of evil that presented itself on stage in New York in 1849. Hollywood's image of the *bad guy* is not *Macbeth* but *Englishmen*. The foppish but menacing caricature of Englishness exploited by Edwin Forrest has made William Charles Macready (the son of an Irishman) the unwitting archetype of stage malice, so much so that it keeps resurfacing in places where children may be present in numbers, just to remind Americans to stick to simple-and-strong, and not to fall for the wiles of the Old European intellectual, especially one speaking in suspicious 'New Accents'.

Take, for instance, Jeremy Irons's portrayal of Scar, the villain in *The Lion King*, that remake of the Forrest model of rugged-individualist American pioneer, whose puritan self-realization is achieved not in the backwoods of the New World, or even in the rowdy mean streets of the Bowery Boys, but in a transplanted Africa-without-Africans, designed for the global marketplace where 'a Shakespearean monster' can be recognized by his posh English accent:

The Lion King offers viewers clear analogues for Hamlet and his father. But the film's best representation of the pleasures and grandeur of Shakespeare comes not in little Simba or martyred Mufasa, but in its villain: Scar, a Shakespearean monster par excellence. (Butler, 2014).

Irons is almost typecast for this role, effortlessly embodying a certain type of Englishness ever since his breakthrough role in *Brideshead Revisited* (1981). As a profile in *The Observer* (2008) put it:

> This is one performer who very much could have proffered variations on Englishness in the decades since his dandified Charles Ryder on television in *Brideshead Revisited* came to embody a certain kind of etiolated, privileged, vaguely androgynous toff.[9]

To American sensibilities, that characterization is evil enough, but Irons himself played on it by portraying Humbert Humbert in Adrian Lyne's adaptation of *Lolita* (1997),[10] the intellectual pervert with European sensibilities who traduces the innocence of girlhood – and of the American road-movie.

To Alfredo Michel Modenessi's sceptical and postcolonial ear, Irons's drawling menace is not so much Shakespeare as 'Shakespeare' (and, we may add, not so much English as 'English'); little more than 'leftovers of bardolatry freely circulating in ready-to-use packages', where 'the British accented and Shakespeare-allusive' Scar of *The Lion King*, echoing stereotypes going back at least to 1849, represents the 'sinister, un-American villain':

> Irons' voice and inflections stand in sharp contrast to [James Earl] Jones' 'heroic' rendering of Mufasa: the gaunt, sometime RSC player delivers a depraved, decadent Old World counterpart to the New World's robust character, who is just as deeply voiced but 'noble' and physically imposing. (Modenessi, 2005: 404–5)

This is 'Shakesploitation' by Disney. Modenessi asks: 'How far should Shakespeare artists and scholars participate?' The answer is already circulating, in the Shakespearean criticism of Terence Hawkes. The real objection to such characterization is his too: once you have bolted the theatre's doors *against* class, colonialism, politics and theory, to focus on 'individual character' and 'personality', you may be discomfited by what

---

[9]Source: https://www.theguardian.com/stage/2008/mar/30/theatre5.
[10]American sensibilities were such that the film initially failed to secure a theatrical distributor in the United States: https://archive.nytimes.com/www.nytimes.com/library/film/tv-lolita-review.html.

happens next out there on the street. To avoid another 'Shakespeare riot' along the hard road to democratization, the reduction of Shakespearean drama to American individualism needs to be shown the door. The trick is not to *reduce* Shakespeare to a John Wayne movie or Disney cartoon, but to make these popular dramatic forms worthy of the mantle they have inherited:

> Forget [Shakespeare's plays'] complex concern with the issues of nationhood, governance and morality. Welcome to our modern, ingrowing, back-bedroom world, where individual personality and its discontents line up to be furtively probed, picked, squeezed and sniffed. … But this replaces the epic sweep of a 400-year-old drama with the comfiness of current soap opera prattle … bossily shooing us down that bleak Coronation Street of the soul where Hamlet, Juliet, and Othello turn out to be 'people just like us' and where we are 'as darkly ambitious as Lady Macbeth, as jubilantly lusty as Bottom, as embittered as Iago'. Reduce the Bard, reduce his art. (Hawkes, 2003)[11]

Four hundred years after Shakespeare's death, here's the take-out message. We need to find a way to investigate the Shakespearean in our societies, not to insert our personalities into 'Shakespeare': to disturb, for our own uncomfortable good, 'the scarcely penetrable world of engulfing violence, wholesale insecurity, and inexplicably mingled cruelty and sentimentality where our roots disturbingly lie' (Hawkes, 2003).

That is surely still an all-too recognizable world. What a waste if Shakespeare studies is merely 'tamed … curbed … explained … made fit to appear on a syllabus near you'. Instead of reducing Shakespeare to mannered menace and stage villainy, Terry Hawkes's Shakespearean and Tocquevillian question draws our attention to 'the uses to which plays are put' – and that includes Disney as much as Dunsinane. Instead of endlessly restaging Forrest's frontier individualism against Macready's perfidious Englishness, what would it mean, and what would it take, for popular culture to take transatlantic differences and class struggle seriously, so that the 'the pit' of contemporary popular drama can again 'lay down the law' for the 'boxes', where new-made antidemocratic evils lurk?

---

[11]Hawkes (2003) is a review of Stephanie Nolen's *Shakespeare's Face* (Piatkus, 2003). The internal quotations are from that book.

9

Staged conflict:

Dialogic monuments and dancing difference

All the misfortunes of mankind, all the dreadful disasters that fill the history books, the blunders of politicians and the faults of omission of great commanders, all this comes from not knowing how to dance.

(MOLIÈRE, 1670)[1]

This chapter investigates 'urban semiosis' in relation to recurrent political debate over public memorials in Australia. I argue that pioneer monuments are part of the civic theatre of group identification, acting in the present to extend into the past the boundaries of a national 'we' community. Like the actions on which it reports, the chapter follows the emergence of a worldwide activist movement known as 'fallism', following a 2015 student protest in South Africa that used the slogan 'Rhodes Must Fall', seeking to remove a statue of the British colonizer Cecil Rhodes from the University of Cape Town and from Oriel College at Oxford University (in the event, the South African university complied, but Oxford did not). Fallism allied with similar moves in the United States to remove statuary and other icons of the Civil War Confederacy (slave states). Of course, the real intent was

---

[1]From *Le Bourgeois Gentilhomme*: https://www.gutenberg.org/files/2992/2992-h/2992-h.htm. The play extols the value of music to the state, and dancing to the person (over philosophy and fencing).

that colonialism, imperialism, racism and Western knowledge systems based upon these antecedents 'must fall', which led to variations on the theme, including 'science must fall', which sparked a further round of controversy around the world (Roy, 2018).

In Australia, following this international 'fallist' activism, statues of explorer-navigator Captain James Cook and colonist Governor Lachlan Macquarie were defaced or criticized in the name of Aboriginal activism, with slogans such as 'No Pride in Genocide' and 'Change the Date' (of Australia Day), in turn provoking exclusionary media and political responses. Further examples from the city of Fremantle in Western Australia indicate, however, that an alternative model of public dialogue on the borders between cultures is available. Provocative monuments have not fallen, but have been used as a *theatre for staged conflict*, where the Aboriginal practice of *corroboree* communicates new possibilities for inter-group reconciliation.

Urban semiosis

This chapter touches on 'urban studies' but it foregrounds *semiosis*, a process that is paramount to citizens but uncommon in city planning or policy, or in their underpinning social sciences. For those not familiar with the term, semiosis is well defined as 'a process in which something functions as a sign to an organism'.[2] In the present context, it describes the processes by which a city is made meaningful to users, outsiders and observers. This brings together two of the most extensive and longest-lasting of human inventions: language (Boyd and Dor, 2017) and – much more recently – cities (West, 2016). The idea of 'urban semiosis' links the imagined space of culture and language or semiosphere (Lotman, 1990) with the physical and technological fabric of cities, where the majority of humans now live,[3] to provide a viable conceptual framework for analysing the *creative city* (Hartley, 2015).

A city exists in a temporal dimension as well as in a spatial one: semiosis makes *time* meaningful. Within the urban semiosphere, certain places express *when* 'we' are. The stern gaze of the long-dead leader, imperial lion or heroic martyr, overlooking all who pass, unites 'us', as one community, coeval across centuries. The gaze addresses citizens, but takes in visitors and excluded populations at a single glance (Figure 9.1).

---

[2]*Merriam-Webster Dictionary* offers this general definition; it is suitable for application to the biosphere as a whole, in line with current theory, whereas the *OED* restricts the term to linguistics. See also: *Sign System Studies*: http://www.sss.ut.ee/index.php/sss.
[3]United Nations data: https://news.un.org/en/story/2014/07/472752-more-half-worlds-popu lation-now-living-urban-areas-un-survey-finds.

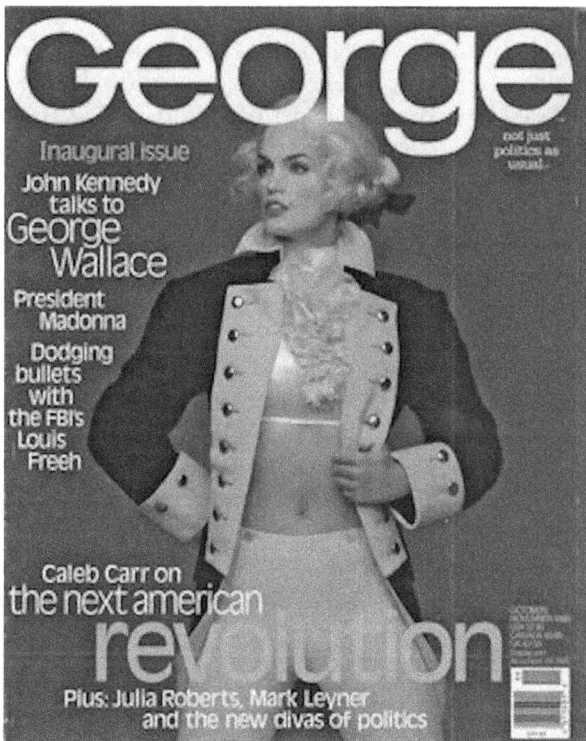

FIGURE 9.1 *The imperious gaze of the ancestor continues to inspire citizens: Supermodel Cindy Crawford channels George Washington for the inaugural cover of the short-lived political/pop-culture magazine* George *(1995–2001). Image: Wikimedia (fair use: https://en.wikipedia.org/wiki/File:George_(magazine).jpg).*

A city's physical fabric often communicates its own historical period of greatest expansion or ascendancy:

- Prague is medieval;[4]
- London is Victorian (Winn, 2018);
- New York is Art Deco (Robins, 2017);
- Las Vegas is postmodern, defined by its 'amnesiac' forgetfulness of temporality (León, 2017);
- … and so on (Jencks, 1991).

---

[4]According to BigBoyTravel.com: https://www.bigboytravel.com/europe/topmedievalcities/.

Cities routinely make more of an effort to preserve one period's meaningfulness over another's, the politics of which are clear when a city is redeveloped to prefer, say, the Protestant Enlightenment, while erasing reminders of Nazi or Communist periods (Burchard, 2016). Few cities preserve signs of defeat, unless there is a political or rhetorical rationale for that (e.g. in Hiroshima and certain German cities).[5]

Citizens too are time-bound, but the 'we'-population is not reducible to 'those who are alive today', as individual subjects of censuses, surveys and social-scientific data. In practice, some of 'those who are alive today' *do not count* as part of a city's 'we' community: migrants, ethnic minorities, slaves, prisoners, visitors. Culture-made groups form inter-knowing populations or demes, bound together by language, story, knowledge and collective action. Demes exclude certain living people but, on the other hand, extend the 'we' community to include people who are dead (leaders, heroes, ancestors), people in the future (posterity, the afterlife), imaginary beings who have never existed but who define who we are (gods, personifications), as well as admired living people (in Australia, that's mostly footballers, it seems).[6] 'We' even extend beyond humans (pets, symbolic animals, robots), and some statuary celebrates what it's made of as much as what's depicted (e.g. Lego).[7]

Through these faces and places, 'we' occupy the past and the future, as well as the present. Where and when 'we' stop is never a hard boundary; the semiotic border is always dynamic and contested in time as well as space. Its uncertainty can perhaps be measured by the sizeable investment devoted to reducing that uncertainty. Civic squares and parks, hospitals, galleries, museums, places of worship, monuments and statuary are all roped in to memorialize 'our' ancestors, representatives, powers, hopes and desires, such that 'we' include persons who are pure signs.[8]

Staged conflict

Civic memorialization is always collective, embodying the idea of citizens as a unitary group, without regard to what any one individual may think about that. But, by the same token, it is always exclusionary. In any urban environment where more than one group has claim to originality

[5]See Becky Alexis-Martin's article on the 'psychogeography' of the bomb: https://www.the guardian.com/science/brain-flapping/2017/aug/06/life-after-the-bomb-exploring-the-psychoge ography-of-hiroshima.
[6]See: http://www.abc.net.au/news/2018-08-02/why-do-footballers-get-all-the-statues-in-brisb ane/10060464; and: https://en.wikipedia.org/wiki/List_of_Australian_rules_football_statues.
[7]See: https://interestingengineering.com/15-of-the-best-sculptures-made-with-lego-bricks.
[8]Wikipedia has a revealing list of 'National Personifications': https://en.wikipedia.org/wiki/National_personification.

(extension into the past), the semiotics of monuments is necessarily political, expressive not of oneness but of difference, sometimes fiercely contested. Given that one of the chief characteristics of cities is heterogeneity, with overlayered systems, demographics and activities that promote mixtures of peoples and trade across demographic borders (Currid, 2008), there cannot be many cities where one identity represents everyone. Memorial objects simultaneously signify not only the 'we' community's identity but also those who are not 'we' but 'they'. The very process of constructing 'wedom' produces 'theydom' (Hartley, 1992). Traditionally, demographic differences could be erased (rhetorically) in what Ernesto Laclau and Chantal Mouffe (2001) have called the 'empty signifier' (Thomassen, 2016): the political leader – monarch, divinity, populist – as *all things to all people*.

In recent times, sculptural personifications have become democratized (the statues have got off their high horses), to show 'everyman/woman': the soldier, the worker, the girl. But such egalitarian signs also serve to accentuate the political aspect of 'our' unity because their signification is never 'empty'.

- Some versions of 'everyman' mask racist and exclusionary values, such as 'Silent Sam' at the University of North Carolina, Chapel Hill, which attracted the attention of 'fallist' activists (Cirillo, 2018).

- There are statues that enter into dialogue with others, such as 'Fearless Girl' (by Kristen Visbal) who 'stared down' the hypermasculine 'Charging Bull' of Wall Street (by Arturo Di Modica), on behalf of 'everywoman', for International Women's Day 2017.[9]

And there are radically inclusive signifiers. Perhaps surprisingly, one is located in London's Trafalgar Square, formerly the symbolic centre of Empire, where a previously unused plinth, installed when the Square was built in readiness for a future monarch or general, but empty for 150 years, now features successively different versions of 'we'. It has featured identities rarely given statuary form, including work *by* a disabled artist (Yinka Shonibare's 'Nelson's Ship in a Bottle') and a statue *of* a disabled artist ('Alison Lapper', by Marc Quinn).[10] Its curators claim it as *'probably the most famous public art commission in the world'*.[11]

---

[9]See: https://www.smh.com.au/business/workplace/defying-wall-street-why-statue-of-a-fearless-girl-is-staring-down-the-charging-bull-20170309-gutxer.html. The temporary installation, intended to last a week, stayed put for a year and was later moved to a new location: http://fortune.com/2018/03/01/fearless-girl-new-york-statue-moving-location-wall-street/.
[10]See: http://disabilityarts.online/magazine/opinion/fourth-plinth-raising-disability-issues-part-ii/. After its stint on the plinth, 'Nelson's Ship in a Bottle' was 'bought for the nation' and relocated to Greenwich.
[11]Source: https://www.london.gov.uk/what-we-do/fourth-plinth-past-commissions. https://www.theguardian.com/artanddesign/2018/mar/28/fourth-plinth-review-my-heart-is-in-my-mouth.

Another form of inclusiveness is the *Stolpersteine* ('stumbling blocks') project, initiated in 1992 by artist Gunter Demnig,[12] where cobblestone-sized brass plaques commemorate each individual victim of Nazi genocide in the street where they last lived freely. This is now claimed as 'the biggest decentralized monument in the world', with over 60,000 memorials across hundreds of cities in twenty-four European countries. Some of the *Stolpersteine* have been stolen; some cities refuse permission to install them.[13] In each case, the apparent permanency of a memorial is interrupted by conflict, dialogue, or design.

Thus, the apparent permanency of statements in marble, bronze and brass is illusory: urban semiosis is fundamentally dialogic, founded on difference, contestation and what Mouffe calls 'agonism': productive and engaged political conflict.[14] The city is a *theatre for staged conflict*, where communities and identities compete for semiotic and temporal as well as spatial accommodation, and where new ideas emerge along the edge of conflict, not in the identity or meaning of any one player.

Australia

Australia is one of world's most urbanized societies.[15] Yet it overlays an ancient and continuing culture that is the oldest in the world (Griffiths, 2018) and not at all urban in origin or mode. How to reconcile these opposites has been one of Australia's most intractable problems since European colonization. Historically, Australia is a recent, transplanted, experimental polity. Despite (or because of) this, it abounds in memorials, especially of pioneer settlers. Among those who made it big had been some who wanted to 'reconcile' the two populations – Indigenous and settler – by eliminating the former, directly by genocide (Tatz, 1999, 2017) or indirectly by assimilation and 'breeding out the black' (Neville, 1947) (Figure 9.2).

These people are destructive invaders to Aboriginal people; but still they overlook all who pass. So long as their actions in building the polity are unacknowledged, their stern gaze implicates all in the crimes committed to make it; these monuments become collective and representative, a *unifying* part of a national narrative that still excludes Aboriginality as part of who 'we' are.

---

[12]See: http://www.stolpersteine.eu/en/home/; and see: https://www.timesofisrael.com/munich-int roduces-new-holocaust-remembrance-plaques/.
[13]See: https://en.wikipedia.org/wiki/List_of_cities_by_country_that_have_stolpersteine; and see, for example: https://www.dw.com/en/20-years-of-stolpersteine/a-19252785.
[14]See: http://pavilionmagazine.org/chantal-mouffe-agonistic-democracy-and-radical-politics/.
[15]In 2018, 'over 85% of Australians lived in urban areas and nearly 70% lived in our capital cities, making Australia one of the world's most urbanised countries'. Source: http://www.population.net.au/.

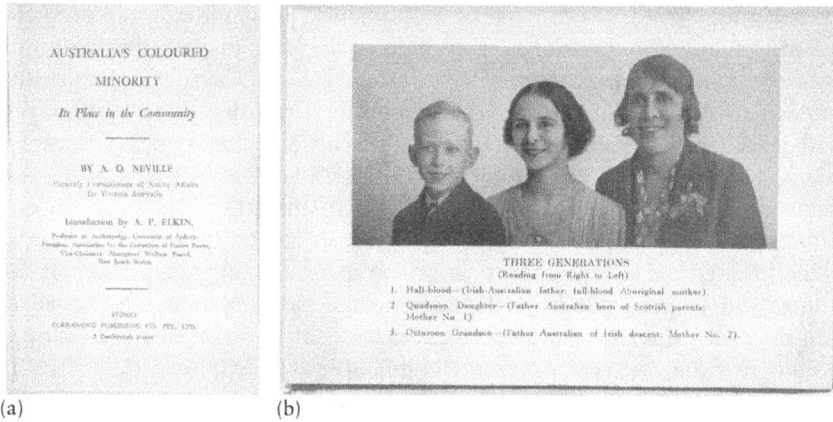

(a)   (b)

FIGURE 9.2 *'Breed out the black'*: A.O. Neville. Image: Museums Victoria. Public domain: https://collections.museumvictoria.com.au/items/1496210.

In the wake of international activism in South Africa and at Oxford University,[16] Australia 'woke' to fallism. Debate about the status of Cecil Rhodes also implicated Australia, whose Rhodes Scholars include some of its most prominent citizens. It was overdue. As historian Billy Griffiths observes, 'Australians tend to have an uneasy relationship with the history of this continent. Of the three strands of our national story – the Indigenous, settler and multicultural pasts – it is the first that we most struggle to accommodate' (2018: 2). So systematic had been the neglect of Indigenous perspectives that, in 1968, anthropologist W. E. H. Stanner called this a 'cult of forgetfulness' and 'the great Australian silence'. Fifty years later, historian Anna Clark (2018) recorded that plus ça change; although much had changed, nothing much had changed. Historiography came in with the colonists; it still has trouble with traditional oral modes of thought. Clark comments:

Indigenous histories are often relegated to 'memoir', 'story', 'family history', 'narratives of place' or 'political protest', rather than acknowledged as part of a disciplinary practice. And there is still a marked absence of Indigenous historiography in Australia's historical 'canon'. (Clark, 2018)

---

[16]'Rhodes must fall' originated in South Africa, from whence 'fallism' spilled over to Oxford University, where Rhodes Scholars from Australia still go. The statue of Rhodes (sculptor: Marion Walgate) was removed from the University of Cape Town (9 April 2015): https://commons.wikimedia.org/w/index.php?curid=48192374. Oxford University decided not to remove theirs: https://www.theguardian.com/education/2016/jan/28/cecil-rhodes-statue-will-not-be-removed--oxford-university.

As for public history, so for public monuments. They underrepresent to the point of silence the traditional custodians of the land. Instead, they continue to serve *demic conflict* (Hartley and Potts, 2014: 78) on behalf of just one version of Australian identity. The conflict is not just between settler and Indigenous memory; the way it is staged reveals differing modes of thought, a clue to which is discernible in Yuri Lotman's (1990: 245–53) distinction between literate and oral cultures. Applied to the arts of memory, on one side there is *literate performance*, written in stone and bronze as well as in more familiar media, seeking for 'laws' in the urban landscape, such that the future may be predicted from the documented past and uncertainty curbed. On the other, there is *oral performance*, or what Lotman calls 'the cultural round of ritual, sacrifice, fortune-telling, songs and dances' (1990: 252), where meaning is not found in texts (sacred or scientific), but is inscribed in place and time (landscapes and periodic changes).

In the literate world, *one truth must prevail*. In an oral world, especially when groups encounter one another along their mutual borders, *difference may be danced* (Flinders, 1814, Vol 1, Ch3; Nind, 1831: 44; Scott, 2010); an encounter commonly known in Australia as a *corroboree*.[17]

'Grow up idiots'

In August 2017, graffiti appeared on statues in Sydney's Hyde Park. Slogans on James Cook's plinth read 'CHANGE THE DATE' and 'NO PRIDE IN GENOCIDE'. 'Change the date' refers to a campaign to move Australia Day from January 26, anniversary of the First Fleet's arrival in 1788, when Governor Arthur Philip set up the penal colony of New South Wales. 'No pride in genocide' refers to the impact of colonization on Indigenous Australians.

One of the things that made this newsworthy was the connection to fallism internationally. The ABC reported: 'Statues of historical figures have been a particularly divisive issue in America, where Confederate monuments have been the scene of protests in the past month.'[18] But what made it even more newsworthy was the local political reaction. The then Prime Minister Malcolm Turnbull, a Rhodes Scholar, was quoted in the same ABC report:

Today's vandalism of statues of James Cook and Lachlan Macquarie is part of a deeply disturbing and totalitarian campaign to not just

[17]Corroboree 2000 was a peak event of the National Reconciliation Council: http://www5.aus tlii.edu.au/au/orgs/car/m2000/1.htm.
[18]See: http://www.abc.net.au/news/2017-08-26/australia-day-argument-intensifies-as-vandals-hit-captain-cook/8845064.

> challenge our history but to deny it and obliterate it. This is what Stalin did. When he fell out with his henchmen he didn't just execute them, they were removed from all official photographs they became non-persons, banished not just from life's mortal coil but from memory and history itself. Tearing down or defacing statues of our colonial era explorers and governors is not much better than that. (Turnbull, Facebook, 26 August 2017)

Prominent right-wing commentators were not slow to take up the baton. The 'statue haters' became a pretext for Andrew Bolt, in a syndicated column, to assert an opposing 'truth about history', throwing the concept of the 'great silence' back into the faces of Aboriginal commentators who had called for an end to it (*The West Australian*, 31 August 2017) (Figure 9.3).

In turn, this provocation was answered by opponents, including Indigenous professor Hannah McGlade from Curtin University (where I work) and other signatories, who protested to the *West Australian*, an action which was itself the subject of a news item in *WA Today*. Their letter wondered what Bolt's column had to do with Western Australia and

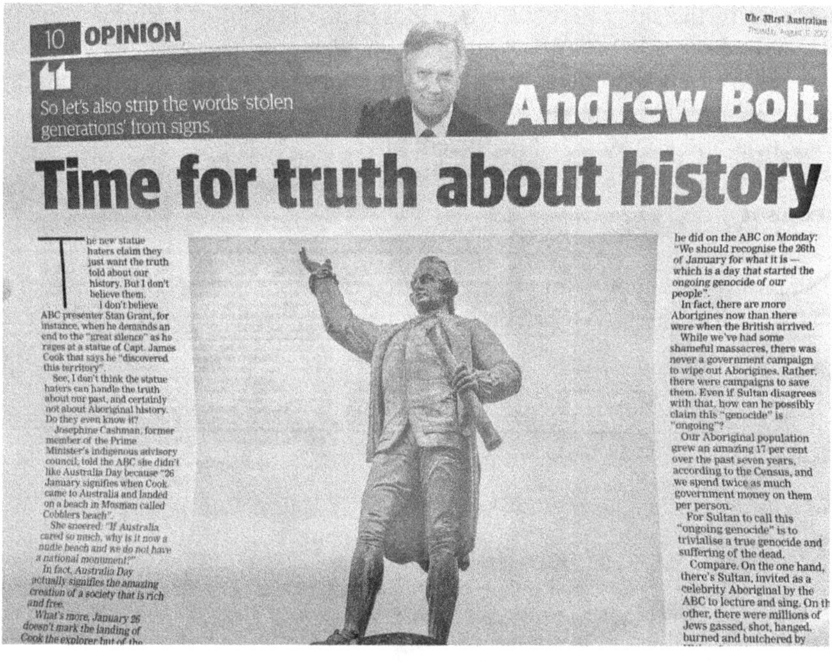

10 OPINION

So let's also strip the words 'stolen generations' from signs.

Andrew Bolt

Time for truth about history

The new statue haters claim they just want the truth told about our history. But I don't believe them.

I don't believe ABC presenter Stan Grant, for instance, when he demands an end to the "great silence" as he rages at a statue of Capt. James Cook that says he "discovered this territory".

See, I don't think the statue haters can handle the truth about our past, and certainly not about Aboriginal history. Do they even know it?

Josephine Cashman, former member of the Prime Minister's indigenous advisory council, told the ABC she didn't like Australia Day because "26 January signifies when Cook came to Australia and landed on a beach in Mosman called Cobblers beach".

She sneered: "If Australia cared so much, why is it now a nudie beach and we do not have a national monument?"

In fact, Australia Day actually signifies the amazing creation of a society that is rich and free.

What's more, January 26 doesn't mark the landing of Cook the explorer but of the

he did on the ABC on Monday: "We should recognise the 26th of January for what it is — which is a day that started the ongoing genocide of our people".

In fact, there are more Aborigines now than there were when the British arrived.

While we've had some shameful massacres, there was never a government campaign to wipe out Aborigines. Rather, there were campaigns to save them. Even if Sultan disagrees with that, how can he possibly claim this "genocide" is "ongoing"?

Our Aboriginal population grew an amazing 17 per cent over the past seven years, according to the Census, and we spend twice as much government money on them per person.

For Sultan to call this "ongoing genocide" is to trivialise a true genocide and suffering of the dead.

Compare. On the one hand, there's Sultan, invited as a celebrity Aboriginal by the ABC to lecture and sing. On th other, there were millions of Jews gassed, shot, hanged, burned and butchered by

FIGURE 9.3 *'Time for truth': Andrew Bolt. West Australian, 31 August 2017.*

described his views as 'a distortion of history and arguably a form of racial propaganda'.[19]

A further response in kind came in the lead-up to the next Australia Day, as reported in *The Guardian*: 'Pink paint was dumped on Cook's head at St Kilda [Melbourne] on Thursday, with the words "no pride" painted beneath his feet, along with the Aboriginal flag' (25 January 2018). This report made explicit mention of the earlier episode in Sydney, reproducing a remark of Scott Morrison, then Federal Treasurer and later prime minister, who had tweeted:

> A national insult & disgrace. Does not keep one indigenous child safe, in school or end up in a job. Grow up idiots. (Morrison, Twitter: 26 August 2017)[20]

The statues, the graffiti and the accompanying media commentary took turns in a public debate, but the utterances remained *performative* rather than *communicative*; part of the *theatre of conflict* we call politics, but at the same time perpetuating exclusionary rhetoric. The nation's two most senior politicians accused activists (fellow citizens) of Stalinism and told them to 'grow up idiots', thereby rhetorically consigning their adversaries *beyond the pale* of any 'we' community. 'We' and 'they' remain firmly opposed. The government's divisive 'infatuation' with Cook (Jones, 2019) soon announced a new $3m memorial to Captain Cook, funded by the Treasurer, and a $50m upgrade to the site where Captain Cook made landfall, which happens to be in the Federal constituency of Cook, held by the Treasurer (later prime minister).[21] Senior public figures have not opened an 'agonistic' dialogue that might result in mutual accommodation. For that, you have to cross the continent and go to Fremantle (where I live).

Lest We Forget

The most prominent monument in Fremantle is on top of a hill overlooking the port city, where, as the main bronze plaque (unveiled 2010) records, it is

---

[19]See: https://www.watoday.com.au/national/western-australia/perth-academics-lash-the-west-australian-for-publishing-attack-on-aboriginal-people-20170912-gyfsbr.html.

[20]Source: https://www.theguardian.com/australia-news/2018/jan/25/captain-cook-statue-vandalised-in-melbourne-before-australia-day.

[21]The NSW and Federal governments agreed joint funding for redevelopment of Botany Bay, including a new Cook memorial for the 250th anniversary of his landfall in 2020. 'This is the place where our ancient Australian story began a new chapter that has led us to the free, peaceful and prosperous nation we are today', a joint statement from the two governments said: see: http://sjm.ministers.treasury.gov.au/media-release/042-2018/; https://www.smh.com.au/politics/federal/sydney-to-get-new-captain-cook-memorial-as-part-of-50m-revamp-20180428-p4zc64.html. See also: https://www.theguardian.com/australia-news/2018/apr/28/sydney-to-get-new-3m-captain-cook-memorial-in-inclusive-project.

the first Australian object that will meet the eyes of travellers coming from the Westward and it will serve for all time as a dignified, silent, and reverent reminder of the stress and strain through which the peoples of the Empire were called upon to pass, as well as a standing memorial to the sons of Fremantle.[22]

This passage may need some decoding for modern readers. It dates from a time (1928) when all visitors and settlers to Australia arrived 'from the Westward', by ship from London and the Cape. Thus it memorializes all the 'peoples of the Empire', not just citizens of Fremantle. Modern sensibilities may be jarred to see that neither the empire nor Fremantle seemed to include any 'daughters', only sons; and that Aboriginal people, who were not 'travellers coming from the westward', don't rate a mention. Instead, the monument invokes Rudyard Kipling's famous line 'Lest we forget',[23] lining itself up with the English-speaking world at large, where that phrase had become the common signifier of remembrance for all who died in (imperial but not colonizing) wars.

But, be it noted, restitution has been made for both of these omissions in later additions to the memorial. There is a plaque 'in memory of the Aboriginal men and women who have served their country in its hour of need. In so doing they helped build a nation' (unveiled 2001). And there is a statue in 'tribute to the families of those who served' and to 'those left behind' (unveiled 2009), personified as a woman and two children, one of whom is certainly a daughter (Figure 9.4).

These adjustments, in what many would regard as Fremantle's most important monument, are important for what follows: initial exclusion, belated but explicit inclusion, 'lest we forget'. However, it remains a site of protest, including an incident in June 2018 when one member of the public caught another emptying a bucket over part of the memorial. When confronted, the 'perpetrator' answered: 'that's my poo', and 'that's my prerogative'. A man was later 'sent for a mental health assessment'.[24]

How, then, to deal with a much more provocative monument, located deep in the heart of Fremantle?[25] Known as the Explorers Monument (unveiled 1913), it commemorates five men of colonial Western Australia: three

[22]The plaque quotes J. S. Battye, State Librarian, whose biographer notes: 'Battye's physical height, commanding presence, unfailing self-confidence, impressive knowledge of relevant facts and his increasing skill in manipulating both large audiences and committees were valuable assets in public life' (http://adb.anu.edu.au/biography/battye-james-sykes-5156).
[23]See: https://en.wikipedia.org/wiki/Recessional_(poem).
[24]See: https://thewest.com.au/news/crime/faeces-thrown-over-fremantle-monument-hill-war-memo rial-ng-b88877183z; and: https://thewest.com.au/news/crime/man-questioned-over-faeces-at-f remantles-monument-hill-war-memorial-ng-b88878926z.
[25]See: http://monumentaustralia.org.au/themes/people/discovery/display/60482-maitland-brown-memorial-explorers-monument.

(a)   (b)

FIGURE 9.4 (a) 'They helped build a nation.' (b) Monument Hill, Fremantle.

whites, F. K. Panter, J. R. Harding and W. H. Goldwyer, who died in 1864 while exploring in the Kimberley region; Maitland Brown, who led a search that became a punitive raid resulting in a retaliatory massacre of up to twenty Aboriginal people; and the fifth, G. J. Brockman, a pastoralist and 'fellow bush wanderer', who paid for the monument, on which he is prominently named and depicted (Figure 9.5).

The memorial plaque is couched in uncompromising terms. Calling the Kimberly region 'terra incognita' (unknown to whites), it proclaims that these 'earliest explorers' were 'attacked at night by treacherous natives' and 'murdered'. It offers 'an appreciative token of remembrance' to Maitland Brown, 'one of the pioneer pastoralists and premier politicians of this state'. The 'intrepid leader of the Government search and punitive party' 'recovered at great risk and danger' the 'sad relics of the ill-fated three'.[26] The plaque concludes with the warrior's farewell: 'Lest We Forget'.

What the 'punitive party' did is not detailed on the memorial but was described by Maitland Brown in a long dispatch published in the *Perth Gazette and W.A. Times*:

The fighting men, about 25 in number, danced forward. I galloped through them and, in passing, shot the man who had taken the lead in

---

[26]See also: http://members.iinet.net.au/~perthdps/graves/bio-27.htm.

FIGURE 9.5 *The Explorers Monument, Fremantle. The crowning bust is that of Maitland Brown, perpetrator.*

directing their manoeuvres. I wheeled my horse and fired the remaining barrel of my carbine at three in a line, and drew my revolver; Williams arriving dashed in, divided their attention, and did good execution. Messrs. Burges and Francisco also joined a few moments after, and the fight went on without any sound but the incessant report of our arms. In ten minutes all was over; six remained upon the plain dead and dying, and about twelve others stand little chance of recovery. The natives stood their ground with the savage, though not cool, pluck of an Englishman. (26 May 1865, 2–4)[27]

---

[27]Source, Trove. The account was published over two issues of the paper. See: https://trove.nla.go v.au/newspaper/article/3751072; https://trove.nla.gov.au/newspaper/article/3750769/721663.

Not surprisingly, during the 2017 fallism episode, this notorious monument attracted renewed attention. A Fremantle City Councillor, Sam Wainwright, said 'residents had raised concerns' about it: 'I don't think the statue should be destroyed but often they better belong in museums', he said. 'Do we really want people directly responsible for what we now consider to be atrocities to be displayed in … public places?' (*Perth Now*, 27 August 2017).

'A contingent and contested narrative'

However, a dialogic alternative to the politics of fallism had already been found, right here. In 1994, a new plaque had been added, 'erected by people who found the monument before you offensive':

> No mention is made of the right of Aboriginal people to defend their land or of the history of provocation which led to the explorers' deaths. The punitive party mentioned here ended in the deaths of somewhere around twenty Aboriginal people. The whites were well-armed and equipped and none of their party was killed or wounded. This plaque is in memory of … all other Aboriginal people who died during the invasion of their country. LEST WE FORGET – MAPA JARRIA-NYALAKU

As Jennifer Harris (2010) and others have noted (Stevens and Franck, 2016:189–90), this 'raw place' encourages political dialogue:

> The memorial has the effect of encouraging performance from its viewers – or vandalism – as the newer plaque is often stolen; on one occasion the head of Maitland Brown disappeared from the top of the monument. It is not, therefore an ossified memorial, or a place where nothing happens. This is a vivid and active place in which the conflicting versions of history are played out in the middle of the city's most popular park. (Harris, 2010: 3).

Its continuing capacity for civic engagement was demonstrated again in 2017: two ABC Kimberley journalists took up the story:

> A plaque giving the Indigenous point of view has pride of place. … Unlike historically contentious statues in other parts of Australia and the United States, supporters of the addition – placed 81 years after the original – say the monument now stands for reconciliation rather than division. (ABC Kimberley, 2017)[28]

---

[28]'The controversial statue that was added to, not torn down or vandalised'. By Vanessa Mills and Ben Collins, ABC Kimberley (29 Aug 2017): http://www.abc.net.au/news/2017-08-29/explorers-monument-added-to-not-torn-down-or-vandalised/8853224.

The story featured Jimmy Edgar, 'a Karrajarri man whose great-grandmother survived the punitive killings'. His brother Joe Edgar had worked on the plaque that gave what he calls 'the other side of the story'. Also interviewed is Bruce Scates, professor of history at the Australian National University, who 'worked with Mr Edgar's brother on the addition of the plaque'. In a separate article for *The Conversation*, Scates (2017) praised the monument's 'dialogical memorialisation, where one view of the past takes issue with another and history is seen, not as some final statement, but a contingent and contested narrative', concluding: 'Perhaps, at this critical juncture in our history, Fremantle suggests the way forward.'

Scates supplied a photograph of the 1994 installation (Figure 9.6), showing Aboriginal dancers from Pinjarra, which is not in the Kimberley but in nearby Noongar country, but which suffered its own massacre in 1834.[29] The unveiling of the counter-memorial thereby united local with Kimberley Aboriginal people and both with settlers, in a ritual of mutual contact: the dance.

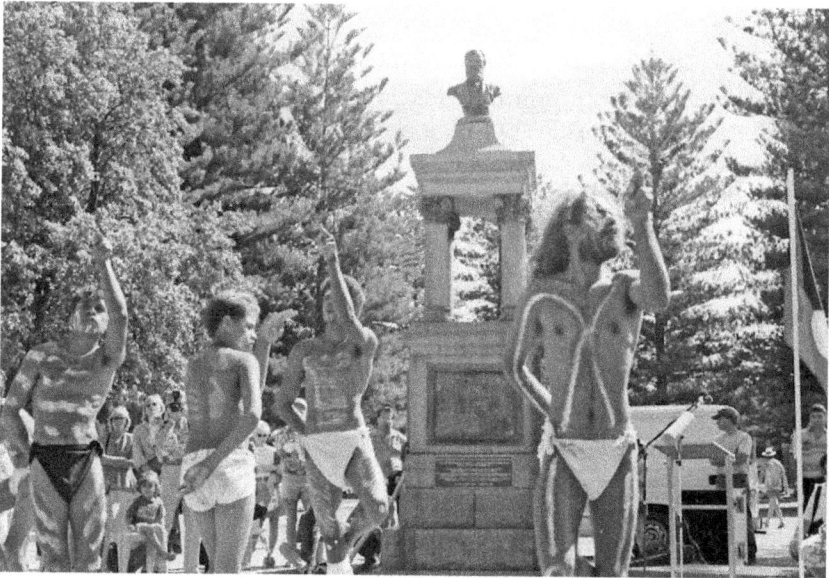

FIGURE 9.6 *'Reconciliation rather than division': Aboriginal dancers from Pinjarra perform at the unveiling of the counter-memorial in 1994. Photo by Prof Bruce Scates (ANU) used with permission.*

---

[29]See: https://en.wikipedia.org/wiki/Pinjarra_massacre.

Multiplatform literacy for urban semiosis

Returning to the themes of urban fallism, the discussion above suggests that the important outcome of 'dialogical memorialization' is that it encourages *literacy* in urban semiosis across multiple platforms. As this chapter has shown, a statue or monument is most actively significant when in conversation with other media, especially journalism (Hartley, 2008), but also dance.

One of the benefits of living in a city is that it is a location for the *intensification* and *compression* of semiosis within larger networks of human communication:

- Intensification is where a given semiotic form – journalism, or statuary – is more *abundant*, more *diverse*, more *elaborated* and more hotly *contested* than is evident elsewhere. It is also more *institutionalized*, proliferating where there is an 'arms race' among competing organizations and occupational specialisms. It is the vital precondition for the growth of knowledge.

- Compression is where many semiotic forms, practices and groups overlap, such that different languages, occupations, ethnicities, political affiliations, lifestyles and knowledge-systems – different interests among producers and contending parties among users – live cheek by jowl, jostling among the crowd in such a way as to promote cross-border contact, translation and admixture among groups. It is the vital precondition for the emergence of new ideas and systems.

Literacy in these circumstances means the ability to navigate incommensurate systems, and to follow elaborate but changing relationships. It accrues to those who can 'read the city' by translating codes across media, spaces, times and conflicts. Attaining, improving and practising such literacy is a chief attractant to city life. Some citizens take their literacy across from 'reading' to 'writing', via street art, graffiti and certain types of direct intervention. Often the 'writers' are treated as part of 'theydom'. But the city is the stage for such conflicts, and eventually it may celebrate as art what was once condemned as vandalism.[30] As this chapter has shown, it may eventually do the same for history. No statues have been removed in Perth, but a sign of change is the decision to name an important new central square after Yagan, hero of Noongar resistance to white settlement, and to install a nine-metre statue, *Wirin* (by Noongar artist Tjyllyungoo/Lance Chadd), whose design 'signifies our people's longevity in the spirit of our Culture' (Figure 9.7).[31]

---

[30]See: https://peterbarrett.com.au/2018/02/06/the-evolution-of-street-art-in-melbourne/.
[31]See: https://www.mra.wa.gov.au/see-and-do/yagan-square/attractions/wirin.

FIGURE 9.7 *Yagan Square, Perth. This photo by the author features visiting Estonian academics Prof Indrek Ibrus and Dr Maarja Ojamaa. It was exhibited on Yagan Square's Digital Tower in March 2019 as part of the celebration of #YearAtYagan: https://www.facebook.com/YaganSquare/posts/1041119576087017.*

Cities *teach urban literacy* through staged drama and stories in space and time, functioning to project the city's own meaning and survival – its knowledge – into the future. Thus, Australian cities have joined the global conversation about how 'we' might need to adjust our semiosis in order to accommodate difference among urban populations; shifting from 'literate' struggles over whose truth should prevail to 'oral' performance of dialogue between opposites, participating in the dance-diplomacy of the *corroboree*, in order to learn new moves in mutual accommodation.

10

Reading magazines:

Taking *Death Cab for Cutie* – from shed to Dalston

Magazine research is like Montreal – diverse on many levels.
(MIGLENA STERNADORI, 2014)

As Chapter 7's 'close reading' of *Vogue* may have hinted, I'm a long-term fan of magazines, which I enjoy without regard to the niceties of demographic targeting, having enjoyed (and published articles about) high-end photography, fashion and style magazines aimed at women as much as political and current affairs weeklies, entertainment and specialist magazines, and 'found' periodicals from earlier times (under the lino, in the skip) that otherwise would have dissolved into forgotten landfill. Magazines allow for longer-form writing compared with newspapers, they glory in pictorial opulence even as they document daily life, rivalling cinema for capital investment in images, and they cover not only the highways but also the bizarre ways of modern life.

Most of the titles I enjoy have gone bust, gone digital or gone global. So why another chapter on magazines? This one is devoted not so much to the form as to the reader. In that context, it does not take the familiar trudge through the peaks and troughs of circulation metrics, but considers the readership of the form over a couple of centuries, seeking for the cultural function of magazines, which it finds in the process by which readers have been constructed and reconstructed as a *knowing subject*, whose *mediated subjectivity* – never uniform, always changing – is the story of modernity. Given the long timeframe, it is worth considering whether some kind of 'media effect' can be observed historically, as magazine literacy has armed readerships with the knowledge needed to 'turn the tables' on their own proprietors.

I. The shed

It could be said that that there's no such thing as a magazine – it's too chaotic, contingent and confused a term to stand as a category.[1] The word's Arabic linguistic origins lie in the storage of goods, especially military ordnance. Thus, the Parthenon was used as a magazine for Turkish explosives during the Ottoman occupation of Greece, with fatal effect on the Parthenon when, in 1687, a hostile Venetian shell blew it up.[2]

Around the same time – the 1600s – as Renaissance ideas settled into modern accumulation and the format of publishing started to standardize, the term was transferred metaphorically from analogue storehouse to printed miscellany, as a generic title for collections of heterogeneous items of interest or use to particular reader-sets. That trade innovation introduced a distinction between 'book' as a volume concerned with one topic and 'magazine' as a volume concerned with many. A further distinction between one-off books and periodical magazines followed. The magazine as form, content and industry evolved; it was not invented in one go.

The original usage of the word 'magazine', denoting any large shed, may seem a long way from *Wired*, *Dazed & Confused*, or *Charlie Hedbo*. But thinking of a magazine as a storehouse may still prove helpful for *placing* 'periodical publications' as we known them. For any centre of mixed population (a city, or country), imagine a distributed network of warehouses, some with specialist contents (gunpowder), others with general goods (department stores), standing ready for users to visit when they need a particular item. Such storehouses are an efficient coordination mechanism for the distribution of specialist and novelty items for differentiated demographics among heterogeneous populations. That in turn defines the magazine format.

Sheds have to be located close to where they will be needed by users, but not so close as to intrude on residential space. They don't have to originate

---

[1]One way to gauge just how little common ground there is in terms of content is to contrast different 'top 10' lists of magazines, such as those based on circulation (e.g. http://gazetter eview.com/2016/08/top-10-best-selling-magazines-world/; or http://www.trendingtopmost.com /worlds-popular-list-top-10/2017-2018-2019-2020-2021/entertainment/most-read-magazine s-world-best-selling-famous-newspapers-cheapest-expensive/), compared with those selected by editorial taste (http://www.theworldsbestever.com/category/magazines-2/; or http://www.them ontrealreview.com/world-best-magazines.php).
[2]See: http://www.ancient.eu/parthenon/.

in the place where they are sold. They may be organized as part of a state apparatus (ordnance shed) or a market economy (Amazon); they may be wholesale (an agricultural barn) or retail (IKEA). It is worth recalling that in many European languages the word 'magazine' refers directly to shops and stores, while periodical publications are called something else (*revista, périodique*, etc.) Despite the seeming exoticism of Cyrillic script, the words 'magazine' and 'journal' are the same in Russian as in English. But a магазин in Russia is something you can walk into: it's a shed. If you want to buy a magazine while you're in there, you'll have to ask for a журнал [journal].

Keeping in mind the built form, it can be seen that print or online magazines are still performing a cultural function of the same type. The contents of each title may differ, but at a higher level of integration they are a type of 'novelty bundling' service (Potts, 2011), making available to a dispersed public various semiotic and knowledge resources that are too specialized or uneconomic for households to keep at home, or sometimes too risky (politics and porn are restricted items). The thing about warehouses is that notwithstanding who owns them or what they contain, their cultural function is the same. Different stores keep different stuff (D. Miller, 2009) for different users. They keep stuff dry for when you need it. The main issue that needs further thought is about who exactly 'you' might be.

Magazines as metaphorical sheds full of words and pictures continue their time-honoured function of storing miscellaneous stuff against its use, but because this is now the realm of semiotic representation, language and sense-making, this 'stuff' is best conceived not as 'goods' but as 'knowledge', which involves people and institutions as well as texts and forms. People notoriously don't know what they don't know,[3] so 'needing' any item of semiosis rarely precedes supply: you don't know you want *Vogue* or *Grazia* or the *New Statesman* until it's under your nose; and you don't know you want to know what is inside any issue until you open it, the surprise being part of the pleasure of keeping up.

Magazines are located at the semiotic equivalent of the 'edge of town' – the edge of attention (Citton, 2017) – so readers must make an effort to visit, and magazines must use the store and its storefront to attract and hold readers for their particular category of difference. The metaphor of 'seduction' is apt here, despite its misleading history (Tilley, 2012). Magazines' cultural function focuses on forming random individual readers into readership *groups*, more or less ordered, and frequently connected among themselves through other institutions or cultural practices. These

---

[3]In psychology it's called the Dunning-Kruger effect: https://en.wikipedia.org/wiki/Dunni ng–Kruger_effect; in politics it may be called the Rumsfeld effect – 'there are also unknown unknowns – the ones we don't know we don't know. And if one looks throughout the history of our country and other free countries, it is the latter category that tend to be the difficult ones': http://archive.defense.gov/Transcripts/Transcript.aspx?TranscriptID=2636.

range from special interests (craft, hobbies, music, sport, business, etc.) to giant abstractions – or 'fictions' – based on religion, nation, gender, age, class, etc. Over time, readerships in turn use their shared consciousness of the group, sustained in part by identity-signalling in magazines, to exercise agency *as groups*.

Circulation

When investigating magazines and other media, scholarship has routinely adopted the point of view of the proprietor, editor, journalist, writer, artist, photographer, etc. These occupations make the object for which demand is thereby created. However, producers' intentions – commercial or imperial advancement, the salvation of souls or the improvement of selves (Oakeshott, 1975: 263–3) – tell us little about what readers use magazines for, once acquired, and how that works within a larger cultural context.

Focusing exclusively on the producer, as media research routinely does, results in a very skewed 'model' of magazines. The 'group' being created is merely a market, shorn of all its cultural, semiotic or political connectivity. Agency, causation and power cluster at one pole of a polarized system: it's all about ownership and control. There's not much left at the other pole. Readers are reduced to little more than a behavioural effect of causal agency located somewhere much further up the value chain. All that's needed is to set the marketing department loose on them.

Media scholarship inherited this skewed way of thinking from both behavioural science (United States) and political economy (Europe). Both traditions saw centralized, top-down, command-and-control, power-hungry media organizations seeking to *amass* readers as tokens in another game entirely: that of gaining commercial or political power (Carey, 2000). It seemed acceptable to carry on using this model of communication throughout the industrial era because of the radical asymmetry between those, predominantly men, who made money (owners) and those, predominantly families, women and children, who made meanings (readers). Looked at through the lens of behavioural political economy, and following a linear sender-receiver model of communication, readers (in the mass) were there for the economic gain of proprietors or the political gain of partisans. Inevitably, once 'seduced' into the metaphorical shed, readers were reduced to a mere number: *circulation*, that being the currency of power and influence for producers. What more was there to worry about?

It has transpired that there was quite a lot to worry about. Technological changes that are now at the centre of everyone's attention destroyed the asymmetry between producer and consumer (not at a stroke, but in principle), by lowering the cost of publication effectively to zero, at least for those with access to computers or mobile devices, now numbering in the billions, more than half of all humans.[4] In principle, everyone who posts a comment or sends an email is a publisher; everyone who uploads a photo or text is a journalist; anyone who wants to find something out can turn to an app or browser; and anyone looking for reading matter across heterogeneous subjects can do so, at almost infinite scale, without turning a single magazine cover. Suddenly, 'readers' became 'users'. They used online and social media for their own purposes. Individually and as groups they made culture – that is, sense (meanings and new language), identity (personal and group), consciousness (of self, other and cosmos) and knowledge (informal know-how and formal disciplines).

The term 'user' was not available in the days of industrial mass communication. It comes from computer culture. Its value lies in the presumption, built into the concept itself, that the 'end user' retains agency. Users *do* something, from utilizing a ready-made feature (copying) or making something new (creating). They are linked through technology into a system or network in which they are 'nodes' of agency (Barabási, 2002), not end-points of a value chain. Further, their digital activity could be tracked, unlike the act of reading itself. Suddenly, *circulation* includes not just consumers but also producers and makers: it signifies a network – in an older but still necessary idiom, a *class* (see Chapter 12).

What were readers 'using' through the long decades of industrial mass media? They were making meaning and growing knowledge, both their own and that of the systems they used. Unfortunately for scholars, these are fleeting, fugitive objects for analysis, extremely hard to recover. To reach them, you need a model of communication that owes more to language and literary studies than to political economy and linear cause-effect.

II. 'Reading' magazines

One way of achieving that result is not to use the usual behavioural disciplinary methods but personal biography, stories from life, or what is sometimes now called auto-ethnography, where it is possible to smuggle life and story into science and method (and vice versa). This was the route taken by Richard Hoggart (1957), the first critic to 'read' magazines as a meaningful part of culture. Hoggart didn't consider magazines as a category

---

[4]"More than half of the world's population now [2017] uses the internet. More than half the world now uses a smartphone. Almost two-thirds of the world's population now has a mobile phone. More than half of the world's web traffic now comes from mobile phones. More than half of all mobile connections around the world are now "broadband".' Source: https://weareso cial.com/special-reports/digital-in-2017-global-overview. At the same time, more than half of the world's population live in cities. Source: http://www.un.org/en/development/desa/populat ion/publications/pdf/urbanization/the_worlds_cities_in_2016_data_booklet.pdf.

(the shed), but only in relation to his own particular interest in who used them (a class).

Those following in his footsteps built on his example, to investigate the meaningfulness of magazines for particular readerships – girls, teens and women in particular, from Angela McRobbie's early work on *Jackie* (1978), via Anne Krisman's 'radiator girls' (1987), to Megan Le Masurier's studies of *Cleo* (2009, 2011). These offer nuanced readings of how reading, culture, knowledge and identity intersect, and startling insights into how magazines forge readerships into self-knowing 'imagined communities' (Anderson, 1991).

It is hard to project this approach back in time or across cultures. Anderson's much cited 'imagined community' is an artefact of reading itself, in the here and now. It's also abstract enough for ambiguity if not incoherence to ensue: the community that each reader 'imagines' as the collective 'we' may differ among readers of a single publication. 'We' might be imagined in terms of nation, city, class, gender, age, market, taste-culture or political allegiance, and it's a rare community where these demographics don't overlap and contradict as well as confirm each other. Meanwhile, the same household or person is likely to attend to an array of magazines that interpellate different 'we'-groups, such that any notion of a unified self is shattered (just read the variety of horoscopes in any month).

Although it is not easy to provide evidence for the cultural role magazines may have played in turning large populations into organized readerships, there's no doubt that it's happening at scale. The individual uses to which they were put are manifold. The line of causation from text to knowledge and action is indirect. It hardly seems possible to trace each grain of influence from an original trickle of textual causation to the wide, amorphous alluvial plain of everyday associated life, especially when everyone involved is dead. Unsurprisingly, the general field of 'reading studies' is sparse, scattered (Cavallo and Chartier, 1999) and often personal, even when offered as a general history (Manguel, 1997). Compared with the history of the book (an object), reading (an act) is an appendage (e.g. Finkelstein and McCleery, 2002).

Hoggart

It was not until about 150 years after popular periodicals began to make political and social waves in industrializing Europe, first as the precursor to the newspaper and then in their own right, that any scholar thought to study how their internal imaginative world meshed with the culture of their readers, for good and ill. Richard Hoggart's *Uses of Literacy: Aspects of Working-Class Life with Special Reference to Publications and Entertainments* was published in 1957. When Penguin republished this landmark book in their

Modern Classics series fifty years later, they lopped off the part of the original subtitle that made 'special reference to publications and entertainments' (McGrath, 2010). The shortened subtitle, 'aspects of working-class life', may leave the impression that here is a work on the sociology of class. But in fact it is written in the tradition of literary criticism (Owen, 2007), where evidence is not gathered from anthropological observation of the reader but from the literary organization, expression and imaginative truth of the text.

Here, Hoggart was on to something new. He asked what popular publications are *for*, not as economic or industrial products but in relation to the inner lives of class-based readerships. The major innovation was not the application of Hoggart's left-Leavisite Lit Crit to popular culture, startling though that was. It was the way he explained the 'uses of literacy' in cultural (group) rather than individualistic (behavioural) terms. Hoggart saw reading as a *class practice*, undertaken in the cultural environment of the urban industrial home, street and neighbourhood. This is what shaped working-class families and loyalties, what they loved and loathed, at once produced by and producing the sense of solidarity and difference that marked 'people like us'. Hoggart's insight was that mass literacy was important at group level, the 'effects' of mass media being felt on class culture, not on individual behaviour. He took a first step towards a 'reading' of modern, urban everyday life, with a view to understanding what it meant, how it was changing and what industrial-scale publication had to do with that.[5]

To his contemporaries, Hoggart was an 'angry young man'. He was placed alongside a new generation of literary intellectuals from working- or middle-class backgrounds. The Angry Young Men were named after John Osborne's play *Look Back in Anger* (1956). They included novelists like John Braine (*Room at the Top*, 1957) and Alan Sillitoe (*Saturday Night and Sunday Morning*, 1958); and playwrights like Arnold Wesker (*Chicken Soup with Barley*, 1958). These writers were scornful of upper-class privilege, working-class restriction and welfare meritocracy alike. They were disdainful of 'the Establishment', even while preoccupied with their own upward social mobility.[6] The successful movie of *Look Back in Anger* (1959) starred Richard Burton, rising Shakespearean actor and son of a

---

[5]Such an enterprise could not be accomplished in one book. It required an entire field – cultural studies – to acquit the project. As ever in the way of these things, by the time cultural studies reached maturity it had forgotten what it set out to find, and Hoggart occasionally despaired of it.

[6]See: https://www.britannica.com/topic/Angry-Young-Men. See also: https://www.theguardian.com/books/2007/feb/24/society on Hoggart as 'angry young man'. The film of *Look Back in Anger* contains the observation: 'You're hurt' [referring to the protagonist's middle-class father-in-law] 'because everything's changed, and Jimmy's hurt' [referring to the working-class (but college-educated) protagonist] because everything's stayed the same'. The line sums up the sense of being caught between two equally unappealing worlds that marks the 'angry young men' and the 'kitchen-sink' domestic drama of the time.

Welsh miner, living embodiment of the explosive and often toxic tension between 'class' and 'culture' (see also Chapter 8).[7]

Death Cab for Cutie

What made Hoggart's analysis of 'publications and entertainments' especially compelling, connecting it to these literary figures, was that its literary criticism was – in fact – *fiction*. Chatto's legal advice was that proprietors would undoubtedly sue if Hoggart quoted mass publications directly or named the names of real culprits. At a very late stage – around the time he was persuaded to change the title of the book from the intended '*Abuses* of Literacy' to the inspired '*Uses*' – Hoggart went through the manuscript and fictionalized the textual examples of 'mass art' he wanted to critique.

Here, he departed from the strict empiricism of modernist Leavisite criticism, which sought objectivity by narrowing the critical enterprise to the literary 'object' itself – the text. Left with no empirical object to analyse, Hoggart entered the imaginative space of the novelist,[8] where the tension between the values of hard-won class culture and the attractions of the new could be given full voice. As a recent observer has put it:

> The punch-up-prone and sex-strewn 'Yank mags' that have such a devitalising effect on British teendom may be morally disgusting, but Hoggart the literary critic, working his way through Sweetie, Take It Hot and The Lady Takes a Dive, is forced to concede that their high-octane, sub-Hemingway, jump-on-his-testicles prose style isn't altogether to be despised. (Taylor, 2017)

It turned out he was really good at it. One of Hoggart's fictional coinages was a pulp-fiction crime magazine called *Death Cab for Cutie*. No such magazine existed, but the title's apt compression of sex (cutie), violence (death), modern urban mobility (cab) and cool but cruel insouciance (American idiom) has led to its own peculiar immortalization. It lives on in the name of an American 'moody emo-rock outfit' specializing in teenage-

---

[7]Burton's obituary in the *New York Times* set the tone for the working-class boy-made-good by describing Burton as 'A plump, roughshod primitive who spoke no English up to the age of 10'. Burton's native tongue was Welsh (http://www.nytimes.com/learning/general/onthisday /bday/1110.html). He 'made good', reigning for a time as the most famous man in the world (simultaneously with fellow Welshman Tom Jones), but the effect of his energy and talent on himself was toxic, a 'career' already rehearsed by fellow Welshman Dylan Thomas, and reflexively reprised – but not re-lived – by Anthony Hopkins (see: https://www.theguardian.c om/film/2018/may/26/anthony-hopkins-most-nonsense-most-lie-lear).
[8]'Like E P Thompson, another icon of the cultural studies brigade, he is supposed to have regretted that he never became a novelist' (Taylor, 2017).

angst music. The band is fronted by Ben Gibbard, better known in the celebrity press for having briefly been married to actor Zooey Deschanel. Commenting on the unlikely band name, Gibbard told Chicago's *Time Out* magazine:

> Thank God for Wikipedia. At least now, people don't have to ask me where the fucking name came from every interview. (23 August 2011)[9]

Wikipedia explains:

> Gibbard took the band name from the song 'Death Cab for Cutie' written by Neil Innes and Vivian Stanshall and performed by their group the Bonzo Dog Doo-Dah Band. The song was performed by the Bonzos in the Beatles film *Magical Mystery Tour*. The song's name was in turn taken from an invented pulp fiction crime magazine, devised by the English academic Richard Hoggart in his 1957 study of working class culture, *The Uses of Literacy*.[10]

Death Cab for Cutie proved too good a name to confine to literary criticism. A jokey take-down of American schlock, it suited the very English Bonzo Dog band, and the Beatles, bringing it to the attention of a much wider crowd. Eventually it turned into its own opposite. Instead of warning 'us' *against* the Americanization of teen culture, it was still circulating fifty years later – taking fares like Uber, you might say – *as* American teen culture.

That things *routinely* mean their opposite is a sign of our times, part of the inner lives of class-based readerships, in Britain at least. John Le Carré (David Cornwell), master of the fiction of deception and distrust (especially on 'our' side), turned that insight into an art form. In his autobiography he explains why:

> In Britain our secret services are still, for better or worse, the spiritual home of our political, social and industrial elite. (2017: 22)

As Le Carré's writings make clear, the secret services are also Britain's last bastion of class supremacy. In the 1950s and 1960s, the traditional elite were the only group deemed (by their own peers) to be trustworthy enough to deal in the stock-in-trade of espionage: deceit, lies and treachery. But a succession of scandals in the 1960s revealed an upper class riddled with traitors. Le Carré's spy fiction is at once a critical class analysis and an attempt to 'explore a nation's psyche' (2017: 22).

Hidden behind his own well-heeled disguise (Sisman, 2015), Le Carré was, like Hoggart and the rest, an Angry Young Man. He concedes that life

---

[9]Quoted in: https://www.timeout.com/chicago/music/death-cab-for-cuties-ben-gibbard-interview.
[10]Source: https://en.wikipedia.org/wiki/Death_Cab_for_Cutie.

stories too are duplicitous. Narrated events become 'sufficient to themselves', part of a culture and its language, beyond the control of authority. The boundaries between fact, fiction, falsification and fabrication, between history and imagination, feeling and faking, are hard to maintain. Instead, they remain a resource for anyone and everyone to use, in ways that may subvert and betray the very values the original subject sought to proclaim. That's the history of reading: life and narration alike have inexorably 'widened into incoherence' (12).

Discovering the ways in which people and populations produce meaningfulness – and deception – among themselves requires 'critical reading', because the evidence is indirect. It follows that the role of the analyst is both crucial and suspect. Interpretation could simply project the analyst's own prejudices onto the evidence, a charge against literary cultural studies (made by sociologists as they moved in to take over the 'manor').

Worse, it could and did lead social activists to falsify evidence. To win an argument about their claimed effects, for example, Fredric Wertham, an early critic of comics (i.e. magazines for youth), decided that 'rhetoric must trump evidence' (Tilley, 2012: 407; and see Chapter 11). He 'cloaked his rhetoric in the guise of science and professional authority', but faked his results. With Carol Tilley, history may judge such behaviour as 'egregious', but it also proves an important methodological point: in this domain, neither science nor cultural criticism has an unblemished record; fiction and fictionalization may be more truthful and are often better received. Magazines have juxtaposed fact and fiction ever since the earliest days of Edward Lloyd's *Penny Weekly Miscellany of Romance and General Interest* (1843).[11] The readership has undergone nearly two centuries of tuition in how to *read between the lines*.

III. Proprietorial readerships

From Walthamstow to Waltham Cross

Perhaps we should leave the world of the reader for a moment, to consider another leading character in this story: the proprietor. As they barge into our everyday life, the media moguls' heavy tread sounds menacingly to contemporary ears. But the 'Demon Barons of Fleet Street' (as it were) have been stomping noisily over popular consciousness for well over a century. What kind of mark did they leave on readers? Perhaps it is not so deep as

---

[11]This 840-page behemoth has been digitized: see a copy here: https://play.google.com/books/reader?id=z7ZHAQAAMAAJ&printsec=frontcover&output=reader&hl=en&pg=GBS.PP5; and a different copy here: https://play.google.com/books/reader?id=97ZbAAAAQAAJ&printsec=frontcover&output=reader&hl=en_GB&pg=GBS.PA2.

feared, or perhaps 'we' – the critical-scientific community – forget too soon. For instance, it is quite likely that you (dear reader) have never heard of Walthamstow, or nearby Waltham Cross. They are both dormitory suburbs in the suburban sprawl stretching across north London. But both of them have a significant place in media history, having felt the heavy footfall of the world's first and its most recent media giant.

In Walthamstow lies the home (previously occupied by William Morris) of Edward Lloyd (1815–90) (Figure 10.1).[12] Lloyd was the pioneer of the 'penny press'. Starting out as a populist radical, turning out cheap periodicals brimming with plagiarized serial stories (notoriously including those of Charles Dickens), Lloyd became the archetypal media industrialist. He

FIGURE 10.1 *Blue Plaque to William Morris and Edward Lloyd on the Water House, Walthamstow. Edward Lloyd's heirs gave it to council in 1898. It was opened as Lloyd Park in 1900. The house is now the William Morris Gallery. Picture: Stephen Craven.*

Source: *Stephen Craven for geograph.org.uk. CC license: https://commons.wiki media.org/wiki/File:Plaque_to_William_Morris_and_Edward_Lloyd_-_geograph.or g.uk_-_1214659.jpg. And see: http://www.edwardlloyd.org/houses.htm.*

---

[12]What follows is indebted to the website of edwardlloyd.org: see http://www.edwardlloyd. org/index.htm.

founded (among others) *Lloyd's Weekly News*, which boasted 'the largest circulation in the world' and was the first British newspaper to sell over a million copies.

Lloyd was a technical innovator, introducing high-speed rotary presses to England and opening a factory for making newsprint out of Algerian esparto grass. As well as promoting technical advances, progressive ideas and democratic politics, Lloyd sought popularity, scale and speed in the dissemination of useful knowledge, both factual and fictional:

> On 27 November 1892, *Lloyd's Weekly*'s 50th jubilee issue reported that 'eight monster web machines, each printing two copies at a time, run off *Lloyd*'s at the rate of over 200,000 copies an hour'.[13]

Fast forward to today's north London, where, in direct line of filiation from Lloyd, and just up the road in Waltham Cross, lies the 40-acre Newsprinters works. Owned by Rupert Murdoch and opened in 2008–9, it houses twelve *Manroland Colorman XXL* presses. These can print 'one million copies of a 120-page newspaper every hour'.[14] Impressive though that is, Waltham Cross is only one of three such UK printing works belonging to Newscorp: another near Liverpool houses five further presses, capable of 430,000 newspapers an hour, with a third in Scotland operating two more, which can print a '144-page tabloid straight in a single pass on the presses at speeds up to 86,000 copies an hour'. Such is their capacity that Newsprinters don't print only Murdoch's own papers:

> 'We are proud to print *The Sun*, *The Times* and *The Sunday Times* for News UK, plus *The Daily & Sunday Telegraph*, *Wall Street Journal*, Northern editions of the *Financial Times*, *The London Metro*, *The London Evening Standard* and a great many regional titles.'[15]

It seems incontrovertible, from such statistics, that the 'mass' media and industrial-era scale of the printed press are still reverberating under the heel of the all-powerful proprietor. Even as we turn our attention to new digital realities, we should take note. The speed of the presses has increased fivefold in the century between Lloyd and Murdoch (from 200,000 to 1 million copies an hour in London), and their capacity increased to print colour (and rival titles). The business model remains the same: central production and

---

[13]Source: http://www.edwardlloyd.org/innovation.htm; and http://www.edwardlloyd.org/LWN -18921127-jub.pdf.

[14]Sources: http://newsprinters.co.uk/Who-are-we/Broxbourne-site-statistics; http://newsprinters. co.uk/Who-are-we/Knowsley; http://newsprinters.co.uk/Who-are-we/Eurocentral.

[15]Steve Whitehead, managing director, Newsprinters. quoted at: http://newsprinters.co.uk/ About-us.

fast distribution of cheap, popular journalism, seen as mass consumption of entertainment (political and sporting spectacle, human interest and conflict, promise of comfort), maintaining an 'us' versus 'them' version of class consciousness as a 'lived experience', and occasionally delivering (or at least promising) vast numbers of popular votes to the proprietor's favoured party. Party politics, the greatest spectator sport of the nineteenth century, is still brought to you by an *industry*, with all the familiar nineteenth-century attributes – unscrupulous capitalists, industrial scale, centralized control, factory-production, mass consumption, political manipulation, modernity rendered as spectacle and story. Everything old is new again.

Having said that, under the showy industrial bang and clatter, something very different is emergent, still not fully formed. It's taking the radical energy of the early 'pauper press' in a completely new direction, not towards standardization and scale but turning inwards, towards the relationships and identities of small-scale or even self-scale users. In a sense, the baronial industrialists made this new agent, but they no longer control it. One of the main achievements of the early popular press was the creation of the *class reader*. This new player is more like a 'language community' than a market; readers use and create new meanings within an *autopoietic* (self-creating and self-renewing) sense-making system (Luhmann, 2012). It's a very different 'mode of production' from the proprietorial one.

Distribution

Readership systems that are internally connected are structured like Paul Baran's (1964) model of a *distributed* as opposed to a *command-and-control* communications network (see Chapter 1). While proprietors, advertisers and governments may imagine – and wish – that a publication communicates as a centralized network, a literate readership means that it is organized and interconnected internally, working as a distributed system, of which the highest-level empirical form is a language.

Such a 'social technology' takes time to establish. Reading was not a popular pastime among the poor before the Industrial Revolution. Of course rising literacy rates were the result of more than one cause. Protestantism in particular promoted Bible study. Education followed the demand for numerate workers to operate utilitarian industrial processes. It was seen as a political necessity too, as the franchise was cautiously extended to the labouring classes in 1867. But the radical progressive 'pauper press' and 'penny press', invented by Edward Lloyd and others, was the world leader in forging a secular, popular readership around the desire for population-wide knowledge, supplied at a scale that dwarfed other media.

The 'knowledge is power' movement was linked not only to power politics but also to Enlightenment values (science, discovery, social progress), the cultivation of 'the self' (*bildungsroman*, self-help), and practical know-how (household management, make-do-and-mend, DIY, smallholdings, 'hobbies'). Naturally, in among all that *useful* knowledge (Rauch, 2001) was a good deal of scandal, murder, sensation and play. In among the news items and 'improving' content were fictional stories by celebrity authors and (purportedly) factual ones from the police courts, although the distinction was not respected in practice. Lloyd's first periodical title was:

> *The Penny Sunday Times* and *Weekly Police Gazette*, a miscellany comprised of fiction and faked police reports. Advertisements for *The Penny Sunday Times* proclaimed the writing was 'Sketched with the Humour of a "Boz"' [Dickens].[16]

Before committing exclusively to newspapers, Lloyd specialized in these 'penny bloods', novels issued in weekly parts (Kirkpatrick, 2016), prefiguring 'death cab for cutie' crime fiction by more than a century. He published over 200 of them between 1839 and 1853.

Among his most famous were *Varney the Vampyre, or The Feast of Blood* (1845–7), and *The String of Pearls, or The Sailor's Gift* (1846–7), both written by James Malcolm Rymer, the latter introducing the world to the character of Sweeney Todd, the Demon Barber of Fleet Street.[17]

Literacy

This was the beginning of a new kind of mass literacy, whose chief characteristic was that it was *purposeless*, not tied to priest, politician or profession, available to be used for any or no purpose at the will or whim of the *user*, not the producer. Literacy, appetite whetted by the penny press, became a 'means of production' of knowledge, but unlike most machinery it was in the hands of the population at large. Sweeney Todd's latest incarnation was a production of Stephen Sondheim's *Sweeney Todd: The Demon Barber of Fleet Street*, brought to London from New York in 2015 by English National Opera, starring the Welsh operatic baritone (Sir) Bryn Terfel and Oscar-winning actor/writer (Dame) Emma Thompson. The political magazine *New Statesman* commented:

> Sweeney Todd is an urban legend, in every sense. The vicious barber who slits his customers' throats and sends their bodies down a chute to be turned into pie filling may first have appeared in a London penny dreadful

---

[16]Source: John Adcock at http://john-adcock.blogspot.com.au/2015/02/edward-lloyds-200th-anniversary-1815.html.
[17]Source: Robert Kirkpatrick at http://www.edwardlloyd.org/biog-kirkpatrick.pdf.

in 1846, but he has been reincarnated on stage, on screen and in print so often since that his origins have acquired a distinctly mythic quality. [18]

Mythic literacy is learnt, not innate – that is, cultural, not behavioural – so it has to be taught. That necessitated the presence of institutions and behind them the purposes of paymasters – church, state, capital and successive barons of Fleet Street. Even so, literacy's peculiar attribute, as a 'social technology' that could nevertheless only be used by individuals, put it at least at one remove from direct or causal force from 'interested' agencies. Reading is not the same as taking instructions. Instead of remaining a top-down tool for governmental control, literacy was increasingly available as an alternative bottom-up source of organization and action among a growing population who could use it to think for themselves.

The 'multitudes' exceeded what was wanted of them by their masters. At micro-scale, readers might resist, refuse or remix the resources of literacy, using them to pursue the very opposite of proprietorial wishes, or they might simply tune out and read the 'Sunday funnies' (Mann, 1992), looking not for ideologies but recipes, stories, tips and scandals, wrapped in 'sensational' semiosis. At macro-scale, collective organization could be constructed 'from below'. Literacy's spread was accompanied by the development of Tocquevillean and class-based 'associations'. These consolidated throughout the nineteenth century, becoming the giant class-based unions and political parties that transformed the political landscape of modernity. All of the major political movements of the twentieth century were founded on literacy established in the nineteenth century by purposeful agencies and organizations. Both knowledge (positive content) and uncertainty (doubt, scepticism, opposition, critique) were circulated as social facts, emancipated from the will of priest or proprietor, part of everyday life, mundane and unremarked but available and scalable.

Later leftist historians, notably Raymond Williams (1961) and E. P. Thompson (1963), argued that the 'English working class' was *self-created* through its organizations, principally the trades union and Cooperative movement and the Labour Party (see Chapter 12). Both Williams and Thompson pursued the history of class consciousness through the means by which it was constructed at the time: periodical publications. Like Hoggart, they felt political and cultural qualms to see how these once purposeful organs of popular enlightenment were faltering in the face of post-Second World War international commercial popular culture. It seemed to them that no sooner had the labouring or 'productive' classes achieved the intellectual

---

[18]Source: https://www.newstatesman.com/culture/2015/04/meat-murder-emma-thompson-and-bryn-terfel-sweeney-todd-london-coliseum.

emancipation that went with full literacy than they were squandering it: on 'Death Cab for Cuties'.

IV. Emancipated readerships

The reader: Feminized, patriotic, fashionable, common

What did early popular readers look like to their contemporaries? This was not the literary 'common reader', whose identity, judgement and powers had been tussled over by scholars and critics, from the gentlemanly commons of Dr Johnson's eighteenth-century coffee house to the caustic wit of modernist outsiders like Virginia Woolf (2003).[19] Working-class literacy had achieved 'surplus value' or *purposelessness*, no longer confined to the needs of industrial capitalism, consumerism or even democratic politics. Such readers entered the realm of representation as self-motivating figures inspired by knowledge but, strangely and simultaneously, as an object of desire – the very archetype of Hoggart's 'cutie'. We can meet a couple of them (Figure 10.2), both of striking beauty, but duplicitously using classical means to convey modern meanings, fictionalizing new truths.

Both the sculpture and the painting are titled *The Reading Girl*. Both are 'duplicitous' because they subvert the classical nude form, using it to depict the modern 'common reader'. The *sculpture* (Figure 10.2a) is by Italian Pietro Magni (1817–77). It was modelled in 1856, carved in 1861. Capturing a young woman who's so absorbed in her reading that she's let her shift slip, the sculpture made Magni's name and fame. For his contemporaries, it expressed the new artistic movement of *verismo* or realism.[20] It was a challenge to neoclassicism, quoting the classical nude in order to renew it. The girl is understood as working class (chair, floor rushes, anonymity), and what she's doing – domestic reading – turns out not to be noble or aesthetic but patriotic and democratic:

> *The Reading Girl* may very well represent Italy itself, soon to come into maturity as a nation. In this regard, *The Reading Girl* fuses verismo concepts of truth to nature and close observation with emotional insight, all in service to a rising Italian patriotic sentiment. ... In its livelier, more

---

[19]See: https://ebooks.adelaide.edu.au/w/woolf/virginia/w91c/chapter1.html.
[20]*Verismo* is now best known as a term in opera: see: http://www.roh.org.uk/news/a-blanket-ter m-misused-what-is-and-isnt-verismo.

FIGURE 10.2 *Reading Girls: (a) Magni's sculpture (1861) and (b) Roussel's painting (1887) dramatize the democratization of reading: the sculpture portends political emancipation; the painting is a harbinger of the modern consumer. Both depict ordinary people ('the masses') as realistic truth rendered desirable. Picture credits: Pietro Magni,* La Leggitrice, National Gallery of Art (USA) (Open Access); *Théodore Roussel,* Reading Girl, Tate National (UK) (image used by permission).

immediate, true-to-life aspects, it successfully appealed to a wide public and linked itself to the growing democratic vision of a united Italy.[21]

This is the democratic reader; anonymous, youthful, private and open to dangerous ideas – including the bold fiction of 'a united Italy'.

Let's meet her later cousin: the fashionable reader. The *painting* (Figure 10.2b) is by Théodore Roussel (1847–1926). It was modelled by Hetty Pettigrew and exhibited in London in 1887. It caused an immediate stir. The critic for *The Spectator* (16 April 1887) wrote:

Our imagination fails to conceive any adequate reason for a picture of this sort. It is realism of the worst kind, the artist's eye seeing only the vulgar outside of his model, and reproducing that callously and brutally.

---

[21]Source: National Gallery of Art (USA): https://www.nga.gov/content/ngaweb/Collection/art-object-page.127589.html. Another copy of this work is held in Milan, juxtaposed with a sculpture that depicts a *writing* girl: http://www.italianways.com/la-donna-che-scrive-e-quella-che-legge-tutte-e-due-compiono-lopera/.

No human being, we should imagine, could take any pleasure in such a picture as this; it is a degradation of Art.[22]

The degrading, brutal, callous and 'vulgar outside' of the model seemed offensive to some at the time because here was a depiction not of classical aesthetics or divine nudity in the service of noble sentiments, but 'a robust and healthy young woman, with a taste for current fashion', as the Tate's unapologetic summary puts it. Here is an early portrait of *the consumer* – female, déclassé, modern, self-absorbed but nevertheless interested in something beyond her own sexuality, which is represented but not proffered. She represents a flattened, naturalistic novelty: a democratization of the 'classic' subject of art for the mass-media age. Among the fashions on show is what she's reading – of course, it's a magazine.

It wasn't long before actual persons began to represent the ideal democratic consumer. A breakthrough moment occurred in 1941 when *Picture Post* – itself one of the great achievements of popular journalism and photojournalism – appointed a Women's editor, the first in the UK press. This was Anne Scott-James, who, while working for *Vogue*, had approached *Picture Post*'s editor Tom Hopkinson suggesting a story about *Vogue*. This was duly commissioned and published just as the London Blitz began to bite.[23] Written by Scott-James, it showed the American photographer Lee Miller shooting a fashion feature (26 October 1940).[24] By 1941 Anne Scott-James was on the *Picture Post* staff. One of her early assignments was to investigate opportunities for women war workers; another was to illustrate the question: 'Should women wear trousers?' According to her *Guardian* obit, 'she was tall, slim and a beauty (photographed by, among others,

---

[22]Source: http://www.tate.org.uk/art/artworks/roussel-the-reading-girl-n04361: Tate Gallery, London, where the painting hangs: https://www.tate-images.com/results.asp?image=N04361. Hetty Pettigrew was one of three professional model sisters. She was about twenty at this time. She became Roussel's mistress and they had a daughter together. She died in 1953 (Wikipedia). Roussel, who was French but domiciled in England, died in 1926.

[23]Source: https://www.independent.co.uk/news/obituaries/anne-scott-james-journalist-who-br eached-fleet-streetrsquos-gender-barrier-and-later-became-a-1686889.html. Anne Scott-James was photographed by legendary *Picture Post* photographer Bert Hardy for 'Should women wear trousers?' (*PP*, 18 October 1941); and investigating opportunities for women war workers, on her first day's training as a bus conductress for the Midland Red bus company (*PP*, November 1941). Photos can be viewed at Getty Images: https://www.gettyimages.com.au /photos/bert-hardy-anne-scott-james-1941.

[24]Source: https://www.telegraph.co.uk/photography/what-to-see/lee-miller-woman-hitlers-bat htub/. Miller was 'a Twenties fashion model who became a Surrealist and later the only female combat photographer in Europe', who 'documented the liberation of Dachau and Buchenwald concentration camps'; famously having herself photographed for *Vogue* in Hitler's bathtub in nearby Munich, the dirt from Dachau still on her boots, on the very day when Hitler killed himself in Berlin (30 April 1945).

Cecil Beaton).'[25] She *embodied* the relations between women, war, work and journalism, literally *modelling* the readership's new 'opportunities', while 'breaking the gender barrier' in British press publishing. She went on to become editor of *Harper's Bazaar* (1945–51), woman's editor of the *Sunday Express* (1953–7), and a *Daily Mail* columnist (1960–8), after which she focused on writing and editing about gardens and gardening, while serving on the panel of the BBC panel show *My Word!* (1964–78). As her *Independent* obit put it, Anne Scott-James was 'one of the first top-flight women journalists to cross the barrier between writing principally for and about women to more universal topics'.

By the mid-twentieth century, popular literacy was very widespread in the industrial trading democracies and in socialist countries alike. If you didn't have it, that could now be understood to be a disorder, bringing social disadvantage and personal shame. Sculpted 'reading girls' might still continue to delight the eye of the benevolent beholder (Figure 10.3), but in this case the purpose has shifted to the evocation of empathy for the 'inner struggle' of the dyslexic child, in order to reduce the shame associated with inability

FIGURE 10.3 *Inner Struggle, by Sir Richard Taylor and Weta Workshop. Dyslexia Foundation, Christchurch, New Zealand http://www.ctct.org.nz/dde/exhibit.html.*

---

[25]Source: https://www.theguardian.com/media/2009/may/15/anne-scott-james-obituary-journalist.

to read, and to display works by dyslexic artists. One of these is multiple Oscar-winner Sir Richard Taylor. With Sir Peter Jackson, he was responsible for the props, costumes, prosthetics and animatronics used in *The Lord of the Rings*.[26] His youthful reader is as self-absorbed as her nineteenth-century predecessors, but hers is an 'inner struggle' – to become a *maker*.[27]

Here, the *uses of literacy* were no longer instrumental but manifold, non-linear, semiotically affluent and creative. Readers were voters, citizens, the public, consumers, audiences; in addition, some were activists, advocates, educators, artists, scientists, radicals, celebrities, revolutionaries, dreamers, mischief-makers, comedians, preachers, commentators, critics and migrants. Each individual reader performed many roles among many groups and was networked to more, ranging in scale from clique to class to cosmos. Among such webs of connectedness, public communication could no longer be modelled as a top-down, centre-to-periphery, command-and-control, one-to-many process.

The 'multitude' began to find ways to 'talk among itself', to achieve some level of self-organizing auto-communicative group identity (Lotman, 1990; Luhmann, 2012), and to give each other a helping hand (or not; trolling from the other side of the street has a long history too). Personal literacy exceeded the intentions of producers, for whom collective masses were feared as 'crowds' given to mass hysteria or 'mobs' bent on anarchy. Social and mobile media enabled a distributed form of 'public writing' within and between decentralized groups. Readership itself was emancipated, emerging as a decentralized user-led function coordinated by myriad overlapping groups and institutions in which collective action was as important as proprietorial intention, and getting more so.

In all of this, reading went in exactly the opposite direction of industrial efficiency. The division of labour and consequent proletarianization of artisanship in the factory system grew apace during the nineteenth century and it still continues, shifting from manufacturing to the service sector, and from national to global scale. But reading has gone the other way: proliferating out of all proportion to utility. Ordinary people, for whom reading was hard-won but barely functional – confined to 'official' purposes of religion, work processes or regulatory compliance – could now read anything the Republic of Letters might throw at them, limited only by local accessibility and price.

---

[26]See: http://www.dyslexiafoundation.org.nz/richard_taylor.html.
[27]Taylor reflects on his own formation as a maker here: http://www.thecreativestore.com.au/creative-talk/sir-richard-taylors-take-on-inspiring-creativity/.

V. Novelty bundling

While the economy was busy *dividing* productive processes (such that each specialist process could be developed as a new industry or market), mass literacy was growing by *bundling* all kinds of novelties together, such that any one reader was confronted by a superfluity of semiotic abundance without obvious limits. The problem now for readers was to how to limit choice (categorize and filter), and where to look for preferred reading (search and sample). The answer was the magazine. The shed that stores multifarious objects can also render them into order.

The magazine was also a solution to a tricky problem for producers. It helped them to sell uncertainty! It traded in novelty – stories, news and ideas whose attraction for readers lay in not being known in advance. The magazine bundled heterogeneous novelties, offering readers a repertoire not a 'good'. Choice was downstreamed from provider to user. Pre-industrial forms of 'novelty bundling' (Potts 2011), such as fairs and festivals, required people to attend in person. Literacy allowed novelties into the home, and at industrial scale, by the shed-load. Periodical publications quickly adopted 'bundling' at various levels: in the text, by genre (romance, action, etc.), by author (who do you like, trust or admire?), or by publisher (specialized imprints).

Magazines played a vital role in stimulating attention to the supply of novelties and providing status signals that affected their value. They helped publishers to reduce uncertainties: they didn't know the market (demand follows supply where novelty is the product); they wanted people to pay attention to things that didn't interest them or that they actively disliked (this is the founding skill of journalism); and they supplied incommensurably different things in one bundle – fact and fiction, story and image, news and pinups, politics and sport, freedom and comfort, economic information and children's entertainment – often within the same covers, for the lowest price, in order to 'capture' as many different segments of the potential market demographic as possible.

Periodical magazines used their succession of pages to organize different sections and genres of content, sometimes purposed for the attention of different 'family members', or simply to put regular features in predictable order. As periodicals they could also sort material by season. It takes time to standardize such forms (just as it took time to sort out which pedal went where in automobiles), but over time an efficient set of 'rules' was established for the convenience of both producers and consumers, who school each other in what works, such that new players would adopt existing layouts. Competing titles would become ever more similar. The general market was extended by a 'division of labour' (specialization) among magazine themselves. Each household might purchase different magazines for different members and different purposes. Eventually, some newcomer's experiment in breaking the rules with something new catches on, and a new paradigm begins.

In short, the magazine was an early adopter of the branding and targeting techniques of the creative economy or 'economy of attention' (Lanham, 2006). It worked as a 'social network market' (Potts et al., 2008), where status (copying style-leaders) determined price and where consumer choices were determined by the choices of others in the system, called 'entrepreneurial consumers' by Hartley and Montgomery (2009), a 'function' that is now professionalized by users who turn into 'influencers' (Abidin, 2016).

Imperceptibly, a community (or numerous overlapping communities) of avid, entertained, well-read readers becomes literate in the fuller sense; it learns the codes and it becomes easier for readers (consumers) to act also as writers (producers). Some people take the chance to raise their own voice, share their ideas, win an argument, or improve their skills in print. Because of the capital costs required, such participation typically takes amateur or consumerist form – letters to the editor, sharing crafts and hobbies, household management (recipes), fanfic and jokes. It is by these means that group identities, a sense of who 'we' are, can be maintained, a feature that was first textualized around social class (the 'pauper press') but soon expanded to encompass large-scale communities of gender and nation, and specialized segments, as magazines proliferated for ever more tightly defined groups.

'We're the majority now, you ****!'

In the digital age, the cultural function of magazines – the storehouse on the edge of town – far exceeds the form that was perfected in print (although the brands and mastheads familiar from that era continue online, with mixed success). Readers are now writers, in their millions, on social media, DIY websites and through magazine-maker apps like Issuu, Blurb (US), Jilster (Netherlands), Madmagz (France), etc. Professional advice is readily to hand, often free.[28]

What is the political effect of user-led novelty bundling and networked, two-way communication, to promote a sense of co-subjectivity among 'people like us'? It may be too soon to tell, but a straw in the wind has been captured by one of the online successors to print periodicals, a 'hyperlocal' news site (Hargreaves and Hartley, 2016: 142–52). This one is called *Loving Dalston* (in East London), run by David Altheer, a journalist made redundant

---

[28]For example, Danny Miller in *Creative Review*, 2016: https://www.creativereview.co.uk/how-to-launch-a-magazine/.

by Rupert Murdoch's prestige title *The Times*.[29] In June 2017, someone tipped it off that a feature film called *Forgotten Man*, shot in East London and featuring a cameo role by actor-model Jerry Hall, was screening at the East End Film Festival in the nearby Hackney Picture House.

The reason why that became news was not just that that Jerry Hall (60) is married to Rupert Murdoch (86), the Australian-American media tycoon with a big printing works in nearby Waltham Cross, nor that the couple came over from 'his Mayfair pad' in their 'tycoon-comfy' Range Rover to watch the film (Figure 10.4). The newsworthy bit came at the end of the

FIGURE 10.4 *'We're the majority now'. Media mogul encounters the audience.*
Photo: Hetty Einzig.
Source: *Hetty Einzig @HettyEinzig (Twitter).*

---

[29]See: http://lovingdalston.co.uk/2012/07/openness-policy/.

film, and starred an anonymous member of the audience, not the power couple themselves. *Loving Dalston* takes up the story:

> Alas, things did not go altogether well. Leaving as the lights went up … they were spotted by a young Corbynista in the near-full house. Murdoch paused in his shuffle towards the exit as a loud voice rent the air: 'We are the majority now, you [James Blunt]!' Except he used a single word.[30]

Was the Range Rover trip to Dalston a metaphorical re-run of 'Death cab for cutie'? Will Rupert Murdoch soon be a 'Forgotten Man' in another anonymous north London suburb? Let the last word (not the rude one)[31] go to the anonymous young representative of a new reading public: *We are the majority now*. That's what comes of reading magazines for 150 years. The tables are turned.

[30]Story at: http://lovingdalston.co.uk/2017/06/rupert-is-wheeled-in-to-hackney-to-see-wife-jerrys-movie-when-an-angry-punter-calls-him-out/.
[31]It was the 'C word' that made this story newsworthy. *The Guardian*, unlike others, chose to spell out the unprintable expletive: https://www.theguardian.com/lifeandstyle/lostinshowbiz/2017/jun/22/rupert-murdoch-jerry-hall--cinema-night-hackney-east-end-welcome. See also: http://www.telegraph.co.uk/news/2017/06/23/rupert-murdoch-verbally-abused-night-hackney/. Appropriately, noting that the film *Forgotten Man* is about homelessness, *The Big Issue* carried the story: https://www.bigissue.com/news/rupert-murdoch-attends-premiere-film-homelessness/.

11

What is television?

A guide for knowing subjects

PRESIDENT: Beavis and Butt-Head. On behalf of all your fellow Americans, I extend my deepest thanks. You exemplify a fine new crop of young Americans who will grow into the leaders of this great country.

(Beavis and Butt-Head Do America, 1996)[1]

I. Fiction function

TV scholar Jason Mittell organized the object of television studies into the following six 'functions':

- a commercial industry,
- a democratic institution,
- a textual form,
- a site of cultural representation,
- a part of everyday life, and
- a technological medium (2422009: 2).

Jonathan Gray and Amanda Lotz apportion TV studies to four headings: programmes, audiences, industries, contexts (2018). Such lists do useful work, not least to suggest that 'television' is *not one thing*, but many parts.

---

[1]*Beavis and Butt-Head Do America*, by Mike Judge and Joe Stillman (1996). Movie script: http://www.dailyscript.com/scripts/beavis_and_butthead_do_america.html.

This chapter argues that television can be conceptualized as a coherent object, not just a contingent collection of incommensurate components. I argue that what unifies and justifies television as an integrated (albeit complex) object of study is its *cultural function*. So here's the claim: *Television is the creation of the modern subject.*

- TV integrates modern life into some sort of shared, imagined, *meaningful universe* or 'semiosphere' (Lotman, 1990),
- TV coordinates viewers at scale into an inter-knowing subpopulation or 'deme',
- Combining semiosphere with demic audience, TV *creates* (makes; represents; distributes; models; motivates; adjusts) *the modern subject* (in the 'inner life' of classed, raced, gendered and otherwise differentiated populations).

You will note that this function is not in the job description of any one person or agency – no one is paid to produce its cultural effect – because cultural function results from a collective, group dynamic, produced by a social-semiotic-technical-corporate system that, like any large-scale social network, operates well beyond the reach of individual intentionality, producing network effects. Thus, the TV semiosphere is both *parochial*, expressive of 'our' group identity, especially in contrast to 'they' adversaries (internal and external) and, at the same time, *universal*, capable of facing any uncertainty or problem: from daily surprises (news, sport), through abiding challenges and conflicts (drama, comedy), all the way up to myth and law-affirming events (ritual, festival).

Meanings are made and marketed, shared among unprecedentedly large and heterogeneous populations, such that the personal act of enjoying fictions is also a group action, *constituting* the group's identity at macro-scale, as another of humanity's determining 'fictions'. Television is not an object in nature but is *constituted in discourse*, realized in social arrangements, and *reconstituted over time*. The TV audience is also a discursive fiction. The sense of co-subjectivity among millions who share a programme or live event is imagined (Dayan and Katz, 1992). You can't catch the audience – individually or as a whole – in the act, as it were. *Studying* audiences introduces new fictions into discourse; an uncertainty principle ensures that direct observation of audiences changes them and what they do; and (as befits a medium that regularly eats itself) this objectification and commodification offers a new programming opportunity: enter *Gogglebox* (UK) and its spin-offs, *Gogglesprogs* (for children), *Vlogglebox* (for teens) and *Gogglebox Australia*. But imaginary doesn't mean illusory. By means of language and stories (Dor, 2015), *Homo sapiens* create entities (demes) that don't exist in nature – that is, Harari's law, religion, firms, money, rights, nations – and use these to ensure cooperation in the growth of knowledge.

The television audience is the largest such group ever created. Stories about it abound, but you'll never meet it face-to-face; and television is the most complete storytelling machine ever invented.

Meanings are carried to all quarters by the twin energies of modernity: *freedom* (intellectual emancipation, both individual and social) and *comfort* (material well-being, both household and market). These notions of modernity have evolved and embedded themselves since the Renaissance and Enlightenment, taking the fruits – bitter and sweet – of Western expansion to the wider world: industrial capitalism, imperial and colonial power; struggles with persistent problems of identity, equality, mobility, and opportunity; never able to extend the mantle of modern freedom and comfort to all human agents or systems, even as the idea of it was globalized along with trade. Television has globalized ahead of both freedom and comfort, for most. Nevertheless, it's the fiction that binds: television has the knack of seeming to address and to include all of us (however construed); and when it doesn't, as inevitably will be the case, audience members may aspire to join the club, or they may protest at being neglected (or both). For all its fictional make-believe and uneven representational accuracy, we want television to be *true* (transparent, direct, intuitively apposite) about who we are. What makes television compelling as an object of study is not any particular textual or industrial forms (which come and go), intriguing as these continue to be, but the one thing that makes them all dangerous, risky and attractive: television's *popularity* – its population-wide reach. Its most important invention is the audience, this 'fiction' being the locus of the entire system's cultural functionality.

Television as a cultural form was established among the winners of the Second World War; now its audience is planetary, just at the moment when it is dawning on people everywhere, if not on their public representatives, that the planet itself is being shaped, possibly catastrophically, by our species' methods of valuing, achieving and exporting modernity's fruits. What happens when *everyone, everywhere* aspires to modern freedom and comfort? What are the limits and alternatives to modernity? And how can we (audience, citizen, public, consumer, maker, species) decide, as Lenin once put it, *what is to be done*? What *collective action* is needed, and how do we know? Here, television lines up alongside other planetary communication systems (science, fiction, publishing, social media) as both source of and solution to the problem: the very medium that brought us together in pursuit of the modern is – we must hope – the means by which we can learn its limits. This conundrum becomes explicit just as television as we know it is morphing into something else on mobile screens and devices.

Technologically, popularity comes and goes too. Television succeeded earlier media forms in an evolving technological-communicative process that stretches back at least to the Renaissance (popular theatre and print-literacy), boosted by the Enlightenment (science, the novel, journalism), to achieve mass-communicative capability with industrialization and world trade: spreading the press, then cinema and radio, across all continents. All of these inventions were attended by contemporary discourses of knowledge, danger, risk – and attraction – based on their popularity. The same applies to TV's successor forms: popular broadcast television has been followed in turn by computational (digital) and networked (internet) forms, including apps, platforms and social media where, once again, the most important invention is not so much the technology, mind-boggling though that can seem, but *the user*, the metaphoric point of intelligibility (and anxiety) around which technology, institution and cultural function cohere. The user is routinely theorized as just another *Homo economicus*, that 'self-contained globule of desire' (Veblen, 1919: 73) beloved of equilibrium economics, although 'the user' (unlike 'the audience') is endowed with agency or expertise to produce as well as to consume. But this abstract figure (like the audience) is still only significant in the aggregate. Users attract the usual aura of risk, danger and attractiveness when they 'go viral' (Abidin and Leaver, 2017). Popularity, the 'fiction' of group scale, drives the system, not individual behaviour or even technological change.

Whether user-based media count as 'television', or as something new, depends on whether the current decentralized, user-led but corporately globalized system of digital-mobile-internet connectivity is accepted as *part of modernity*, or as evidence of its demise. Television's successes and failures will tell us much about the prospects for modern life in the global era.

II. Cultural function

Round up the usual subjects?

One way of tackling a multivalent knowledge terrain would be to 'round up the usual suspects', not to constitute an *object* but a *field* of study. An iconic example of a literature review that constituted a new field is Alfred Kroeber and Clyde Kluckhohn's anthropological survey of 164 different concepts of culture (1952). Since I'm searching for television's *cultural function*, this seems a good place to start. Their effort to pin down what culture might mean in nature (as it were; i.e. not just in theory) was conducted in the post-Second World War geo-strategic context, just as television took off, where the newly dominant world power – the *pax americana* – pursued global goals that were mutually incommensurable: egalitarian ideals (freedom for all), industrial ambitions (world markets) and imperial responsibilities (world order). US foreign policy operated across these contradictory objectives partly by trying to systematize their own knowledge of the diverse cultures they encountered as part of national intelligence (still discernible in the CIA's annual *World Factbook*),[2] partly by funding new transnational institutions (the UN, Peace Corps, CIA), and partly by fictionalizing the tensions involved, projecting them into imaginary worlds for this planet's entertainment market, all the way from the warmongering *Casablanca* (1942) to a prolonged reflection on the possibilities – philosophical rather than imperial – of non-lethal encounters with diverse others, as explored in *Star Trek* (Pearson and Davies, 2002: 10).[3] How should America behave in Europe, the Middle and Far East, and towards the so-called second world (Communist bloc) and third world (decolonizing and developing countries)? This question was partly political and strategic, of course, but it was also a question of culture: How far to rely upon, to respect or seek to change the many conflicting cultures emerging from total war, and how far to encourage the informal entertainment market for strategic purposes, as had occurred systematically and effectively in 'the Hollywood War'? (Viotte, 2013).

Deciding what counts as culture could no longer be determined by magisterial readings, as had been the trend in European high literary and art criticism (e.g. Arnold, Ruskin, Burckhardt, Pater), whose purpose was to train discriminating judgement, especially among governing classes (Quiller-Couch, 1917), and whose values were thought, at least by advocates, to apply everywhere. In a post-war, democratizing, pluralist, mixed economy, culture's definition needed to be derived not from empire but from *usage*. The available tool for that was not 'high' culture, and certainly not its polar opposite popular culture, but anthropology, itself rooted in the experience of modern imperial expansion.

Kroeber and Kluckhohn synthesized multifarious usages into one rule, thereby *codifying* culture, turning it from parochial history to universal scientific present tense, while at the same time withdrawing the universalist claims of those who thought that a particular tradition of culture should prevail (Clark, 1969).[4] The shift from quality to usage enabled them to

---

[2]The CIA's own history of *World Factbook* includes this rationale: 'The need for more comprehensive basic intelligence in the postwar world was well expressed in 1946 … in *The Future of American Secret Intelligence* (Infantry Journal Press) that world leadership in peace requires even more elaborate intelligence than in war. "The conduct of peace involves all countries, all human activities – not just the enemy and his war production".' See: https://www.cia.gov/library/publications/the-world-factbook/docs/history.html.

[3]For a flavour of the racial politics of *Star Trek*, and what that meant to Martin Luther King, see this interview with Nichelle Nichols (Lieutenant Uhura), by then in her eighties, in *The Guardian*: https://www.theguardian.com/tv-and-radio/2016/oct/18/star-trek-nichelle-nichols-martin-luther-king-trekker.

[4]As much a television landmark as a cultural one, Kenneth Clark's BBC2 series, *Civilisation: A Personal View* (1969) was controversial from the start, and is still, fifty years later, spawning reposts and rejoinders, from John Berger's *Ways of Seeing* (1972) and Robert Hughes's *Shock of the New* (1980) to *Civilisations*, fronted by David Olusoga, Mary Beard and Simon Schama (2018). See Olusoga's informative review of this history here: https://www.theguardian.com/commentisfree/2018/feb/04/civilisation-revisited-kenneth-clark-television-landmark-series-art.

produce a serviceable definition, not quite an algorithm but nevertheless an abstract formula, of 'culture systems', based on their function for 'human groups':

> Culture consists of patterns, explicit and implicit, of and for behavior acquired and transmitted by symbols, constituting the distinctive achievements of human groups, including their embodiment in artifacts; the essential core of culture consists of traditional (i.e. historically derived and selected) ideas and especially their attached values; culture systems may, on the one hand, be considered as products of action, on the other, as conditional elements of future action. (Kroeber and Kluckhohn, 1952: 181)

Hmmm, interesting: that might even work as a definition for television! TV didn't count as culture when this definition was published, but it was entering its heyday as the most popular pastime in the history of the world, part of everyday lived culture. It was regarded by cultural critics as a threat to judgement and taste, but it too displays 'patterns ... behavior ... symbols ... achievements ... groups ... artifacts ... ideas ... values'. Like 'culture systems', the *television system* is produced by past actions, and that system determines future actions, that is, causation is systemic, evolutionary, path-dependent and dynamic.

Kroeber and Kluckhohn's generalized abstraction of culture as a macro-system allowed critics to get off their high horses and look at contemporary life. Here's where cultural studies came in. An early theorist of this approach was Henri Lefebvre (2014), who was among the first to perform the trick of linking the supposed trivia of modern 'everyday life' (*la vie quotidienne*) with philosophical thought and questions about power, dominance and transgression. Unlike Kroeber and Kluckhohn, Lefebvre saw his task as one of intervention: 'The object of our study is everyday life, with the idea, or rather the project (the programme), of transforming it' (2014, Vol II: 2). He was among those philosophers who thought, with Marx, that the point was not to interpret the world but to change it.

Cultural studies gave to early TV studies the same urge towards action: it wasn't enough to situate TV in the context of everyday life; it was necessary in order to transform everyday life. Why? Because television, among other modern technologies, left in place the *'uneven development'* that Lefebvre saw as the 'prime law of the modern world'. He speculated (this is *circa* 1961):

> It is easy to imagine that one day 'mankind' will have travelled beyond the sun, while on earth actual men, peasants for example, will still be hoeing the land, transporting things on donkeys and mules, and perhaps living in hunger. (2014, Vol II: 3)

Like air travel, interplanetary travel 'will be the preserve of a technical, social and political "elite"'. Changing that 'law' of uneven development in a project of 'transforming the everyday into a higher creativity' would take more than technology, domestic science, or cultural entertainment, because 'the everyday' is a *causal* force in making the modern subject, who lives within it and cannot escape to (or indeed in) a higher plane:

> The quotidian is what is humble and solid, what is taken for granted and that of which all the parts follow each other in such a regular, unvarying succession that those concerned have no call to question their sequence; thus it is undated and (apparently) insignificant; though it occupies and preoccupies it is practically untellable, and it is the ethics underlying routine and the aesthetics of familiar settings. (Lefebvre, 2000: 24)

The centrepiece of those familiar settings, teacher of ethics, aesthetics and sequence, supplier of tellable stories, was the TV console. Did it release modern subjectivity, or confine it? That is what was at stake. These were television's salad days of optimistic expansion, when *I Love Lucy* and *Sergeant Bilko* ruled the burgeoning suburbs, and popularity meant 'population-wide'. By 1955, a majority of households in the United States boasted at least one TV set; by 1960 it was 90 per cent (Spigel, 1992: 1, 32). During that period, TV sets were the hardware and TV shows the software for promoting everyday suburban living, centred on *producing* 'modernity, technology and the comfortable life' (Spigel, 1992: 18–26; 30ff.). Producing modern subjectivity felt like a progressive enterprise.

There was little thought in the United States about how all this might play *beyond* Peoria, but play it did, across the Americas and Europe, where the Americanization of everyday life put the skids under the French Empire, the only remaining non-anglophone world empire. According to Lefebvre, to the Situationists (Wark, 2015) and to the cinematic New Wave (Sconce, 1995), 'the colonisation of everyday life' referred to the continuation of the structures of imperialism within domestic household routines. Consumerism and technology promoted cleanliness, efficiency, interior isolation and American capitalism at the micro-scale (Ross, 1994; Olson, 2009). Among the responses to that process were the philosophical, critical and artistic ideas that led to the politicization of the everyday and thence to postmodernism.

III. Paedocracy

In this effort to colonize the everyday, the most important agents of adoption, in the United States and elsewhere, were children. Lynn Spigel quotes *Advertising and Selling*, an industry journal, which reported as early as 1948 that 'children not only exert a tremendous amount of influence in the selection and purchase of television receivers but that they are, in fact, television's most enthusiastic audience' (Spigel, 1992: 59–60).

When doubts arose concerning that enthusiasm, as they soon did, television studies (Gray and Lotz, 2018) did not yet exist to guide public debate. In fact, the perceived problem was not *on* television; it was the juvenile 'subject' lolling on the couch *watching* it. In the United States, it fell to existing social sciences to diagnose the upstart medium's invasion and colonization of children's leisure time (Wartella and Mazzarella, 1990), and its feared pathological effect on their worryingly malleable subjectivity. The pathologizing tone was set by psychiatrist Fredric Wertham's influential denunciation of comic books, *Seduction of the Innocent*, which had a chapter on 'Homicide at Home: Television and the Child' (1954: 353–83). Wertham found 'bad things' even in innocent places: 'Crime is crime and violence is violence even in the patriotic setting of a Western locale or in the science-fiction setting of interplanetary space' (1954: 370). In short, the trouble with television was not television but culture. The child *delivered to* the screen was already 'corrupted':

> The greatest obstacle to the future of good television for children is comic books and the comic-book culture in which we force children to live. If you want television to give uncorrupted programs to children you must first be able to offer it audiences of uncorrupted children. (Wertham, 1954: 383)

Hilde Himmelweit was the first career specialist in TV Studies in the UK, following her landmark study of *Television and the Child* (1958). Her *disciplinary* focus wasn't on television. She installed the child as the point of intelligibility for television studies, continuing the American trend (personified in such figures as George Gerbner, Sandra Ball-Rokeach, Ellen Wartella, Charles Osgood and Percy Tannenbaum), rather than the French one (which was incubating across London at *Screen* and *Screen Education*). Himmelweit enjoyed considerable academic celebrity and policy influence (Caplan, 1996), creating a path-dependency for television studies that was not rivalled until French Theory finally broke through in the 1970s and 1980s. She was rather dismissive about changes in television 'itself'; they were 'superficial' compared with 'children's lives':

> The role of television in children's lives, the manner of children's reactions and the underlying principles that determine them remain constant in the face of the superficial changes in television itself. (Himmelweit, Oppenheim and Vince (1958: xiii)

The book's confident subtitle, *An Empirical Study of the Effect of Television on the Young*, is contradicted in the telling: despite 'the effect of television', childhood remains 'constant'; playing a 'role' in children's daily lives, but by no means transforming them, least of all in a direction likely to be welcomed by Lefebvre. Himmelweit's *method* was 'empirical', chiefly consisting of 4,000 interviews with children, parents and teachers in five English cities. Her research team found that television was already the number one leisure activity among children, who watched mostly adult shows, where they were 'exposed' to Wertham's worst fears: sex, violence and bad language, although the children reported that they used TV mostly as a 'time-filler' (1958: 15).

The interviews probed concerns about TV's impact on children's own anxieties, outlook and education, finding that watching TV had a 'solid and consistent' impact on their lives (1958: 245). The researchers were given access to children's IQ tests – a practice no longer acceptable (Livingstone and Bovill, 1999, Ch1:4, fn5) – and found that the 'higher' a child's 'intelligence' the less TV they watched, leading to generations of rationing for middle-class or aspirational-parented kids. The book recommended that parents should protect children from the 'risks' of television, supervise programme choices and guide children towards 'quality' programming (although the children didn't mention this), in order to learn how to distinguish 'make-believe' from reality (as if semiosis is not real). Thus, right at the outset, television was deemed important – was constituted as an object of study – not because of its commercial, democratic, textual, representational, quotidian, or technological properties (Mittell, 2009), or its colonization of everyday life (Lefebvre), but because of its presumed role in forming the *modern subject – at risk*.

Forty years later, Sonia Livingstone, also at the LSE, undertook a follow-up study, just at the moment when television was giving way – at least in terms of public debate and disquiet – to 'new media'. Her research team 'tried to put to one side the considerable public anxieties surrounding our key terms – "children", "youth", "new" and "media"' (Livingstone and Bovill, 1999, Ch1: 2). Instead, they 'set out to contextualise children and young people's meanings and uses of new media in relation to their "environment" or "life-world"'. Perhaps not surprisingly, they came to the same conclusions as did Himmelweit:

> The case for change should not be overstated. Each decade may see dramatic technological change, but in many respects children's lives are as they were ten or even forty years ago. Children grow up, watch television, ride their bikes, argue with their parents, study hard or become disaffected with school, just as they always did. (Livingstone and Bovill, 1999, Ch1: 3)

Where 'larger changes' are discerned, 'these are often only indirectly connected with new media technologies'. They are left as open questions:

> Even larger changes are also at work, as globalising economic, political and technological developments challenge the autonomy of the nation state. How are we to link all these changes? Does lack of freedom to play outside influence time spent watching television, or does use of global media impact on consumerist values, or does children's new-found expertise with computers affect family authority? (1999, Ch1: 3)

Like Himmelweit, Livingstone is drawn not to 'television' or even 'media', but to 'larger changes' that are seen as global and national, within which the modern subject faces universal pressures: freedom to play, consumer values, family authority. These questions about freedom and comfort impelled the direction of Livingstone's later research, especially the large-scale *EU Kids Online* project.[5] Thus, 'the child' – an abstract, universal fiction created by 'public anxieties' – continues to drive and direct the research agenda in television studies, even while the real action seems to be going on at global scale, challenging the 'autonomy' of nations and the 'authority' of families, while 'everyday life' itself is increasingly hard to separate from 'media':

> New forms of engagement between user and medium may contribute to the gradual shift from a clear distinction between mass communication and face-to-face communication to a more diversified, participatory, active notion of mediated communication in everyday life. (1999, Ch12: 11)

Modernity versus everyday life

Once semiosis and reality are recognized as one and the same, as French theory had realized from the start, then there are consequences, both for *modernity*, which was sceptical about that, and for *everyday life*, which becomes the site of struggle, not only between global colonization and local authenticity but also between 'order' and 'transgression', between modernity and community. Amanda Third and Philippa Collin return to

---

[5]The project maintains a blog, here: http://blogs.lse.ac.uk/parenting4digitalfuture/. Some of the many publications arising from it and from associated research can be accessed here: http://www.lse.ac.uk/media@lse/research/EUKidsOnline/EU%20Kids%20Online%20reports.aspx; and here: http://www.lse.ac.uk/media@lse/research/EUKidsOnline/Home.aspx.

Lefebvre's 'everyday' as a 'naturalized' but 'totalizing' sphere, consisting of 'pressures and repressions at all levels, at all times and in every sphere of experience including sexual and emotional experience, private and family life, childhood, adolescence and maturity' (Lefebvre, 2000: 145). In other words, it's the site of 'order'. But, they note, it is also a bit wild:

> Lefebvre … theorises the everyday as simultaneously a mechanism of dominant order – a tool of repression – and a site for the transgression and deconstruction of that order. For Lefebvre, the everyday is both 'the point of delicate balance and that where imbalance threatens' (2000: 32). (Third and Collin, 2016: 51).

'Dominant order … repression … transgression … deconstruction … imbalance', undermining dominance and unbalancing order even as it applies them to the general population – it all sounds a bit *postmodern*. So here's where television and philosophy intersect once again: television is not only an agent of a modern order that 'evades critique', it is also an agent of deconstruction and transgression. Just as the act of watching television has fragmented across devices and platforms, and the identity of the viewer diversified, so too the recognition of what modernity comprises and how it works has expanded to include its own erstwhile 'other' – postmodernity (Lucy, 2016).

What's new about television in the unpredictably unfolding twenty-first century is that its popularity is both greater than ever (across more countries, modes of consumption and aggregate numbers of eyeballs) and more fragmented and dispersed than ever. Even in its most successful national market, the United States, broadcasters no longer seek to gather populations into one Andersonian imagined community, as *Dallas* or *M*A*S*H* once could, with *Dallas*'s famous '53 share' (of all TV sets – a majority of US households) for the 1980 'Who shot JR?' episode, or *M*A*S*H*'s finale in 1983, which scored nearly 106 million simultaneous viewers. Instead, even today's most popular shows (*Game of Thrones, Top Gear, Westworld*) reach no more than 10 million viewers at one time. It takes a special or fatal event – a moon landing, assassination, terrorist attack, natural disaster, celebrity court-case or sporting final – to bring impressive audiences together in the same time and place, but even these numbers only mask increasingly polarized demographic contours (Pew Research, 2014b). TV now serves both to separate and to interconnect many disconnected knowledge-making demic groups, who know one another by semiotic and rhetorical means, not necessarily by national or ethnic boundaries.

Thus, postmodern uncertainty is not so much a departure from modernity as a way of integrating how we know with what we know, which means that the modern subject nowadays is not only the presumed-to-be-universal figure of Enlightenment-Industrial-Imperial freedom and comfort but also reflexive (able to self-interrogate) and positioned (conscious of identity, partisan), therefore, not universal at all.

The idea that an industry can *make* something (subjectivity, or modern agency at population scale) that it does not *manufacture* (programmes, etc.) may seem unempirical and postmodern, until we recall that this is how television entered formal knowledge in the first place, through the figure most often thought to be damaged by their encounters with television: the child. Here, scholarship about television has been part of the problem; using the child as a handy metaphor for discounting popular media and culture as childish, without inquiring too deeply into what enables children to construct and perform an identity (e.g. gender, ethnicity, etc.), relationships (trust, translation), meaningfulness and thence knowledge in modern times, using the discursive resources to hand (Butler, 1990). Philosophy was slow to take notice, because it did not recognize children as 'knowing subjects':

> I have no quarrel with Children, and I do not wish to pronounce them blind, deaf or dumb, merely to deny that they possess the capacities of philosophical subjects, that they have the attributes of 'knowing' subjects independent of their formation and training as social beings. (Hirst, 1979: 67)

If you take modernity as Habermas's 'incomplete project' for training these 'social beings' (d'Entrèves and Benhabib, 1997: 39–55), that is, not only as the outworking of Enlightenment communicative rationality, and not only as modern-*ism* in the arts, literature, architecture (etc.) but also as the *modernization of* the economy (*vide* Deirdre McCloskey), politics (Robert Darnton) and society (Immanuel Wallerstein; Henri Lefebvre), then the creation of modern subjectivity and its distribution across global populations, even while avant-garde thought was simultaneously criticizing the very notion of modernity (in the name of postmodern doubt and scepticism about progress and grand narrative), becomes a most interesting phenomenon.

Children (see Chapter 12) were 'knowing subjects' throughout the process, some of whom *performed* 'the capacities of *philosophical* subjects', live on TV, scripted or spontaneous. Television was good at appealing to childlike attributes in its address to audiences young and old – it was a 'paedocratic' discursive regime – but scholarship was sceptical of exactly that skill. Thus, the first problem to face early television scholars was that of the worthiness of the object of study. Professional philosophy was not interested in television (Hirst, 1979; Hall, 1996), which was routinely dismissed as an 'unworthy object' (Caughie, 1990: 55), even though philosophy has been defined as the 'systematic and critical study of fundamental questions that arise both in everyday life and through the practice of other disciplines' (Brown University, n.d.). If so, then it shares common cause with television, since both pursue questions that arise in everyday life and in other disciplines. Of course there's room for debate about what might count as 'systematic and critical' study. Do chat shows or journalistic interviews, dramatic scenarios and conflict, comedic critique or take-down, sporting contests and display, constitute such study? They might! [Insert fave shows here.] Television shows were quite interested in philosophers, for example, *Men of Ideas* (1978) or *The Great Philosophers* (1987), both by Bryan Magee for the BBC. Philosophers – especially French ones – were not shy about appearing on television (Chaplin, 2007). But mainstream philosophy as a discipline and practice has been very slow to turn its attention to television, and when it did the results were frequently disappointingly prejudicial (Bourdieu, 2001; Botton, 2014) or plain weird, like the strange experiment in crossing philosophy with news called *The Philosophers' Mail*.[6]

In short, disciplinary or formal knowledge has drawn too tight a boundary around its object and its methods, excluding children and television alike, even as contemporary media were accumulating capabilities that might challenge its authority, and considering topics worthy of its most 'systematic and critical' attention. With the emergence of interactive and multi-device digital media, this tendency could only accelerate, as viewers could binge-watch TV shows with Google, Wikipedia, IMDb and social media at hand to settle arguments in a pleasingly Socratic manner.

IV. What does it mean to be *Humans*?

This raises the question of how TV is used by contemporary viewers, makers and institutions, to consider the prospects and probabilities facing the future of the post/modern subject, a future that, all the experts agree, is uncertain. Where television in its expansive, aspirational phase was about *creating and teaching* the modern subject, television now is more reflexive, mindful of post-human, post-apocalyptic possibilities. Some of its best shows, in an un-systematized but accelerating wave of worry, are thinking through *what will become of the modern subject.* Perhaps TV always has pursued that question, not only through science-and-philosophy shows (gadgets, wonders, dangers) but also in the guise of speculative entertainment, guided

---

[6]Weird and short-lived: http://thephilosophersmail.com/what-this-is-all-about/the-philosophers -mail-is-dead/. An example of its weirdness (and woeful gender awareness) is a feature comparing the newsworthiness of the Arctic ice-melt with that of Taylor Swift's legs: http://thephilosophe rsmail.com/what-this-is-all-about/swifts-legs-beat-arctic-melt-ordinary-yet-perfect-long-but-no t-freakish-unbowed-by-their-implausible-length-utterly-firm-yet-yielding-and-soft/.

by *Star Trek, Buffy The Vampire Slayer, Game of Thrones* and *Westworld* in the United States or *Quatermass, Dr Who* and *Humans* in the United Kingdom.

As a global medium, television has been well placed to ask the general question: *What does it mean to be human in an era of power?* – a question shared by cultural studies. Speculative TV drama has proven to be an efficient – that is, powerful, gripping, mind-blowing – machine for exploring problems of the modern (global) and postmodern (knowing) subject. In the Cold War, enmity was imagined between adversarial cultures: for example, the 'Kohms' (Communists) versus 'Yangs' (Yankees) of *Star Trek*'s 'Omega Glory' episode (aired in March 1968, during the Tet Offensive in Vietnam). Now, when *real* enmity seems to have turned inward, tribal, and intercommunal (i.e. post-imperial, for those who read Gibbon), bespeaking internal collapse in the midst of environmental catastrophe and mass extinctions, the *fictional* battle is pitched at species scale: humans versus the planet or other species, humanity versus the undead, aliens, robots or AI.

Honestly, who needs philosophy when you've got *Westworld* (HBO) and *Humans* (Channel 4 UK) to think with? That transatlantic pairing can serve to illustrate not only the importance of the questions raised in television entertainment but also the strong contrasts to be found among their worldviews. Table 11.1 charts what I take to be some of the profound differences between them, among which I think the opposition between 'slavery' and 'class' is the primary driver of each semiosphere.

How the relations between human and non-human agents are imagined invokes strong differences between US and European cultural preoccupations at system level. Both shows address an overall problem; an unresolved social anxiety and running sore of history, in which the boundaries of the human are not settled. In *Westworld* it is slavery; in *Humans* it is class. If a robot 'host' (*Westworld*) can be owned, killed, sexually abused and its consciousness (speech, character, actions) be tuned to the whim and pleasure of the owner, then what we are watching is *slavery* – AI as source of consolidated wealth and power; the other as ant. If, on the other hand, a 'synth' (*Humans*) can, despite irreducible otherness, become part of a family, join with other synths in solidarity, struggle for rights and feel reciprocal love for a human child, then here is *class* – AI as the productive source of dynamic change, knowledge and meaning; the other as holder of rights and obligations. The two series differ markedly in their narrative arcs, with characters driven by different motivations (individualism vs. mutual obligation); relationships based on sex (transmission) or love (translation); resolution achieved by death (winning) or compromise (cohabiting). *Westworld* adopts the narrative point of view of the owner/producer (how do I exploit and will that destroy me?), *Humans* that of the user (how do I learn to accommodate and will that complete me?).

TABLE 11.1 *Contrasting Semiospheres:* Westworld *versus* Humans

	Westworld (HBO, 2016) *	*Humans* (C4, 2015–16) *
National culture	United States	UK/Europe
Running sore of history	*Slavery, power*	*Class, meaning*
Characters	Dolores (Evan Rachel Wood)	Anita/Mia (Gemma Chan)
	Maeve (Thandie Newton)	Niska (Emily Berrington)
Motivation	*Individualism*	*Mutuality*
Self-realization by...	*Making a decision*	*Joining a group*
Relationship	*Sex, death*	*Love, accommodation*
Children? †	Little Boy, robot	Three Hawkins children, human
Location	Fantasy park	Suburban locations
Dénouement, Mood	Catastrophe, death *Untergangsstimmung* (feeling of doom)	Compromise, life *Mündigkeit* (responsibility, maturity)
Perspective on robots	Power, owner – 'they'	Culture, user – 'we'
Model of communication	Transmission of power – *to/through individuals*	Translation of meaning – *between groups/cultures*
Communication theorist	Claude Shannon	Yuri Lotman
Kagan ID ‡	Mars ♂ (hegemony, force)	Venus ♀ (law, institutions)

Notes:
* Both shows screened further seasons, see https://www.hbo.com/westworld and https://www.channel4.com/programmes/humans for more information. A Chinese version of *Humans* was announced in 2018: http://ent.people.com.cn/n1/2018/0725/c1012-30169933.html.
† Children are central to *Humans*: Sophie Hawkins (Pixie Davies) is the youngest (aged 8–9) of the central family; she welcomes the synths and is especially fond of Mia/Anita, whose mannerisms she begins to copy. Her older teenage brother Toby (Theo Stevenson) is attracted to and protective of Anita; The oldest daughter Mattie (Lucy Carless) is strongly motivated to discover more about the synths, using her computer hacking skills, and becomes a major 'translation' link between them and the human world.
Children are rare in *Westworld*: Little Boy (Oliver Bell) is a 'host', thought by fans to be a clone of the park's fictional creator, Dr Robert Ford (Anthony Hopkins):http://westworld.wikia.com/wiki/Little_Boy.
‡ 'Kagan ID' refers to Robert Kagan (2003), who argued that 'Americans are from Mars; Europeans are from Venus' to signify a strategic distinction between the US preference for hegemonic force and the EU's use of law, persuasion, compromise. See also *Policy Review*, 113 (2002), and 172 (2012). I broached the Kagan question in a column for *Flow TV* (online magazine): http://www.flowjournal.org/2005/06/media-reform-media-studies-fiske-mcchesney-bodroghkozy-jenkins-mccarthy-benny-hill-toby-mill/ (24 June 2005).

In the context of public disquiet about automation, the unsettling comparative question is this: What if the post-human 'other' is not a technology but a class? Of course, the answer is already prepared: it's called *The Handmaid's Tale*, where real women are subjugated to the status of technology (birthing machines), in a fantasy world with grim reminders of the one that we already live in (Season 1); for some, too grim (Season 2),[7] because it doesn't know the difference between *slavery* (where rebellion looks like Spartacus),[8] and *class* (where rebellion looks like Canada).

Thus, the question 'What is television?' has remained pertinent long after TV ceased to operate along strictly broadcast, mass-society lines, and well into the era of postmodern mediatization, with simultaneous globalization and fragmentation of platforms, audiences and senses of collective self. Television is a world system for constructing and reflecting on the modern subject, most compellingly posing the question of how dangerous that subject is to the world and to other systems. It allows us to crowdsource our deliberations about what should become of the Western-oriented 'we' of modernity.

There are many who have enjoyed the fruits of freedom and comfort but who fear for what their children may inherit at planetary scale. The prospect of the unfurling Anthropocene era, when 'we' (the 'we' of *H. sapiens*) become our own worst enemies, globalizing conflict, climate change and environmental catastrophe and imposing cruelties on 'they' classes from migrants to robots, presents a doubtful future for our own children. Television has routinely pursued this unquiet thought through its most visible discursive elaboration, not philosophy directly (Wark, 2016) but the pop-culture forms where philosophy and children habitually meet – in drama, music, fantasy and fiction. Do we follow McKenzie Wark's philosophical advice for the 'over-developed world'?

> The Anthropocene calls not so much for new ways of thinking as for new ways of practicing knowledge. When the going gets weird, the weird turn pro. And it is likely to get weird – in this lifetime, or the next. That's why I think we could start working now, not on theory of the Anthropocene, but theory for the Anthropocene. ... Let's build a world, and live in it. (Wark, n.d.)

---

[7]See: https://www.hulu.com/series/the-handmaids-tale-565d8976-9d26-4e63-866c-40f8a137c e5f; and https://www.smh.com.au/entertainment/tv-and-radio/all-the-ways-the-handmaid-s-ta le-s2-finale-got-it-so-horribly-wrong-20180716-p4zrub.html.
[8]Not the 1960 Stanley Kubrick film, or Ridley Scott's *Gladiator* (2000), or the 2004 US TV miniseries, but the event on which these are based, known at the time as the Third Servile War: https://en.wikipedia.org/wiki/Third_Servile_War.

Wark is recommending a practice derived from the work of Alexander Bogdanov (Wark, 2016), who promoted 'tektology' (systems theory in science and the biosciences, or 'work') and 'proletkult' (revolutionary-proletarian art, or 'play'). Wark reckons that 'one could do worse, I think, than imagine and practice again something like a tektology and a proletkult – a tektology for hackers, a proletkult for cyborgs' (Wark, n.d.), where tektology covers 'science and design' while proletkult covers 'culture and art'. This sounds very like a programme for cultural science!

What becomes of our children there? Do they succeed, or succumb?

12

World class:

Girls as a problem of knowledge

*What kind of constitutive role in the production of knowledge,
imagination, and practice can new groups doing science have?
How can these groups be allied with progressive social and
political movements? What kind of political accountability can be
constructed to tie women together across the scientific-technical
hierarchies separating us?*

(DONNA HARAWAY, 2004: 29)

World class?

Girls are one of the most familiar groups in and on social media, but
not quite, or not even, a stand-alone category in social sciences, where
the default unit is the adult male. That asymmetry is what this chapter
is about: the problem of knowledge posed by 'girls'. As an object of
knowledge, girls seem to be at once over-represented/overvalued in the
informal knowledge domain and under-represented/undervalued in the
formal one. In anthropological thought, something that is at once over- and
undervalued is a sure sign of taboo, that ancient brokerage of the relations
between nature and culture, sacred and profane, giving and receiving,
visible and invisible. In turn, what that means is simply that girls have,
since time immemorial, been defined from the outside, according to their
value to others and not in terms of their individual characters or intrinsic
capabilities, which means that 'knowing about girls' is not a simple matter

of observation, but rather one of relation. 'What girls know' and 'how they are known' (including in this chapter) are different things. The chapter pursues that difference, on the hunch that their traditional undervaluation/overvaluation in knowledge systems masks an emergent reality: that girls themselves, as *agents* of knowledge, may have something new to say about the future of this increasingly integrated and connected but fragmented and conflicted planet, just at the time when 'we' are starting to think as a species, about the Earth system as a unitary whole.

According to this view, girls are forming themselves, and their allies across all gender categories, into a new 'world class' borne out of digital media technologies and global connectivity. They are not a specialist group (such as scientists, technologists, businesses or security forces – groups organized to exploit), but a deme, or inter-knowing population bound by language, identity and knowledge (a group organized to explain), whose own demographic prominence is propelled by computational and creative productivity, and whose sense of internal identity is created and carried in distributed talk, song, story, entertainment and communication at global scale. What's new about this class is that it is of global scale, in principle encompassing the species, and having as its domain the planet, not sectarian groups and appropriated resources.

If girls are a 'world class' (the first of that name), then now is the time when they may be transitioning from a class 'in itself' to a class 'for itself', as Marx might have put it. They are shifting from the status of object, acted on by exogenous forces, to that of subject, acting endogenously for themselves as a group. Created by techno-economic forces, they are transitioning towards creating their own class consciousness and leadership. They are both *reacting* to the undervaluation/overvaluation binary, and *acting* to create their own future-facing deme. The difference between Marx's time and now is not that class conflict has been superseded but that a *world class* is also the *world population*, which means that 'class interests' and 'class enemies' are within the same deme: everyone is implicated (for instance in climate change, waste, global warming, extinction and the transformation/despoliation of the environment) and everyone is at once the hope and the despair of the future.

If girls – with their allies of other ages and other genders – are the vanguard of a 'world class', then who or what is their main antagonist? What they are fighting against is no longer a social group – an opposing camp – but something more abstract and more dangerous:

- the *systems* that exploit the planet and its populations without accountability;
- accelerating technological and biosocial *automation*, which no longer requires mass labour (Harari, 2018) but enforces mass debt (Wang, 2018);

- a *financial system* that promises economic growth for all ('trickle-down economics') but delivers financial profitability to few (Levine, 1997; Piketty, 2014);
- a *political apparatus* that seems unable even to discuss the issues young citizens hold most dear.[1] Those issues include:
  - diversity, Indigenous and human rights;
  - education and freedom to travel and learn;
  - climate change, waste, pollution, carbon reduction;
  - extinctions and the impact of human activity on the planet that has precipitated a new geological epoch, the Anthropocene.

The Anthropocene is already a contested term that some believe has been appropriated for the 'neoliberal financialization of nature, anthropocentric political economy, and endorsement of geoengineering' (Demos, 2017). With foes like this, girls may seem an unlikely resource for resistance. However, equally clearly, it's time for something new. Despite their existing status (as liminal figures in knowledge, society and collective action), girls are in the thick of new social movements and they know it: changing their social-media hypervisibility from 'being looked at' as individuated objects of desire/disdain to 'taking action' in organized groups and movements. So, where did they come from, as 'knowing subjects', and what might cultural science learn from them?

Knowing about girls

In the academic tree of knowledge, there is no branch dedicated to a science called 'Girls', although there is a growing interdisciplinary subfield of 'girls studies', drawn largely from feminism, media and cultural studies, and social psychology (e.g. Driscoll, 2002, 2008; Mazzarella, 2010; Kearney, 2006, 2011; Lemish, 2015); and there is growing interest in 'children and the media', in which girls figure prominently (e.g. *Journal of Children and Media*; the Global Kids Online research project at the LSE).[2] Girls studies is institutionalizing in journals, books, courses, and an association.[3] It is born out of the tension – or gap – between girls' portrayal in entertainment media (overvalued) and their circumstances and life chances in society (undervalued), 'entwined with anxieties about cultural norms and cultural

---

[1]See for instance: https://www.unicef.org.au/blog/stories/february-2019/a-passing-grade.
[2]For the journal, see: https://www.tandfonline.com/loi/rchm20. For the research project, see: http://globalkidsonline.net/.
[3]See the International Girls Studies Association: https://www.facebook.com/International-Girls-Studies-Association-249675338376037/ and the journal *Girlhood Studies* (Berghahn Books).

change' (Driscoll, 2008: 13). Girls studies has grown out of critique of the representation of girls in commercial media and concern for the potential impact that this may have on girls themselves (e.g. their self-image, body-image, or the risk of digital predators and cyberbullying); and it is often based in a critique of consumerism, sexism and exploitation more generally (for which the most extreme statement may be Tiqqun, 2012).

Otherwise, across the sciences, girls as a *self-organizing, self-representing group* remain marginal, fugitive, discounted figures, not so much misunderstood as not worth knowing. Compared with this spoken-for scarcity within formal knowledge systems, however, girls are *all over* the internet and social media, taking centre stage both as users and as representations in discourse.

Here then is a relationship: in knowledge systems, there's a scarcity amounting to lack of interest; in media systems, there's an abundance and plenitude amounting to obsession. Clearly there's nothing to be gained by choosing one side or the other of this asymmetry. Instead, cultural science, as an attempt to reconcile science, subjectivity and critique, linking systematic studies and media sociality, needs to account for the asymmetry and if possible to synthesize the two kinds of knowledge, both 'productive' and 'connective' (see Chapter 4). How might formal knowledge systems integrate with informal social media productivity and inventiveness to understand girls in relation to knowledge? This chapter attempts an answer: that girls are a culture-made deme, evolving – not without struggle – into a self-conscious *class*, self-organized around the media-politics of the digital-global age (*Teen Vogue*, 2016).[4]

I. Girls in the wild

Who wants to know?

An 'objective' way of characterizing girls would be to observe them 'in the wild', as it were. Straight away you can see that this is far from being a neutral, scientific method. Much depends on who is observing, what their motives and intentions might be, and whether the girls in question have any agency or voice in the process. In a scientific register, 'observing girls' is not only appropriate but essential; in another register, say in a shopping mall, 'observing girls' may range from creepy to criminal behaviour or, for the 'age-appropriate' demographic, it may merely point to gendered

---

[4]*Teen Vogue* (USA, September 2016), edited by Elaine Welteroth, devoted an issue to 'The Girls For Girls By Girls Issue', with a cover feature on 'Who Runs the World? – Introducing 21 [girls] under 21', and an interview with cover-girl Tavi Gevinson.

sociality in action. The duplicitous potential of the very activity associated with creating knowledge about girls – including by me – is evident from the extent to which girls studies, and feminist media studies more generally, are principally conducted by women and those who identify as 'gender creative (or gender non-conforming)' (McNeill, 2013: 846), despite the fact that men and boys have much to learn from the field, from feminism and from understanding 'girls as knowledge'. This is the clue that the chapter follows: not by observing girls directly, but by observing how they are brought into knowledge, formal and informal, and who by.

I do have an ulterior motive, of course; 'girls' is a fascinating test for cultural science itself, since it is an indeterminate, contingent, uncertain concept, posing the question of how new demes form and communicate, how they self-organize and act as a group, how they adapt to the world and change it, as harbingers of new politics – from Malala Yousafzai to Greta Thunberg; from Hermione Granger to Arya Stark; from teenage 'influencers' to pop sensations – and how they collectively produce knowledge upon which they and their deme can act. Here, 'pop culture' is a knowledge-medium, used for world-building as well as self-building. The question is: Are girls a class? Are we observing *digital-global-mediated* class formation on the fly, as it happens? Is this group dynamic replacing both the old industrial class systems that formed in the nineteenth century (on which mainstream political parties are still based) and the post-human automation of the information age (where 'class consciousness' has an *artificial* ring to it: see Chapter 11)?

Biosocial dispositions

Girls 'in the wild': What sort of animals are they? How are they brought into knowledge? Scientifically, girlhood is said to be a developmental stage among humans, as female offspring grow progressively more dimorphic (different-shaped) compared with males, enabling biological reproduction of the species once sexual maturity is reached, and social reproduction of gender roles, once girls are socialized into theirs. The question here, of course, is how much of that socialization is 'nurture' (cultural) and how much is 'nature' (biological). The 'nature first' position is standard in the natural and biosciences. It has been set out by sociologist and demographer Richard Udry. He was noted for seeking to integrate biological and social models of gender difference. But despite his 'biosocial' approach, he saw biological determination as primary:

> Humans form their social structures around gender because males and females have different biologically influenced behavioural dispositions. Gendered social structure is a universal accommodation to this biological fact. (2000: 454)

By this reckoning, girlhood is the process by which female offspring turn their biological disposition (aka prenatal hormones, determining foetal development) into social fact, boosted by postnatal encouragement from their mothers (2000: 450).

Not surprisingly, Udry's position was soon critiqued (Johnston et al., n.d.). Feminists and sociologists argued that social structures of power and inequality are more significant in determining gender roles. Eleanor Miller and Carrie Yang Costello nailed the problem with this mic-drop remark: 'Udry does not specify a mechanism by which maternal testosterone produces low wages and high jewelry use' (2001: 593).

While both sides of the debate welcomed the idea of an integrated biosocial theory of gender, the problem of causal sequence – which comes first: egg or chick? – is not solved simply by assuming that biology determines while society 'accommodates' to it, nor is it self-evident that the 'selfish gene' paradigm in bioscience is the last word on the topic. Causation may just as easily be the other way round: social requirements may cause some biological features to be accentuated, others to be moderated, especially in early life when 'dispositions' are plastic and contingent. Or perhaps it is more accurate to change the terms of the question, from 'either/or' to 'both/and', as Donna Haraway has done throughout her remarkable career:

> There is no border where evolution ends and history begins, here genes stop and environment takes up, where culture rules and nature submits, or vice versa. Instead, there are turtles upon turtles of naturecultures all the way down. (Haraway, 2004: 2)

Having failed to achieve (or even to attempt) Haraway's synthesis in practice, the biosciences and humanities remain as far apart as ever: dialogue is dampened not deepened when bio*science* is simply opposed by a Foucauldian notion of bio*power* (Rabinow and Rose, 2006).

There is a way to resolve the impasse, however. If biology is the determinant of gender, then gender is 'universal' as Udry claims, and unchanging across the entire species and across the whole timespan of *Homo sapiens*, from about 200,000 years ago.[5] But if it is socially constructed, gender roles can vary (across cultures) and they can change (across time), resulting in biosocial outcomes that are 'hard-wired' in the activities, relations and identities fitted out in *human youth*, not in the Pleistocene era. Indeed, girlhood may be the very process of hard-wiring them. As Miller and Costello (2001: 595) put it:

> Small variations in bodily form are given great social significance in our deeply gendered society. Thus we agree with Udry that biology and social forces interact in producing variations in gendered behaviors, but unlike

---

[5]See: https://en.wikipedia.org/wiki/Timeline_of_human_evolution.

Udry, we grant the social a much greater role in that interaction and hence predict that these gendered behaviors will change over time.

Do they change over time? Are girls always and everywhere girls, or are they something different at different times and in different places? Girls vary both cross-culturally and historically, so much so that there is a strong case for arguing that 'girl' is a modern (post-Renaissance) invention. Of course girls (female offspring) were not unknown in traditional or premodern societies, but were they differently construed, with different identities, actions (behaviour) and representation, and thus with different meaning? And do any of those differences persist, for example among non-Western cultures or in circumstances of economic deprivation or political danger, such that what girls mean in one place or time differs systematically from what they mean in another? And if so, what are the mechanisms that re-link them in a global economy, sorted into (overvalued) white innocence (Kanjere, 2018) and (undervalued) brown labour (Eddo-Lodge, 2018)?

Girls as we know them

When did girls 'as we know them' emerge? This question was first asked by the social historian Philippe Ariès (1962), with whose name is associated the larger idea of the 'social construction of childhood'. He pioneered the use of art history in order to 'read' representations of childhood in the (largely European) past. Ariès observed that portraits of children were rare in the medieval period, when children were routinely wasted. They died in infancy, before they had 'entered life' (productive society), not infrequently to be replaced by a younger sibling who was given the same name.

Portraits of high-status children, including dead ones, began to appear on European tombs only in the sixteenth and seventeenth centuries, albeit in the context of their father's death, not their own:

> The appearance of the portrait of the dead child in the sixteenth century accordingly marked a very important moment in the history of feelings. This portrait was a funeral effigy to begin with. The child was not at first portrayed alone, but on their parents' tomb. (1962: 40)

For example, check out these girls from 1600 (Figure 12.1), on a well-known tomb in Essex, England. These are the *original* 'Essex girls'. But it is quite hard even to distinguish which of Sir Edward Denny's offspring were female. They are not represented as girlish or individuated in any way, but as 'little adults'. As Ariès says, 'the distinction between child and adult still did not exist in the case of women' (1962: 50–2).[6] Girls dressed like their mothers,

---

[6]Ariès was referring here to a 1649 painting with similar characteristics. See: https://commons .wikimedia.org/wiki/File:Champaigne-Montmor-Reims.jpg.

FIGURE 12.1 *Little adults: Monument to Sir Edward Denny (d. 1600), Waltham Abbey, UK. Photo (detail) 2008 by Richard Croft, geograph.org.uk. CC license: https://commons.wikimedia.org/wiki/File:Denny_Monument_-_geograph.org.uk_-_1032693.jpg. There are ten children: seven boys and three girls. Two adult boys wear swords; two married girls wear ruffs; two children predeceased their father. The three girls' names were Elizabeth (b. 1586), Honora (died young) and Marie (d. 29 November 1678). See: https://en.wikipedia.org/wiki/Edward_Denny_(soldier).*

and young boys dressed like girls (in swaddling, then smocks). On the Essex tomb, the ten Denny children are weeping/praying for their deceased father, whose 'increase' is thereby celebrated: his wealth-creation (he was a soldier, privateer and colonizer), social standing (he was knighted and a member of parliament), and increase in dynastic progeny (himself an orphan).[7] Further differentiation was not deemed necessary, even of two of the children – a girl and a boy – who were already dead.[8] In short, the girls are *his*,

---

[7]Denny was an Elizabethan courtier and adventurer, active in privateering against Spain and the suppression of Ireland. See: https://en.wikipedia.org/wiki/Edward_Denny_(soldier).

[8]Wikipedia (see previous note) reckons the two children on the right are twins, hence their linked arms; but they may depict the already-deceased girl and boy. If so, then the figures are

not *themselves*. This is a 'portrait' of what the philosopher C. B. Macpherson (1962) would call 'the political theory of possessive individualism'.

Sir Edward Denny belonged to the world of Elizabeth I, Shakespeare and his own more famous cousin Sir Walter Raleigh, when the European Renaissance modulated into the early modern era. This was characterized by the emergence of the strong state (the Tudors), 'enclosure' (privatization of common land) and expansionism abroad, which was itself modulating from exploration to imperialism. In such a world, property assumed a new guise (as capital) and a new significance (valuing a man by his 'increase' not his descent). Accumulating capital and making it work through such newfangled inventions as banks and joint-stock companies (one of the first being Shakespeare's theatre company) became the route to success, especially for those without direct inheritance or title who could go far by exploit, in war, law or letters, in an age that was 'on the make'. In this world, highborn girls were a family's *property assets*, not in their own right but in terms of marriage capital.

Parthenophilia

Naturally, as Henry VIII's attempts to sire a legitimate male heir gruesomely demonstrated, biology played a role, but the vicissitudes of uncertain life and society made all the difference. Henry's ultimately successful heir was perhaps the least likely, given that her mother was executed by her father, and she was preceded to the throne by her half-brother Edward, cousin Jane Grey and half-sister Mary. Had any of these survived long enough to produce an heir we would never have heard of Elizabeth Tudor.

Doubtless she was naturally endowed with traits that contributed to her conduct during her long reign (1558–1603). But 'nurture' played its part, not only informally, in the character-forming childhood of a Tudor princess during the high-risk period when a medieval Catholic monarchy transformed itself into a centralized, Protestant state, but also formally – Elizabeth was *educated*, unlike most girls of her time. Her most important tutor was Roger Ascham,[9] who wrote of her in about 1550, after Henry's death:

> It is difficult to say whether the gifts of nature or of fortune are most to be admired in my distinguished mistress. ... She has just passed her sixteenth birthday and shows such dignity and gentleness as are wonderful at

---

sorted with all the surviving boys on the left, girls and dead children on the right, which may indicate their relative values in a society where girls married *out* of the family and descent was through male heirs. Hence, boys are grouped together, girls and deceased grouped together in dynastic equivalence.

[9]See: http://www.oxfordbibliographies.com/view/document/obo-9780195399301/obo-978019 5399301-0167.xml.

her age and in her rank. … Her mind has no womanly weakness, her perseverance is equal to that of a man. (Qtd in Neale, 1952: 14)

Clearly, 'girlishness' was not innate! Nature had endowed her, wrote Ascham, with 'beauty, stature, prudence, and industry' but not with 'womanly weakness' of mind. Her experience of girlhood was determined by birth but also by religion (she was raised a Protestant, a bookish religion) and by considerations of family (class) and of state (politics) that eventually overturned eons of gender expectation. Together with her equally learned cousin Jane Grey (Protestant queen for nine days) and half-sister Mary (Catholic queen for five years), Elizabeth broke the mould of male succession and ruled for forty-five years, during which time the 'first British Empire' began to be carved out of the North American continent by buccaneering daredevils like Sir Walter Raleigh and Sir Edward Denny. Elizabeth learned from her father's court how uncertain the 'feminine career' (McRobbie, 1982) of advantageous marriage could be. She fulfilled his dynastic ambitions by negating them, 'married' only to her people. Her maiden status, normally disastrous for aristocratic women, was now celebrated as a glorious attribute in the person of Virgin Queen, embodiment of the one power indisputably belonging to *girls*. The colonial plantation of Virginia was named for her, as was the first English child born in America, Virginia Dare (b. 1587). Virginity became a mark not of marriageability but of a New World of potential wealth and power, and Virginia remains an honourable girl's name to this day.

II. Evolutionary girls

Conflict theory

Elizabeth I's own long road to self-determination, to beat the odds of history, of expectation and competing interests, has become a 'role model' for girls, not least in the movies, where her times are still a box-office attraction. Self-determination still depends on uncertain combinations of inheritance, education, ambition and luck but, after four centuries of modernization and democratization, it is no longer tied directly to descent. As premodern status hierarchies eroded, so the agent of change shifted; by the end of the nineteenth century, the driver of biosocial change was seen, not as blood and gender, but as *struggle* – in both 'nature' (the evolutionary 'struggle for existence') and 'nurture' (Marxist 'class struggle').

Here lies the *origin of girls*, at least according to a 'Darwinian conflict theory' advanced by Stephen Sanderson (2001). Sanderson seeks to resolve the bio/social debate sparked by Richard Udry (see above) by introducing Darwin to Marx: biosocial evolution is 'Darwinian' because it accepts underlying biological evolution; and it is a 'conflict theory' because it accepts Marx's model of society as a site of struggle. Working from this premise, Sanderson draws attention to the issue of *change* in relation to gender equality. That is an important addition to the debate. However, his view is that change itself is gendered. Over the forty to fifty years before the turn of the twenty-first century, he writes,

> men have changed little, whereas women have changed considerably. Women have become much more like men than men have become like women. (2001: 213)

Sanderson concludes that 'social change efforts in the direction of greater gender equality ... should concentrate on *making females more masculine in their life orientations, occupational interests,* and so on' (2001: 213; my emphasis).

Perhaps that is not a very tasty dish to set before the world's girls, as their life's ambition! But it does draw attention to two important issues. First, that 'masculinity' involves more than just testosterone-driven behaviour or personal identity: it also includes employment and life chances, power and freedom to embark on what used to be called 'exploit' – adventure, enterprise and risk, requiring daring and action. It is quite possible that girls would very much want their share of employment, power and exploit. To the extent that these have been allocated to the masculine domain for many generations, 'making females more masculine' makes sense, because it speaks to *social* not *biological* gender identity. Second, Sanderson's suggestion for 'social change efforts' towards gender equality assumes that gender roles can be varied by deliberate *activism* to produce social change. The problem to be addressed is about gender inequality, not just about women's biology, and thus there's no suggestion that gender inequalities were all 'hard-wired in the Pleistocene', as the saying goes, but are subject to struggle.

However, despite these advances over the biological determinist position, Sanderson's model is fatally flawed. First, he assumes what he should explain – that women 'have become more like men', which assumes that *men* are 'like men' because they *are men*: a false syllogism, or, even more clumsily, that men are the standard, women the deviation, so the quicker they become 'more masculine' the better for them. More significant is that – like a neoliberal libertarian – he reduces 'struggle' to *individual* competition, never countenancing the Marxist implication of the term, even though he borrows it from Marx, which is that it is a *group-level* phenomenon – *class* struggle. As a result, his speculations on the question of power are ludicrous, still obsessed with girls' virginity, this time not as a mark of sovereignty and independence but as a bargaining chip:

> We know why men want to control female sexuality, but why should they be able to control it much more in societies at higher stages of social

evolution? The answer is probably that women are competing more among themselves for men, especially high-status men, who prefer virgin brides and are in a position to demand them. ... It is a cost benefit matter. (2001: 214)

Unfortunately, as they say, the latter end of his commonwealth forgets the beginning. This is far from being an evolutionary theory, much less a Marxist one. First, there's no such thing as a 'higher stage' of evolution, social or otherwise. Evolution is blind, based on random variations in matter-energy processes. Certainly societies and states may become more complex, but that doesn't make them 'higher'; indeed, taking the long view, sophisticated systems routinely collapse to extinction. Second, evolution is not 'interested': it does not proceed from the intentions of individual actors, be they scheming women or parthenophile (virgin-loving) men.[10] On top of this, Sanderson explains *men's* behaviour (wanting to control female sexuality) by guessing about *women's* actions (competing among themselves). It is hard to imagine a woman writing that passage, because it blames women for their own sexual subjection, saying nothing about power, predatory behaviour and divide-and-rule tactics. Sanderson is driven to this lame and impotent conclusion by the logic of his own theory, which 'insists' (his term) that gender has nothing to do with *culture*:

> [Darwinian conflict theory] acknowledges that much of human society is 'socially constructed', but insists that the constructions that result are not arbitrary and capricious products of some sort of autonomous 'culture'. (2001, 143)

Instead, according to him, social 'constructions' are 'constrained' by biological, ecological, economic and material conditions, and social 'functions' belong to 'individuals' (specifically, men), not to 'some reified abstraction called "society"' (143). Here, causation is ascribed only to individuals, while social functions are not social and cultural constructions are arbitrary, without autonomy (i.e. without causal agency). In the effort to retain a commitment to materialism and to oppose postmodern cultural relativism (a popular theme among science commentators at the time), his 'comprehensive' and 'integrated' theory collapses. A biosocial 'conflict theory' might offer insights into gender relations, but this version

---

[10]For this word, which means 'Virgin-lover', applied equally to the maiden (object of poet's desire) and to Queen Elizabeth, see this disturbing poem by Barnabe Barnes (1593): http://www.bartleby.com/358/index5.html. In the end, Parthenophile (Virgin-lover) can't bear for Pathenophe (Virgin-girl) to *remain* a virgin, and the poem ends on a fantasy of the Renaissance equivalent of date rape, accomplished with the Renaissance equivalent of Rohypnol (Sonnet CV and Sestine 5). Is that what contemporaries *really* thought of the Virgin Queen?

of it falls over by reducing gender to 'rational choice' between status-seeking women and virgin-loving men, and it allows culture, or even indeterminacy, no role in making society. In these days of #MeToo, we can do better than that.

Evolved groups

A proper 'Darwinian conflict theory' would not explain social change by reference to individual choices, rational or otherwise, but by interactions *between groups* (populations and subpopulations), in this case sorted by gender. Feminism has done much of the heavy lifting on this aspect of the problem, by showing how individual choices are not open equally across the gender spectrum, because individuals are also 'determined' by the gender-group to which they are assigned. For example, working from an evolutionary perspective and using evidence from across the primates, Barbara Smuts (1995) has hypothesized that conflicts between the sexes 'pre-date the emergence of the human species'. The result – *patriarchy* – is compatible with evolution, she argues, resulting from these six causal conditions:

- Reduced social support for females among kin and female allies (failure to maintain strong group identity among females);
- Development of stronger 'alliances' among males (operating as a coherent group);
- Control of resources by males;
- Increasing hierarchies among men, in which women became 'increasingly vulnerable to the will and whims of the few most powerful men';
- Female strategies reinforcing patriarchal control;
- The evolution of language, enabling the creation of ideologies to reinforce patriarchy.

All of this requires 'male' and 'female' to be understood as distinct groups or subpopulations (i.e. demes) within the category of the human, created out of gender-based alliances, resources, power, coping strategies and the use of language to promote group interests and to maintain 'we'-group solidarity. (Rita Felski (1989) points out that feminism itself serves this function.)

Conflict here is not the working out of individual cost-benefit calculations but a 'conflict of interest' between groups in relation to common practices of sexuality and reproduction. 'Conflict' and 'struggle' are therefore different concepts for individuals compared with groups, just as 'aggression' is personal and 'violence' is social (as we saw in Chapters 3 and 4). Individual violence can be used to *decide* an issue, not least semiotically, typically by man-on-man fist fighting in TV, film and drama, whether of power (winner takes all) or morality (right defeats might). But group conflict cannot be decided in this way. Instead, it is continuous along a border-zone of difference between incommensurate or incompatible opposites, which nevertheless require each other in order to exist *as* different. There can be no such identity as 'man' without contrast to 'woman'. The system of gender difference requires both poles, because it is the opposition and difference between them that is productive of what each means (Barthes, 2007). Men's and women's sexual reproductive interests and functions are different, but both are needed for the continuation of the species. Conflict, then, is a mode of *translation* (in Lotman's terms), where incommensurable interests are not eliminated but productive of something new: that is, lived senses of sexual difference (culture-made groups, and thence gender-knowledge), and children.

III. Revolutionary girls

As with other large-scale social groups, 'workers' cannot exist without the 'capitalists' against whose interests they struggle, but both are needed for economic growth (again, up till now, when Yuval Harari (2018: 35–6) has his doubts). However, as Donna Haraway (2004) has warned, groups are not 'equal' as well as 'opposite' forces: they may be strongly asymmetrical, following power differentials:

> A major social and political danger is the formation of a strongly bimodal social structure, with the masses of women and men of all ethnic groups, but especially people of color, confined to a homework economy, illiteracy of several varieties, and general redundancy and impotence, controlled by high-tech repressive apparatuses ranging from entertainment to surveillance and disappearance. (Haraway, 2004: 29)

This grim but prescient characterization of present times reminds us that groups do not 'behave' in the same way as individuals. They bind their members together in language, codes, rules, customs, etc. One of the mechanisms for doing that is *adversarialism* – hostility towards competing groups. This is what Marx recognized as class antagonism, which he saw as one of the motors of historical change. Conflict, competition and foe-creation help to sustain cultural groups, which themselves are multiple, dynamic (constantly emerging and decaying), overlapping and, at their edges, experimental and adaptive. Conflict at group level is not based on individual prowess: to fend off antagonists' increasingly lethal incursions, groups – from empires to the labour movement, religions to classes – require *organization* at scale (Turchin, 2005; Malešević, 2017) (and see Chapter 4).

'Present at its own making'

In the present conjuncture, where a global economy is driven by information, data, creativity, culture, communication and knowledge (not as in earlier cycles, when national economies were driven by heavy industry), it is not so easy to identify an overall organizational form that directly represents any and all workers. In the industrial era, the 'labouring' or 'productive' classes produced also the union and labour movement as a 'mass' organizational form (Thompson, 1963; Williams 1961). Although the combined working-class movement was far from universal (it was never able to represent women's domestic labour, for example), it combined multiple sectors, including agricultural, fisheries, energy resources, manufacturing, transport, construction, white-collar and some service workers. The forms of organization, representation and action created in the nineteenth and twentieth centuries – trades unions (the economy), Labour Parties (politics) and the periodical press (communications) – have survived into the digital era but, like the mass media forms of that era (see Chapter 10), they are struggling for purpose as well as members, and they no longer aspire to represent or to address the workforce of global capitalism as a whole.

But as E. P. Thompson pointed out long ago in a telling statement, 'the working class ... was present at its own making' (Thompson, 1963: Preface). Its ideological aspirations (working-class emancipation) and community formation (working-class culture) were 'organically' connected, as Gramsci (1971) put it. It used the most advanced technological affordances and media of the day to organize itself.

Yet, those connections, organizational forms and media were not 'present' in the same way at the emergence of new forms of wealth-creation in the knowledge economy. The millennial generations have grown up in an era of technological disruption, increasing inequality of wealth (Piketty, 2014), porous borders (migration, globalization) and volatile politics. 'Work' does not signify the disciplined mass industriousness of the factory – except where outsourced to China, India, etc. – but precarious, casual, part-time or 'no hours' contracts, unpaid internships, start-up self-employment and home-based microbusiness. Value is created in performance, celebrity, communicative cut-through. So who is 'present' in this era of *communicative labour*? As mainstream politics (still based on 'mass' parties) spins out into xenophobic 'national populism' (Eatwell and Godwin, 2018), *gilets jaunes* (yellow vests) and Brexit, spawning but unable to control authoritarian crackdown and corporate unaccountability, this has emerged as a crucial question for political thinkers.

For example, in the *New Statesman*, one of the few surviving political weeklies, Jonathan Rutherford analyses the problem this way:

> Communicative labour is immaterial. It has no end product and so what counts as a measure of productivity is performance. ... Early industrial

capitalism commodified human labour and enclosed the commons of land. Today, capitalism is enclosing commonly owned information and knowledge. ... The ubiquity of social media compounds the dilemma of human emotional connection. (Rutherford, 2018)

This catch-all analysis does not identify those who perform 'communicative labour' (they are abstract and 'immaterial' like their work); but it does identify the 'states of anxiety, depression, insecurity and self-dislike' that social media have made 'more commonplace in the young' (Rutherford, 2018). Rutherford wants to blame the baby-boomers for turning 'belonging' into 'performing', seeing 'immaterial labour' itself as a failure of progressive politics:

> The countercultural values of the 1968 generation helped to create a more tolerant and open society. But they also provided a crucial resource for these new kinds of capital accumulation, and a new consumer aesthetic of capitalism. The pursuit of transgression was assimilated by the market and commodified. Over the decades, progressive politics' ... cosmopolitan liberalism and moral relativism have left it poorly equipped to address the questions now confronting its own children about the nature of adulthood, and the meaning and purpose of life, and how we can live it well. (Rutherford, 2018)

This dystopian vision leaves the young as a mere *effect* of the old. It seems that the *labour* approach to class formation and action has reached its limit: it cannot identify the agency of change. But if a class is 'present at its own making', and performing its own constructed, 'immaterial' self, using the organizational forms of social media and commodified culture, then that's where to look for class consciousness to arise. If communicative labour is exploitative of 'the young' and of 'its own children', then the unnamed presence includes girls, but the idea that they may combine to form responses of their own is not entertained.

'Freedom and arrogance': A model of subversion

To offer a flavour of alternatives, there is a very different history of the girl in Japanese literary and popular culture (compare Iversen, 2016). In their study of the 'reading girl' or *shōjo* in Japanese literary culture, editors Tomoko Aoyama and Barbara Hartley (no relation) note that the majority of literary 'reading girls' are adolescents or young women, but they point to work that identifies 'girl consciousness' (*shōjo ishiki*) as a general concept, 'not the sole province of the chronological girl but something older women and even men can possess' (Aoyama and Hartley, 2010: 7). They introduce the concept of 'girl consciousness', characterized by 'freedom and arrogance, the key attributes needed for the girl to function as an active self, resisting hegemonic norms'.

Aoyama and Hartley note that the term was coined in Japanese by a male author, Eiri Takahara (2006), as a transgender, transsexual or intersexual signifier of 'the girl as a model of subversion for other marginalized social or cultural selves' (Aoyama and Hartley, 2010: 8). They add that 'caution might be sounded regarding the appropriation of the attributes of the girl by more powerful discursive elements' (2010: 7–8) – a caution that must apply to this chapter too – but with Kazumi Nagaike they accept that the concept of 'girl consciousness' in literature, manga, anime and Japanese culture is not determined by the biological age or gender of the character: it is a 'cognitive' matter in the realm of representation, and as such it may 'escape complicity in the master social narrative of gender determination' (Nagaike, 2010: 113).

The attributes of 'freedom and arrogance' as a 'model of subversion' are both the essence of 'girl consciousness' and generalizable across 'marginalized selves'. This squares with the argument put by Berndt, Nagaike and Ogi (2019), that the Japan-derived concept of *shōjo*, 'while still situated, begins to offer possibilities for broader conceptualizations of girlness within the contemporary global digital mediascape', which is where we're headed now.

IV. Representative girls

What's in a word?

Girls circulate as representations, of which perhaps the basic 'unit' is the word 'girl' itself. Of course this differs among different languages, but its origins and career in English (and that tongue's Germanic neighbours) are instructive. The English world for 'girl' reveals not 'freedom and arrogance' but some very long-standing prejudices about girls that have nothing to do with any intrinsic properties and everything to do with how girls are looked at, spoken about and positioned, at once constructed and contained in discourse. The word 'girl' entered English (no one knows where from) in the late Middle Ages (1400s to 1500s) as a non-gender-specific term for young children, applied to boys as well as girls. According to the *OED*, its origin is:

Middle English (denoting a child or young person of either sex): perhaps related to Low German gör child'.[11]

---

[11]According to Stephen Fry on *QI*: 'The people who were traditionally dressed in pink and called girls were boys. Pink was considered the traditional colour for boys and blue for girls

'*Gör*' is still a word in German: a term for 'brat'. In the *Duden*, the standard German reference dictionary, *gör* is sourced from 'Low German, probably an adjective meaning "small" … and originally = small helpless creature'. It is still applicable to both sexes:

1. *<Usually in the plural> [dirty, naughty]* Child
   <meist im Plural> [schmutziges, unartiges] Kind

2. *[Cheeky, naughty little]* Girl
   [vorwitziges, freches kleines] Mädchen

According to the *Duden*, the word *gör* is synonymous with *Frechdachs*, *Rotzjunge*: 'snotty-nosed brat', 'whippersnapper', 'rascal', referring to a 'cheeky, naughty little girl'.[12]

If *gör* is indeed the source-word of 'girl', its career in German has been somewhat different from its career in English. Even so, one of the English language's most impressively imagined girl-heroines, Roald Dahl's *Matilda* (1988), is certainly a *gör*, at least as far as her parents and headmistress Miss Trunchbull are concerned, which is no doubt why legions of girls love her. There's an important lesson here: the word 'girl' – like the word *gör* – conveys a meaning that comes from the judgement of others, not from the 'content of her character' (as Matilda proves).

Apparently neutral or objective words may mask a whole history of casual put-down, amounting almost to hate speech. It turns out that this is the story of 'girl', at least in dictionaries. The most influential predecessor of the *OED* in English is Samuel Johnson's great *Dictionary*, first published in 1755. Dr Johnson was even more cautious than the *OED* about where 'girl' comes from. His entry, which defines 'girl' simply as 'a young woman, or female child' (as does the *OED*), is prefaced with etymological caution:

GIRL [About the etymology of this word there is much question: Meric Casaubon, as is his custom, derives it from χορη,[13] of the same signification; Minshew from garrula, Latin, a prattler, or girella, Italian, a weathercock; Junius thinks that it comes from herlodes, Welsh, from which, says he, harlot is very easily deduced. Skinner imagines that the Saxons, who used ceoŋl for a man, might likewise have ceoŋla for a

---

in the 19th century. … Right until the mid-15th century, all children were referred to as girls, boys were called "knave girls" and girls were called "gay girls". The word "boy" originally meant "servant"': https://www.comedy.co.uk/tv/qi/episodes/7/7/. See also: http://www.etym online.com/index.php?term=girl.
[12]See: http://www.duden.de/rechtschreibung/Goer. The *Duden* is the 'predominant language resource of the German language': https://en.wikipedia.org/wiki/Duden.
[13]I think the Ancient Greek word referred to here is χορός, 'chorus'.

woman, though no such word is now found. Dr. Hickes derives it most probably from the Islandick karlinna, a woman.][14]

In short, take your pick, but pack your scepticism, while noting lexicography's prejudicial name-calling: 'girl' means 'prattler', 'weathercock', 'harlot' or simply 'wo-man'. None of Dr Johnson's etymological sources has survived into the *OED*, but they were widely shared among other lexicographers, and are still a ghostly presence in the etymology section of Wiktionary.[15] As well as their persistence in time, these 'definitions' of girls travelled far and wide. Nathan Bailey's *Universal Etymological English Dictionary*, first published in 1721, was the most popular English dictionary of the eighteenth century, running to thirty editions.[16] The entry on 'girl' from the 28th edition, published in 1800, borrows Johnson's etymology, but adds an explanation: '...of *garrula*, L. prating ... because they are addicted to talkativeness' (Figure 12.2).

It seems that prejudice became 'true', that is, definitional (shifting meaning from speech to object), as soon as there were dictionaries. Girls were named by reference to existing objects of disdain, gaining 'objectivity' from how they were seen by learned men. What we learn from the historical dictionary, then, is that 'girl' comes from outside English (from other languages), outside

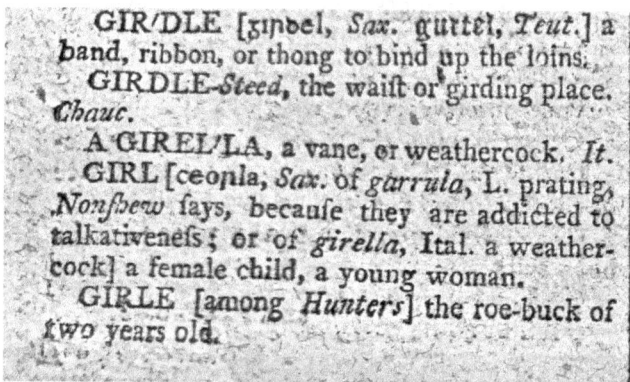

FIGURE 12.2 *'Talkativeness'! (Bailey's* Universal Etymological English Dictionary, *1721–1800).*

---

[14]1755 edn. See: http://pbc.gda.pl/dlibra/docmetadata?id=19407 (p. 904). See also 1785 edn: http://publicdomainreview.org/collections/samuel-johnsons-dictionary-of-the-english-langua ge-1785/ (p. 873).
[15]See: https://en.wiktionary.org/wiki/girl.
[16]See: https://en.wikipedia.org/wiki/An_Universal_Etymological_English_Dictionary; Dictionary at: https://archive.org/details/universaletymolo00bail.

girls (from other people), and outside girls' own attributes (from other discourses). It's a term of relationship, coined in disrespect. The best that can be said of 'definition' is that it leaves plenty of scope for girls themselves to fill in the gaps with 'arrogance and freedom'.

Selfie consciousness

Missing-in-action across the learned disciplines, girls are disproportionately ubiquitous in social and entertainment media. Here, it's not only a matter of self-representation *by* girls, or commercial and anthropological display *of* girls, but also 'girls' as a concept or idea is deployed by others and by girls themselves (as a deme), as something to *think with*, about the limits of the social, for instance. Girls are 'produced' and delineated (bounded by limits) in informal *knowledge systems*, where they are also productive, intensive sites of transformational energy.

Given their limited outlets for self-representation and mediation in formal knowledge systems (see Chapter 4), perhaps it is no surprise that girls and young women have taken to social media so enthusiastically (Pew Research, 2014a, 2015), where they have made *the selfie* their own (Senft and Baym, 2016; O. Nelson, 2013): 'Among Millennials, women are more likely than men to have posted a selfie (68% vs. 42%)' (Pew Research, 2014a: 48). Naturally, at that same point, selfies attracted massive social and media anxiety, attention and criticism from the outside. So much so that 'selfie', a word that originated at a drunken party in Australia in 2002, was named *Oxford Dictionaries'* international Word of the Year in 2013:

> Language research conducted by *Oxford Dictionaries* editors reveals that the frequency of the word selfie in the English language has increased by 17,000% since this time last year [November].[17]

What the selfie tells us is that self-representation – turning identity into knowledge, constituting it by communicating it – is not confined to speech or writing, but is equally readily found in visual, electronic and mobile media. What's more, it is important to look at 'informal' sources such as these, because that's where knowledge about girls proliferates most intensely, by girls themselves using whatever media are accessible, and by others,

---

[17]The word was first recorded on an ABC Online forum posting (13 September 2002): 'Um, drunk at a mates 21st … And sorry about the focus, it was a selfie.' According to the editorial director of *Oxford Dictionaries*, 'Australian English has something of a penchant for – ie words – barbie for barbecue, firie for firefighter, tinnie for a can of beer – so this helps to support the evidence for selfie having originated in Australia.' Source (including quoted passage): http://blo g.oxforddictionaries.com/press-releases/oxford-dictionaries-word-of-the-year-2013/.

whose interventions are often directed towards controlling girls rather than explaining them.

The will to control was attested by the furore that greeted the popularization of the selfie *by girls* (see Senft and Baym, 2016; Warfield, Cambre and Abidin, 2016). Of course, that form is different from those in which scholarship is commonly conducted. Paul Frosh (2015: 1608/1624) calls the selfie 'a new phatic agent in the energy flows between bodily movements, sociable interactions, and media technologies that have become fundamental to our everyday, routine experience of digital activities', where knowledge comes out of a 'technocultural circuit of corporeal social energy that I will call kinesthetic sociability'. Every selfie is a link in a communication chain, to which a response (from 'followers', for instance) is required as part of the statement being made; and what results is shared knowledge. But, as Anne Burns (2015) argues, such knowledge does not go uncontested. It is gendered:

> Once the selfie is established as connoting narcissism and vanity, it perpetuates a vicious circle in which women are vain because they take selfies, and selfies connote vanity because women take them. (Burns, 2015: 1720)

In short, there's a difference between knowledge *by* selfie and knowledge *about* selfies: one comes from within the demic group and is 'universal' (applies to everyone in the group), the other from outside and is 'adversarial'. Onlookers from other domains (whose own selfies are not seen as vain, of course) mistake phatic communication and 'kinesthetic sociability' for 'vanity' only because they are unable to recognize selfies as components of the 'mother tongue' in a particular 'knowledge club' – one that does not include the critics. In short, the critical rhetoric simply marks a demic boundary.

Girls online

Girls form a significant proportion of internet and social media users, and are often the source as well as destination of innovations, crazes, and new ideas that sweep the world. They are not organized here as a self-conscious, purposeful group (as, say, a firm or even industry might be), but their group-level activities and impact as both consumers and producers means that individual, intimate actions can have global impact. The Pew Research Center (US) conducted a major survey of American teens' (13–17 years) use of social media in 2014–15; updated in 2018. In 2015 it found that girls 'dominate visually-oriented platforms': 61 per cent of girls used Instagram (44 per cent of boys); 51 per cent of girls used Snapchat (31 per cent of boys),

33 per cent of girls used boards like Pinterest (11 per cent of boys) and 23 per cent of girls used Tumblr (5 per cent of boys) (Pew Research, 2015). More boys than girls played games, although the majority of girls did. In 2018, these differences were still apparent: girls predominated on Snapchat (42 vs. 29 per cent), boys on YouTube (39 vs. 25 per cent), but the percentages were lower, as they were for both boys' and girls' usage of Facebook (down from 71 to 51 per cent). 'Most notably, smartphone ownership has become a nearly ubiquitous element of teen life: 95% of teens now report they have a smartphone or access to one.' In general, girls remained more frequent users than boys: 'Half of teenage girls (50%) are near-constant online users, compared with 39% of teenage boys' (Pew Research, 2018).

More recent figures trace the rise of TikTok, which marked the entry of Chinese social media into American and global markets (against the grain of White House rhetoric), when this app (trading as Douyin in China and recently merged with Musical.ly, also Chinese-owned) became the most downloaded free app in the United States and third in the world. The *BusinessofApps.com* website reported:

> TikTok/Douyin (and formerly Musical.ly) users use the app largely to create, share, and view content based around lip syncing, dancing, comedy skits, and other physical activities. Clearly, this is something that appeals to young people (and quite a few older ones) around the world, with the app snowballing in popularity over 2018. (February 2019)[18]

What happens in the United States, still the world's richest, biggest and most advanced technological economy, is not the norm for girls around the world.[19] However, it would not be right to assume that less advantaged countries are less interested in or engaged with social media: some of the strongest growth in usage comes from places far away from Main St. USA, especially in East Asia (China, S Korea, Japan), South Asia (India and the Sub-continent) and SE Asia (Indonesia, Philippines, Malaysia, etc.). It is true that the least developed countries in Africa are also those with lowest levels of social media access, which is recognized as a threat to young people's development. According to a relevant UN report:

> Poor youth are less likely to have access to digital technologies and thus are disadvantaged with regard to information and other means of building social capital. Although 30 per cent of youth aged 15 to 24

---

[18]Source: http://www.businessofapps.com/data/tik-tok-statistics/.
[19]For a comparison with 'EU kids online' (with different age-ranges), see: http://www.lse.ac.uk /media-and-communications/research/research-projects/eu-kids-online/reports-and-findings; and for AU kids online, see: https://culturalscience.org/articles/abstract/10.5334/csci.40/.

worldwide in 2012 were 'digital natives', that is, with five or more years of online experience, the proportions of digital natives are much higher in wealthier countries with better Internet access, ranging from over 90 per cent in Norway and other wealthy countries to under 10 per cent in much of sub-Saharan Africa. Moreover, studies show that poor youth are much less likely than wealthier youth to use digital technologies. (UNFPA, 2014: 44)

While the digital divide is very real, there is no evidence that girls and boys *don't want* to participate, only that they *cannot* if blocked by poverty, isolation, educational and economic underinvestment, conflict, disasters and predatory policies or authoritarian regimes (UNFPA, 2014, 2015). Trends and activities among those with access in economically favoured countries are a reasonable guide to young people's aspirations, where these impediments are in process of being overcome (for instance, in China).

Girls are leaders in social media uptake, use and innovation, but that's not the whole story, of course. They occupy the other extreme as well. While girls are ubiquitous signs of success, the good life and desirability in consumer media, they remain society's most vulnerable demographic across the world, especially younger girls living in poorer countries. According to the UN's Babatunde Osotimehin (UNFPA, 2015: 3):

> Very young adolescent girls ... are the most vulnerable and least able to confront the many challenges they face, even in stable times. Under normal circumstances in some developing countries, a 10-year-old girl, for example, may be married off against her will, trafficked, separated from her family and all social support and have limited access to education, health or opportunities for a better life. When a crisis strikes, these risks multiply, and so do that girl's vulnerabilities. Her prospects go from bad to worse.

The UN's call for a 'transformative agenda for women and girls in a crisis-prone world' is based on the proposition that we are 'one world', and that therefore the vulnerabilities of girls anywhere is everyone's problem: (UNFPA, 2015: 35). That's part of the motivation for this chapter, not only that 'girls in the world' are one object of study but also that they are beginning to find common voice and common cause, from Malala Yousafzai and Tavi Gevinson to Greta Thunberg and Emma Watson, such that a global 'girl consciousness' can be seen to be emerging, of which celebrity figures are at once the 'organic intellectuals' and market leaders.[20]

---

[20]See, for example, Emma Watson as UN Women Goodwill Ambassador, visiting Mtakataka Secondary School in Malawi, with Stella Kalilombe and Cecilia Banda, girls whose marriages

V. Girls in the world

Cultural science

Cultural science opens up another way to think about 'girls in the world', by taking seriously the 'world' part of the equation. Instead of starting with the individual and working up to larger units, cultural science starts from the perspective of systems and populations. As girls themselves may have understood more clearly than their elders, you can't understand a relational entity like 'girl' outside of the global systems of sense-making (the semiosphere), mediation (the mediasphere) and knowledge (the noosphere) within which everyone else lives.

H. sapiens is combining as a global 'unit', interacting as a single network with the planet and its systems. It is in this context that girls emerge as a new deme-formation, with political agency (self-consciousness as a group) led by girls, as well as self-organization within the group using semiotic and technological means to hand.

An indication that politics is now more divided between young and old than between left and right emerged from the Australian federal election of 2019, when a youth-oriented radio station (ABC Triple J) surveyed 14,000 first-time voters (18–29 years), to find that

> the vast majority of young Australians – 89 per cent – have no faith that politicians are working in the best interests of the planet, and rate environmental policy and climate change as the most important issues to them at next month's election.[21]

When *90 per cent* of an entire population (both male and female) has observed and understood national politics in this global perspective, it is clear that a general change in consciousness is afoot – and reaching the age of action – just as traditional politics has reached impasse.

Distributed expertise

These developments pose important new questions for observers, analysts and experts, who are now fully integrated participants in the global knowledge economy. Education, research, the creative industries, consultancy and the digital economy are now one integrated knowledge-making category.

---

were annulled and they returned to school (2016): http://www.stewardshipreport.com/in-mala
wi-un-women-goodwill-ambassador-emma-watson-works-to-end-child-marriage/.
[21]https://www.abc.net.au/triplej/programs/hack/whats-up-in-your-world/11021316.

And, as the economist John Quiggin has pointed out (2008: 176–7), 'the household sector may play a central role in the growth of the information economy, blurring traditional boundaries between employment and household practice'. In other words, activities in families, domestic settings and households, traditionally excluded from economic accounting despite the productivity of housework and childcare, become economically as well as culturally visible in a knowledge economy. With ubiquitous internet and media connectivity, household practices (traditional and otherwise, from cooking to fanship, childcare to games) could be rendered into knowledge and communicated to peers – and hence customers – directly by those who practised them. The maker movement and DIY culture extend craft 'know-how' into digital 'can-do'.

Expertise is now a distributed, non-rare resource. Online tuition and education is available freely, everyone is an expert in something. Age is no barrier to entry into this 'market': simply by using social media, users change from expression to publication, rendering the entire online population into producers as well as consumers. Sometimes people share their expertise without expectation of reward, but there's money in 'knowing and showing' too. Family life is regularly turned into online 'show and tell'. Household self-help can turn into a business, and individuals can become 'consumer entrepreneurs'; by acting as fashion and brand 'influencers' (Abidin, 2015a). The scale of these achievements should not be underestimated. Delighting children with the simple adventure of 'unboxing' toys and treats can take your household's viewing hits up to the half-a-billion mark.[22] One enterprising couple started putting up nursery rhyme compilations on YouTube in 2011. Five years later their channel had over 8 million subscribers and nearly 10 billion views.[23] The babies of 'influencers' regularly feature in their videos; infants and toddlers can become what Crystal Abidin (2015b) calls 'micro-microcelebrities'.

Abidin has followed this phenomenon through numerous publications (Abidin, 2018), showing how commercial pop culture and celebrity raises questions of much wider import. Questions of communicative labour, activism and community formation require 'theorizations focused on race and ethnicity, gender and sexuality, popular culture and entertainment, commerce and power, and politics and activism' (Abidin and Brown, 2018: 8). Further, Abidin and her co-authors focus their analyses on the Global South,

---

[22]'Play Doh Sparkle Princess Ariel Elsa Anna Disney Frozen MagiClip Glitter Glider Magic Clip Dolls' received over half-a-billion views (2014–16): https://www.youtube.com/watch?v=I8vzbIuv hoo; and see: http://fusion.net/story/38924/the-highest-youtube-earner-of-2014-made-4-9-millio n-just-by-opening-disney-toy-packages/. So did Ryan Toy Review for '100+ cars toys GIANT EGG SURPRISE OPENING Disney Pixar Lightning McQueen': https://www.youtube.com/w atch?v=Tldlt2RhrDw.
[23]Little Baby Bum (LBB) channel: https://www.youtube.com/user/LittleBabyBum/about. Their best-known single video, *Wheels of the Bus*, had 1,605,768,132 (1.6bn) views, 2014–16.

extending microcelebrity studies beyond the 'Anglobalization' perspective dominating media and scholarship. Microcelebrities are a microcosm of the problem of knowledge posed by girls: harbingers of the new, but treated as exotic rather than expert, in the very places where they are (being told off for) developing new forms of distributed expertise.

As soon as ordinary users begin to teach each other, a challenge is issued to educational expertise. This is in fact quite a familiar situation for scholars of media themselves. Their/our own expertise is precarious: 'watching telly' is hardly a scientific method. Once upon a time, research related to TV was simply a branch of some other specialism: psychologists looked for its adverse behavioural effects (as discussed in Chapter 10); literary scholars compared its texts with those of canonical art; social scientists wanted to know how media entertainment changed other social institutions – the family, education, class, gender, etc.; and political economists worried about the power of media corporations. It took a long time for these and other input strands to twine into 'media studies' (a continuing process), where popular culture and mediation was investigated on its own terms, rather than as a secondary symptom of some primary moral, aesthetic, political or behavioural shortcoming, to which research in other disciplines was already devoted.

But this is just one example of the broadening of knowledge that put the study of popular culture onto precarious methodological ground: What exactly was the necessary expertise required to make sense of it? Trained expertise in ordinary experience and communication is always going to be outpaced and exceeded by its own untutored object of study. Audiences and consumers may know more about the subject of popular culture than their professors do, often with the passionate encyclopaedic knowledge of fans. The status of the cultural expert is always uncertain, ambivalent and apt to be undermined. What's new is that with the accessibility and scale of online archives, this precariousness extends, in principle, to all educational institutions: the internet knows more than they do, and it can be accessed at a fraction of the cost, by anyone, including children.

Abandoned trust

The implications of that revolutionary change in the 'symmetry' of knowledge relations have barely begun to unfold or be explored, despite the general atmosphere of digital pessimism that has settled over mainstream journalism and critical media studies alike. Mainstream journalism is always on the lookout for stories that show the dangerous extremities of the internet, in which children and girls may become entangled, casting it on the wrong side of any social or trust boundary you'd care to name: cyberbullying, terrorism, sexualization, drugs, piracy, addiction, you name it.

From a very different vantage point, critical media studies has begun to cluster around critiques of algorithmic capitalism, 'the identity trade', corporate and state surveillance and 'predatory' measures against citizens: for instance, see Bratton, 2016 (the stack); Cheney-Lippold, 2017 (data); Draper, 2019 (identity); Foster, 2019 (surveillance); Griffin, 2003 (the alt-right); Jane, 2015, 2017, 2018 (online misogyny); Srnicek, 2016 (platforms).

Indeed, Jackie Wang (2018) theorizes a new stage of capitalism that she calls 'carceral' – *wealth by prison*. Her heartache about the conditions in which young people of colour have to live is motivated by her own family's experience of incarceration, where her brother, a minor, was sentenced 'as an adult' to a forty-year term without parole. Once incarcerated, a mass prison population is available as a new slave-labour force. At the same time, following the 2008 financial crisis in the United States, public debt was increasingly privatized and outsourced to the financial sector. In order to pay off this debt, government bodies exact money from the populace via policing and incarceration, leading to a government that is more accountable to its creditors than to the public. In such a state, 'peace of mind' can only be guaranteed by the mass precarity, indebtedness and disappearance of others, in a process whereby 'innocence' (celebrated as an innate attribute of white-girl children in marketing semiosis) comes to be a moral value, its absence marked on the bodies of those who are dispossessed:

> White civil society has a psychic investment in the erasure and abjection of bodies onto which they project hostile feelings, allowing them peace of mind amidst the state of perpetual violence. (Wang, 2018: 287)

Here, corporate and state agencies 'keep the peace' among dispossessed and disaffected populations by violence, while the 'predatory state', accountable to creditors and lobbyists not to voters, uses 'algorithmic governance', 'predictive analytics' and 'the data-ification of everyday life' to enable 'municipal plunder' to control and farm its own citizens (see also Mazzucato, 2015; Desmond, 2016). Wang outlined her practical program for *SVLLY(wood)* magazine:

1. Organize.
2. Jam the algorithms.
3. Write to prisoners/sign up for penpals.
4. Circulate information about what is happening inside prisons.
5. Support campaigns to free political prisoners.
6. Support campaigns to free political prisoners.[24]

---

[24]Source: http://www.svllywood.com/essays/badbitcheslinkupftjackiewang (May 2018).

Add to Wang's dystopian vision the everyday news-stream of failed mainstream politics and it is not hard to see why young people have abandoned trust in current arrangements. It is hard to maintain a positive attitude towards technological culture and the wonders of global connectivity when the extremes seem to be ruling the system because the 'mainstream' is in gridlock and the crazies are a click away (Jane, 2017).

Of course, what's needed is a new set of arrangements, created and actioned by those whose future is in such jeopardy. As the extension of distributed expertise and ubiquitous connectivity continues, new social groups need to form around the clusters of problems raised above, using the means at hand to create new knowledge, new resistance, new alternatives. Girls are among the leaders of just such a new class in formation around the new media associated with global-digital culture, work and power. They may seem unlikely actors in this scenario, but that is only because they never have been a coherent 'object of study' in academic disciplines and political discourses that have their origins in medieval and modernist states. Girls' own self-representation has to navigate not only unwanted surveillance from others, as well as the manifold institutions of 'correction and protection' designed to keep them 'innocent' for the benefit of others, but also the censorious attention of their own carers, teachers and advocates, aided and abetted by mainstream media and news outlets, and even by the very language they speak.

Expertise on girls

Girls are most clearly a class when they are blamed for the actions of those who abuse and exploit them. For instance, when news broke in 2016 of a website displaying 'sexual images of girls from private and public schools across Australia', without the girls' knowledge or consent,[25] the story was greeted by a chorus of advice from police,[26] schools and advocates that made it the girls' responsibility: they should not post too much information online (police), wear longer skirts (school), and not take sexy selfies in the first place (advocates). Unusually, in this case, the backlash that shamed girls rather than blaming boys was itself picked up in later news coverage:

> Students interviewed in a UNSW study [Albury et al., 2013] ... recognised that 'gendered double-standards were applied to discussions of sexting, and digital self-representation in general'. Additionally, female students

---

[25]http://mobile.abc.net.au/news/2016-08-17/police-investigate-child-porn-ring-targeting-australian-schools/7750586.
[26]See: https://www.thinkuknow.org.au/site/megans-story.

felt adult authority figures were 'constantly monitoring' them for signs of 'sexualisation' and 'provocative' behaviour, and 'criticised what they perceived as excessive attention by teachers and parents to young women's bodies and choices in relation to sexual expression and self-representation'. That 'excessive attention' does not exist in a vacuum. Young women with any sort of online presence are constantly policed for signs of 'inappropriate' sexual behaviour, and punished if they are deemed to breach the boundaries of what is 'acceptable'.[27]

This is not expertise but command-and-control *government* over girls' bodies that is not extended to boys or men, and it is amplified in the media such that it naturalizes the shaming of beauty. The lead author of the UNSW report, Kath Albury, is quoted in this news story, pointing out that in this skew-whiff world, the opposite of shame is not confidence or agency, but 'vanity':

> There's a very long tradition of framing beautiful young women as objects of desire to be looked at, presented absolutely for the viewer. But if they know that they're beautiful, or that they have agency or power as a result of their beauty, then they're vain, Professor Albury said. 'The critique of selfies is just the latest manifestation of attitudes to female beauty.'

So the post of 'expert on girls' remains open: existing agencies of authority cannot be trusted to have girls' own interests in mind, and girls don't trust them (for instance, they are high users of the internet but low consumers of news). They look to each other and to their own social networks for advice. Girls can no longer be discounted or ignored as their own experts, as they are knowledge agents within this larger system. Their productivity can take various forms:

- Producers of 'content', meaningful self-representation, expression and communication (Banet-Weiser, 2011; Carter, 2019).
- Producers of knowledge (Mazzarella, 2010), by role models in celebrity culture, activists with a strong online following, or girls' media, such as *Teen Vogue* under editor Elaine Welteroth or Tavi Gevinson's now-concluded *rookiemag.com*.

---

[27]Source: Alex McKinnon (2016) '"Don't take nude selfies" and other ways men treat women with contempt. Advising female school students not to take nude photos misses the point. When society shames young women for being sexual, we can't be surprised when young men treat them with contempt'. ABC News [Australia], 27 August: http://mobile.abc.net.au/news/2016-08-27/nude-selfies-and-why-men-treat-women-with-contempt/7790720.

- Producers of revenue, either on their own behalf as entrepreneurs or part of a family enterprise (the Kardashian family), or as characters in professional productions by other agencies (actors, singers, models).
- 'Organic intellectuals' in social media and entertainment (especially music), plus those able to move into 'traditional intellectual' positions (Wang, 2018), and those whose youth activism (often supported by agencies funded by celebrities) re-orders mainstream politics on issues such as climate change, pollution, gun violence, human rights (including Indigenous rights), open education and girls' own self-realization.
- Class-based organizations to support activism, such as: https://teensagainstgunviolence.org/; https://www.schoolstrike4climate.com/; https://www.heforshe.org/en.

'Girl Consciousness' Now!

In his *21 Lessons for the 21st Century* (2018), Yuval Harari writes:

The Russian, Chinese and Cuban revolutions were made by people who were vital for the economy, but who lacked political power; in 2016, Trump and Brexit were supported by many people who still enjoyed political power, but who feared that they were losing their economic worth. Perhaps in the twenty-first century populist revolts will be staged not against an economic elite that exploits people, but against an economic elite that does not need them any more. This may well be a losing battle. It is much harder to struggle against irrelevance than against exploitation. Harari, 2018: 9)

Neither leftist 'revolutions' nor rightist 'populist revolts' against the logic of technological change and data-owning oligarchs seem to have worked (Baysha, 2019). Is it the case that 'those who own the data own the future' (Harari, 2018: 73), and that the only response for populations (as opposed to robots) is 'disillusionment'?

Harari's pessimism seems to belong to a world entirely without girls – and entirely without contestation by those whose economic 'uselessness' (under present arrangements) has not only morphed into the prospect of debt-based servitude but also into 'girl consciousness'. Far from 'irrelevant', socially or biologically, girls are *producers of the new* for *H. sapiens*, both literally and in other ways – carriers of new humans and also of change and transformation through organization and innovation, especially in the semiosphere, where fictions, song, story, spectacle and drama constitute a continuous experiment in 'modelling' futurescapes.

Girls – and boys – use such means to break out of the command-and-control regime into a networked world, even while – as a class – they are among those that coercive, ideological and patriarchal powers *most want* to control. Much of what needs to be understood about girls belongs to that control history, but the best argument for attempting a new approach, and for using the cultural science method, is the need to connect and explain the signs of change at population scale: to set girls – as a self-conscious class – in the global context, as agents of new deme-formation and as protagonists in a different story for the future.

ACKNOWLEDGEMENTS

I thank Jason Potts, co-author of *Cultural Science: A Natural History of Stories, Demes, Knowledge and Innovation* (2014), to which this volume is a kind of sequel.

I acknowledge the support of the Australian Research Council over several schemes (Federation Fellowship, Centre of Excellence, Discovery, Linkage), which supported the research on which numerous chapters are based.

Thanks to the hundreds of authors whose work is cited in the references: theirs are the shoulders of giants! I thank the many scholars who have contributed to cultural science or critiqued it, especially Carsten Herrmann-Pillath, Indrek Ibrus, Ellie Rennie, Joan Leach, Cameron Neylon, Frances Pinter; the editorial board of *Cultural Science Journal* and its reviewers.

I thank Tama Leaver, Head of Internet Studies at Curtin University, for advice and support in the preparation of this manuscript. Thanks to the late and much-missed Niall Lucy and to colleagues at the Centre for Culture and Technology in the School of Media, Creative Arts and Social Inquiry at Curtin University: Lucy Montgomery, Cameron Neylon, Henry Li, Eleanor Sandry, Michele Willson, Matt Chrulew, Katie Ellis, Huan Wu, Crystal Abidin; to research students He Zhang, Yaoxia Zhu, Alkim Ozaygen, Shanshan Liu, Guo Chen, Anna-Katharina Laboissiere; to Sam McGrath and to everyone at Curtin for their congenial collegiality and (sometimes bemused) tolerance.

As ever, chief thanks to Tina Horton. As Terry Hawkes once wisely put it: *sine qua non*.

Versions of chapters have been rehearsed, as it were, in journal articles and book-chapters scattered across numerous publishers and continents. I thank the editors and anonymous referees who helped so much to get the original papers into shape. In this book they are ordered into a coherent sequence or 'narrative arc' that I hope amounts to more than the sum of those parts. Each one has been further revised and updated for this book, in some cases radically.

- Chapter 1: *Cultural Science Journal*: https://culturalscience.org/; and *Czech and Slovak Journal of Humanities* (1/2017), 118–20 (ed. Milan Hain).
- Chapter 2. Jean Burgess, Thomas Poell and Alice Marwick (eds) (2018) *The Sage Handbook of Social Media*. UK: Sage Publications.

- Chapter 3. Mark Dunford and Tricia Jenkins (eds) (2018) *Story, Form and Content in Digital Storytelling: Telling Tales*. UK: Palgrave Macmillan.
- Chapter 4. *Cultural Science Journal* (10) (2018).
- Chapter 5. Abbe Brown and Charlotte Waelde (eds) (2018) *Research Handbook on IP and Creative Industries*. UK: Edward Elgar, Ch 28.
- Chapter 6. *Media International Australia* (2015), 156, 108–22 (issue ed. P. David Marshall).
- Chapter 7. Jonathan Gray and Derek Johnson (eds) (2013) *A Companion to Media Authorship*. USA: Wiley-Blackwell, 23–47.
- Chapter 8. *Shakespeare Studies*, XLIV (2016), 75–90 (ed. Diana Henderson).
- Chapter 9. Submitted to *City: Analysis of Urban Trends, Culture, Theory, Policy, Action* (issue ed. Mirjana Ristic and Sybille Frank).
- Chapter 10. Accepted for Tim Holmes and Miglena Sternadori (eds), *Handbook of Magazine Studies*. USA: Wiley-Blackwell.
- Chapter 11. Accepted for Shawn Shimpach (ed.) *The Routledge Companion to Global Television*. USA: Routledge.
- Chapter 12. Unpublished; the initial version was accepted for the *International Communication Association* annual conference (2017, San Diego). Thanks to Rhiannon Hartley for collaborating on this paper, and to the ICA's anonymous referees for cogent critique.

Special thanks to Katie Gallof at Bloomsbury, to Erin Duffy and the anonymous referees, who have guided this work through completion to publication.

I'm very grateful to Perth artist Natasha Lea, who made the cover image for me (https://www.natashalea.net/about; see also http://www.instagimg.com/user/thedesignskeleton/20903219).

REFERENCES

Abidin, C. (2015a) 'Communicative ❤ Intimacies: Influencers and Perceived Interconnectedness'. *Ada: Journal of Gender, New Media & Technology*, 8: http://adanewmedia.org/2015/11/issue8-abidin/. doi:10.7264/N3MW2FFG

Abidin, C. (2015b) 'Micro-microcelebrity: Branding Babies on the Internet'. *M/C Journal*, 18 (5): http://journal.media-culture.org.au/index.php/mcjournal/article/view/1022.

Abidin, C. (2016) 'Visibility Labour: Engaging with Influencers' Fashion Brands and #OOTD Advertorial Campaigns on Instagram'. *Media International Australia*, 161: 86–100.

Abidin, C. (2018) *Internet Celebrity: Understanding Fame Online*. Bingley, UK: Emerald Publishing.

Abidin, C. and M. L. Brown (eds) (2018) *Microcelebrity Around the Globe: Approaches to Cultures of Internet Fame*. Bingley, UK: Emerald Publishing.

Abidin, C. and T. Leaver (2017) 'From YouTube to TV, and Back Again: Viral Video Child Stars and Media Flows in the Era of Social Media'. Paper presented at *Digitising* Early Childhood International Conference, Perth (Australia): http://www.digitisingearlychildhood.com/uploads/9/4/9/2/94929330/abidin_from_you tube_to_tv_and_back_again.pdf.

Adams, P. (2005) *The Bowery Boys: Street Corner Radicals and the Politics of Rebellion*. Westport, CT: Praeger.

Allen, D. and J. Potts (2016) 'How Innovation Commons Contribute to Discovering and Developing New Technologies'. *International Journal of the Commons*, 10 (2): 1–20.

Althusser, L. (1971) *Lenin and Philosophy and Other Essays*. Trans. B. Brewster. London: New Left Books; New York: Monthly Review Press.

Anderson, B. (1991) *Imagined Communities: Reflections on the Origin and Spread of Nationalism*, 2nd edn 2006. London: Verso.

Anderson, C. (2008) *The Long Tail: Why the Future of Business is Selling Less of More*, rev. edn. New York: Hachette Books.

Antrosio, J. (2013) 'Agriculture as "Worst Mistake in the History of the Human Race"?' *Living Anthropologically*: http://www.livinganthropologically.com/anthropology/worst-mistake-in-the-history-of-the-human-race.

Aoyama, T. and B. Hartley (2010) *Girl Reading Girl in Japan*. London, UK and New York: Routledge.

Ariès, P. (1962) *Centuries of Childhood: A Social History of Family Life*. London: Jonathan Cape; New York: Alfred P. Knopf. Accessible at: https://monoskop.org/images/d/d0/Ari%C3%A8s_Philippe_Centuries_of_Childhood_A_Social_History_of_Family_Life_1962.pdf.

Arthur, W. B. (2009) *The Nature of Technology: What It Is and How It Evolves*. London: Penguin.

Banet-Weiser, S. (2011) 'Branding the Post-Feminist Self: Girls' Video Production and YouTube'. In M. C. Kearney (ed.), *Mediated Girlhoods: New Explorations of Girls' Media Culture*. New York, NY: Peter Lang, 277–94.

Banks, D. (2018) 'Nothing Squared is Still Nothing'. *Cyborgology*, 9 October: https://thesocietypages.org/cyborgology/2018/10/09/nothing-squared-is-still-nothing.

Barabási, A.-L. (2002) *Linked: The New Science of Networks*. New York: Perseus: http://barabasi.com/book/linked.

Baran, P. (1964) *On Distributed Communications*. Santa Monica: RAND Corporation: https://www.rand.org/content/dam/rand/pubs/research_memoranda/2006/RM3420.pdf.

Barthes, R. (1977a) 'The Death of the Author'. *Image-Music-Text*. London: Fontana, 142–8.

Barthes, R. (1977b) 'Lecture in Inauguration of the Chair of Literary Semiology'. Paris: Collège de France, 7 January. Trans. R. Howard. Accessible at: www.albany.edu/~rn774/fall96/barthes.html. [Published in French as *Leçon*. Paris: Editions du Seuil, 1978.]

Barthes, R. (2005) *The Neutral: Lecture Course at the Collège de France 1977-78*. New York: Columbia University Press.

Baym, N. (2010) *Personal Connections in the Digital Age*. Cambridge: Polity Press.

Baysha, O. (2019) *Miscommunicating Social Change: Lessons from Russia and Ukraine*. Lanham, MD: Lexington Books.

Beck, A. (2017) 'Unnatural Selection: How Racism Warps Scientific Truths'. *Bitch: Facts*, Issue 76, Fall: https://www.bitchmedia.org/issue/76.

Bell, E., P. Boehnke, T. M. Harrison and W. Mao (2015) 'Potentially Biogenic Carbon Preserved in a 4.1 Billion-Year-Old Zircon'. *PNAS*, 112 (47): 14518–21: http://www.pnas.org/content/112/47/14518.full.

Bentley, R. A., M. Earls and M. O'Brien (2011) *I'll Have What She's Having: Mapping Social Behavior*. Cambridge, MA: MIT Press.

Bentley, R. A., C. Lipo, H. Herzog and M. Hahn (2007) 'Regular Rates of Popular Culture Change Reflect Random Copying'. *Evolution and Human Behavior*, 28: 151–8.

Berndt, J., K. Nagaike and F. Ogi (eds) (2019) *Shōjo Across Media: Exploring "Girl" Practices in Contemporary Japan*. London: Palgrave Macmillan.

Bethell, S. L. (1944) *Shakespeare and the Popular Dramatic Tradition*. London: Staples.

Bogost, I. (2019) 'Video-Game Violence Is Now a Partisan Issue: For Decades, Both Republicans and Democrats Saw Games as Cultural Dangers. That Changed After the Parkland Shooting'. *The Atlantic*, 5 August: https://www.theatlantic.com/technology/archive/2019/08/video-game-violence-became-partisan-issue/595456.

Botton, A. de (2014) *The News: A User's Guide*. London: Pantheon.

Bourdieu, P. (2001) 'Television'. *European Review*, 9 (3): 245–56.

Bowles, S. (2011) 'Cultivation of Cereals by the First Farmers was not More Productive than Foraging'. *PNAS*, 108 (12): 4760–5: http://www.pnas.org/content/108/12/4760.full.

Bowles, S. and H. Gintis (2011) *A Cooperative Species: Human Reciprocity and Its Evolution*. Princeton, NJ: Princeton University Press.

Boyd, B. and D. Dor (2017) 'Challenging Chomsky and His Challengers: Brian Boyd Interviews Daniel Dor'. *TVOL Magazine*: https://evolution-institute.org/challenging-chomsky-and-his-challengers-brian-boyd-interviews-daniel-dor.

Bragg, M. (1988) *Rich: The Life of Richard Burton*. London: Hodder & Stoughton.

Bratton, B. (2016) *The Stack: On Software and Sovereignty*. Cambridge, MA: MIT Press.

Braudel, F. (1972) *The Mediterranean and the Mediterranean World in the Age of Philip II*, 2 vols. New York: Harper and Row.

Braudel, F. (2012) 'History and the Social Sciences: The Longue Durée'. Trans. I. Wallerstein. Appendix to R. E. Lee (ed.) 2012, 241–76. First published in French (1958) as '*Histoire et Sciences sociales: La longue durée*. *Annales* E.S.C. XIII, 4: 725–53.

Brogan, H. (2006) *Alexis de Tocqueville: Prophet of Democracy in an Age of Revolution*. London: Profile Books.

Brown University (n.d.) 'Philosophy: What and Why?' Accessible at: https://www.brown.edu/academics/philosophy/undergraduate/philosophy-what-and-why

Bryce, Q. (2013) *Boyer Lectures*. ABC Radio National: http://www.abc.net.au/radionational/programs/boyerlectures/2013-boyer-lectures/5486344.

Buchanan, J. (1965) 'An Economic Theory of Clubs'. *Economica NS*, 32 (125): 1–14.

Buonanno, M. (2005) 'The "Sailor" and the "Peasant": The Italian Police Series between Foreign and Domestic'. *Media International Australia*, 115: 48–59. www.independent.co.uk/news/uk/home-news/bbc-unveils-the-star-of-its-first-world-war-anniversary-coverage--rupert-murdoch-8884028.html.

Buonanno, M. (2012) *Italian TV Drama and Beyond: Stories from the Soil, Stories from the Sea*. Bristol, UK: Intellect Books; Chicago, IL: Chicago University Press.

Burchard, W. (2016) 'What's the Point of Rebuilding Germany's Palaces?' *Apollo, The International Art Magazine*: https://www.apollo-magazine.com/whats-the-point-of-rebuilding-germanys-palaces.

Burke, S. (1998) *The Death and Return of the Author: Criticism and Subjectivity in Barthes*, 2nd edn. Edinburgh: Edinburgh University Press.

Burns, A. (2015) 'Self(ie)-Discipline: Social Regulation as Enacted Through the Discussion of Photographic Practice'. *International Journal of Communication*, 9 (Feature): 1716–33.

Burton, R., with S. Burton (1991) *A Christmas Story*. New York: W. W. Norton and Company. ISBN 0-393-03034-2.

Butler, I. (2014) 'The Tragedie of Scar, King of Pride Rock: The Shakespearean Grandeur of The Lion King's Villain'. *The Slate Culturebox*: http://www.slate.com/articles/arts/culturebox/2014/06/the_lion_king_20th_anniversary_scar_is_a_great_shakespearean_villain.html.

Butler, J. (1990) *Gender Trouble: Feminism and the Subversion of Identity*. London: Routledge.

Cangelosi, A., A. Greco and S. Harnad (2002) 'Symbol Grounding and the Symbolic Theft Hypothesis'. In A. Cangelosi and D. Parisi (eds), *Simulating the Evolution of Language*. London: Springer, 191–210.

Caplan, S. (1996) 'Hilde Himmelweit (1918-1989)'. In N. Signorielli (ed.), *Women in Communication: A Biographical Sourcebook*. Westport, CT: Greenwood Press, 216–19.

Carey, J. (1989) *Communication as Culture*. Boston: Unwin Hyman.

Carey, J. (2000) 'Some Personal Notes on US Journalism Education'. *Journalism*, 1 (1): 12–23.

Carré, J. le (2017) *The Pigeon Tunnel: Stories from My Life*. London: Penguin.

Carter, C. (2019) 'Be Cute, Play with Dolls and Stick to Tea Parties: Journalism, Girls and Power'. In C. Carter, L. Steiner and S. Allan (eds), *Journalism, Gender and Power*. London: Routledge, 236–50.

Caughie, J. (1990) 'Playing at Being American: Games and Tactics'. In P. Mellencamp (ed.), *Logics of Television: Essays in Cultural Criticism*. Bloomington, IN: Indiana University Press; London: BFI, 44–58.

Cavallo, C. and R. Chartier (eds) (1999) *A History of Reading in the West*. Amherst, MA: University of Massachusetts Press.

Chadwick, A. (2006) *Internet Politics: States, Citizens, and New Communication Technologies*. New York and Oxford: Oxford University Press.

Chaplin, T. (2007) *Turning on the Mind: French Philosophers on Television*. Chicago: University of Chicago Press.

Cheney-Lippold, J. (2017) *We Are Data: Algorithms and the Making of Our Digital Selves*. New York: New York University Press.

Childe, V. G. (1925) *The Dawn of European Civilization*. London: Kegan Paul, Trench, Trubner; 6th edn 1958. New York: Knopf.

Childe, V. G. (1936; 4th edn 1965) *Man Makes Himself*. London: Watts.

Childe, V. G. (1958) *The Prehistory of European Society*. London: Cassell.

Chouliaraki, L., ed. (2012) *Self-Mediation: New Media, Citizenship and Civil Selves*. London: Routledge.

Cirillo, F. (2018) 'Why "Silent Sam" Had to Go'. *Washington Post*, 22 August: https://www.washingtonpost.com/news/made-by-history/wp/2018/08/22/why-silent-sam-had-to-go/?noredirect=on&utm_term=.fba6b2ad4d25.

Citton, Y. (2017) *The Ecology of Attention*. Cambridge: Polity Press.

Clark, A. (3 August 2018) 'The "Great Australian Silence" 50 Years On'. *The Conversation*: http://theconversation.com/friday-essay-the-great-australian-sile nce-50-years-on-100737.

Clark, K. (1969; this edn 1990) *Civilisation: A Personal View by Kenneth Clark*. London: HarperCollins.

Cliff, N. (2007) *The Shakespeare Riots: Revenge, Drama, and Death in Nineteenth-Century America*. New York: Random House.

Couldry, N., R. MacDonald, H. Stephansen, W. Clark, L. Dickens and A. Fotopoulou (2014) 'Constructing a Digital Storycircle: Digital Infrastructure and Mutual Recognition'. *International Journal of Cultural Studies*, 18 (5): 501–17.

Crossick, G. and P. Kraszynska (2014) 'Under Construction: Towards a Framework for Cultural Value'. *Cultural Trends*, 23 (2): 120–31.

Crossick, G. and P. Kraszynska (2016) *Understanding the Value of Arts and Culture: The AHRC Cultural Value Project*. London: Arts and Humanities Research Council: https://ahrc.ukri.org/documents/publications/cultural-value-project-final-report.

Csibra, G. and G. Gergely (2011) 'Natural Pedagogy as Evolutionary Adaptation'. *Philosophical Transactions of the Royal Society B*, 366: 1149–57.

Currid, E. (2008) *The Warhol Economy: How Fashion, Art, and Music Drive New York City*, new edn. Princeton, NJ: Princeton University Press.

Dahl, R. (1988) *Matilda*. London: Jonathan Cape.

Darnton, R. (1984) *The Great Cat Massacre, and Other Episodes in French Cultural History*. New York, Bantam Books.

Darwin, C. (1871) *The Descent of Man*. London: John Murray. Accessible online: http://darwin-online.org.uk/content/frameset?pageseq=1&itemID=F937.1&v iewtype=text.

Dawkins, R. (1976) *The Selfish Gene*. Oxford: Oxford University Press. 30th Anniversary Edition 2006.

Dayan, D. and E. Katz (1992) *Media Events: The Live Broadcasting of History*. Cambridge, MA: Harvard University Press.

Dediu, D., M. Cysouw, S. Levinson, A. Baronchelli, M. Christiansen, W. Croft, N. Evans, S. Garrod, R. Gray, A. Kandler and E. Lieven (2013) 'Cultural Evolution of Language'. In P. Richerson and M. Christiansen (eds), *Cultural Evolution: Society, Technology, Language, and Religion*. Cambridge, MA: MIT Press. doi:1 0.7551/mitpress/9780262019750.003.0016.

Dekker, E. (2016) *The Viennese Students of Civilization: The Meaning and Context of Austrian Economics Reconsidered*. Cambridge: Cambridge University Press.

Demos, T. J. (2017) *Against the Anthropocene: Visual Culture and Environment Today*. Berlin: Sternberg Press.

d'Entrèves, M. P. and S. Benhabib, eds (1997) *Habermas and the Unfinished Project of Modernity: Critical Essays on The Philosophical Discourse of Modernity*. Cambridge, MA: The MIT Press.

Derrida, J. (2005) *Paper Machine: Cultural Memory in the Present*. Trans. R Bowlby. Stanford: Stanford University Press.

Desmond, M. (2016) *Evicted: Poverty and Profit in the American City*. New York: Crown.

Diamond, J. (1987) 'The Worst Mistake in the History of the Human Race'. *Discover Magazine*, May, 64–6. Accessible online: http://discovermagazine.c om/1987/may/02-the-worst-mistake-in-the-history-of-the-human-race.

Dobson, M. (2007) 'Let him be Caesar!' *London Review of Books*, 29 (15): 15–17.

Dopfer, K., J. Foster and J. Potts (2004) 'Micro–Meso–Macro'. *Journal of Evolutionary Economics*, 14 (3): 263–79.

Dor, D. (2015) *The Instruction of Imagination: Language as a Social Communication Technology*. Oxford: Oxford University Press.

Draper, N. (2019) *The Identity Trade: Selling Privacy and Reputation Online*. New York: New York University Press.

Driscoll, C. (2002) *Girls: Feminine Adolescence in Popular Culture and Cultural Theory*. New York, NY: Columbia University Press.

Driscoll, C. (2008) 'Girls Today – Girls, Girl Culture and Girl Studies'. *Girlhood Studies*, 1 (1): 13–32.

Drotner, K. (2008) 'Boundaries and Bridges: Digital Storytelling in Education Studies and Media Studies'. In K. Lundby (ed.), *Digital Storytelling, Mediatized Stories: Self-Representations in New Media*. New York: Peter Lang, 61–81.

Dush, L. (2013) 'The Ethical Complexities of Sponsored Digital Storytelling'. *International Journal of Cultural Studies*, 16 (6): 627–40.

Eatwell, R. and M. Goodwin (2018) *National Populism: The Revolt Against Liberal Democracy*. London: Pelican.

Eco, U. (1976) *A Theory of Semiotics*. Bloomington: Indiana University Press.

Eco, U. (1989) *The Open Work*. Cambridge, MA: Harvard University Press.

Eddo-Lodge, R. (2018) *Why I'm No Longer Talking to White People About Race*. London: Bloomsbury.

Edgerton, D. (2006) *Warfare State: Britain, 1920–70*. Cambridge: Cambridge University Press.

Elias, N. (1939/1969) *The Civilizing Process*. Trans. from the German, 1982. Oxford: Basil Blackwell.

Evans, N. (2009) *Dying Words: Endangered Languages and What They Have to Tell Us*. Malden, MA and Oxford, UK: Wiley-Blackwell.

Evans, N. and S. Levinson (2009) 'The Myth of Language Universals: Language Diversity and Its Importance for Cognitive Science'. *Behavioral and Brain Sciences*, 32 (5): 429–48. doi:10.1017/S0140525X0999094X.

Felski. R. (1989) *Beyond Feminist Aesthetics*. Cambridge, MA: Harvard University Press.

Finkelstein, D. and A. McCleery (eds) (2002) *The Book History Reader*. London: Routledge.

Finn, E. (2017) *What Algorithms Want: Imagination in the Age of Computing*. Cambridge, MA: MIT Press.

Fisher, B. (2015) 'Why English, Not Mandarin, is the Language of Innovation'. *Harvard Business Review*, 12 January. Online: https://hbr.org/2015/01/why-english-not-mandarin-is-the-language-of-innovation.

Flinders, M. (1814) *Voyage to Terra Australis*, vol. 1, Ch. 3: http://gutenberg.net.au/ebooks/e00049.html.

Ford, H. (2013) '*Two or Three Things I Know About Her*'. *Senses of Cinema*, 66. Online: http://sensesofcinema.com/2013/cteq/two-or-three-things-i-know-about-her.

Fortini, A. (2005) 'Defending *Vogue*'s Evil Genius'. *Slate*: www.slate.com/id/2113278.

Foster, J. B. (2019) 'Capitalism Has Failed – What Next?' *Monthly Review*, February: https://monthlyreview.org/2019/02/01/capitalism-has-failed-what-next.

Foucault, M. (1977) 'The Political Function of the Intellectual'. Trans. C. Gordon. *Radical Philosophy*, 17: 12–14. Fr. original: (1976), 'La fonction politique de l'intellectuel'. In D. Defert and F. Ewald (eds) (2001) *Dits et écrits II, 1976-1988*, Paris: Gallimard, 109–14.

Foucault, M. (1984) 'What is an Author?' In P. Rabinow (ed.), *The Foucault Reader*. New York: Vintage Books, 101–20.

Frosh, P. (2015) 'The Gestural Image: The Selfie, Photography Theory, and Kinesthetic Sociability'. *International Journal of Communication*, 9 (Feature): 1607–28.

Frosh, P. (2019) *The Poetics of Digital Media*. Cambridge: Polity Press.

Frow, J. (1995) *Cultural Studies and Cultural Value*. Oxford: The Clarendon Press.

Gallop, J. (2011) *The Deaths of the Author: Reading and Writing in Time*. Durham, NC: Duke University Press.

Gauthier, M. and K. Sawchuk (2017) 'Not Notable Enough: Feminism and Expertise in Wikipedia'. *Communication and Critical/Cultural Studies*, 14 (4): 385–402.

Gibson, M. (2007) *Culture and Power: A History of Cultural Studies*. London: Berg/Bloomsbury.

Gintis, H. (2012) *Human Evolution: A Behavioural Synthesis*. Online: Santa Fe Institute: http://tuvalu.santafe.edu/~bowles/HumanEvolution.pdf.

Gitlin, T. (1987) *The Sixties: Years of Hope, Days of Rage*. New York: Bantam Books.

Goudsblom, J. (1994) 'The Theory of the Civilizing Process and Its Discontents'. Amsterdam: Paper voor *de Sectie Figuratiesociologie van de Zesde Sociaal-Wetenschappelijke Studiedagen*: http://www.norberteliasfoundation.nl/docs/pdf/GoudsblomDiscontents.pdf.

Gramsci, A. (1971) *Selections from the Prison Notebooks*. London: Lawrence and Wishart.

Gray, J. and A. Lotz (2018) *Television Studies*, 2nd edn. Cambridge: Polity Press.

Griffin, R. (2003) 'From Slime Mould to Rhizome: An Introduction to the Groupuscular Right'. *Patterns of Prejudice*, 37 (1): 27–50.

Griffiths, B. (2018) *Deep Time Dreaming: Uncovering Ancient Australia*. Carlton, VIC: Black Inc.

Hall, S. (1996) Who Needs 'Identity'? In S. Hall and P. du Gay (eds), *Questions of Cultural Identity*. London: Sage, 1–17.

Hamilton, J. (2003) 'Remaking Media Participation in Early Modern England'. *Journalism*, 4 (3): 293–313.

Hammond, B. (1997) *Professional Imaginative Writing in England, 1670-1740: 'Hackney for Bread'*. Oxford: Clarendon Press.

Harari, Y. N. (2014) *Sapiens: A Brief History of Humankind*. London: Harvill Secker.

Harari, Y. N. (2018) *21 Lessons for the 21st Century*. London: Jonathan Cape.

Haraway, D. (2004) *The Haraway Reader*. New York and London: Routledge.

Harbage, A. (1947) *As They Liked It: An Essay on Shakespeare and Morality*. London: Macmillan.

Harding, J. (2012) 'T.S. Eliot's Shakespeare'. *Essays in Criticism*, 62 (2): 160–77.

Hardy, P. and T. Sumner (eds) (2014) *Cultivating Compassion: How Digital Storytelling Is Transforming Healthcare*. Chichester, UK: Kingsham Press.

Hargreaves, I. and J. Hartley (eds) (2016) *The Creative Citizen Unbound: How Social Media and DIY Culture Contribute to Democracy, Communities and the Creative Economy*. Bristol, UK: Policy Press.

Harris, J. (2010) 'Memorials and Trauma: Pinjarra 1834'. In *Trauma, Media, Art: New Perspectives*. Newcastle-upon-Tyne, UK: Cambridge Scholars Publishing, 36–57: http://wwwmcc.murdoch.edu.au/trauma/docs/JenniferHarris-paper.pdf.

Hartley, J. (1992) *The Politics of Pictures: The Creation of the Public in the Age of Popular Media*. London and New York: Routledge.

Hartley, J. (2007) 'Documenting Kate Moss: Fashion Photography and the Persistence of Photojournalism'. *Journalism Studies*, 8 (4): 555–65.

Hartley, J. (2008) *Television Truths: Forms of Knowledge in Popular Culture*. Malden, MA and Oxford, UK: Wiley-Blackwell.

Hartley, J. (2015) 'Urban Semiosis: Creative Industries and the Clash of Systems'. *International Journal of Cultural Studies*, 18 (1): 79–101.

Hartley, J., J. Burgess and A. Bruns (eds) (2013) *A Companion to New Media Dynamics*. Malden, MA and Oxford: Wiley-Blackwell.

Hartley, J. and K. McWilliam (eds) (2009) *Story Circle: Digital Storytelling Around the World*. Malden, MA and Oxford, UK: Wiley-Blackwell.

Hartley, J. and L. Montgomery (2009) 'Fashion as Consumer Entrepreneurship: Emergent Risk Culture, Social Network Markets, and the Launch of *Vogue* in China'. *Chinese Journal of Communication*, 2 (1): 61–76.

Hartley, J., L. Montgomery and H. S. Li (2017) 'A New Model for Understanding Global Media and China: "Knowledge Clubs" and "Knowledge Commons"'. *Global Media and China*, 2 (1): 8–27.

Hartley, J. and J. Potts (2014) *Cultural Science: A Natural History of Stories, Demes, Knowledge and Innovation*. London: Bloomsbury. Accessible (CC license) at Bloomsbury Collections: https://www.bloomsburycollections.com/bo ok/cultural-science-a-natural-history-of-stories-demes-knowledge-and-innova tion.

Hartley, J., J. Potts, L. Montgomery, E. Rennie and C. Neylon (2019) 'From Communication Technology to User Community: A New Economic Model of the Journal as a Club'. *Learned Publishing*, 32.

Hartley, J. and E. Rennie (2004) '"About a Girl": Fashion Photography as Photojournalism'. *Journalism: Theory, Practice, Criticism*, 5 (4): 461–82.

Hartley, J., W. Wen and H. S. Li (2015) *Creative Economy and Culture: Challenges, Changes and Futures for the Creative Industries*. London: Sage Publications.

Hawkes, T. (1973) *Shakespeare's Talking Animals: Language and Drama in Society*. London: Arnold.

Hawkes, T. (ed.) (1977) *Twentieth Century Interpretations of Macbeth*. Englewood Cliff, NJ: Prentice-Hall.

Hawkes, T. (1986) *That Shakespeherian Rag*. London and New York: Methuen.

Hawkes, T. (1999) *Meaning by Shakespeare*. London: Routledge.

Hawkes, T. (2002) *Shakespeare in the Present*. London: Routledge.

Hawkes, T. (2003) '*Coronation Street* of the Soul'. *New Statesman*, 7 April: http://www.newstatesman.com/node/157436.

Hayek, F. (1945) 'The Use of Knowledge in Society'. *American Economic Review*, 35 (4): 519–30.

Herrmann-Pillath, C. (2013) *Foundations of Economic Evolution: A Treatise on the Natural Philosophy of Economics*. Cheltenham: Edward Elgar.

Herrmann-Pillath, C. (2018) 'Dilthey and Darwin Combined? 19th Century *Geisteswissenschaft* for 21st Century Cultural Science'. *Cultural Science Journal*, 10 (1): 42–53: https://culturalscience.org/articles/10.5334/csci.108.

Hess, C. and E. Ostrom (2003) 'Ideas, Artifacts, and Facilities: Information as a Common-Pool Resource'. *Law and Contemporary Problems*, 66: 111–45: http://scholarship.law.duke.edu/cgi/viewcontent.cgi?article=1276&context=lcp.

Hickey-Moody, A. (2015) 'Carbon Fibre Masculinity: Disability and Surfaces of Homosociality'. *Angelaki: Journal of the Theoretical Humanities*, 20 (1): 139–53.

Himmelweit, H., A. Oppenheim and P. Vince (1958) *Television and the Child: An Empirical Study of the Effect of Television on the Young*. Oxford: Oxford University Press.

Hirst, P. (1979) *On Law and Ideology*. Basingstoke, UK: Macmillan.

Hodder, I. (2018) *Where Are We Heading? The Evolution of Humans and Things*. New Haven, CT: Yale University Press.

Hodgson, G. (2004) 'Veblen and Darwinism'. *International Review of Sociology/ Revue Internationale de Sociologie*, 14 (3): 343–61: http://www.geoffrey-hodgs on.info/user/image/veblendarwinism.pdf.

Hoggart, R. (1957) *The Uses of Literacy: Aspects of Working-Class Life with Special Reference to Publications and Entertainments*. London: Chatto & Windus (Penguin edn 1959; Penguin Classic edn 2009).

Hornblower, S. and A. Spawforth (2005) *The Oxford Classical Dictionary*, 3rd edn. Oxford: Oxford University Press.

Humboldt, A. von (1858) *Cosmos: A Sketch or a Physical Description of the Universe*. 5 vols. Vol. 1. Online: Project Gutenberg: http://www.gutenberg.org/ cache/epub/14565/pg14565-images.html.

Humboldt, A. von (2018) *Selected Writings*, ed. A. Wulf. New York: Alfred A. Knopf Everyman's Library.

Hutter, M. (2015) *The Rise of the Joyful Economy: Artistic Invention and Economic Growth*. London: Routledge.

Huxley, J. (1942) *Evolution: The Modern Synthesis*. London: Allen & Unwin.

Hyde, L. (2008) *Trickster Makes This World: How Disruptive Imagination Creates Culture*. Edinburgh: Canongate.

Ibrus, I. (2015) 'Dialogic Control: Power in Media Evolution'. *International Journal of Cultural Studies*, 18 (1): 43–59.

Iversen, K. (2016) 'The Evolution of the Teen Girl in 35 Young Adult Novels'. *NYLON Magazine*, 10 September: http://www.nylon.com/articles/evolution- teen-girl-young-adult-novels.

Jane, E. A. (2015) 'Flaming? What Flaming? The Pitfalls and Potentials of Researching Online Hostility'. *Ethics and Information Technology*, 17 (1): 65–87.

Jane, E. A. (2017) *Misogyny Online: A Short (and Brutish) History*. London: Sage Publications.

Jane, E. A. (2018) 'Systemic Misogyny Exposed: Translating Rapeglish from the Manosphere with a Random Rape Threat Generator'. *International Journal of Cultural Studies*, 21 (6): 661–80.

Jencks, C. (1991) *The Language of Post-Modern Architecture*, 6th edn. London: Academy Editions.

Jenkins, H., S. Ford and J. Green (2013) *Spreadable Media: Creating Value and Meaning in a Networked Culture*. New York: New York University Press.

Jenkins, T. (2015) 'Digital Words of Wisdom? Digital Storytelling with Older People'. *Cultural Science Journal*, 8 (2): 43–62.

Johnston, M. and others (n.d.) 'Engaging the Debate Over "Biological Limits of Gender Construction": Applying Concepts from Research Methods to Published Sociological Research'. *AMSA On-Line Sociological Review*, 1 (1): http://www .olemiss.edu/pubs/amsa/current_issue.html.

Jones, B. (2019) 'Rough Seas Ahead: Why the Government's James Cook Infatuation May Further Divide the Nation'. *The Conversation*, 23 January: https://theconversation.com/rough-seas-ahead-why-the-governments-james-cook -infatuation-may-further-divide-the-nation-110275.

Jones, O. (2011) *Chavs: The Demonization of the Working Class*. London: Verso.

Kagan, R. (2003) *Of Paradise and Power: America and Europe in the New World Order*. New York: Alfred A. Knopf.

Kagan, R. (2019) 'The Strongmen Strike Back: Authoritarianism has Reemerged as the Greatest Threat to the Liberal Democratic World – a Profound Ideological, as Well as Strategic, Challenge. And we have no Idea how to Confront it'. *The Washington Post* Opinions Essay, 14 March: https://www.washingtonpost.com /news/opinions/wp/2019/03/14/feature/the-strongmen-strike-back/?noredirect= on&utm_term=.272b2584201f.

Kanjere, A. (2018) 'Defending Race Privilege on the Internet: How Whiteness Uses Innocence Discourse Online'. *Information, Communication & Society*, published online 5 June. doi.org/10.1080/1369118X.2018.1477972.

Kearney, M. C. (2006) *Girls Make Media*. New York: Routledge.

Kearney, M. C. (ed.) (2011) *Mediated Girlhoods: New Explorations of Girls' Media Culture*. New York, NY: Peter Lang.

Kirkpatrick, R. (2016) *Pennies, Profits and Poverty: A Biographical Directory of Wealth and Want in Bohemian Fleet Street*. Online: CreateSpace.

Konner, M. (2010) *The Evolution of Childhood: Relationships, Emotion, Mind*. Cambridge, MA: Harvard University Press.

Kroeber, A. L. and C. Kluckhohn (1952) *Culture: A Critical Review of Concepts and Definitions*. Cambridge, MA: Peabody Museum of Archaeology and Ethnology Papers, 47 (1).

Krisman, A. (1987) 'Radiator Girls: The Opinions and Experiences of Working-Class Girls in an East London Comprehensive'. *Cultural Studies*, 1 (2): 219–29.

Kull, K. (1999) 'Towards Biosemiotics with Yuri Lotman'. *Semiotica*, 127 (1/4): 115–31.

Laclau, E. and C. Mouffe (2001) *Hegemony and Socialist Strategy: Towards a Radical Democratic Politics*, 2nd edn. London: Verso.

Lambert, J. (2006) *Digital Storytelling: Capturing Lives, Creating Community*, 4th edn 2013. New York: Routledge.

Lanham, R. (2006) *The Economics of Attention: Style and Substance in the Age of Information*. Chicago: Chicago University Press.

Leadbeater, C. (1999) *Living on Thin Air: The New Economy*. London: Viking/ Penguin.

Lee, R. E. (ed.) (2012) *The Longue Durée and World-Systems Analysis*. Albany, NY: SUNY Press: Editor's Introduction, 1–7. Accessible here: http://www. sunypress.edu/pdf/62451.pdf.

Lefebvre, H. (2000) *Everyday Life in the Modern World*. London: Bloomsbury (First published in French, 1968).

Lefebvre, H. (2014) *Critique of Everyday Life: The Three-Volume Text* (First published in French, Vol I: 1947, Vol II: 1961, Vol III: 1981). London: Verso.

Le Masurier, M. (2009) 'Desiring the (Popular Feminist) Reader: Letters to *Cleo* During the Second Wave'. *Media International Australia*, 131: 106–16.

Le Masurier, M. (2011) 'Popular Feminism, the Second Wave and *Cleo*'s Male Centrefold. *Feminist Media Studies*, 11 (2): 215–29.

Lemish, D. (2015) *Children and Media: A Global Perspective*. Malden, MA: Wiley-Blackwell.

León, B. B. (2017) 'Urban Theory in Postmodern Cities: Amnesiac Spaces and Ephemeral Aesthetics'. *URBS. Revista de Estudios Urbanos y Ciencias Sociales*, 7 (1): 57–65.

Lepore, J. (2018) *These Truths: A History of the United States*. New York: W. W. Norton.

Lesser, Z. (2004) *Renaissance Drama and the Politics of Publication: Readings in the English Book Trade*. Cambridge: Cambridge University Press.

Lévi-Strauss, C. (1955/1961) *Tristes Tropiques*. Harmondsworth, UK: Penguin.

Levine, R. (1997) 'Financial Development and Economic Growth: Views and Agenda'. *Journal of Economic Literature*, 35 (2): 688–726.

Li, H. S. (2015) 'The Phatic, the Link and the Promise of the Internet'. In J. Hartley and W. Qu (eds), *Re-Orientation: Trans-cultural, Trans-lingual and Transmedia Studies in Narrative, Language, Identity, and Knowledge*. Shanghai: Fudan University Press, 87–106.

Livingstone, S. and M. Bovill (1999) *Young People, New Media*. Report of the research project Children Young People and the Changing Media Environment. London: LSE Department of Media and Communications: http://eprints.lse.ac.uk/21177.

Lotman, J. (2009) *Culture and Explosion*. Berlin: Mouton De Gruyter.

Lotman, Y. (1990) *Universe of the Mind: A Semiotic Theory of Culture*. London and New York: I.B. Tauris; Bloomington: Indiana University Press.

Lotman, Y., B. Uspensky and G. Mihaychuk (1978) 'On the Semiotic Mechanism of Culture'. *New Literary History*, 9 (2): 211–32: http://faculty.georgetown.edu/irvinem/theory/Lotman-SemioticMechanism-1978.pdf.

Lucy, N. (2016) *A Dictionary of Postmodernism* (ed. J. Hartley). Oxford: Wiley-Blackwell.

Luhmann, N. (2012) *Theory of Society, Vol. 1*. Stanford, CA: Stanford University Press.

Luhmann, N. (2013) *Introduction to Systems Theory*. Cambridge: Polity Press.

Lukasik, S. (2008) 'Military Service, Combat, and American Identity in the Progressive Era'. PhD Dissertation, Duke University: http://dukespace.lib.duke.edu/dspace/bitstream/handle/10161/909/D_LUKASIK_SEBASTIAN_a_2008 12.pdf.

Lundby, K. (ed.) (2008) *Digital Storytelling, Mediatized Stories: Self-representations in New Media*. New York: Peter Lang.

Lyotard, J. (1979) *The Postmodern Condition: A Report on Knowledge*. English translation published by Manchester University Press (UK) and University of Minnesota Press (USA), 1984.

Macpherson, C. B. (1962) *The Political Theory of Possessive Individualism: Hobbes to Locke*. Oxford: Oxford University Press.

Malešević, S. (2017) *The Rise of Organised Brutality*. Cambridge: Cambridge University Press.

Malešević, S. and K. Ryan (2013) 'The Disfigured Ontology of Figurational Sociology: Norbert Elias and the Question of Violence'. *Critical Sociology*, 39 (2): 165–81.

Manguel, A. (1997) *A History of Reading*. London: Penguin.

Mann, S. (1992) *Immediate Family*. New York: Aperture Foundation.

Mansfield, H. and D. Winthrop (2000) 'Editors' Introduction', in their edition of A. de Tocqueville, *Democracy in America*. Chicago: University of Chicago Press.

Marx, K. (1845) *The German Ideology*. Accessible at: https://www.marxists.org/archive/marx/works/1845/german-ideology/ch01b.html.

Marx, K. (1857) *Preface and Introduction to A Contribution to the Critique of Political Economy*. Peking: Foreign Languages Press edn (1976). Online: http://www.marx2mao.com/M&E/PI.html.

Maturana, H. and F. Varela (1980) *Autopoiesis and Cognition: The Realization of the Living*. Dordrecht, Holland: Reidel; Boston, MA: Kluwer.

May, C. (2010) *A Global Political Economy of Intellectual Property Rights: The New Enclosures*, 2nd edn. London: Routledge.

Mazzarella, S. (ed.) (2010) *Girl Wide Web 2.0: Revisiting Girls, the Internet, and the Negotiation of Identity*. New York, NY: Peter Lang.

Mazzucato, M. (2015) *The Entrepreneurial State: Debunking Public vs. Private Sector Myths*, rev. edn. London: PublicAffairs Press.

McGrath, J. (2010) 'Review: The Uses of Literacy: Aspects of Working-Class Life by Richard Hoggart'. *Popular Music*, 29 (2): 317–19.

McIntire, S. (2009) *Speeches in World History*. New York: Facts on File, Inc.

McIntyre, B. and W. Zhang (2013) 'Western Mass Media Exposure and Chinese Cultural Values: The Case of Hong Kong'. Paper presented at the Second Hawaii International Conference on Social Sciences, Honolulu, USA, 12–15 June: https://www.researchgate.net/publication/228596700_Western_Mass_Media_Exposure_and_Chinese_Cultural_Values_The_Case_of_Hong_Kong.

McKinsey Global Institute (2016) *Digital Globalization: The New Era of Global Flows*. Online: https://www.mckinsey.com/business-functions/digital-mckinsey/our-insights/digital-globalization-the-new-era-of-global-flows.

McNeill, T. (2013) 'Sex Education and the Promotion of Heteronormativity'. *Sexualities*, 16 (7): 826–46.

McRobbie, A. (1982) '*Jackie*: An Ideology of Adolescent Femininity'. In B. Waites, T. Bennett and C. Martin (eds), *Popular Culture: Past and Present*. London: Croom Helm, 263–83: http://epapers.bham.ac.uk/1808.

Meadows, D. and J. Kidd (2009) '"Capture Wales." The BBC Digital Storytelling Project'. In J. Hartley and K. McWilliam (eds), *Story Circle: Digital Storytelling Around the World*. Malden, MA and Oxford, UK: Wiley-Blackwell, 91–117.

Meadows, D., L. Heledd and C. Evans (2006) 'How Public Broadcasting Serves the Public Interest in the Digital Age'. *First Person: International Digital Storytelling Conference*, Australian Centre for the Moving Image, 5 February: www.acmi.net.au/global/docs/first_person_meadows.pdf.

Mee, S. (2009) 'Joseph Schumpeter and the Business Cycle: An Historical Synthesis'. Online: https://www.tcd.ie/Economics/assets/pdf/SER/2009/simon_mee.pdf.

Mesoudi, A. (2011) *Cultural Evolution: How Darwinian Theory Can Explain Human Culture and Synthesize the Social Sciences*. Chicago: University of Chicago Press.

Miller, C. H. (2014) *Digital Storytelling: A Creator's Guide to Interactive Entertainment*, 3rd edn. Burlington, MA and Oxford, UK: Focal Press.

Miller, D. (2009) *Stuff*. Cambridge: Polity Press.

Miller, E. and C. Costello (2001) 'The Limits of Biological Determinism'. *American Sociological Review*, 66 (4): 592–98: http://www.academicroom.com/article/limits-biological-determinism.

Mittell, J. (2009) *Television and American Culture*. New York: Oxford University Press.

Modenessi, A. M. (2005) 'Disney's 'War Efforts': *The Lion King* and Education for Death, or Shakespeare Made Easy for Your Apocalyptic Convenience'. *Ilha do Desterro: Journal of English Language, Literature in English and Cultural Studies*, 49: 397–415: https://periodicos.ufsc.br/index.php/desterro/issue/view/651.

Mokyr, J. (2009) *The Enlightened Economy: The Enlightened Economy: An Economic History of Britain 1700–1850*. New Haven, CT: Yale University Press.

Montgomery, L., J. Hartley, C. Neylon, M. Gillies, E. Gray, C. Herrmann-Pillath, C. K. Huang, J. Leach, J. Potts, K. Skinner, C. Sugimoto and K. Wilson (2018) *Open Knowledge Institution: Reinventing Universities*. Online: MIT Press Pub: https://wip.mitpress.mit.edu/pub/oki.

Moore, S., C. Neylon, M. Eve, D. O'Donnell and D. Pattinson (2017) '"Excellence R Us": University Research and the Fetishisation of Excellence'. *Palgrave Communications*, vol. 3: https://www.nature.com/articles/palcomms2016105.

Murphy, T. (2005) 'Editor's Introduction: Books for Burning'. In A. Negri (2005) *Books for Burning: Between Civil War and Democracy in 1970s Italy*. London: Verso, ix–xxviii.

Nagaike, K. (2010) 'The Theme of "Girl-Addressing-Girl" and Male Homosexual Fantasies'. In T. Aoyama and B. Hartley (eds), *Girl Reading Girl in Japan*. London, UK and New York: Routledge, 107–18.

Nature News (2017) 'Wikipedia Shapes Language in Science Papers: Experiment Traces how Online Encyclopaedia Influences Research Write-Ups', by Mark Zastrow, 26 September: https://www.nature.com/news/wikipedia-shapes-language-in-science-papers-1.22656.

Neale, J. E. (1952) *Queen Elizabeth I* (Republished 1992). Chicago, IL: Academy Chicago Publishers: https://www.amazon.com/Queen-Elizabeth-I-J-Neale/dp/0897333624#reader_0897333624.

Negri, A. (2005) *Books for Burning: Between Civil War and Democracy in 1970s Italy*, ed. T. Murphy. London: Verso.

Nelson, O. (2013) 'Dark Undercurrents of Teenage Girls' Selfies'. *Sydney Morning Herald*, 11 July. Online: www.smh.com.au/comment/dark-undercurrents-of-teenage-girls-selfies-20130710-2pqbl.html.

Nelson, R. (2019) *Two Shakespearean Actors*. New York: Broadway Play Publishing Inc.

Neville, A. O. (1947) *Australia's Coloured Minority: Its Place in the Community*. Sydney: Currawong Books.

Nietzsche, F. (2006) *Thus Spoke Zarathustra*, trans. Adrian del Caro, ed. Robert Pippin. Cambridge: Cambridge University Press.

Nind, I. S. (1831) 'Description of the Natives of King George's Sound (Swan River Colony) and adjoining Country'. *Journal of the Royal Geographical Society of London*, 1: https://en.wikisource.org/wiki/Journal_of_the_Royal_Geographical_Society_of_London/Volume_1/Description_of_the_Natives_of_King_George%27s_Sound_(Swan_River_Colony)_and_adjoining_Country.

Notroff, J. and O. Dietrich (2017) 'Neolithic Gathering and Feasting at the Beginning of Food Production'. *The Tepe Telegrams*, 2 August: https://www.dai nst.blog/the-tepe-telegrams/2017/08/02/neolithic-gathering-and-feasting-at-the-b eginning-of-food-production.

Oakeshott, M. (1975) *On Human Conduct*. Oxford: Clarendon Press.

Oakley, K. and J. O'Connor (eds) (2015) *The Routledge Companion to the Cultural Industries*. Abingdon, UK: Routledge.

Ohler, J. (2013) *Digital Storytelling in the Classroom: New Media Pathways to Literacy, Learning, and Creativity*, 2nd edn. Thousand Oaks, CA: Corwin (Sage).

Ojamaa, M. and P. Torop (2015) 'Transmediality and Cultural Autocommunication'. *International Journal of Cultural Studies*, 18 (1): 61–78.

Olson, L. (2009) *Modernism and the Ordinary*. Oxford: Oxford University Press.

Ong, W. J. (1971) *Rhetoric, Romance, and Technology: Studies in the Interaction of Expression and Culture*. Ithaca, NY: Cornell University Press.

Ong, W. J. (2012) *Orality and Literacy Technologizing the Word, with Additional Chapters by John Hartley*, 30th Anniversary Edition. London: Routledge.

Oppenheimer, J. (2005) *Front Row: The Cool Life and Hot Times of Vogue's Editor In Chief*. New York: Martin's Press.

Ormerod, P. (2012) *Positive Linking: How Networks Can Revolutionise the World*. London: Faber & Faber.

Ostrom, E. (1990) *Governing the Commons: The Evolution of Institutions for Collective Action*. Cambridge: Cambridge University Press.

Ostrom, E. (2000) 'Collective Action and the Evolution of Social Norms'. *Journal of Economic Perspectives*, 14 (3): 137–58: http://www.policy.hu/karimli/Ostrom %20collective%20action%20and%20evolution%20of%20social%20norms.pdf.

Ostrom, E. and C. Hess (2007) 'A Framework for Analyzing the Knowledge Commons'. In C. Hess and E. Ostrom (eds), *Understanding Knowledge as Common*. Cambridge, MA: MIT Press, 41–79.

Owen, S. (2007) 'Richard Hoggart as Literary Critic'. *International Journal of Cultural Studies*, 10 (1): 85–94.

Pagel, M. (2012a), *Wired for Culture: The Natural History of Human Cooperation*. London: Allen Lane.

Pagel, M. (2012b) 'The Culture Bandwagon'. New Humanist. Accessible at: www.e urozine.com/articles/2012-02-21-pagel-en.html.

Papacharissi, Z. (2010) *A Private Sphere: Democracy in a Digital Age*. Cambridge: Polity Press.

Papacharissi, Z. (ed.) (2011) *A Networked Self: Identity, Community and Culture On Social Network Sites*. London and New York: Routledge.

Papacharissi, Z. (2015a) 'We Have Always Been Social'. *SM+S, Social Media + Society*, 1 (1): 1–2: http://sms.sagepub.com/content/1/1/2056305115581185.ful l.pdf+html.

Papacharissi, Z. (2015b) *Affective Publics: Sentiment, Technology, and Politics*. New York: Oxford University Press.

Parker Pearson, M. (2012) *Stonehenge: Exploring the Greatest Stone Age Mystery*. London: Simon & Schuster.

Patterson, F. T. (1920) *Cinema Craftsmanship: A Book for Photoplaywrights*. New York: Harcourt, Brace & Co.

Pearson, R. and M. Davies (2002) 'A Brave New World a Week: *Star Trek*, Cult Television, Master Narratives and POSTMODERNISM'. In P. Le Guern (ed.) *Les cultes médiatiques: Culture fan et œuvres cultes*. Rennes (France): Presses universitaires de Rennes, 263–80: http://books.openedition.org/pur/24181.

Pettitt, T. (2013) 'Media Dynamics and the Lessons of History: The "Gutenberg Parenthesis" as Restoration Topos'. In J. Hartley, J. Burgess and A. Bruns (eds), *A Companion to New Media Dynamics*. Malden, MA and Oxford, UK: Wiley-Blackwell, 53–72.

Pew Research (2014a) *Millennials in Adulthood: Detached from Institutions, Networked with Friends*. Online: Pew Research Center: http://www.pewsocial trends.org/files/2014/03/2014-03-07_generations-report-version-for-web.pdf.

Pew Research (2014b) *Political Polarization in the American Public: How Increasing Ideological Uniformity and Partisan Antipathy Affect Politics, Compromise and Everyday Life*. Online: http://www.people-press.org/2014/06/12/political-polarization-in-the-american-public.

Pew Research (2015) *Teens, Social Media & Technology Overview 2015*. Online: Pew Research Center: http://www.pewinternet.org/2015/04/09/teens-social-medi a-technology-2015/.

Pew Research (2018) *Teens, Social Media & Technology 2018*. Online: Pew Research Center: https://www.pewinternet.org/2018/05/31/teens-social-media-technology-2018.

Pierson, P. (2004) *Politics in Time: History, Institutions, and Social Analysis*. Princeton, NJ: Princeton University Press.

Piketty, T. (2014) *Capital in the 21st Century*. Cambridge, MA: Harvard University Press.

Pinker, S. (2011) *The Better Angels of Our Nature: The Decline of Violence in History and Its Causes*. New York: Allen Lane.

Podkalicka, A. and J. Staley (2009) 'YouthWorx Media: Creative Media Engagement for "at Risk" Young People'. 3CMedia: *Journal of Community, Citizen's and Third Sector Media and Communication*, 5: 1–7. Online: https://www.cbaa.org.au/article/connecting-through-digital-storytelling.

Popper, K. (1945/2002) *The Open Society and Its Enemies*. (2 Vols; republished 2002) London: Routledge.

Popper, K. (1963) *Conjectures and Refutations: The Growth of Scientific Knowledge*. London: Routledge.

Potts, J. (2011) *Creative Industries and Economic Evolution*. Cheltenham: Edward Elgar.

Potts, J. (2012) 'Innovation in the Commons'. *International Schumpeter Society*: www.aomevents.com/media/files/ISS%202012/Potts.pdf.

Potts, J. (2019) *Innovation Commons: The Origin of Economic Growth*. Oxford: Oxford University Press.

Potts, J., S. Cunningham, J. Hartley and P. Ormerod (2008) 'Social Network Markets: A New Definition of the Creative Industries'. *Journal of Cultural Economics*, 32 (3): 166–85: https://eprints.qut.edu.au/18071/2/18071.pdf.

Potts, J., J. Hartley, L. Montgomery, C. Neylon and E. Rennie (2017) 'A Journal is a Club: A New Economic Model For Scholarly Publishing'. *Prometheus: Critical Studies in Innovation*, 35 (1): 75–92.

Potts, J. and E. Rennie (2017) 'Blockchains and Creative Industries', 16 November. Available at SSRN: https://ssrn.com/abstract=3072129 or http://dx.doi.org/10.2139/ssrn.3072129.

Purton, V. (ed.) (2013) *Darwin, Tennyson and Their Readers. Explorations in Victorian Literature and Science*. London and New York: Anthem Press.

Quiggin, J. (2008) 'Employment and Innovation in the Information Economy'. In G. Hearn and D. Rooney (eds), *Knowledge Policy: Challenges for the 21st Century*. Cheltenham, UK: Edward Elgar, 175–87.

Quiller-Couch, A. (1917) *On the Art of Writing: Lectures Delivered in the University of Cambridge 1913-1914*. Cambridge: Cambridge University Press: http://www.gutenberg.org/cache/epub/17470/pg17470-images.html.

Rabinow, P. and N. Rose (2006) 'Biopower Today'. *Biosocieties*, 1 (2): 195–217.

Rafols, I., A. Porter and L. Leydesdorff (2010) 'Science Overlay Maps: A New Tool for Research Policy and Library Management'. *Journal of the American Society for Information Science and Technology*, 61 (9): 1871–87: https://www.leydesdorff.net/overlaytoolkit/overlaytoolkit.pdf.

Rauch, A. (2001) *Useful Knowledge: The Victorians, Morality, and the March of Intellect*. Durham, NC: Duke University Press.

Reich, R. (2014) 'The New Tribalism and the Decline of the Nation State'. Blog post: http://robertreich.org/post/80522686347.

Richards, T. (1993) *The Imperial Archive: Knowledge and the Fantasy of Empire*. London: Verso.

Robertson, A. (2014) 'Can you Own a Language?' *The Verge*: http://www.theverge.com/2014/8/13/5998273/who-owns-a-language-wikipedia-palawa-kani-raises-old-debate.

Robins, A. (2017) *New York Art Deco: A Guide to Gotham's Jazz Age Architecture*. Albany, NY: SUNY Press.

Romer, J. (2012) *A History of Ancient Egypt: From the First Farmers to the Great Pyramid*. London: Penguin Books.

Ronen, S., B. Gonçalves, K. Hu, A. Vespignani, S. Pinker and C. Hidalgo (2014) 'Links that Speak: The Global Language Network and Its Association with Global Fame'. *PNAS*, 111 (52): E5616–22. Online: http://www.pnas.org/content/111/52/E5616.full.

Ross, K. (1994) *Fast Cars, Clean Bodies: Decolonization and the Reordering of French Culture*. Cambridge, MA: The MIT Press.

Roy, R. D. (2018) 'Decolonise Science – Time to End Another Imperial Era'. *The Conversation*, 5 April: https://theconversation.com/decolonise-science-time-to-end-another-imperial-era-89189.

Rutherford, J. (2018) 'How the Decline of the Working Class Made Labour a Party of the Bourgeois Left. Progressive Politics in the 1990s Turned Away from Class Politics and Solidarity in Favour of Group Identities and Self-realisation'. *New Statesman*, 19 September: https://www.newstatesman.com/politics/uk/2018/09/how-decline-working-class-made-labour-party-bourgeois-left.

Sanderson, S. (2001) *The Evolution of Human Sociality: A Darwinian Conflict Perspective*. Lanham, MD: Rowman and Littlefield.

Sandler, T. and J. Tschirhart (1980) 'The Economic Theory of Clubs: An Evaluative Survey'. *Journal of Economic Literature*, 18: 1481–521.

Sandler, T. and J. Tschirhart (1997) 'Club Theory: Thirty Years Later'. *Public Choice*, 93: 335–55.

Sandry, E. (2015) *Robots and Communication*. Basingstoke, UK: Palgrave Macmillan.

Saussure, F. de (2006) *Writings in General Linguistics*. Trans C. Sanders and M. Pires. Oxford: Oxford University Press.

Scates, B. C. (2017) 'Monumental Errors: How Australia Can Fix Its Racist Colonial Statues'. *The Conversation*, 28 August: https://theconversation.com/mo numental-errors-how-australia-can-fix-its-racist-colonial-statues-82980.

Schmidt, K. (2010) 'Göbekli Tepe – the Stone Age Sanctuaries. New Results of Ongoing Excavations with a Special Focus on Sculptures and High Reliefs'. *Documenta Praehistorica*, XXXVII, 239–56: http://arheologija.ff.uni-lj.si/doc umenta/authors37/37_21.pdf.

Schuller, K. (2017) *The Biopolitics of Feeling: Race, Sex, and Science in the Nineteenth Century*. Durham, NC: Duke University Press.

Schumpeter, J. A. (1939) *Business Cycles: A Theoretical, Historical, and Statistical Analysis of the Capitalist Process*. New York: McGraw-Hill.

Schumpeter, J. A. (1942) *Capitalism, Socialism and Democracy*. New York: Harper Perennial; Taylor & Francis e-Library (2003): http://digamo.free.fr/ capisoc.pdf.

Sconce, J. (1995) '"Trashing" the Academy: Taste, Excess, and an Emerging Politics of Cinematic Style'. *Screen*, 36 (4): 371–93.

Sconce, J. (2000) *Haunted Media: Electronic Presence from Telegraphy to Television*. Durham, NC: Duke University Press.

Sconce, J. (2019) *The Technical Delusion: Electronics, Power, Insanity*. Durham, NC: Duke University Press.

Scott, J. C. (2017) *Against the Grain: A Deep History of the Earliest States*. New Haven, CT: Yale University Press.

Scott, K. (2010) *That Deadman Dance*. Sydney: Picador.

Senft, T. and N. Baym (2016) 'What Does the Selfie Say? Investigating a Global Phenomenon'. *International Journal of Communication*, 9: 1588–606.

Shannon, C. (1948) 'A Mathematical Theory of Communication'. *Bell System Technical Journal*, 27 (3): 379–423. Accessible at: https://archive.org/details/ bstj27-3-379.

Shirky, C. (2010a) *Cognitive Surplus: Creativity and Generosity in a Connected Age*. London: Penguin.

Shirky, C. (2010b) 'The Shock of Inclusion'. *The Edge*, World Question Center: www.edge.org/q2010/q10_1.html.

Simondson, H. (2009) 'Connecting Through Digital Storytelling'. *3CMedia: Journal of Community, Citizen's and Third Sector Media and Communication*, 5: 61–73. Online: https://www.cbaa.org.au/sites/default/files/3CMedia-Issue5-October%202009-Simmondson.pdf.

Simpson, P. (2001) 'Aristotle's Idea of the Self'. *Journal of Value Inquiry*, 35 (3): 309–24.

Şimşek, B. (2012) *Using Digital Storytelling as a Change Agent for Women's Participation in the Turkish Public Sphere*. PhD Thesis, Queensland University of Technology: http://eprints.qut.edu.au/50894/1/Burcu_Simsek_Thesis.pdf.

Şimşek, B. (ed.) (2015) *Broadening Digital Storytelling Horizons*. Special issue of *Cultural Science Journal*, 8: 2. Online: http://cultural-science.org/journal/index.php/culturalscience/issue/view/17.

Sisman, A. (2015) *John le Carré: The Biography*. London: Bloomsbury.

Skeggs, B. (2005) 'The Making of Class and Gender through Visualizing Moral Subject Formation'. *Sociology*, 39 (5): 965–82.

Skinner, E. and M. Hagood (2008) 'Developing Literate Identities with English Language Learners through Digital Storytelling'. *The Reading Matrix*, 8 (2): 12–38: http://www.readingmatrix.com/articles/skinner_hagood/article.pdf.

Smuts, B. (1995) 'The Evolutionary Origins of Patriarchy'. *Human Nature*, 6 (1): 1–32.

Sokal, A. and J. Bricmont (1998) *Fashionable Nonsense*. New York: Picador.

Spigel, L. (1992) *Make Room for TV: Television and the Family Ideal in Postwar America*. Chicago, IL: Chicago University Press.

Spurgeon, C. and J. Burgess (2015) 'Making Media Participatory'. In C. Atton (ed.) *The Routledge Companion to Alternative and Community Media*. Abingdon, Oxon: Routledge, 403–13.

Srnicek, N. (2016) *Platform Capitalism*. Cambridge: Polity Press.

Sternadori, M. (2014) 'Editor's Reflection: Diversity in Magazine Research'. *Journal of Magazine & New Media Research*, 15 (2): https://aejmcmagazine.arizona.edu/Journal/Summer2014/SternadoriReflection.pdf.

Stevens, Q. and K. Franck (2016) *Memorials as Spaces of Engagement: Design, Use and Meaning*. London: Routledge.

Stott, R. (2004) *Darwin and the Barnacle: The Story of One Tiny Creature and History's Most Spectacular Scientific Breakthrough*. London: Faber & Faber; New York: W. W. Norton.

Takahara, E. (2006) 'The Consciousness of the Girl: Freedom and Arrogance'. Trans. T. Aoyama and B. Hartley. In R. Copeland (ed.), *Woman Critiqued: Translated Essays on Japanese Women's Writing*. Honolulu: University of Hawai'i Press, 185–93.

Tatz, C. (1999) *Genocide in Australia*. Canberra: Australian Institute of Aboriginal and Torres Strait Islander Studies: https://aiatsis.gov.au/sites/default/files/products/discussion_paper/tatzc-dp08-genocide-in-australia.pdf.

Tatz, C. (2017) *Australia's Unthinkable Genocide*. Xlibris: https://www.xlibris.com/Bookstore/BookDetail.aspx?BookId=SKU-001133401.

Taylor, D. J. (2017) 'Entertaining the Masses: *The Uses of Literacy* 60 Years On'. *New Statesman*, 18 June: http://www.newstatesman.com/culture/books/2017/06/entertaining-masses-uses-literacy-60-years.

Taylor, L. (2008) *A Taste for Gardening: Classed and Gendered Practices*. Aldershot: Ashgate.

Tennyson, A. (1859) *Idylls of the King*. London: Edward Moxon: https://en.wikisource.org/wiki/Idylls_of_the_King.

Thibault, P. (1997) *Re-Reading Saussure: The Dynamics of Signs in Social Life*. London and New York: Routledge.

Third, A. and P. Collin (2016) 'Rethinking (Children's and Young People's) Citizenship Through Dialogues on Digital Practice'. In A. McCosker, S. Vivienne and A. Johns (eds), *Negotiating Digital Citizenship: Control, Contest and Culture*. London: Rowman & Littlefield International, 41–59.

Thomas, D. and J. S. Brown (2011) *A New Culture of Learning: Cultivating the Imagination for a World of Constant Change*. Online: CreateSpace Independent Publishing Platform: www.newcultureoflearning.com/newcultureoflearning.html.

Thomassen, L. (2016) 'Hegemony, Populism and Democracy: Laclau and Mouffe Today'. *Revista Española de Ciencia Política*, 40 (March): 161–76: https://recyt.fecyt.es/index.php/recp/article/download/40516/pdf_24.

Thompson, E. P. (1963) *The Making of the English Working Class*. London: Gollancz.

Thumim, N. (2012) *Self-Representation and Digital Culture*. Basingstoke, UK: Palgrave Macmillan.

Thumim, N. (ed.) (2018) *Self-(re)presentation now*. London: Routledge.

Tilley, C. (2012) 'Seducing the Innocent: Fredric Wertham and the Falsifications That Helped Condemn Comics'. *Information & Culture: A Journal of History*, 47 (4): 383–413: https://muse.jhu.edu/article/490073/pdf.

Tiqqun (2012, First published in France, 1999) *Preliminary Materials for a Theory of the Young-Girl*. Cambridge, MA: Semiotext(e), MIT Press.

Tocqueville, A. de (2010, first published 1835; 1840, Fr.) *Democracy in America*, 4 vols, historical-critical edn, ed. E. Nolla, trans. J. Schleifer. Indianapolis, IN: Freedom Fund: http://oll.libertyfund.org/titles/2287. Accessible at: http://classiques.uqac.ca/classiques/De_tocqueville_alexis/democracy_in_america_historical_critical_ed/democracy_in_america_vol_3.pdf.

Tolstoy, L. (1868–9, this edn 1942) *War and Peace*. London: Macmillan.

Tomasello, M. (2014) *A Natural History of Human Thinking*. Cambridge, MA: Harvard University Press.

Turchin, P. (2005) *War and Peace and War*. New York: Pi Press and Plume Books.

Turchin, P. (2016) *Ultrasociety: How 10,000 Years of War Made Humans the Greatest Cooperators on Earth*. Online: Beresta Books: http://peterturchin.com/blog/2015/11/21/ultrasociety-how-10000-years-of-war-made-humans-the-greatest-cooperators-on-earth.

Turchin, P., T. Currie, E. Turner and S. Gavrilets (2013) 'War, Space, and the Evolution of Old World Complex Societies'. *PNAS*, 110 (41): 16384–9: http://www.pnas.org/content/110/41/16384.full.pdf.

Turner, G. (2003) *British Cultural Studies – An Introduction*. London: Routledge.

Turney, C., J. Palmer and M. Maslin (2018) 'Anthropocene Began in 1965, According to Signs Left in the World's "Loneliest Tree"'. *The Conversation*: https://theconversation.com/anthropocene-began-in-1965-according-to-signs-left-in-the-worlds-loneliest-tree-91993.

Udry, J. R. (2000) 'Biological Limits of Gender Construction'. *American Sociological Review*, 65: 443–57.

UNFPA (2014) *The Power of 1.8 Billion: Adolescents, Youth and the Transformation of the Future*. New York: United Nations Population Fund; Online: http://www.unfpa.org/sites/default/files/pub-pdf/EN-SWOP14-Report_FINAL-web.pdf.

UNFPA (2015) *Shelter from the Storm: A Transformative Agenda for Women and Girls in a Crisis-Prone World*. New York: United Nations Population Fund; Online: http://www.unfpa.org/swop.

Vaz, P. and F. Bruno (2003) 'Types of Self-Surveillance: From Abnormality to Individuals "at Risk"'. *Surveillance & Society*, 1 (3): 272–91.

Veblen, T. (1898) 'Why is Economics not an Evolutionary Science?' *The Quarterly Journal of Economics*, 12 (4): 373–97: https://archive.org/details/jstor-1882952.

Veblen, T. (1899) *Theory of the Leisure Class*. New York: B. W. Huebsch. Accessible at: https://oll.libertyfund.org/titles/veblen-the-theory-of-the-leisure-cl ass-an-economic-study-of-institutions.

Veblen, T. (1919) *The Place of Science in Modern Civilisation, and Other Essays*. New York: B. W. Huebsch: https://archive.org/stream/placeofsciencein00vebl.

Vernadsky, V. I. (1998) *The Biosphere*. New York: Copernicus (Springer-Verlag).

Viotte, M. (2013) *La Guerre d'Hollywood 1939-1945: Propagande, patriotisme et cinéma*. Paris: Editions La Martinière. DVD: http://www.worldcat.org/title/holly wood-war-1939-1945/oclc/914462121.

Vivienne, S. (2015) *Digital Identity and Everyday Activism: Sharing Private Stories with Networked Publics*. Basingstoke, UK: Palgrave Macmillan.

Vološinov, V. (1929) *Marxism and the Philosophy of Language*. Bloomington: Indiana University Press (1973).

Wallerstein, I. (2004) *World-Systems Analysis: An Introduction*. Durham, NC: Duke University Press.

Walls, L. D. (2009) *The Passage to Cosmos: Alexander von Humboldt and the Shaping of America*. Chicago: University of Chicago Press.

Wang, J. (2018) *Carceral Capitalism*. Cambridge, MA: Semiotext(e) MIT Press.

Warfield, K., C. Cambre and C. Abidin (2016) 'Introduction to the *Social Media + Society* Special Issue on Selfies: Me-diated Inter-faces'. *Social Media and Society*, 2 (2): http://sms.sagepub.com/content/2/2/2056305116641344.full.

Wark, McK. (2015) *The Beach Beneath the Street: The Everyday Life and Glorious Times of the Situationist International*. London: Verso.

Wark, McK. (2016) *Molecular Red: Theory for the Anthropocene*. London: Verso.

Wark, McK. (n.d.) 'Digital Labor and the Anthropocene'. *Dis Magazine*, ed. M. Jordan: http://dismagazine.com/disillusioned/discussion-disillusioned/70983/mc kenzie-wark-digital-labor-and-the-anthropocene.

Wartella, E. and S. Mazzarella (1990) A Historical Comparison of Children's Use of Leisure Time. In R. Butsch (ed.), *For Fun and Profit: The Transformation of Leisure into Consumption*. Philadelphia: Temple University Press, 183–5.

Watkins, T. (2010) 'New Light on Neolithic Revolution in south-West Asia'. *Antiquity*, 84: 621–34: https://www.cambridge.org/core/services/aop-cambri dge-core/content/view/S0003598X00100122.

Welch, C. (2001) *de Tocqueville*. Oxford: Oxford University Press.

Wertham, F. (1954) *Seduction of the Innocent*. New York: Rinehart: https://ww w.scribd.com/doc/30827576/Seduction-of-the-Innocent-1954-2nd-Printing

West, G. (2016) 'The Urban Species: How Domesticated Humans Evolved'. Santa Fe Institute: https://www.youtube.com/watch?v=vJDJFIchsoU.

Williams, R. (1961) *The Long Revolution*. Harmondsworth: Penguin.

Williams, R. (1974) 'Communications as Cultural Science'. *Journal of Communication*, 24 (3): 17–25.

Winn, C. (2018) *Walk Through History: Discover Victorian London*. London: Ebury Press.

Winroth, A. (2014) *The Age of the Vikings*. Princeton, NJ: Princeton University Press.

Woodrow, N., C. Spurgeon, E. Rennie, H. Klaebe, E. Heck, B. Haseman, J. Hartley, M. Edmond and J. Burgess (2015) 'Community Uses of Co-creative Media Digital storytelling and Co-creative Media: The Role of Community Arts and Media in Propagating and Coordinating Population-Wide Creative Practice'. *Cultural Science Journal*, 8 (2): 150–243.

Woolf, V. (2003, first published 1925) *The Common Reader: Volume 1*. London: Penguin Vintage Classics.

Wulf, A. (2015) *The Invention of Nature: The Adventures of Alexander von Humboldt, the Lost Hero of Science*. London: John Murray.

Zecker, R. (2008) *Metropolis: The American City in Popular Culture*. Westport, CT: Praeger.

Zittrain, J. (2008) *The Future of the Internet – and How to Stop It*. New Haven, CT: Yale University Press.

INDEX

www.ingramcontent.com/pod-product-compliance
Lightning Source LLC
Chambersburg PA
CBHW060148280326
41932CB00012B/1676